Employability and Skills Handbook for Tourism, Hospitality and Events Students

This handbook provides students with an essential understanding of the skills and knowledge needed to work in the tourism, hospitality and events industries. It offers reflective, reflexive and critical analysis on personal, academic and professional development.

Not only looking at how to develop the skills, attributes and prospects for employment in these competitive industries, this handbook also focuses on what the employers in tourism, hospitality and events sectors require of graduate employees. Highly illustrated, the chapters contain think points and activities, and case studies are integrated throughout offering first hand advice from both employer and graduate perspectives.

Being the first book to focus on skills and employability in tourism, hospitality and events, this is a must read for all students studying these fields.

Dr Miriam Firth has worked, researched and taught in tourism, hospitality and events management programmes for over 15 years. Building upon a career in hotel, restaurant and festival management she specialises in supporting the employability of students and professional development for management in these sectors. From working, and the continued research, in these industries, her publications are informed from both published research and active experience in the contexts into which students will graduate. She is currently Senior Lecturer at the University of Manchester (ranked 27th in the world in 2019), Programme Director of BA (hons) Management, Leadership and Leisure, and Director of Teaching and Learning Strategy.

Employability and Skills Handbook for Tourism, Hospitality and Events Students

MIRIAM FIRTH

Routledge
Taylor & Francis Group

LONDON AND NEW YORK

First published 2020
by Routledge
2 Park Square, Milton Park, Abingdon, Oxon OX14 4RN

and by Routledge
52 Vanderbilt Avenue, New York, NY 10017

Routledge is an imprint of the Taylor & Francis Group, an informa business

British Library Cataloguing-in-Publication Data
A catalogue record for this book is available from the British Library

Library of Congress Cataloging-in-Publication Data
Names: Firth, Miriam, author.
Title: Employabilty and skills handbook for tourism, hospitality and events students / Miriam Firth.
Description: Abingdon, Oxon ; New York, NY : Routledge, 2020. | Includes bibliographical references and index.
Identifiers: LCCN 2019033563 (print) | LCCN 2019033564 (ebook)
Subjects: LCSH: Tourism–Vocational guidance. | Hospitality industry–Vocational guidance.
Classification: LCC G155.5 .F589 2020 (print) | LCC G155.5 (ebook) | DDC 910.23–dc23
LC record available at https://lccn.loc.gov/2019033563
LC ebook record available at https://lccn.loc.gov/2019033564

ISBN: 978-1-138-49394-0 (hbk)
ISBN: 978-1-138-49397-1 (pbk)
ISBN: 978-1-351-02694-9 (ebk)

Typeset in Vectora
by Swales & Willis, Exeter, Devon, UK

Visit the companion website: www.routledge.com/cw/firth

Dedicated to David and Pauline

For supporting my own personal, academic and professional development.

Contents

Figures

Tables

Think points

Activities

Case studies

Preface

Writing this as a senior lecturer in Higher Education in the United Kingdom, this handbook has come from my experience in teaching and training candidates to work within tourism, hospitality and events management. I have operated as a manager, business owner, employee and researcher within these industries, so I am aware of the recruitment and staffing issues present within the fluctuating demands for these industries.

Instead of writing a book on how to manage or develop employees, I wanted to write an informed text for students on tourism, hospitality and events (THE) management to aid their skills and knowledge development for successful graduate roles. Employability is not a single set of skills and knowledge that is developed and fixed, it is fluid and emergent from completing a range of experiences. The skills for THE are equally varied and present in different customer and management contexts. The usual focus in published literature and research is upon how to manage or fit employees into these roles for customer service, rather than placing the employees and management development as the focus. This handbook offers reflective, reflexive and critical analysis on personal, academic and professional development.

Although this handbook was written within two years, it has been in process for around six years (within the same time I started and completed my own doctoral studies focussed upon the employability of THE students). My motivation for offering this handbook is to enable students theoretical consideration of employability and skills for personal, academic and professional development in THE, whilst enabling reflection and consideration of alternative ways to see employability. Are you employable after completing a course successfully? Or is your personality a factor in your employability? Is it who you know or what you know? How does your self-awareness affect your employability and skills? Which research philosophy affects your position to THE theory and current knowledge? Is your experience embedded in these positions? These are the types of questions I ask students in my classes and I wanted to further this by writing a handbook to support their critique and development of reflexivity in their studies. Equally, issues concerning leadership, influence and sustainability are emerging in recruitment practices for THE. I intended to embed consideration of these within a book for employability and skills to ensure they are positioned in line with employment, rather than as an adjunct within studies of THE human resources.

I have been lecturing since the age of 23 and regard my own industry expertise as essential in teaching THE. Whilst teaching I have completed further qualifications culminating in my doctorate whilst continuously teaching, working and researching in THE. I have, therefore, been fortunate in my own career as I have been able to manage, work, teach and research in areas I am passionate about. Within my own roles I have taken on duties and positions which have not been within a specific career map. Having the flexibility to complete different tasks has led to the development of my own skills and knowledge. If you were to ask my colleagues, friends or family what defines me it would be boundless enthusiasm for employability in THE.

How to read the book: with a critical and curious eye. Do not take the content to be pure fact and truth. In some areas I have been facetious in noting how to satisfy usual conventions and then written this incorrectly to show you how it looks when it is wrong. As a handbook I have summarised and condensed a number of theories in order to allow a basis of knowledge from which to apply reflective and reflexive thinking. Therefore, the handbook is in itself a teaching and learning aid for any student on a THE, or related, course. Use this book as a starting point on key theory linked to personal, academic and professional development to then complete further research and data collection.

There are roles which are not present in THE contexts yet. Therefore, this handbook has not been written for a specific role or level of employment experience. Instead it is written with a range of employment for THE in mind: permanent, fixed term, temporary and portfolio. There exists a historical tension between acknowledging THE research as high ranking and industry roles as being professional. Through writing this handbook I am celebrating the complex, demanding and varied professional roles within industries associated with THE. The research completed in support of THE are of importance not only to economic success but societal, philosophical and psychological issues.

With respect and praise given for those studying THE and looking to complete brilliant careers in tourism, hospitality and events management.

Miri

Acknowledgements

This handbook has been written with the support of a number of colleagues, friends and family members. The following are acknowledged for their support:

Catherine Powell

Phil Tragen
Emma Livesey
Steve Courtney

Helen Gunter

Tom Baum

Emma Absson

John Swarbrooke

Nigel Hemmington

Susan Horner

Jonah Firth-Kendal

Lydia Kessell

Holger Jansen

James Brook

Neil Symon and also the staff and management at Bevano Lounge in Manchester

Emily Griffiths

Natalie Howman

Tom Charles

Elliott Matthews

Lucy Davis

Holly Ledger

Jessica Atter

Andi Ferguson

Shobana nair Partington

Anne Millan
Shaun Litler
Paul Walters

Rita Ralston

Richard Smith

Tammy Goldfeld

Paul Gratrick

Juup Stelma

Liz Smith

Richard Fay

Su Corcoran

In addition to the people listed above I would like to acknowledge the colleagues and students I have worked with in industry and education over the last 20 years. Your support, advice and guidance has all led to me being able to write this handbook. Thank you!

Final thanks are offered to Thorsten Jansen for assisting in the final stages of creating the manuscript and for drawing the owls for think points, activities and case studies.

Abbreviations

AHLE	American Hotel and Lodging Association
AI	Artificial Intelligence
AL	Aesthetic Labour
ANT	Actor Network Theory
CAP	Creative Analysis Practice
CAS	Council for the Advancement of Standards in Higher Education
CPD	Career Professional Development
CV	Curriculum Vitae
DEA	Development Education Association
DfID	The Department for International Development
EL	Emotional Labour
EU	European Union
EWTD	European Working Time Directive
GCE	Global Citizenship Education
GDP	Gross Domestic Product
GDPR	General Data Protection Regulations
GROCERS	Gentle, Realistic, Objective, Clear, Enthusiastic, Reflexive, Selfish
HR	Human Resources
IC	Intercultural Competence
MARS	Motivation, Ability, Role perceptions, Situation
MEA	Meetings and Events Australia
MNC	Multinational Company
NGO	Non-Governmental Organization
NLP	Neuro-Linguistic Programming
NVQ	National Vocational Qualification
OECD	Organisation for Economic Co-operation and Development
PDP	Professional Development Planning
PDR	Professional Development Review
QAA	Quality Assurance Agency
SL	Sexualised Labour
SMART	Specific, Measurable, Achievable, Realistic, Timely
SME	Small to Medium Enterprise
SNIP	Source Normalized Impact per Paper
SWOT	Strengths, Weaknesses, Opportunities and Threats

T&T	Travel and Tourism
TEQSA	Tertiary Education Quality and Standards Agency
THE	Tourism, Hospitality and Events
TTRA	The Travel and Tourism Research Association
URL	Uniform Resource Locator (web address)
VET	Vocational Education and Training
WTO	World Trade Organization

Part 1

Employability skills for tourism, hospitality and events management

Part 1 will introduce the text and situate the sectors of tourism, hospitality and events management and appraise their relation to recreation and leisure sectors. An overview of each of the industries will clarify their specific context within global economies. This context will lead to explanation of the specific types of business within which tourism, hospitality and events management students can obtain employment. As the majority of these industries rely on small- to medium-sized businesses, the skills are also identified as specific to the industries. Theory on communication, society and entrepreneurial skills will be described to clarify some of the industry specific skills needed to obtain employment in tourism, hospitality and events management. The structure and content of the following three parts is then identified.

Chapter 1
Introduction to the textbook

LEARNING OBJECTIVES

1. To understand the practical and theoretical scope of this textbook.
2. To examine definitions on employability and skills.
3. To outline how this text can support professional development in tourism, hospitality and events management.

INTRODUCTION

This chapter begins with an overview of the scope of the textbook. The scope will outline the theoretical and practical uses, and audiences which the publication seeks to support. This is followed with an analysis of definitions on employability and skills, the two key terms framing the publication. A description on how students can use the book in professional development for tourism, hospitality and events is then identified via outlining each chapter's structural components (think points, activities, revision questions and further website support).

TEXTBOOK SCOPE

This textbook aims to support students in tourism, hospitality and event management studies to reflect and improve their professional development. As an academic source, it accomplishes this aim using both practical and theoretical detail and activities. Practical and theoretical components of the chapters and parts are noted here first. This is followed with lists of the types of programmes of study the text is aimed at. Limitations, or contextual reflection, is then noted to allow readers to understand the position from which the text is written.

So, firstly, what do I mean by practical and theoretical details? Here, I am identifying a traditional divide in knowledge required when studying vocational courses: knowledge of information verses using knowledge to complete a task. This can also be linked to definitions on explicit and tacit knowledge. Explicit knowledge is information we can repeat and tacit knowledge is that which we cannot tell (Polanyi, 1966). An example of explicit knowledge can be demonstrated in examination contexts. You will sit an exam and write out information learnt on a particular topic. It is explicit as you can write or inform another person (via verbal communication) about the information. Tacit knowledge, on the other hand, is seen in three components:

1.   Relational tacit knowledge.
2.   Somatic tacit knowledge.
3.   Collective tacit knowledge.

To explain these each in turn, relational tacit knowledge is information learnt through relational exchanges. Politeness and manners are examples of these. You automatically complete polite acts and behaviour without necessarily being able to verbalise why these are important and how they are completed. Somatic tacit knowledge is whereby you complete a task using muscle memory. Riding a bike is an example of this as, once learnt, you will be able to complete this action without re-training. Again, it would be difficult to explain verbally what each of your muscles do in this activity. You simply ride the bike! Finally, collective tacit knowledge is knowledge learnt through collective or small group behaviour. To situate in context, one amusing example of this from the UK is queue formation. In a customer service scenario in the UK, you will find that people automatically form an orderly line behind one another. This is particularly amusing in a public house where there is one bar to stand at and often people will queue in a line extending from one point. No one has informed these people to behave this way and if you asked individuals why they joined or started the queue they may simply say it was the polite or right thing to do.

ACTIVITY 1.1 EXPLICIT AND TACIT KNOWLEDGE

Identify examples of explicit and tacit knowledge (including the three forms of tacit knowledge discussed). Identify:

1.   How you learnt this knowledge/skill.
2.   What you needed to learn this knowledge/skill.
3.   How you can improve this knowledge/skill.

Compare your answers with each other and identify how these may differ according to your skills or level of ability.

As you can note, explicit and tacit knowledge manifests in behaviour. I have linked these to the practical and theoretical elements in this book as it aims to address and develop your own professional behaviours to ensure successful graduate employment in tourism, hospitality or events management.

KEY DEFINITIONS: EMPLOYABILITY AND SKILLS

Employable:

1. Suitable for paid work.
2. Able to be used.

Skill:

1. The ability to do something well: expertise.
2. A particular ability.

(Oxford Dictionary, 2019)

The above dictionary definitions are useful starting points from which to consider what it means to be employable and skilled. However, it must be noted that in academic writing, using dictionary definitions is considered subpar. Acknowledgement of these is offered here to clarify the position from which people might usually understand the words, prior to academic analysis. This textbook conforms to these definitions as its aim is to enable successful paid employment via evidence of expertise.

THINK POINT 1.1 I'LL WIKIPEDIA THAT!

In your usual search for definitions or information related to a particular topic, do you refer to Google, Wikipedia or another search website?

Do you find this information to be correct and factual? If so, how do you know?

Why do you think academic (textbooks or journal articles) sources of information are considered to be more valid in their factual claims? Do you agree that they are?

(See Chapter 15 on academic writing to consider this position further.)

In order to define employability and skills for tourism, hospitality and events management positions, it is important to clarify that these require vocational education and training, and that this differs to traditional training for non-vocational roles. That being noted, there are roles within tourism, hospitality and events companies which could be seen as non-vocational. Table 1.1 is offered to clarify this position.

Table 1.1 Vocational and non-vocational roles in tourism, hospitality and events

Vocational roles	Non-vocational roles
Customer service agent in a tour operator	Finance officer
Chef at a hotel	Marketing executive
Medical doctor for an event	Lawyer

Table 1.1 was created to clarify that, although the main routes into employment in tourism, hospitality and events require vocational education and training, there are some roles which can be completed from more traditional educational qualifications (like law, for example). This is an important distinction here and one which supports more generic use of this textbook. Although this textbook is aimed at tourism, hospitality and events management students, due to the varied working roles completed in these businesses it can be used by a range of students and working professionals who have not yet completed higher university or college education. It can also be utilised by new management entering these sectors who need to understand the types of professional development required in their staff.

To clarify employability skills for THE, this chapter will offer a review of generic employability skills, then outline vocational employability skills and finally move to the specific THE employability skills. This will enable readers to understand the wide array of generic transferable skills required for any successful employment, against the job specific vocational skills needed in THE industries. This enables clarification on the context within which the parts of this textbook are written.

Employability skills in employment and education

Employability skills are defined here through acknowledgement of employer requirements and linked to how education supports these. This is due to all education qualifications supporting transferable, job-specific skills for life, as required by all employers. To establish common skills required for employability, Hinchliffes (2013) data is offered in Table 1.2.

Table 1.2 clarifies the ranking importance of specific employability skills as seen by a range of employers. This suggests that interpersonal skills and written skills are most important for employment and commercial/business awareness, and experience of the work environment is seen as least important. The need for interpersonal skills is a consistent finding by employers and scholars in THE (see Garavan, 1997; Baum, 2006; Chan, 2011 for examples), and this is highlighted as a focal component of this textbook in a number of chapters.

Table 1.2 Employer rankings of employability skills

Rank (1 being most important)	Employability skill
1	Interpersonal skills
2	Written communication skills
3	Numeracy
4	IT skills

Source: based on Hinchliffe, 2013: p.56

Clarifying employability skills through maps, frameworks and themes has been a consistent scholarly activity since the 1980s. This is partly due to economic drivers in the need for a more flexible and adaptive labour market. It can also be seen as a result of the increase in service sector economies. This has parity with the focus of this textbook as the employability skills for all employment noted in these models recognise core THE skills as paramount (particularly interpersonal and communication skills). The ways in which employability skills are addressed in scholarly outputs are various. In Canada, McLaughlin (1995) offered a model of skills which addressed the economic needs of the whole country to include academic, communication, thinking, learning, attitudes, behaviours, responsibility, adaptability and working with others. In conjunction with this, educators such as Atkins (1999) noted the teaching practices required to develop employability skills: enterprise, core, common, transferable, generic and key. These two sources outline how employability skills are not simply seen through employer's demands but through economic needs, and are supported in education practices. This textbook will support these positions as it offers frameworks and models within common employability skills, situated and focussed in THE industries.

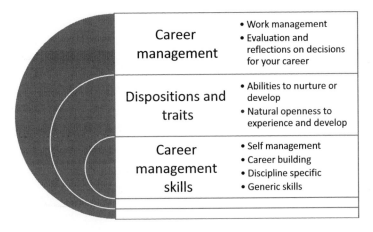

Figure 1.1 Skills for employability: a figure on career management
Source: based upon Bridgstock, 2009: p.36

Figure 1.1 enables clarification on where employability skills are required in career management. An important element of this figure is the acceptance and awareness of underpinning traits and dispositions (like personality, drive and motivation). These are paramount in employability skills as you cannot divorce the employee from their personality and natural aptitudes from which they are appraised and manifest. Career management is supported within this textbook as it enables personal reflection and appraisal of current and desired employability skills whilst enabling individual reflection on how traits and dispositions may inhibit or support these.

ACTIVITY 1.2 CAREER AND EMPLOYABILITY SKILLS

Zinser's (2003) research on employability skills in America noted that any course or publication that seeks to support employability skills requires applied academic skills, career planning, the development and presentation of information, problem solving, personal management, organisational skills, teamwork, negotiation skills, an understanding of systems and the use of employability skills.

Task: identify a recent piece of work you have completed in support of your studies. Using the ten areas noted above from Zinser (2003), align how this piece of work has developed or supported these. N.B. you may find that you use external experience or knowledge in order to complete all of these and not just skills developed from the piece of academic work.

Skills in the 21st century is an overarching term used in acknowledgement of skills for employment. This is a contemporary term used in consideration of employability skills for any industry or profession. This term originated from research carried out in America in which scholars identified that student skills needed analysis due to recent technological advances in society and employment. Trilling and Fadel's (2009) book on this topic identified that these skills could be placed into three categories: learning and innovation skills, digital literacy skills, and career and life skills. Each of these categories of skills is defined with specific attributes, such as communication and collaboration, flexibility and adaptability, or media literacy. This term and framework of skills has since been used by a range of other scholars. Griffin et al. (2012) identified the following ten skills in four area groupings in support of skills in the 21st century:

Ways of thinking

1. Creativity and innovation
2. Critical thinking, problem solving, decision making
3. Learning to learn, metacognition

Ways of working

4. Communication
5. Collaboration (teamwork)

Tools for working

6. Information literacy
7. ICT literacy

Living in the world

8. Citizenship – local and global
9. Life and career
10. Personal and social responsibility – including cultural awareness and competence.

(Griffin et al., 2012: pp.18–19)

The skills noted in Figure 1.1 identify how employer skills can be themed and categorised to support contemporary employability skills. These are all evident in this textbook to ensure that students are able to evaluate and reflect on their employability skills.

CASE STUDY 1.1 DIGITAL SKILLS FOR THE 21ST CENTURY

A university course taught in the UK requires students to understand economic principles in order to ascertain different approaches to economic frameworks. Showcasing skills and knowledge for this could be completed in a range of standard assessment types:

- Essays
- Reports
- Examinations

However, instead of using standard assessment forms, one course requires students to offer a selfie to explain the economic concept. A selfie is a photograph which includes the person taking the photo.

Support for the development of employability skills through and within education is worldwide. In the UK, for example, there are reports for educators in particular disciplines (mathematicians employability skills see Stirling, 2002; Challis et al., 2009; Hibberd and Grove, 2009). There are also notes on how pedagogy (academic practice) can support employability skills: blogs (Dunne and Ryan, 2014), online learning portals (Bateman, 2014), project-based learning (Whatley, 2012) and alumni collaborative work (Russell, 2014). These examples identify that educators are not simply required to develop knowledge (tacit and explicit) but support the development of and reflection on employability skills for all graduate transitions. Atkins (1999) supports this in noting that it was in the 1990s that universities started to address the economic and social needs for employability skill development within higher education curriculum in the UK.

In acknowledgement that employability skills are needed for all students, Van Der Heijde and Van Der Heijde (2006) stated that careers are no longer stratified within set hierarchies. For example, a promotion within a company can be moving to a different department rather than moving up within the chain of command of one department. This has direct links to the noted change in employee's psychological contracts (Rousseau, 1989). A psychological contract is defined as the mutual beliefs between an employee and employer (Rousseau, 1989). Historically, employees were seen to have relational psychological contracts and that they would remain in one career and organisation for life. This was partly due to the reduced access to education and life expectancy (if considered in the 1900–1950s). Contemporary employees now have aspirations to move and gain promotions in a range of careers and positions. This means that their psychological contracts are seen as transactional. However, it is not simply that all employees have transactional psychological contracts. It is that employees will come with a range of career trajectories and that with a full set of employability skills, employees are now able to move positions and companies more easily. This is an important consideration acknowledged in this textbook. The employability skills appraised in working through the parts within this textbook will enable students to apply and address generic employability skills needed for 21st-century employment in a range of industries.

Vocational employability skills

Vocational education is the 'social development of labour' (Clarke and Winch, 2007: p.1). It is referred to as vocational education and training (VET) and, ultimately, prepares a person for work. This differs from liberal or civic education as it requires students to develop specific skills and competencies for specific employment. This is important in the consideration of employability skills for THE, as these industries are noted as requiring VET in support. Skills for successful employment are noted as vocational skills also. Moodie (2002) notes there are tensions in the links between vocational employability skills and traditional higher education knowledge and skills due to the practical application of these needed in training. There is a perceived snobbery around vocational training in comparison to traditional academic education in that VET is seen as less academic. In response to this, this chapter will identify how this textbook will support employability (vocational) skills through the application of academic frameworks, which support the critical thinking and academic knowledge needed in employment and education.

To begin, Habermas's (1971) theory on ways of knowing is utilised throughout this textbook. Habermas is seen as an important scholar when writing about employability skills for THE as he has written extensively on the philosophy and sociology of communication and education. He has also written on the epistemologies around critical theory and so is in a useful position from which to identify knowledge development for employability skills for THE. In terms of VET, his 'ways of knowing' is also useful as it allows for practical application:

1. Technical reflection (know how and know what).
2. Practical reflection (know what to do).
3. Critical reflection (development of relational autonomy).

(Habermas's work cited in Moodie, 2002: p.250)

As noted in this chapter, employers require knowledge, critical reflection, critical thinking and innovative, entrepreneurial thinking for successful employment. Habermas's theory on ways of knowing has been used in other discussions on vocational education (see Ewert, 1991; James, 1995), as it enables clarification of the link between knowledge learnt and then used in the practical application of skills for employment. Technical reflection can be identified through the appraisal of skills and identification of appropriate actions to complete in mind of knowledge. For example, if a customer has a complaint an employee is aware of the potential ways to act in response. Practical reflection then allows the employee to choose an appropriate response in the specific context. So, in a customer complaint example, being aware of the context and circumstances of the issue and resolving it within the business, societal and social contexts present. Critical reflection is then the higher ability to critically reflect on a range of positions and outcomes from a situation (individually and within team or organisational contexts). The tension between academic knowledge and practical application in using skills is acknowledged here. It is also confirmed that vocational skills can often be an outcome of traditional education forms (see a research case study from Malaysia by Bakar and Hanafi, 2007).

Through acknowledging the nature of vocational education and situating it within Habermas's knowledge definitions, it is clear that VET both supports employability skills and can also enable a person to critically appraise their knowledge of skills in employment contexts. This textbook will achieve this through the use of a range of academic frameworks (knowledge), requiring readers to critically reflect on these through activities, think points and revision questions. In support of VET it is noted that this textbook can be used in combination with studies and experience in the THE industry.

Employability skills for THE

To clarify why tourism, hospitality and events have been grouped for this publication, it is important to outline how the employability skills for these industries link and overlap. You may be studying a course that explicitly notes one of these industries, but the skills for employment will be relevant for all. This is because careers within these industries are seen to be *'boundaryless'* (Van Der Heijde and Van Der Heijde, 2006: p.449). This is an important position taken in this textbook as it is written for students on any course associated with tourism, hospitality or events management. With this intention, any chapter of this textbook can be used and applied to employment in these industries and their associated fields. The final section in this chapter states the various employment roles that will benefit from using this textbook but, for the moment, this chapter will outline knowledge on the particular employability skills needed for tourism, hospitality and events management.

As noted earlier in this chapter, interpersonal and communication skills are seen as paramount to all employers (Hinchliffe, 2013). Interpersonal, or soft skills, are addressed in Part 2 of this textbook and are noted as vital for successful employment in THE. The following model clarifies the importance of soft skills within tourism:

Figure 1.2 Conceptual model of soft skills for tourism employability skills in Malaysia
Source: based on Chan, 2011: p.7

Figure 1.2 clarifies how a number of the employability skills (noted earlier in this chapter) can be situated within specific employability skills for an area of THE. Critical thinking (e.g. knowledge) and vocational skills (e.g. team working) are all present here in order to understand how soft skills can be evident in tourism employees.

Soft skills are seen as competencies and these are consistently noted as core to employment skills for THE. Baum (1991) supports this in hospitality and tourism. However, as noted previously, you cannot divorce an individual from the competencies. Their aptitude, behaviour and attitude is ever present. Using Van Der Hiejde and Van Der Heijde's (2006: pp.475–476) model of competencies for employability, Activity 1.3 enables students to appraise their competencies (employability skills) for THE employment.

ACTIVITY 1.3 COMPETENCY APPRAISAL FOR THE EMPLOYMENT

Read through the following five areas on employability skills. Within each list tick each one that applies to you and add them up for a total in each area. If you do not have current employment, you can use a piece of academic work or team within which to base your answers.

Appraisal based on working within: (clarify employment position, student or team role)

Occupational expertise

1. I consider myself competent at engaging in in-depth, specialist discussions in my career interest and industry.
2. During the past year, I was, in general, competent to perform my work accurately and with few mistakes.
3. During the past year, I was, in general, competent at making prompt decisions with respect to my approach to work.
4. I consider myself competent at indicating when my knowledge is insufficient to perform a task or solve a problem.
5. I consider myself competent at providing information on my work in a way that is comprehensible.
6. In general, I am competent to distinguish main issues from side issues and to set priorities.
7. During the past year, I was, in general, competent at carrying out my work independently.
8. I consider myself competent at providing practical assistance to colleagues with questions about the approach to work.
9. I consider myself competent at weighing up the pros and cons of particular decisions on working methods, materials and techniques in my job domain.

Total out of 9 =

Anticipation and optimisation

1. I spend a lot of time improving my knowledge and skills for employment in THE.

2.   I take responsibility for maintaining my labour market value (i.e. competitive advantage against others applying for similar roles).
3.   I approach the development of correcting my weaknesses in a systematic manner.
4.   I am focused on continuously developing myself.
5.   I consciously devote attention to applying my newly acquired knowledge and skills.
6.   I have clear career goals.
7.   In formulating my career goals I take account of external market demand.
8.   During the past year I was actively engaged in investigating adjacent job areas to see where success could be achieved.
9.   During the past year I associated myself with the latest developments in my job domain.

Total out of 9 =

Personal flexibility

1.   I adapt to changes in work easily (for example if a group changes membership or if tasks change in nature or requirements).
2.   I am able to change the location of my work easily (apply to part-time work if necessary here).
3.   I adapt to developments within my organisation.
4.   I anticipate and take advantage of changes in my working environment.
5.   I generally anticipate and take advantage of changes in my sector (for example if in hospitality, being aware of legislation changes and changing your approach in advance of this knowledge).

Total out of 5 =

Corporate sense

1.   I am involved in achieving my organisation's/department's mission.
2.   I do that extra bit for my organisation/department, over and above my direct responsibilities.
3.   I support the operational processes within my organisation.
4.   In my work, I take the initiative in sharing responsibilities with colleagues.
5.   In my organization, I take part in forming a common vision of values and goals.
6.   I share my experience and knowledge with others.
7.   I use my influence to support and develop others in the company.

Total out of 7 =

Balance

1.   I suffer from work-related stress.
2.   My work and private life are evenly balanced.
3.   My working, learning and living are in harmony.
4.   My work efforts are in proportion to what I get back in return.

5. The time I spend on my work and career development, on the one hand, and my personal development and relaxation, on the other, are evenly balanced.
6. I achieve a balance in alternating between a high degree of involvement in my work and a more moderate one at the appropriate moment.
7. After working, I am generally able to relax.
8. I achieve a balance in alternating between reaching my own work goals and supporting my colleagues.
9. I achieve a balance in alternating between reaching my own career goals and supporting my colleagues.
Total out of 9 =

Review your totals within each area and reflect on your current experience and ability within these competencies. What action do you want to take as a result?

In terms of current knowledge around specific skills for employment in THE, there are scarce frameworks available. Knowledge is evident on skills, knowledge and competencies for employment and vocational employment, but as THE requires fluctuating customer and management demands there are no specific skills universally accepted. In order to appraise some of these, the following will outline some frameworks on employability skills seen as lacking or present in THE contexts.

Table 1.3 Skills and knowledge gaps in THE UK 2011/2013

2011	2013
Job-specific, practical skills 59%	Safety management 40% Ensuring compliance/regulation 37% Financial/budgetary control 23%
Problem-solving skills 47% Customer-handling skills 65%	Monitor and solve customer problems 37% Capability to help customers with disabilities 33%
Teamwork skills 56%	Teamwork 37%
Oral communication skills 52% Written communication skills 27%	Professional communication skills 35%
Management skills 39%	Management and leadership 34% Ability to coach and motivate others 35%
Numeracy skills 25%	Basic numeracy 22%
Literacy skills 22%	Basic literacy 21%
	Positive attitude and commitment 38%
	Professional-looking appearance 28%
	Intercultural sensitivity 21%

Source: People 1st, 2011: p.87, 2013: p.62

Table 1.4 Skills and knowledge for THE employment

Skills	Knowledge
• Interpersonal skills: interact with different people, communicate with different people and manage different people. • Maintaining professionalism: smiling appropriately, remaining calm, responding appropriately. • Communication: verbal and non-verbal forms. • Entrepreneurial skills: using initiative, adapting service to suit a range of guests, adhering to company standards whilst maintaining customer satisfaction. • Society skills: team working, awareness of others, adapting behaviour. • Acting. • Positive attitude. • Numeracy: handling bills. • Professionalism. • Self-motivation and initiative. • Ethical behaviour (linked to environmental and sustainable skills). • Digital skills. • Flexibility and adaptability.	Explicit knowledge: • Operations within the area of work. • Communication knowledge: phonetic alphabet. • Legal issues. • Human resource management. • Food and beverage operations around the leisure experience. • Customer types and their requirements. • Nationality, culture and religion. • Health and safety in the workplace. Relational tacit knowledge: • Empathy and understanding customers' needs. • Colleague and management expectations and requirements. • Customer reactions and expectations. Collective tacit knowledge: • Organisational cultures. • Customer behaviour. • Appropriate reaction and behaviour with others. Somatic tacit knowledge: • Behaviour which happens automatically in reaction to a context (e.g. smiling or laughing).

Source: based on information from Arcodia and Barker, 2002; Christou, 2002; Busby, 2005; Tribe, 2005; Warhurst and Nickson, 2007; Munar and Montano, 2009; Dhiman, 2012; Firth, 2020

Table 1.3 showcases research conducted in the UK with employers in THE businesses. The purpose of this is to highlight perceived missing skills needed in applicants to roles in these businesses. This textbook addresses all of these skill gaps in order to support employer requirements (noted in chapter numbers aligned to each area).

On the other hand, other publications clarify the employability skills of graduates from THE courses. The list in Table 1.4 shows employability skills required for THE and is based on a range of research sources.

USING THE TEXTBOOK FOR PROFESSIONAL DEVELOPMENT IN TOURISM, HOSPITALITY AND EVENTS MANAGEMENT

This chapter has offered definitions and positions on employability skills for THE industries in order to situate and offer context on the scope of its use. This final area now considers the practical application and use of the textbook in support of employment in these fields (and ones linked or associated with). To begin, a list of the industries and businesses in which this textbook will support is noted below:

Industries:

1. Wholesale and retail trade – restaurants and hotels.
2. Transport, storage and communications.
3. Community, social and personal services.
4. Manufacturing.
5. Finance, insurance, real estate and business services.
6. Agriculture, hunting, forestry and fishing.
7. Industry including energy.
8. Mining and quarrying.
9. Electricity, gas and water supply.
10. Construction.

(Listed using the OECD, 2019a worldwide industry classifications)

Employees within the industries noted above can all use this textbook, due to THE businesses operating within them all. This list is offered in terms of relevance/importance to THE. Evidently, the core industries are those of tourism, hospitality and events management, but, in light of the following quotation, noting only these three industries would be insufficient:

both tourism and hospitality are broad terms or constructs, consisting of a diverse group of industries.

(Ottenbacher, Harrington and Parsa, 2009 cited from Chan, 2011: pp.3–4)

The above quotation is a well-known position within studies for THE. Although you may be studying or working within a known THE sector, it will interlink with a variety of other industries (due to stakeholders and customer needs). Furthermore, in order to fully assess your employability skills for THE, you also need to apply and use these in working contexts:

> It is important to have an essence of hospitality in a school. Without it how do students become socialised into the hospitality environment/way of thinking? With it you have the noise, the smells, the deliveries, the refuse, the issues, the customers, the problems. It's something that you don't normally get in a business school. It makes us different to other departments. (Case 2, Participant 4).
>
> (Alexander et al., 2009: p.62)

This quotation from Alexander et al. (2009) clarifies that employability skills and knowledge for THE cannot be fully assessed without application of the knowledge in industry contexts. This textbook seeks to offer readers opportunities to appraise these skills in working contexts for all roles in businesses associated with THE.

SUMMARY

1.   Understand the practical and theoretical scope of this textbook.

This textbook is applicable to both students and those employed in tourism, hospitality or events management (or interlinked fields of study). Theoretical frameworks (knowledge) are offered alongside employability skills in order to allow readers to reflect and appraise their development for successful employment in THE.

2.   Examine definitions on employability and skills.

Employability is proven via obtaining employment. Skills are used to evidence employability and complete roles within employment. Economies across the globe are interested in developing employability skills to ensure labour markets can improve and individuals can navigate career management across a diverse range of industries and businesses.

3.   Outline how this text can support professional development in tourism, hospitality and events management.

This textbook is aimed at THE students. However, as THE is seen to link to a range of workers in a range of industries, it can also be applied in training and education in other sectors and contexts.

Questions to support your learning and research

1. How would you define explicit and tacit knowledge?
2. What are the three forms of tacit knowledge?
3. Can you identify examples of explicit and tacit knowledge?
4. What do skills for the 21st century include?
5. What are psychological contracts and how do they influence the employability skills present in labour markets?
6. What is vocational education and how does this support employability skills for THE?
7. Why can THE be linked to a range of other industries?

Employability skill questions for career development

1. Overall, how do you see yourself in terms of your work performance?
2. How much confidence do you have in your capabilities within your area of expertise?
3. How would you rate the quality of your skills overall?
4. What proportion of your work would you say you brought to a successful conclusion in the past year?
5. I have a ___ opinion of how well I performed in the past year.
6. During the past year, how sure of yourself have you felt at work?
7. How much variation is there in the range of duties you aim to achieve in your work?
8. I have a _____ (very negative–very positive) attitude to changes in my function.
9. I find working with new people _____ (very unpleasant–very pleasant).

Websites in support of your learning from this chapter

Institute of Hospitality – www.instituteofhospitality.org/
International Hotel and Restaurant Association – www.ih-ra.org/
OECD Tourism – www.oecd.org/cfe/tourism/
Ministry of Tourism (India) – www.tourism.gov.in/
World Trade Organization – Tourism and travel-related services – www.wto.org/english/tra top_e/serv_e/tourism_e/tourism_e.htm

Chapter 2
Sector overviews

LEARNING OBJECTIVES

1. To explore the scope of tourism, hospitality and events businesses within global economies.
2. To examine how leisure and recreation can be seen as overarching sectors within which tourism, hospitality and events are situated.
3. To appraise current knowledge on leisure and recreation.
4. To identify research strands in tourism, hospitality and events management specifically linked to staff professional development in these sectors.

INTRODUCTION

This chapter offers sectoral overviews of tourism, hospitality and events (THE) in order to outline the scope and locations in which employability skills are supported in this textbook. Definitions are offered from industry and economic reports to clarify the size, markets and scope of these industries. This is followed with academic definitions for each sector. As THE is located and aligned with leisure and recreation studies an appraisal of these terms and employment skills are also offered. Industry and world trade reports are used to clarify the scope of these sectors. Within the discussion of academic literature there are some evocative and powerful accounts of how these industries negatively affect gender, race and equality within society. Finally, current research that supports employability skills for THE is noted in the following chapters to further knowledge required for employment in these sectors.

THE SCOPE OF TOURISM, HOSPITALITY AND EVENTS MANAGEMENT BUSINESSES

Tourism, hospitality and events are often linked industries. In this way, the sectoral definitions naturally overlap and include one another. For example, a hotel business can be noted as either part of hospitality (catering), tourism (accommodation for tourists) or events (wedding or private events venue). This interlinking in THE businesses means that a review of tourism alone, for example, will usually include events and hospitality businesses. Recreation and leisure businesses are also seen to link to THE as they support these industries through activity and experience, which naturally link to THE services. There is no singular database nor economic report that offers scope on all of these sectors. As such, this chapter will use tourism and leisure reports to outline the economic input from all THE industries. This will clarify some of the scope of THE within economies and labour market, but is accepted as incomplete.

To begin the identification of the scope of THE, the Organisation for Economic Co-operation and Development (OECD) clarify that tourism accounts for 4.2% of global gross domestic products (OECD, 2019b). Furthermore, tourism is seen to support 6.9% of global employment and 21.7% of service exports (OECD, 2019b). This clarifies that THE sectors offer significant economic support around the world, both in terms of income for countries and the labour market. Torkildsen (2011) clarified that the leisure market was worth just under £224 billion in 2008. This data identifies that THE is a successful group of industries within global economies.

Within different countries, there are disparities in spending on travel due to economic fluctuations and focus within the country:

Australia 12%
France 12%
Japan 14%
UK 19%
USA 12%
Western Germany 14%
                    (Holecek, 1993: p.23)

Although this data is relatively old, it clarifies fluctuations in travel spending within countries. These fluctuations can be due to the form of the economy (commercial, voluntary and public) and also societal contexts present. Issues noted within the fluctuations in travel spending include government changes, societal freedom, social unrest (protests, terrorism and war) and labour market make-up (Van Lier and Taylor, 1993). Within society, Hodge et al. (2015) note that family dynamics can greatly affect leisure spending. They noted that in America, families are reducing in size due to couples choosing to have fewer children. Smaller sized families will naturally spend less on leisure and as couples are choosing to have children later in life, this will mean an increase in leisure activities suitable for couples over a longer period of time and alternative leisure activities for families with older parents.

ACTIVITY 2.1 THE SCOPE OF THE IN YOUR LOCAL AND NATIONAL ECONOMY

As noted above, THE industries are reported in the following areas:

1.   Gross domestic product input.
2.   Sectoral worth.
3.   Labour market size.
4.   Travel spending.
5.   Family size.

Using the five areas above, identify what THE statistics are available in your local area. This could be statistics from the local city, county, country or continent.

LEISURE AND RECREATION: OVERARCHING SECTORAL AND RESEARCH POSITIONS

Leisure and recreation can be seen as linked to, or as a replication of, THE services and organisations. Tourism contexts and businesses are the main ways in which these are seen as linked. This is due to academic publications on recreation and leisure being based within tourism businesses. This chapter will offer an account of leisure and recreation management knowledge in order to clarify how these link to the THE sectors. As they are seen as linked to THE, it is imperative to also offer an account of issues discussed in leisure and recreation management research that link to employability skills needed to work in THE.

Tourism is defined as a special form of leisure (Chang and Gibson, 2010). This is due to tourists choices in travel and experience often relating to their usual leisure time preferences. A key differentiator seen in published research is that tourism research often looks to unique or individual time-specific decisions, versus leisure, which showcases consistent participation in a particular leisure activity. In this way, leisure is seen as overarching and a sectoral position offering insight for THE employment.

THINK POINT 2.1 NON-ACTIVE LEISURE ACTIVITY

Chang and Gibson (2010) suggest that non-physically active leisure activities are defined as watching TV, reading, relaxing, playing cards, creating arts, shopping, dining and visiting museums.

Do you agree with this list? How would you define physical activity? How would this change according to the age of the person or if they have a disability? What level of action would you use for each activity?

To clarify the history and emergence of leisure as an area of study, the professionalisation of this sector will firstly be identified. Henry (1993) noted that professionalising employment within leisure was only emergent in the UK in the 1980s due to city councils creating departments who had to focus on leisure services. Prior to this, workers in leisure sectors were seen as being semi-professional (Henry, 1993). This perceived emergence of leisure as a profession was also seen in THE at the same time (Lashley and Morrison, 2007). These sources are highlighting that employment in THE businesses was not seen as a core, nor highly skilled profession before the 1980s in the UK (Baum, 1996; Burns, 1997; Baum, 2006b). This emergence of a professionalism for THE was due to the changing shift in western economies as they started to increase government funding and support for leisure and tourism services. Western governments were less focussed on manufacturing and production of physical products and were instead interested in supporting the tourism industry.

Following on from this, UK university courses started educating within THE subjects in the 1990s. The UK has been offering higher education within universities for over a century and it was during an education reform that colleges were able to become universities within the UK. This increase in institutions in the UK is known as the post 92 institutions. Offering THE courses (amongst other vocational courses) in universities the 1990s evidences a significant shift in the education level for people interested in working in these sectors.

THINK POINT 2.2 PROFESSIONALISATION OF THE

Working as a waiter or waitress is often seen as a low skilled role within THE. Based on your knowledge of the duties and actions completed in this role, how would it link to other vocational roles such as a nurse, teaching assistant or builder? Can you identify skills and operational knowledge needed in all roles? Why do you think waiting on someone is deemed a low skill in comparison to these others? Do you think this is fair or appropriate?

Leisure, recreation and THE were not all offered in universities in the UK at once. Leisure and recreation were offered within arts and humanities based subjects, and tourism was the first key area of education offered within THE management. Hospitality management programmes emerged in the late 1990s and events management programmes in the mid-2000s. This background account of the professionalisation and increase in higher education for leisure and recreation and THE in the UK identifies how economic shifts have led to an increase in the recognition and appreciation for these sectors, and the roles within them.

ACTIVITY 2.2 **EMERGENCE OF THE COURSES**

Leisure, recreation and THE have been linked to economic development and university courses in the UK. This established how these sectors are linked as well as clarified their relatively emergent importance in education and economy.

Find out when courses in leisure, recreation and THE were first offered within your country:

1. What level of education were these offered at?
2. Were they based upon specific industry roles?
3. Have there been shifts in programme titles linked to these in the last ten years? If so, does this match economic changes surrounding these?
4. Are the programmes aimed at a specific level of employment?
5. How does this information clarify the economic support and drive for more THE professionals?

Discussion linking leisure and recreation to THE so far has noted how professionalisation (due to economic change) and increase in higher education courses (driven by larger service economies) has driven the increase in THE roles in employment. These roles are no longer seen as low skilled and menial, but professional and supportive of western economies.

Moving on to consider theory and issues in leisure knowledge, this field of study is seen to link with social ideologies on what it means to participate in leisure and how each individual is expected to perform within these activities. This is important in understanding the THE business as leisure research can clarify why and how customers choose to participate with their businesses. The following will now offer a brief overview of leisure time, social contexts for leisure, THE businesses supporting leisure activities, and contemporary issues in leisure research to support this in global economies in the 21st century.

Leisure is defined as a time, cluster of activities or a *state of being* (Torkildsen, 2011: p.13). Leisure time refers to activities completed outside of work and home duties. This often links to play, recreation and free time. As such, it is only possible if a person has space within their usual routines to complete leisure activities. The type of leisure activity also depends on what the individual is interested in. Sport, arts and family activities are often noted as key leisure activities completed in this time. As leisure time is noted as being unobligated or unrequired, there is a tension between the mental and physical requirement to complete leisure activities for a 'normal' or 'successful' life and the motivation to complete the activities associated. For example, sport is seen as a component part of leisure activity, but this is not universally liked nor completed. Miles (2016) suggests that leisure is unstable. This is due to leisure activity being completed within specific social and economic contexts. If you live in an area with high employment and living standards it is seen that you are more likely to complete leisure activities. Technology innovations would offer a counterargument to this position as you can now complete shopping and sporting activities within your own home, for example. Miles (2016) notes that leisure activity is based upon consumerism in that engagement requires people to consume (purchasing within THE businesses). Rojek (1989, 1993) supports this position in noting that contemporary society can inhibit leisure activity due to it necessitating consumerism. This is exacerbated with the increase in social media channels such as Instagram and Facebook. People no longer run in a park or eat at a café without linking to their social media accounts and posting an update showing their tourist activity.

CASE STUDY 2.1 KHALIM'S LEISURE TIME

Khalim is a 20-year-old male student studying culinary arts in New York, America. During a usual week he completes the following activities outside of work and home life:

1. Dinner with friends.
2. Grocery shopping.
3. Soccer practice.
4. Band practice.
5. Online browsing for new clothes.
6. Reading fiction books.
7. Writing a graphic novel.
8. Yoga.
9. Drawing sketches of exhibits in local art galleries.

All of these activities fit around Khalim's study and home life, but he feels he does not spend enough time at the gym. This is due to his friend's posting on social media about their own body improvements and gym sessions. Khalim could make time to attend the gym, but he enjoys the current activities he completes in his leisure time. As such he is conflicted in what he should do. Without knowledge of his friend's leisure time at the gym, he would be content in his own leisure choices, but with this knowledge he feels pressure to post and complete the same form of leisure activities.

Questions:

1. How does your leisure time and activities compare to Khalim's?
2. Does peer pressure via social media alter your own leisure state of mind?
3. What is the 'perfect' balance in leisure time and activity? Is this the same for each person?

Some of the activities noted in Khalim's case example clarify how recreation and leisure are linked. In research publications leisure and recreation are used interchangeably to suggest the same activity or occasion. Recreation and leisure can be seen as different to THE in that they address more specifically the outdoor activities associated with hobbies and leisure time (Kelly, 1983). This accepted, it is evident that leisure activities mainly occur within THE venues and businesses (Wall, 1983). Even in consideration of Khalim's leisure activities, all can be seen as linked to THE business or knowledge in the ways shown in Table 2.1.

Table 2.1 Linking Khalim's leisure activities to THE business and knowledge

Khalim's leisure activity	THE business or knowledge
Dinner with friends	Restaurant, bar or café
Grocery shopping	Culinary arts knowledge
Soccer practice	Sports event management
Band practice	Arts management
Online browsing for new clothes	Arts management and consumer behaviour
Yoga	Sports event management
Drawing sketches of exhibits in local art galleries	Arts management and customer behaviour

Reading and writing were not included in the table above as these are seen as activities which could not be directly linked to THE business or knowledge. However, all other activities completed by Khalim have relevance to THE business or knowledge. In this way, every person who completes leisure activities will naturally come into contact with THE business and be aware of the skills and knowledge needed to negotiate these. Skills and knowledge for THE is therefore seen, via Leisure activity, as perpetual in societies.

Moving onto consideration of the societal contexts within which leisure time and activities are seen, Jones and Wills' (2005) text offers an excellent historical account of how parks have been a consistent societal context within which the public can enjoy leisure pursuits. This is an important context in leisure research and it also highlights how sport management and sport theory is linked to THE business also. Parks are seen as a location for play and relaxation freely available for members of the public. Again, these contexts are seen as used by all of society for play activity, leisure pursuits, sporting activities or required for home life activity (such as walking pets). Jones and Wills (2005) link parks to sporting activity as they are used for play activity such as running, football, yoga or outdoor exercise classes. As they incorporate play, there are natural overlaps with sporting activities.

Parks are not only seen as a core context for leisure time and activity, but also depicted as a space of utopia or paradise, which can be different to the local cultures, sights or traditions of an area (Jones and Wills, 2005). This position has parity with contemporary event authenticity research and the hyper reality in event experiences (see MacLeod, 2006). Events are often seen as an activity that allow customers to immerse themselves in new locations or experiences divorced from the societal context within which they are located. For example, themed events, such as historic re-enactments, allow customers to watch or participate in a leisure activity not currently seen in contemporary society. Parks demonstrate this in their use of varied plants taken from around the world and physical structures installed depicting new spaces. Staff working in the management of local parks are therefore seen to be a component part of creating event experiences. A list of the types of THE employment positions within parks are noted below for clarification:

- Gardener or park maintenance.
- Event manager.
- Surveyor.
- Funding manager.
- Horticulturalist.
- Café manager (if within the park).
- Shop manager (if within the park).

The roles noted above are often present in local parks and are seen as important in creating leisure activities associated with leisure time and tourist spending. As parks are often hired or used for events, they will also be the site in which event management roles are also witnessed. As such, a local park, as noted within the leisure management literature, is seen as a context within which THE business is most easily seen across the globe.

Parks are not just green areas. They are also theme parks where tourism spending is most notable:

> Disney embodies one attempt to capture the image of utopia and make it real.
>
> (Jones and Wills, 2005: p.174)

Disneyland parks are accepted by Jones and Wills (2005) as a theme park and, as such, are linked to park contexts for leisure management. Disneyland is of particular relevance in leisure management, linked to THE, as it offers an example of how tourist attractions are created with the specific intention of offering new spaces for tourists to participate within, separate to the society in which they are located.

From outlining definitions on leisure and clarifying parks as a usual context within which leisure is situated, the following will now identify other THE businesses that support leisure activity and time:

- Cinema, theatres, music venues.
- Amusement, themed and wildlife parks.
- Licensed premises (hotels, nightclubs, restaurants and bars).
- Tour operators (virtual and physical).
- Holiday businesses (including tourist experiences).
- Festivals and events.

In the list above, it is also evident that the supply chains to these can also be included as leisure and THE businesses. For example, the food provider for a hotel may not serve the customers directly, but they are a component function in creating dining leisure experiences for the hotel's customers.

ACTIVITY 2.3 CUSTOMER MARKETS AND SUPPLY CHAINS FOR THE BUSINESSES SUPPORTING LEISURE ACTIVITIES

Using the list of businesses noted above, pick one of these areas of business and identify a local business who fits within this category. List the customer markets and businesses in their supply chains for operation of the customer experience. Link each customer and supplier to different experiences provided by the business.

Moving on to consider strands of knowledge within leisure research, we will now consider how participation, social unrest and the family are key issues known in leisure management. After this, an outline of future areas of consideration are noted for leisure research in the 21st century.

Participation in leisure is seen to be encouraged or inhibited due to barriers (Jackson, 2000). There is a great deal of literature available on barriers to leisure participation (see Crawford and Godbey, 1987; Jackson, 2000, for examples). However, Jackson (2000) suggests that analysis of support mechanisms and enhancing entry routes into leisure activity should be considered. If leisure is seen as a *'perceived freedom'* then every person should be encouraged to use this (Jackson, 2000: p.63). Miles (2016) and Rojek (1989, 1993) both support this issue in leisure activity, in that it now requires people to prove their consumption of THE products in order to appear successful and *'enacting'* our freedom (Miles, 2016: p.271). These articles identify that leisure participation can be due to economic contexts and a person's spending ability rather than them using their freedom to complete activities. For example, a family with children visiting a local park will undoubtedly come across an ice cream van or café, which will lead to them consuming hospitality products.

Social unrest is an emotive and powerful element within leisure research. Discussion on this is focussed upon an incident in America where a 12-year-old boy was shot dead in a local park. Mowatt's (2018) article addresses this incident in detail to highlight how parks are locations of social injustice:

> The death of someone, especially a child in a location of play, should be disturbing enough to shock and remind us of the very real, the very structural, and the very systematic nature of racism and that unlike racial discrimination, racism is quite legal.
>
> (Mowatt, 2018: p.56)

The death of this boy was due to a police officer being called to respond to an emergency call. As the child did not do as the officer requested he was shot and fatally wounded. This has parity with THE businesses as there are an increasing number of terrorist attacks and police presence within these businesses in contemporary societies. This position is also interesting considering that leisure is defined as a form of freedom to be used.

THINK POINT 2.3 SOCIAL UNREST IN PLACES OF LEISURE ACTIVITY

If parks and event locations are increasingly locations of social unrest and terrorist activity, how do the public maintain and exercise their freedom safely? How does social unrest and terrorism change public leisure activity?

Furthermore, Mowatt (2018) notes that parks are also locations within which people choose to commit suicide. As such, leisure locations, such as parks, are seen to be sites of social unrest. Knowledge of this is important for people working by and creating events or building THE businesses within parks.

Finally, the family unit are often considered within leisure research. This is due to sites of leisure activity being with spaces often utilised by and supporting families. Hodge et al. (2015) noted current themes in family leisure research which can aid employability skills:

- Family well-being can be promoted by leisure experiences.
- Frameworks within the leisure activity can aid positive family outcomes.
- Leisure activities need a range of activities and outcomes to meet the individual needs of family members.
- Costs need to be appropriate, bearing in mind family disposable income.
- Inequality is seen in the time and effort required to support family leisure (notably the mother spends 'intense' time and effort (Hodge et al., 2015: p.588)).
- Non-traditional families within a society may be disadvantaged in usual family time leisure activities (for example a single parent family, a family with religious beliefs different to the local society or a gay couple).

- Omission of key family members perspectives in current research (grandparents and siblings).

Within literature on family participation in leisure, feminism is another key strand of research within leisure management to be considered. This is based around traditional family make-up in that the mother is seen to invest more time in leisure activities than the father. Hodge et al. (2015) noted there is an unequal intensity of time spent on planning family leisure time in activities. In addition, it is seen that regardless of the mother spending more time within these activities, the father may have a more authoritative determining position:

> It is not difficult to imagine a traditional married couple in which the leisure preferences of the wife are subordinated to those of her spouse.
>
> (Crawford and Godbey, 1987: p.122)

The above quotation is time and context bound in its assertion. However, within a family there will undoubtedly be different opinions on how to spend leisure time. In this way, the genders within this will have to negotiate and compromise on decisions. If one party is more interested in specific sporting or leisure activities this will lead to an argument in which to choose. Framing feminist issues in leisure research is a common link to family participation in leisure activity.

Before moving onto recreation management research themes, a summary is offered on future areas of research for leisure management. Jackson (2000) suggested the following four areas of research needed to consider 21st-century leisure management:

1. The process of leisure requires negotiation between the individual and contextual circumstances that enhance or detract from people's ability to achieve their leisure goals.
2. Constraints and transitions: are these constraints particularly pertinent at transitional points in people's lives (e.g., entering high school, marriage, birth of the first child, divorce, death of a spouse, emigration)? Do transitions provide new opportunities for leisure negotiation?
3. Turning constraints into opportunities: why are some people particularly successful in their leisure lives, not only negotiating constraints but also viewing constraining factors more positively as opportunities to develop new leisure interests and pursuits?
4. Constraints and benefits: empirical investigation coupled with theoretical exploration is needed to enhance the integration of these two recent dominant themes in North American leisure studies.

(Jackson, 2000: p.66)

Henderson and Bialeschki (2005) also clarified the following five areas of research continuing within leisure research:

1. Outdoor recreation research notes how people impact the environment rather than how the natural environmental positively impacts people within the experience.
2. The built environment research focusses on management issues, rather than how these support active lifestyles (e.g. gym equipment in parks being vandalised, but conversely being used by a range of local inhabitants).
3. Time spent in active leisure requires more research to understand how the increase in free time is not translating into more time devoted to an active life style (e.g. 30 minutes per day as recommended).
4. Barriers exist and require analysis.
5. How social capital affects interdependent leisure activity and participation.

These four strands of recommended research refer to a need for social interdependence to complete leisure activity. The social and cultural dimensions of parks and recreational spaces require exploration in order to support active lifestyles.

ACTIVITY 2.4 GET POETIC ABOUT THE FUTURE OF LEISURE MANAGEMENT RESEARCH

Sjollema and Yuen (2017) use creative analysis practice (CAP) to help participants explain their opinions on leisure. CAP, as described in their paper, is whereby participants write poems to express their feelings.

Using the eight future areas of research for leisure, create a poem explaining the key areas of research required.

Now moving onto recreation, Torkildsen (2011) noted that recreation is often seen as organised activities. These activities can be seen as leisure or tourist activities completed within leisure time. As recreation literature overlaps with leisure it is important to note a few positions on this from current research in order to understand its link. However, literature on this is limited and so a brief discussion is offered.

The key to recreation, similarly to leisure, is that it is completed in free time. Recreation is often considered an outdoor activity (Lieber and Fesenmaier, 1983) within worldwide contexts (Pigram, 1985). As recreation is often within locations of national heritage or environmental protection, there is a need for management of these sites to create public policy on how people use the spaces:

> Managers adopt regulations not because they are authoritarian personalities or closet storm troopers, but because they are very committed, concerned people who place a high personal value on creating lands and particularly on wilderness.
>
> (Lucas, 1983: p.8)

A key element, therefore, to working in a recreational area is to be aware of the conservational, heritage or environmental issues present in that area. Entrants wanting to work in local government offices concerned with land used for recreation and leisure need to have awareness of this in order to maintain safe leisure activities and businesses that protect the local environment.

Similarly to Lucas (1983), Needham and Szuster (2011) considered how coastal and marine environments are affected by tourists. Wilderness and fringe events, and hospitality businesses, are therefore included in these. Both Lucas and Needham and Szuster outline two approaches to protecting recreation locations:

1. Restrict access via public policy.
2. Outline appropriate behaviour to reduce human impact.

Both of these strategies clarify how customers, businesses and workers require education on how to operate within areas of natural heritage for recreational activity. Recreation sites are advised to complete the following actions in support of maintaining these environments:

1. Improved education and information on the site.
2. Enhanced upkeep and maintenance of the site.
3. More facilities and services (cafés, car parks and toilets).

CASE STUDY 2.2 HOUSTON'S ARBORETUM AND NATURE CENTRE

Houston's Arboretum and Nature Centre is an example of a recreational site that celebrates the natural habitat of the local environment whilst educating customers and offering a site of leisure activity. There are walks available across the site to review local birds and animals and a central visitor centre where visitors can learn about the area and consume catering products. The website for the Arboretum notes:

> Located on the western edge of Memorial Park, the Houston Arboretum & Nature Center offers an escape from the hustle and bustle of city life and the opportunity to experience the natural world. This 155-acre non-profit urban nature sanctuary provides education about the natural environment to people of all ages. It plays a vital role in protecting native plants and animals in the heart of the city where development threatens their survival. The Houston Arboretum is a private non-profit educational facility that operates city land.

This park offers a case example of a city park that operates as a site for leisure and recreation activity to help educate tourists on the natural environment. Unlike theme parks noted earlier in this chapter, this form of park is supported in order to highlight local nature and preserve animals and plants.

The history of this site is noted as follows:

The land on which the Houston Arboretum & Nature Center sits is part of Memorial Park, one of the largest urban parks in the country. From 1917 to 1923, the land was the site of Camp Logan, a World War I Army training camp. After the war, in 1924, the land was deeded to the City of Houston to be set aside as a park dedicated to the memory [of] the fallen soldiers of World War I.

The idea to create an arboretum began with local ecologist and educator Robert A. Vines who advocated carving out a piece of land from Memorial Park to serve as a nature sanctuary. In 1951, City Council agreed to his proposal and set aside 265 acres as an arboretum and botanical garden; since that time, roads and their rights-of-way have reduced the size of the arboretum to 155 acres. Vines' intense botanical research sparked the interest and enthusiasm of Mrs. Susan M. McAshan, Jr., and in 1966, through a major contribution from the McAshan Educational and Charitable Trust, the Aline McAshan Botanical Hall for Children was funded.

On February 17, 1967, ground was broken for a nature center building. In the 1980s, the organization changed its name from the Houston Botanical Society to the Houston Arboretum & Nature Center to better represent the wild and natural quality of the surrounding grounds.

In 1995, funds from a capital campaign provided for a building renovation and the installation of new, state-of-the-art Discovery Room exhibits. This expansion allowed for an increase in the variety of Nature Center program offerings and sparked a surge in attendance.

The Meadow Restoration Project began in 1999 with a gift from Marie and Anthony Kraft. Through cooperation of many state and local agencies, the Arboretum was able to perform a much-needed prescribed burn to renovate soil and improve vegetation in the meadow.

The Charlotte Couch Memorial Birding Walkway was dedicated in the fall of 2000. Designed and built to reduce impact to the forest habitat, this raised walkway allows visitor access to views of Buffalo Bayou and the forest canopy while protecting a fragile ecotone.

A Wildlife Garden, which demonstrates plantings appropriate to attract hummingbirds, butterflies and other wildlife to an urban backyard, and the Carol Tatkon Sensory Garden featuring native plants attractive to the senses are the latest additions to the Arboretum's ever-changing landscape.

Source: https://houstonarboretum.org/

Recreation management research focusses on customer behaviour and site management to ensure the conservation and heritage of the area is maintained. It has been noted that it is important for employees to be aware of environmental concerns in these locations. People who like recreation are termed recreationists (Louviere and Timmermans, 1990). Louviere and Timmermans' (1990) article identified six issues in researching recreation and recreationists:

1.   Customer perception of competitor recreation activities.
2.   Customer preferences for different facilities within recreational businesses.
3.   Predicting customer recreational choices and behaviours.
4.   Predicting customer attendance at unique recreational events.
5.   Predicting customer choices for recreational experience within the existing competitive market.
6.   Estimation of customer perceptions on context effects.

These research strands seen in the early 1990s clarify further the link between recreation theory and customer participation management. Butler (2015) and Getz and Page (2016b) all link recreation management to tourism and events management due to the similar customer markets seen consuming these experiences.

CASE STUDY 2.3 BOARDMASTERS SUPPORTING LOCAL ENVIRONMENTS

For almost 20 years we've worked closely with our long standing partner Surfers Against Sewage to implement sustainable & environmental strategies at Boardmasters, that grow greater year on year. We're learning, and we strive to do our best and improve. From Litter Bonds to the Green Team, beach cleans to the mammoth post-festival clean up operation, banning plastic straws to implementing a cup deposit scheme; our mission is to reduce our environmental impact and run an enjoyable, sustainable festival.

2018 Impact Figures from Boardmasters Festival:

*   16,000 bags of rubbish collected by Litter Bonds.
*   1.5 tonnes of rubbish collected in the annual beach cleans.
*   No single use plastic in the main arenas.
*   £20,000 donated to Surfers Against Sewage.
*   £53,000 donated to local charities.
*   100,000 plastic bottles saved by promoting reusable bottles on site.
*   2 Sustainability awards won at the Cornwall Sustainability Awards.

Source: https://www.boardmasters.com/info/sustainability

This section has clarified the research and industry contexts of leisure and recreation management. It has identified key themes in research linking to employability and skills in

THE. Knowledge of park management, conservation sites and outdoor activity participation are all highlighted as important factors when working in THE businesses located in leisure and recreation. Leisure participation and customer management in recreation sites are important management considerations when operating tourist businesses within these contexts. Therefore, both leisure and recreation are inherently connected to THE due to customer leisure time being used in sites of leisure and recreation.

MANAGEMENT STYLES AND BUSINESS STRUCTURES

Within the leisure and recreation literature, there are assertions made on the form and structure of operating businesses. The structure of these companies is important for employability in THE as it clarifies potential management styles and organisational cultures present. When you are considering employment within a THE company, the structure and management styles present will mould your position, duties and influence within the company. For example, if it is a small independent company you may have significant responsibility and influence on the products and experiences offered. Conversely, looking to work in a multi-national company will naturally mean the operating procedures are static and you would work within larger teams working towards higher income targets. These examples offer insight into two extremes in organisational structure, but they serve to clarify how a company structure will impact management style and employee influence. This is offered here from leisure management literature to clarify the make-up of THE businesses within leisure sectors.

Authors (such as Henry, 1993) have linked leisure company development to public policy. Governments impact upon leisure companies in its governance of operating procedures. For example, Henry (1993) noted that UK monarchs preferred specific forms of recreational activity and, as such, allowed certain types of events and businesses to succeed and thrive in support of these national events.

In Henry's (1993) review of leisure policy and politics it is suggested that external policy affected the structure, management style and business form.

Table 2.2, from Henry (1993), suggests that economic shifts from manufacturing intensive (Fordism) to service sector (Post-Fordism) altered the structure of leisure businesses. It is not simply that all leisure companies became flat and flexible structures with more skilled labour, but that these emerged as a significant portion of businesses within the sector. Torkildsen (2005) affirms this in noting that leisure businesses have particular organisational structures. These structures are dependent on local policy but also affect other THE and service companies.

The structures of companies operating in leisure is an important consideration when seeking employment in leisure-related businesses, as you will need to ascertain which

Table 2.2 Economic impacts of leisure management: Fordism affects

Elements of leisure business	Fordism up to 1970s	Post-Fordism 1970s+
Management type	Corporate management, centralised control	De-concentration, autonomous roles to section/division managers
Manufacturing and markets	Mass production, deskilled labour Mass consumption	Flexible production Skilled labour Market niches
Organisation types	Mechanistic, 'tall', bureaucratic	Oragnismic, 'flat', flexible

Source: based on Henry, 1993: p.181

structure and at what level you want to gain employment. Torkildsen (2005) cited the International City Management Association (1965: p.492) structures in his review of leisure organisational management as follows:

1. Unity of command: each employee has a single manager who manages their duties and performance. An example of this in THE would be an assistant stage manager reporting to the stage manager. One singular manager who works closely with the employee.
2. Logical assignment: employees who complete the same role or duties are grouped and managed by one manager. An example of this in THE would be a restaurant manager who leads all waiting staff.
3. Span of control: a company would identify a maximum number of employees a manager could lead. This dictates how the span of control is organised. An example of this in THE would be within a festival where staff are grouped and managed by different shift managers, even though they are completing the same role. Security staff, for example, are often managed in this way. The shift times and length of shift would also influence the number of employees managed per manager in this example.
4. Authority and power: the form of business dictates the authority used and influence management have on their employees. A THE example would be an independent café with 20 covers and a national chain of cafes. The manager of the small café would have legitimate authority and power on all employees work. Conversely, an area sales manager for a group of cafés would have less legitimacy perceived by employees in each store, but have more power to action significant business changes across the suite of cafés.

There is a well-known question used when coaching employees into new positions: do you want to be a small fish in a big pond, or a big fish in a small pond? The four structures of management control noted above clarify how this is present in leisure businesses. A smaller business will mean employees and lower management will have more flexibility and influence (seen as post-Fordism). Employment in a larger business will lead to reduced autonomy but potentially higher employment stability. Both company and department size can therefore identify the potential authority and influence employees can assert. Torkildsen (2005) further noted that departments in leisure companies are seen as being structured in five ways:

1. Functional: where by work is structured according to operations completed within a department. An example in THE would be in hotels where you have departments like front of house, housekeeping, and food and beverage, as structures to support internal operations. Employees would be based in a single department in support of the products and experiences within particular areas.
2. Clientele: structure of the organisation is based upon specific customer groups. Within tourism, airline classes are supported with specific employees who manage classes of customers. In major airlines like Emirates, Virgin or British Airways, their air stewards are trained and operate according to the class level of their clientele (like economy, business or first class).
3. Geographic: supply companies are created in locations of significant operational need. This can be seen as locally or nationally located. THE examples can be seen in local food produce suppliers to a restaurant whereby local farms are contracted to supply meat or vegetables for catering operations. Alternatively, event production companies may not have a clear base of operations as they need to be mobile to attend and support event operations at a range of venues.
4. Process: similarly to functional, leisure organisations are structured according to processes required in producing the experience or product. Large kitchens in hospitality businesses evidence this in their line management of chefs within the creation of specific menus and dishes. The role within chef de partie's like pantry, pastry, friturier, patissier, poissonnier and boucher, evidence this in kitchen environments. Similarly, in event management there are production, security, artist, tickets and marketing managers for key processes on site.
5. Time or shift: management is structured according to the times of work and shift patterns required to support operations. In an airport arrivals and departure areas management is structured according to key shifts throughout the day. In THE, time or shift structures are often seen in businesses operating 24 hours a day. Management is required to oversee all operations rather than specific departments or processes.

The five structures of management offered from Torkildsen (2005) enable clarification of where employees and management sit within a leisure business. Examples offered within these enable you to consider how employment duties may differ according to the structures present. It is not simply that one of these is applied universally within a company, as a few may be present within the organisation. The role you complete will be situated in one of these and therefore affect your influence, shift pattern, customer contact and autonomy within the company. To exemplify this further, Table 2.3 suggests the appropriate number of subordinates, superiors, shift patterns, organisation size and location, which may all differ according to the structure of the company and department.

Table 2.3 Role variances according to departmental structure

	Function	Clientele	Geographic	Process	Time or shift
Number of subordinates	10+	10+	5+	5+	5+
Number of superiors	1	1	1	2+	2+
Shift pattern per day	2/3	1	1	2/3	2/3+
Organisation size	Large	Large	Small to medium	Any	Any
Organisation location	Central to tourist areas	Located in sites of customer demand and potentially mobile	Mobile to support national companies	Central to tourist areas	Mobile and central to tourist areas

Table 2.3 seeks to outline variances in employee and management numbers within the five organisation structures suggested by Torkildsen (2005).

In terms of employment practices within leisure, Henry (1990) confirmed that leisure companies operate flexible employment practices due to peaks and troughs in consumer demands. Flexible employment relates to the form of contract an employee has within a company or organisation. Employment contracts are usually seen as temporary, fixed term or permanent.

- Temporary contracts are offered to employees in support of fluctuating customer demand. Leisure businesses use these in order to staff operations on a week by week basis and ensure they do not pay wages during months when there may be lower tourist demand. This is seen most acutely within tourist resorts where employees will fly in from a range of locations in order to work for a few weeks or months. Even if they are based in a tourist location, their shift patterns may fluctuate weekly in order to be available for higher tourist demand. Evidently this is in support of business profits, rather than employee's financial stability.
- Fixed-term contracts enable an employee to be paid and complete work within a specified time. Events and hospitality suppliers often work within these contracts to enable focussed support for leisure activities. The length of time in the contract will also depend on the leisure activity. For example, artist liaison managers may be employed for six months before a music festival to support the management of acts. Their contract

would be temporary, but within the dates stipulated they would have stable income and duties to complete. Again, this is appropriate for the form of leisure activity and duties to complete. It would not be financially viable to employ staff permanently for one off events.

- Permanent contracts are the most stable for employees. These are offered as continuous employment in a leisure business. Duties completed may be static if they work in a functional structure or flexible if they are within a small company where all tasks need completion within the shift. A business employing permanent staff would have more fixed or stable business throughout the year.

The brief review of employment contracts given above is offered to support the definition of management styles and business structures, as employment within these will also vary. This can also be linked to the size of a business (MNC to SME).

This section has outlined models of organisational structure in leisure in order to clarify how public policy and economic fluctuations can dictate the frames in which these businesses are created. Knowledge of these differences within the leisure sectors is important in order to understand how THE businesses alter according to customer, management and operational needs.

RESEARCH STRANDS IN SUPPORT OF TOURISM, HOSPITALITY AND EVENTS MANAGEMENT EMPLOYABILITY AND SKILL DEVELOPMENT

This final section of the chapter offers a review of contemporary research strands within THE seen as linked to employability and skills development. This will outline contemporary issues relevant to employability and skills for THE as well as signal existing knowledge linked to development of these industries and professionalisation of employment within.

Table 2.4 clarifies some of the sources used in support of this discussion. It should be noted that these are not all encompassing of all publications and research available. They were chosen due to their extensive analysis of existing publications linked to THE employment and were published in peer reviewed journals. In using these seven articles, 1825 research publications are acknowledged from 1939 to 2016. These are mainly English language publications, but they reflect a range of THE businesses across the world. For example, Omerzel's (2016) article reflects research completed in Europe, Asia, the USA, the Caribbean, Africa and Australia. This table may appear imbalanced in focus upon tourism publications, but as noted previously, the THE sectors overlap in society. In this way, although the table highlights the area of THE published within, it is accepted that the publications will relate to a range of THE businesses and contexts.

Research into tourism and discussion of how visitors and businesses support tourist activities have a long history in English language research publications. As noted earlier, as the professionalisation of these fields was not seen until the 1980s, there is still existing tensions

Table 2.4 Articles used to evidence THE research strands on employability and skills

Author	Publications and years examined	Area of THE observed
Okumus et al. (2018)	462 publications between 1976 and 2016	Hospitality (gastronomy)
Shoval and Ahas (2016)	45 peer reviewed articles between 1995 and 2015	Tourism (tracking technologies)
Getz and Page (2016b)	677 articles between 1970 and 2016	Event tourism
Light (2017)	266 articles between 1996 and 2016	Dark and heritage tourism
Butler (2015)	62 articles between 1933 and 2012	Tourism and tourism research
Omerzel (2016)	152 papers between 1992 and 2014	Innovation in tourism and hospitality
Jin and Wang (2016)	161 articles between 2000 and 2014	Outbound tourism

on the academic value or worth in researching this as a field of study. Tourism and leisure is heavily linked to social participation and economic support for leisure time. In order to situate its history and presence within academic literature, Butler's (2015) article enables clarification of the following key points:

Definition	Tourism is analysing what visitors do.
Characteristics	What tourists do and how they interact.
Themes in tourism	Travel to observe, learn, participate, relax, support and appreciate a local area.
Areas linked	Anthropology, economics, business management, history, sociology, leisure, recreation, geography, development studies, political science, international studies, architecture, urban studies, rural development, language and culture studies.
Active research	Since the 1990s, research on tourism has been seen as a separate field of study.

The above details offer clarification on what tourism research is focussed on, where it is researched and how it is linked to other disciplines of academic study. This will aid readers in finding and understanding known functions, structures and management of tourism businesses in order to seek employment. Getz and Page's (2016b) analysis of event tourism research clarifies not only how these fields of study link and overlap, but how there are clear career paths within tourism and events management.

Table 2.5 can be used to understand how events and tourism careers link and overlap. The key duties enable readers to consider if they would enjoy the work and types of duties within these roles. These were created with knowledge of the event tourism developments

Table 2.5 Event tourism career paths

Typical functions	Major tasks
Event facilitator/ Coordinator	• Research tourism potential of the event destination (funding, advice, marketing). • Venue liaison including request for proposals and negotiation on costs and suppliers. • Networking with other event and tourism management companies and event management contractors.
Event tourism producer	• Production of event concepts and design based upon tourism impact and value. • Supplier, partner and stakeholder management.
Event tourism planner	• Liaise with destination venues and local government to aid the creation of an event tourism strategy. • Utilise tourism product and place marketing as a focus and catalyst for event concepts.
Event tourism policy analyst and researcher	• Review the local government tourism strategy and undertake research to support goals and targets. Research could include destination/product/experience evaluations, feasibility assessments or tourism performance evaluations. • Using your research skills, offer local government tourism departments advice from analysis of data to facilitate new tourism event concepts.
Event bidder	• Identify calls for event destination hosts and assess their suitability for the destination and tourism strategy of the local area. • Research previous successful host destinations for the events and evaluate their bidding processes and supporting infrastructure, which led to their success. • Create the event bid documentation: venue analysis, local public transport infrastructure, risk assessments, feasibility studies and contingency plans.
Event services agent	• Work within a venue offering tourist services linked to event production. • Employment in any supply chain organisation linked to tourist services. These could include leisure and recreation businesses as well as THE ones.

Source: based upon Getz and Page, 2016b: p.596

in research and industry roles over a number of decades. Getz and Page's (2016b) article offers a considerate discussion on key themes in event tourism research and future directions from secondary, desk-based analysis of a considerable number of sources. Within their summary they identify a range of consumer trends linking to event tourism with there also being an alignment to employability and skills to THE:

- Daily experiences are being developed into themed and alternative events. This means there is innovation seen in production and employment forms in event tourism.
- Consumer interest in heritage and history means that tourist activities require more employee knowledge on local traditional and cultural events.
- Increases in leisure participation means that events are seen as a new form of social capital whereby consumer experience is shared as evidence of tourist activity. Knowledge of this will ensure events are connected and supportive of leisure activity.
- Transnational flows of people across the world means that access and work with a range of people is usual and no longer unexpected. In employment this means that services are created in more societies and with a more international labour market.
- Technology, such as social media, used by customers and employees in events means that information on tourist participation is increasing from multiple positions. Employees need to find customer posts and react to these in order to manage customer expectations and feedback.
- Tourists increasingly want what they perceive to be authentic, rather than staged, activities. This requires employees to understand historically accurate production of these activities.
- Individual spending power has seen a significant increase. This means that tourists have access to more money and want to spend more on event tourism. Employees should ensure that their production of tourist activity meets the standards of service appropriate for the cost of these to consumers.
- Populations have seen an increase in average life span. This means that customer market groups are larger in older age categories. Employees must understand the unique requirements of the aging populations in order to satisfy and support their tourist experience.
- Ethical considerations within tourist activity is prevalent across the world. Employees and event tourist businesses need to consider green policy and practice in order to support the local and national environments.
- Instead of participating and enjoying tourist experiences, consumers have an increasing need to share and celebrate their attendance at events using technology platforms. Again, employees need to be mindful of this as they, and their tourist service, may be recorded, photographed and shared on the internet. Instead of completing the event separate from society, technology is now enabling customers to share their perceptions of an event using social media. This means employees need to be constantly aware of their actions and behaviours as they may be more closely monitored.

Getz and Page's (2016a and 2016b) reviews of over 600 articles on event tourism has enabled clarification of both current and future issues in research themes within this joint sector. Most importantly, it enables clarification on the forms of knowledge and skills required for successful employment and business development for tourism and event businesses. Using the list above, readers can both perceive how tourism and events are linked in employment and perceive how current research strands outline working practices for companies producing tourist events.

Omerzel (2016) states that hospitality and tourism sectors are seen to have innovated within employment and growth in recent decades. This is linked to the growth of service sector economies within western countries, but is also seen as natural within THE businesses due to the fluctuations in customer demand. Personal skills, skilled labour, experience of using skills and skill development were all noted as vital within innovation for tourism and hospitality. In consideration of the practical management implications for innovation in tourism and hospitality, the author notes:

> Alertness is also required when hiring employees with multiple skills, training employees for multiple skills and modelling the organisational climate and training plans in developing managerial characteristics, as employees often influence innovation activity and performance.
>
> (Omerzel, 2016: p.543)

Therefore, innovation as a research strand within tourism and hospitality can be seen to be a component employability skill for applicants to showcase as a strength they have to offer in employment. Being aware of, and making suggestions for, improved processes and products within THE businesses will undoubtedly be viewed as a strength in employment.

Okumus et al. (2018) considered research publications from 45 countries across the world within food and gastronomy (the majority in the UK, n=514, with the least amount in Turkey, China, France and Macau, each n=5). Conclusions in this research outlined how traditional courses in tourism and hospitality lack focussed attention to food production, gastronomy, food safety and food production. It was agreed that these areas are of importance within tourism and hospitality knowledge for successful employment, but that due to the decrease in culinary schools these may have resulted in reduced research focus. They assert that these areas would fit within food science, biology and scientific linked disciplines of study. This paper does not align research strands in food and gastronomy with employability and skills for working within associated roles, but it is clear that knowledge of the following is required within food and gastronomy roles:

- Food science.
- Food and health.
- Food and culinary production, food and culture, food safety.
- Food availability.
- Food tourism.
- Food and education.

Although food is mostly aligned to research in hospitality and culinary arts, it is ever present within tourism activities and events. In this way, these areas are noted as important for any role linked to food production and management.

CASE STUDY 2.4 QUALITATIVE RESEARCH IN TOURISM: LINKS TO EMPLOYABILITY AND SKILLS

Wilson and Hollinshead's (2015) article proposes that tourism researchers need to pay further attention to qualitative research within the soft sciences. They clarify eight key themes for future qualitative research for tourism. These have all been linked to employability and skills in this case example in order to clarify how future directions in tourism research may impact upon knowledge for THE employment and skills:

1.   Critical pedagogy.

An approach to research which seeks to re-frame ways in which the world is viewed. Bring critical of ways of seeing things in order to create a more balanced society. This position views employees within tourism as:

> 'cultural' or 'ideological' workers who are often consciously (or unconsciously) furthering an existing hegemony, or who are otherwise cultivating resistance to the ways that a particular place, space, inheritance has been regarded.
>
> (p.35)

Therefore, THE employees should evidence critical pedagogy by critiquing usual positions within societies in order to problematise and equalise issues present.

2.   Critical discourse analysis.

A position which requires discourse and power relations to be addressed in existing published documentation. For example, adverts, guidebooks, magazines and blogs for tourist activities. Analysis of these written documents enables researchers to consider how hosts and guests interact. Therefore, application of critical discourse analysis will reveal attitudes and power relations between workers and consumers of tourism activities.

3.   Feminist research.

Authors accept a range of theories and research befitting feminist themes in tourism. They suggest that the overarching areas of consideration are how gender is socially constructed and how tourism research should look to improve women's lives. Future research in this strand will support employability and skills for THE in addressing social inequality seen for women. Particular consideration on sole female travel, safety and security of women, and how women are viewed in tourist activities is needed to understand how to attract, support and meet the needs of female guests.

4.   Ethnoaesthetics/ethnopoetics.

Research in ethnoaesthetics and ethnopoetics is traditionally seen in postcolonial locations. They rely heavily on understanding cultural understandings of experiences. As such, they would review culture as being a lived, rather than static experience. THE employment will increasingly require employee knowledge on culture, however differences in lived culture, and emergent culture within political governance of an area, are particularly important for maintaining successful tourism businesses.

5.   Autoethnography.

This position is a self-reflective and self-reflexive account of how the research sits within cultural, political and social contexts. How an employee perceives their own position within the environment of a THE business will affect how they are able to relate to, work with and manage the array of employees and customers present.

6.   Performance ethnography.

Based upon the human rights of others, this research position enables a researcher to perform research using vocal, body, symbolic, movement and gesture in order to perform interpretations. Within THE employment you will already complete this within your body and oral reactions to customer and colleague demands. In this way, industry practice in completing performance is being moved into academic research spheres in order to amplify understandings and analysis of tourism contexts.

7.   Paraethnography.

Here, research participants are not simply asked to offer opinions, information or perspectives within an area, but instead are required to participate with the researcher in creation of community-based tasks.

8.   Indigenist research/epistemologies of colour.

Making researchers of indigenous contexts consider empowerment and resistance is core to this position. Emphasis here is on ensuring colonisers confront issues and traumas present as a result of colonisation. As THE businesses emerge within existing colonised locations it is important employees are aware of the historical and political issues present in order to appraise problems local customers may have as a result of colonisation.

In connection to the case study on emerging research positions for tourism offered from Wilson and Hollinshead (2015), Lamers et al., (2017) suggest that tourism is increasingly seen as a 'social practice.' This position is offered to suggest that future research in tourism needs to consider the range of activities and performances present within the industry. Social practices in tourism can be seen in combination with the following elements:

1. Performance of tourism services.
2. Material products offered or used in tourism services.
3. Competences of employees and customers.
4. Rules or social norms within the context of the practice.
5. Policy surrounding the practice (government or business regulations).

Lamers et al. (2017) discuss two key theoretical fields associated to social practices: performativity and actor network.

ACTIVITY 2.5 PERFORMANCE AND ACTING IN TOURISM AS A SOCIAL PRACTICE

Within Lamers et al.'s (2017) discussion of social practice in tourism studies, they suggest two overarching theoretical positions: performativity and actor network. Their discussion on these is offered below for consideration.

Performativity studies and social practice:

Both performativity and practice research draw their inspiration from Erving Goffman's performance approach to social interaction (Spaargaren et al., 2016). Related to tourism, numerous authors have explored the metaphor of performance to investigate how tourism can be studied as a set of activities (e.g. Edensor, 2001; Coleman and Crang, 2002; Haldrup and Larson, 2009). By looking at the contexts in which tourism is regulated, directed and choreographed, or alternatively how tourism is a realm of improvisation and contestation, Edensor (2001) considers the constraints and opportunities that shape the ways in which tourist space and performance are reproduced, challenged, transformed and bypassed. Just as practice theories argue that camping, sailing, backpacking and other tourism activities should be studied in terms of practices, performance studies claim that most everyday tourism practices can be analysed as performances. Both practice theories and performance studies focus on what people do, not in a detached way but through ethnographic involvement. However, whereas performance studies predominantly focus on what practice theories would denote as practices-as-performances, practice theorists are also particularly interested in practices-as-entities and in the ways in which they manage to attract recruits that become more or less faithful practitioners or carriers of the practice (Shove et al., 2012).

Actor network theory and social practices:

The second contemporary theoretical approach within tourism studies that comes close to practice theories is Actor Network Theory (ANT). Authors such as Ren, Jóhannesson, Franklin, Simoni and Van der Duim have inspired tourism studies by utilising insights from ANT (Van der Duim and Ren, 2012; Van der Duim, Ren and Jóhannesson, 2013; see also Van der Duim, 2007). Both ANT and practice theories are relational materialist theories that enable radical new ways of analysing tourism by insisting on a flat ontology, by critically investigating social-material dimensions and by providing toolkits for generating more telling analyses of the heterogeneous relations in tourism, based on a firm grounding in empirical case studies (Souza Bispo, 2016). Similar to the recent interest of practice theories in larger social phenomena (like many tourism associated problems) (Lamers and Van der Duim, 2016; Schatzki, 2016a, 2016b), Latour has argued that

> there are two different ways of envisaging the macro–micro relationship: the first one builds a series of Russian Matryoshka dolls – the small is being enclosed, the big is enclosing; and the second deploys connections – the small is being unconnected, the big one is to be attached.
>
> (Latour, 2005: p.180)

It is the second approach that ANT puts forward that closely resembles the argument of extensiveness in practice theories.

1. Define performativity and actor network theory based on the above discussion from Lamers et al. (2017).
2. How are these two theories important for employee skills and knowledge for work within tourism businesses and environments?

As noted by Getz and Page (2016b), ethical choices in green tourist activity has increased significantly in the last two decades. This is in tandem with consumer spending power and increased choice in tourist activity. Light (2017) offers a similar piece in review of tourism research but concentrates on how dark tourism and heritage tourism are in conflict. In particular, Light highlights that the management of dark tourism activities by employees has been *'rarely'* considered (Light, 2017: p.298). Dark tourism is seen as activities whereby customers view, engage or re-enact historical occasions where mass destruction, death or suffering has occurred. A key part in managing and creating these experiences is that management need to be psychologically and consciously distant to the event. This is due to the highly emotionally charged experiences and events associated with dark tourism (for example, the holocaust or the twin towers attacks). Customer's motivations for attending these forms of tourist activity are numerous and include education, genealogy, personal interest, political discourse and military interest. Clearly, working in a location of dark tourism will mean employees require a knowledge of the disaster or culture being re-created or presented for tourists. If employees have had similar experiences or family connections to the event being created it may enhance the authenticity of the experience for customers, but it will also require a greater amount of psychological strength in order to complete working duties.

Shoval and Ahas (2016) is the last paper to discuss in relation to current research strands supporting employability and skills for THE. Their paper addresses a specific area of research into using tracking technology to ascertain tourist behaviour and movement around tourist destinations. This form of research is important to advise management of THE companies on how their customers move and participate within their leisure experience. The data can aid decisions on locations of key production elements as well as educate employees on how to advise new customers on usual activities completed by previous tourists. There are ethical issues within this strand as some customers will not allow researchers to track their movements, and once they are tracked researchers are unsure if the tracking device, or knowledge of being tracked, alters their usual patterns of movement. As tracking customers is an emergent strand in THE research it is an important consideration for employees and management in these businesses. The data and resulting actions possible from tracking customers comes with caveats around data protection. In the UK, there is improved legislation around personal data use within the General Data Protection Regulations (GDPR). This legislation means that anyone offering their data has to give written consent to agree to have their data tracked and used. This is appropriate practice for any employee or manager looking to track or use customer data as it ensures they are fully informed on the purpose and management of their data.

THINK POINT 2.4 TRACKING EMPLOYEES

This think point serves as a case example and a think point. Fit Together, a South Korean technology company, tracks football and sporting players during matches. This is to enable analysis on their movements and decisions within a game. As Shoval and Ahas (2016) have outlined the use of tracking customers in tourist locations to support THE business, this think point raises questions for discussion in the potential direction of tracking technology:

1. Do you think THE employers will track employees during their shifts?
2. If so, do you think this is cost effective and appropriate?

SUMMARY

1.   Explore definitions on tourism, hospitality and events management.

The opening section offered statistics and quantitative data on the size and locations of THE businesses. This relied on global and national reports on economic elements. Gross domestic products and labour market make-up was noted as key in understanding the sectors of THE. At present THE offers significant economic contribution and support to a range of national economies. In this way, employment within an associated business will be successful and supported as economies are more heavily reliant on services and experiences.

2.   Examine how leisure and recreation can be seen as overarching sectors within which tourism, hospitality and events are situated.

From sectoral reports it is evident that THE are not simply treated as individual sectors. This first acceptance allows readers to acknowledge that even if they are studying tourism, hospitality or events related courses, the employment routes will not stay fixed to these terms. Businesses associated with THE were identified as providing leisure activities within recreational environments. In this way, leisure and recreation are accepted as overarching terms linked to THE. Knowledge of leisure participation and environmental protection in recreation is needed by new entrants into employment to ensure they are aware of how customers interact and are controlled in THE contexts.

3.   Appraise current thought on recreation and leisure.

Leisure is free time wherein activities are completed in public spaces. Parks are often noted and so this links to events management employment. Barriers to leisure participation, social unrest and feminist theory is important. Recreation is based upon outdoor activity in natural environments, which tourists could negatively affect. Conservation and heritage knowledge is required by entrants to businesses seen within recreation sites in order to support the natural environment. Leisure organisations are seen to be affected by national government policy. Their structure and management styles are based upon customer demand fluctuations. Knowledge of company structure can aid decisions on which form and type of company to apply to work within.

4.   Identify research strands in tourism, hospitality and events management specifically linked to staff professional development in these sectors.

- Event tourism literature clarifies how experience economies, aging populations, the increased use of technology and the need for authentic events are driving research projects and investigation into support for employability and skills for staff in these working contexts.
- Skills and knowledge in innovative practice and products are important to aid development of THE businesses.
- Food and gastronomy knowledge is largely unrepresented in academic literature, but still viewed as a core employability skill linking to scientific disciplines.
- Emerging research methods and positions will mean future research will offer a wider range of perspectives in a number of mediums (for example, poetry and performance).

- Businesses which link to environmental protection, dark tourism or use customer tracking (for examples) will need to ensure employees have contemporary and historic knowledge related to the experiences offered. They may also require further training on how to respond to customer queries surrounding contemporary issues linked to THE business (such as climate change and aviation practices).

Questions to support your learning and research

1. How do THE support gross domestic product of major countries?
2. When was THE seen to become professionalised within the UK?
3. What is leisure time and how does this relate to THE businesses?
4. How do public parks create new spaces?
5. How do theme parks differ from public parks and how do the employment roles differ within these?
6. What three strands or research are reviewed in leisure management?
7. What is CAP?
8. In which THE business locations do you need heritage and conservation knowledge?
9. How does organisational structure and management style affect the role and duties to be completed within a leisure business?
10. Why is there a division seen in Fordism and post-Fordism companies? How did the economy affect this?
11. What are the three forms of employment noted with leisure management?
12. How do current research strands in THE aid knowledge of employability and skills development for THE?

Chapter 3

Graduate employment

LEARNING OBJECTIVES

1. To understand what graduate employment means to students and employers.
2. To ascertain applicant skills graduate employers in tourism, hospitality and event management companies look for.
3. To evaluate company types to look for employment within them (multi-national, small to medium, non-profit, public and self).
4. To identify the form of business and role to apply for within THE.

INTRODUCTION

So far, this part has offered an overview of the sectors and skills required for employment in tourism, hospitality and event (THE) management roles. This chapter will identify and examine the skills graduate THE employers look for and show you how to become more entrepreneurial whilst studying. The final sub-sections will then examine employment direction within THE and leisure industries.

WHAT IS GRADUATE EMPLOYMENT?

Graduate employment is obtaining work or travel opportunities, where you are paid or trained within a specific sector or role. It does not relate to a specific salary or level of employment, but signals your ability to gain a contract of employment after completing your studies. Often, my students note they feel under pressure to obtain full-time, paid management positions after graduating from a course. As a lecturer in a UK university I remind my own students that their transition into graduate life will be unique – dependent on their own ambitions and reflective of the work opportunities and labour market in which they seek employment. This chapter will aim to squash any fears around graduate employment by outlining the various directions and positions possible after completing your studies.

Every employer seeking a new employee will know what type of person and skills they are looking for. Whether they need to fill a role that has just been vacated or a new position created through expansion of the company, every role will come with a job description and person specification. To start an appraisal of your own skills please complete reading and tasks provided in Chapter 4 of this part. The job description for a post will identify a range of duties and specifics relating to the role. It may include times of work, uniform, holiday entitlement and even the hierarchy of staff around which the role has been created. The most important part of a job description for any potential employee is the main duties. The main duties on a job description will inform you of the competencies, skills and abilities needed to complete the job. For the purpose of examining key skills for all THE positions I will firstly suggest you need to consider the following main duties:

1.   Liaising with a range of customers/stakeholders/suppliers.
2.   Managing staff/customers whilst on duty.
3.   Upholding the company brand.

These three core duties will be essential to every position within THE. To begin, you will always be dealing with customers, suppliers or stakeholders of the business. Communication skills are therefore a priority for every employer in the THE sector. However, this is not just appropriate communication, but effective communication.

Liaising with a range of customers/stakeholder/suppliers

Effective communication comes from an understanding of language. Verbal and body language are key in every encounter you have in employment. Whether you communicate in person ('service with a smile') or liaise over the phone, every aspect of your body communicates something to the other person. Verbal language is essential to communicate your needs and enable you to liaise with a range of different people. Whether you are understanding a request from a customer or informing staff of their working rota, you need to be able to speak the same language. Within international THE companies, this language is usually English. Please note, however, that the geographic location of the company will change the words and meaning of the English language.

Table 3.1 offers just a few examples of language differences within the English language. You will not be expected to know each and every difference, but it is vital that you are aware that there are differences in English words used, dependent on your geographic location. In the UK alone there are many words that have different meanings dependent on your location (also termed colloquialisms). For example someone in Yorkshire may say they need their 'badly' jumper. This would not mean that the jumper is dirty, it means that they want their jumper that makes them feel better, or a big snuggly jumper. If you were to use this phrase in America 'jumper' can mean a sleeveless dress, thus they may think you need a bad dress!

Table 3.1 British and American word meanings

Word	British	American
Bathroom	A room that contains a bath	A toilet
Chips	French fried potatoes	Potato crisps
First floor	The floor of a building that is one above the ground floor	The ground floor of any building
Pants	Underpants	Trousers
Tea	Hot beverage	Cold beverage (iced tea)
Vest	Underwear worn on the top part of your body	Underwear, or more usually a waistcoat

THINK POINT 3.1 COMMUNICATING EFFECTIVELY

Have you had any situations where you have tried to communicate in English and have found your words or meaning are understood by the other person differently to your understanding of them.

How did you overcome this?

How did this help or interfere with your communication?

Was it amusing or insulting?

What will you do in the future?

To discuss the body language aspect of communication we will now consider the paralinguistic elements of communication (see also Chapter 7 for communication and inter-personal skill development). Paralinguistic elements in non-verbal communication are as follows:

- Haptics – touch (see Hall, 2000; Hertenstein et al., 2006).
- Kinesics – facial gestures and movements (see Birdwhistell, 1955).
- Proxemics – space (often seen as personal space) (see Hall, 1966).
- Chronemics – time (see research on intercultural competences).

ACTIVITY 3.1 PARALINGUISTIC COMMUNICATION WITH FRIENDS AND COLLEAGUES

Thinking about the four paralinguistic elements noted above, write out what touch, gestures, space and timing you use when communicating with a friend or a work colleague.

1.   How do these differ?
2.   What would happen if you swapped the paralinguistic communication you use with a friend to a colleague?
3.   Why do you think these differ? Is it important that they do?

When considering effective communication as an employment skill you also need to consider what type of company it is. For example, if you go to a McDonald's restaurant would you need to stand at the door and greet every customer on entry? Or if you worked for an airline on their planes would you expect customers to come to you to order food and beverages? Both of the questions are answered 'no', as they do not conform to the usual practices in either situation. Customers in McDonald's know to enter the restaurant and approach the counter to communicate with staff over a fixed counter. More recently, McDonald's restaurants require you to place your order using a screen and you do not need to talk to the staff when ordering and paying for your food. If you (as a worker) opened the door and greeted customers directly, they may be confused and not understand what you are trying to do. Equally, with the airline example, if customers had to find staff to order food, one of two things might happen:

1.   No one orders food as they are used to being asked for orders as they are seated on the plane.
2.   All customers stand up and find staff to order food and beverages, creating a queue in the aisle of the aircraft and so posing a health and safety risk.

For outcome 1 the company would not get any profit from the sales of on board services and the second outcome would create a health and safety hazard. Therefore, when considering effective communication you also need to consider customer expectations, practicalities in completing the service and the legal boundaries within which the company operates. If you are to effectively showcase this employment skill within an interview it is important that you offer situational examples. Furthermore, you must clarify how communication needs to be adaptable and flexible to the situation and person with whom you are communicating.

Manage staff/customers whilst on duty

Managing staff or customers requires you to have certain competences and competency to complete set duties.

Having a competence is being able to evidence a learnt skill from experience. Having competency is wherein you can prove your skill via a qualification. Therefore, your degree gives you competency in tourism, events, hospitality or leisure management. An example of competence would be being an effective communicator via evidence in work experience.

In Table 3.2, Suh et al. (2012) have identified key competencies needed to fulfil management positions in hospitality. These are key skills employers need from students and managers. All of these would be needed to manage staff and customers whilst working in THE. In this table, personal integrity and staff training are not noted in the ranked competencies for hospitality students. Does this mean hospitality students do not need these? Of course not! This is something to be aware of when researching and considering skills for employment. What one employer requires, another may feel is invalid for the position.

To complete management tasks it is also important to use your own knowledge. Industry and task knowledge will be evident from your qualifications.

Table 3.3 evidences the UK competency developed within each programme for THE. These are the areas that have been specified due to collaboration and discussion with employers across the sectors, however, for each and every situation in work you will

Table 3.2 Student and manager competencies for hospitality

Rank	Managers	Students
Most important	Listening	Leadership abilities
	Acceptance for change	Listening
	Customer service skills	Customer service skills
	Openness to new ideas	Acceptance for change
	Integrity	Working with others in lower positions
	Working with colleagues who have more responsibility, influence and power	Working with others on a similar level of responsibility and duty
	Working with others on a similar level of responsibility and duty	Working with colleagues who have more responsibility, influence and power
	Leadership abilities	Decision making
	Working with others in lower positions	Flexibility and willingness to try, or consider, new ideas
Least important	Staff training/knowledge in cultural differences	Verbal English communication skills

Source: based upon Suh et al., 2012, p.107

Table 3.3 UK university knowledge development for THE courses

Tourism	Events	Hospitality	Leisure
Sustainable tourism, strategic planning and development of tourism, geography of tourism, impacts of tourism, ethics, international tourism, operation of the tourism industry, passenger transportation, research methods, technology in travel and tourism, tourism and the natural environment, tourism economics, tourism marketing, tourism policy and visitor management.	Events industry, organisational behaviour, event environment, event operations, event planning process, applied technology, management support systems, event design, theming hospitality, event risk management, production, conferencing, support services, event resource management, operations and project management, volunteer management, human resource management, event marketing, consumer behaviour, sponsorship, venue and facilities management, place/destination, safety and security, strategic management, entrepreneurship, creativity, financial management, fundraising, economics, public relations, small business management, event law and licensing, administration, event policy, cultural studies, globalisation, mega-events and spectacle, evaluation, event studies, research methods and market research.	Food and beverage production and service, facilities management, design and planning, food safety, quality assurance, food science and microbiology, operations management, events, human resources management, law, services marketing, consumer behaviour, financial management, organisational behaviour, strategic management, small business management, entrepreneurship, information technology, critical thinking and applied research methods. In addition, students will normally be given the chance for specialist study which might include languages, licensed retail, tourism, leisure management and culinary arts.	Concepts of leisure, the leisure environment, the sociology of leisure, the philosophy of leisure, sports studies, countryside recreation studies, arts and entertainment, recreation, leisure economics, leisure events, leisure operations, leisure development, leisure policy, leisure planning, leisure resources management, leisure facilities management, leisure strategies, and the management of leisure.

Source: based upon QAA, 2008 curriculum content specifications for UK degree courses in THE

need to use a specific process and product knowledge in order to manage the people around you. For example, it is rare for universities to teach you Fidelio or Opera computer systems (used in the front office for hotel reservations). Therefore, employers may expect you to have IT skills but know they will have to train you on specific 'in-house' software for the job.

THINK POINT 3.2 COMPETENCE AND COMPETENCY IN STOCK ORDERING

Imagine you are a chef or kitchen supervisor. You are required to order in the weekly stock. What information do you need in order to complete this? What competence and competency do you need to complete this task?

Uphold the company brand

Within every small- to medium-sized enterprise (SME) and multinational corporation (MNC) there will be a brand and marketing strategy aligned to the company. Therefore, the final skill employers will want to analyse will be your ability to uphold and support these. To show this, knowledge of aesthetic labour (Witz et al., 2003) is needed (also covered within Part 2 Chapter 8).

Aesthetic labour (AL) is about how you look. This does not necessarily refer to beauty or physical features, as researchers mainly consider the clothes people wear. AL is important for THE and retail industries as staff communicate face to face with other people on a daily basis. By communicating face to face, you will literally be the image of the company. Therefore, your aesthetics (how you look) will convey the company brand to the customer.

ACTIVITY 3.2 WHAT TO WEAR FOR AN INTERVIEW

Imagine you are going for an interview at the following companies:

- Manager of Burger King, Sydney Airport.
- Reception Manager, Burj Al Arab, Dubai.

- Artist Liaison Manager, Glastonbury Festival, UK.
- Airline steward for Emirates.

Questions:

1. What would you wear for each interview?
2. What are the differences in your choice of outfit for each interview?
3. Why are these differences necessary?

What do employers expect a graduate to offer?

As a 'graduate,' employers will expect you to have a certain set of skills, competencies, knowledge and behaviour traits. In order to understand what employers perceive as a graduate attribute it is crucial to understand what you as a graduate are actually offering. Within the UK there is the Quality Assurance Agency (QAA), in Australia there is the Tertiary Education Quality and Standards Agency (TEQSA) and in America there is the Council for the Advancement of Standards in Higher Education (CAS). Each country that offers higher education has these specific benchmarks to clarify the competency you will gain within the set qualification.

If you were to research 'graduate employability skills' you would find a mass of literature and findings from academics trying to link graduate attributes to employer needs in a whole range of industries and sectors. There is a huge variation in the recommendations from research in THE. Some suggest the most important skills are leadership and interpersonal skills (Kay and Russette, 2000), others suggest that the graduate and industry skills do not match (Jackson, 2012) or that there is definite parity between management and student skills (Suh et al., 2012). Prospects (2009) in the UK suggest all graduates should have self-reliance, people, general employment and specialist skills. So who is right? And which ones do you need to develop? Help!

Please note, there is not one clear or accurate formula on what THE employers want from you as a graduate. As mentioned in the beginning of this part, every employer wants the skills that get the job done in the most effective and cost efficient manner.

Before moving on to the types of business in which to seek employment for THE, it is important to outline other graduate routes after completing your studies. This textbook will allow you to appraise your skills and understand key issues in employment within THE, but this is seen as a continual and life-long process. You may decide that upon graduation you want to travel or seek further qualifications. Both of these directions are successful graduate employment outcomes. Details on how to use these are noted below.

- Travelling after graduation: as you near the end of your studies you may decide to travel and complete leisure experiences for a time afterwards. This is beneficial for your own understanding of tourist experiences, as well as developing further your intercultural awareness, independence, self-motivation and initiative. As such, travelling is noted as a successful graduate route. Employers interviewing you within or after this experience will want to understand your motivations for travelling and the key skills you developed during this period. Ensure you prepare for these interviews by completing the skills appraisal in Chapter 6 and outline how travelling has enhanced your employability. The knowledge gained from travelling is an asset if it is appraised and considered in full.
- Seeking further qualifications: students completing undergraduate or college education may decide that they want to complete further qualifications after a course in THE. This will enable them to apply their sector knowledge and skills in a more focussed area of business. For example, you may decide to complete a marketing, human resources or industry qualification in support of your employment. These are excellent examples of focussing your passion and interest in a specific employment route. Within these, ensure you complete further work or leisure experiences. Completing further study or research within a specific department or area of work will showcase your drive and determination to work within a specific sector or department of THE. Further qualifications can often lead into more senior employment routes but this will depend on the type of qualification completed. Check with the programme or course leader on the usual graduate employment routes or employability statistics to ensure the course is right for you.

TYPES OF EMPLOYMENT: SME, MNC, NON-PROFIT, PUBLIC AND SELF

In order to become employable it is important to understand what types of businesses offer THE positions and whether these businesses are right for you. To begin we will consider the history and legal terms within employment. The terms small- to medium-sized enterprises (SME), multinational corporations (MNC), non-profit, public and self-employment will then be defined within the THE sectors.

Working practices have developed over a number of years. Being paid for work started in Roman times. The term 'salary' derives from the roman word 'salarium.' This said, they did not have pounds, dollars or the euro in Roman times. Instead people would barter or work in exchange for possessions. It was not until economists such as Benjamin Franklin and Adam Smith started to critique the theory of labour and the values attributed that we started to use currencies.

> Money as bullion, or as land, is valuable by so much labour as it costs to produce that bullion or land.

Money, as a currency, has an additional value by so much time and labour as it saves in the exchange of commodities.

(Franklin, 1729)

These two quotations from Franklin's essay evidence that it was in the 1700s that paper currency was being printed and used in exchange for work. The first quotation shows that money was being seen instead of 'bullion,' which is gold. So, money was valued by the amount of work required to produce the same equal amount in bullion or land. Secondly, that money as a currency had added value, which related to the time it took to complete the discussions on what would be offered in exchange for the work. Today, currency is used in exchange for work, but there are further distinctions like minimum wage, tax, insurance, currency and contract type.

After noting the origins of money being paid in exchange for work it is important to next consider the types of employment contract in existence. This is important for THE sectors, as managers rely on a variety of employees and workers. Firstly, the employment contracts differ in each country. In the UK people who work are either referred to as *employees* or *workers* (Government, 2012). An employee in the UK is someone who has a full-time or part-time contract and works continuously with the same company until the employment contract is terminated. A worker also has an employment contract but there is a defined finish date. Thus, workers can also be known as temporary staff. A third type of staff in the UK is casual workers. These people may not have a contracted number of hours to work but are employed solely by one company. These contracts are sometimes called zero hour contracts. In America, they use at-will employment contracts (Feinman, 1976). This is whereby either the employer or employee can terminate the employment at any time without ramifications. Although countries in the world will offer different employment contracts, Baum (2006a) identified that one contributing factor to flexible contracts for THE will be the need for flexible working hours for the staff and from the staff.

Now you know a rough history of gaining money for work and the different employment types and contracts it is important to understand how these are different within THE SME and MNCs. Small- to medium-sized enterprises (SMEs) are defined as any company that has less than 250 employees and a turnover of less than €50 million per annum (Enterprise and Industry, 2012). This type of company is defined in EU law due to the support available for these smaller companies. As an SME is a small-sized company there are additional risks for the directors to manage. They are an integral part of any economy as they provide support for the MNCs. Multi-national corporations (MNCs) are the corporate giants of business. Walk along any high street in any major city and you will come across these in multitudes. See Table 3.4 for examples of these in the THE sectors.

Table 3.4 SMEs and MNCs in tourism, hospitality, events and leisure sectors

Sector	SME	MNC
Tourism	Invasion Travel Boutique Travel Services, Sydney, AUS The Ride NYC, New York, USA	World of TUI, International Madame Tussauds, International Expedia, International Booking.com, International
Events	Croissant Neuf Summer Party, UK Chilli sauce, UK Bob Gold & Associates, USA Ground Control, UK	Creamfields, International Olympics, International NFL Games, International
Hospitality	Trevinos, Christchurch, NZ Anatolian Grill, Manchester, UK The Chairman, Hong Kong	McDonalds, International Marriott, International Hilton, International

THINK POINT 3.3 YOUR POSITION IN GRADUATE EMPLOYMENT

Do you want to be a small fish in a big pond or a big fish in a small pond? Do you want a fixed, stable and continuous employment contract, or are you happy to work with different companies for a finite amount of time?

Write down your answers to these questions and your reasoning for these answers.

Next, consider your current CV. Align the companies you have worked for in terms of SMEs and MNCs to compare your current experience. Have you so far worked mainly for MNCs? Or have you mainly worked for SMCs?

Working within an MNC will mean that you will gain training and experience from a major company, which will be recognised by future employers. Usually these roles are full time and permanent (no fixed end date). However, they may have restrictive standards and protocols for completing your job. This can be beneficial when learning about a role within the sector, but does not suit all employees. For example, if you want to open your own business it will be of benefit to work for an equivalent MNC to gain knowledge of how a successful business operates before setting up your own SME using the knowledge gained. Beware though, some employment contracts stipulate that you cannot use their intellectual property or take their customers after terminating your employment contract. In an SME you may be a bigger fish in the pond, but this will equally mean you have more responsibility and are more visible. In THE SME businesses seasonal work, which has a fixed end date, is usually preferential as they can manage the amount they are paying for additional staff. This also means that face-to-face contact and who you know is more important.

Non-profit, public and self-employment will now be reviewed to outline how non-traditional business forms are also supportive for employment in THE.

To begin, non-profit companies are often seen as non-government organisations, charities, or cause-related social enterprises. They are created with a specific focus and role in supporting an area, or group, within society. Within THE there are non-profit companies who support employees within these businesses (see Hospitality in Action, for example). However, this chapter considers non-profit companies across an economy, rather than specifically supporting THE. Non-profit companies, or charities, will need to raise awareness and funds by creating events. Therefore, this form of employment will naturally involve the use of events and hospitality skills. Looking for employment in this form of enterprise would require looking into the following linked areas:

- Charity (cause related).
- Education (awareness raising).
- Local government (political event).
- Public service (raising funds for medical treatments or awareness of public services).
- Arts (raising awareness of an arts form and supporting delivery and performance of this).
- Sports (using sports to raise money for a cause, or creating a sporting event to educate and raise awareness of a local sport or team who require funds).

The above list can be used as a starting point to find employment in a non-profit organisation. You may be aware of some of these due to your current hobbies or interests outside your studies. However, some students look specifically to these companies as they prefer working for an organisation whose motivation and strategy is for community and social improvement, rather than profit.

Working for a public organisation is similar to non-profit as their targets and overarching aims will be aligned to local government and supporting a local community. Income is maintained via government investment and employees are accountable to meet set targets in support of the local community. For example, leisure locations like local parks are managed by local government and are seen as a public-funded and managed leisure context. Working within a local park will mean that employees are paid by the government and tasked to maintain the grounds for the local and visiting public. Parks are a clear example of THE employment supported by local government, but there are many more complicated locations of these roles. For example, a paramedic working at a sporting event is working for a public health organisation but within a THE context.

THINK POINT 3.4 **PUBLIC EMPLOYMENT FOR NON-PROFIT ACTIVITIES**

In discussing public employment, it has been noted that there are often publically employed workers present in a range of THE activities and events. What THE skills and knowledge are required by these workers in support of delivering leisure experiences?

Finally, THE graduate employment can also be completed in the form of self-employment. This is traditional within events management whereby a number of workers complete temporary contracts for a range of events and festivals. However, in this chapter I am outlining how you may decide to set up your own company and service in support of THE businesses. During your time studying THE you will have critically analysed operations and positions within key procedures for THE employment. Within this you may have found personal interest within the management of particular leisure experiences. Using this interest and knowledge, you are in a unique position to set up and create your own company. This is a risk intensive position to take upon graduation but can enable you to achieve high profit and satisfaction within employment as you are leading and managing your own time.

This section has offered you a brief overview on the types of companies to look for in support of graduate employment in THE sectors. From experience, graduates are seen to usually seek employment in MNCs and SMEs due to their perceived success and stability in salary and professional development. However, as social awareness, corporate citizenship and entrepreneurialism are taught on THE courses, it is anticipated that work within non-profit, public and self-employment will rise in future years. These are equally important forms and positions of graduate employment for THE students. Furthermore, it may be a necessity for you to offer voluntary work within a THE business in order to command a salary and evidence experience in emergent areas.

EMPLOYMENT AND LABOUR MARKETS

It was noted in Chapter 1 of this part that being employable refers to the skills you have to gain employment. However, Brown et al. (2003: p.111) stipulates that graduate employability is about 'The relative chances of finding and maintaining different kinds of employment.' This quotation is especially apt for today's generation of students (generation X, Y or Z, or A[1]) in college and university, as you will not have one job for life. After graduation you may find an excellent position and be promoted within that company for a number of years. However, research suggests that the majority of students graduating today will have a portfolio of careers rather than the traditional 'job for life' (Patton and Mcmahon, 2002). Bearing this in mind, academics have gone further to suggest that employability is now not just about gaining employment or skills or changing jobs, but is about understanding how to navigate within relevant labour markets (Yorke, 2012).

A labour market is the total number of working-aged people who are employed plus those working-aged people who are not employed. This labour market is examined in every country by economists and government officials to show how successful the economy is running. For example, in 2007 American unemployment had remained at a consistent low rate of 5% (Of and Statistics, 2012). Unemployment rates are usually gathered by finding out how many people are actively seeking jobs, rather than people who are not working. The recession was seen when this employment rate increased between 2007–2009 to a figure of 9.5%, meaning that the recession had fully taken form. These figures were then at 6.8% unemployment at the end of 2008 and 7.8% unemployment in September 2012 (Rogers and Burn-Murdoch, 2012). Although these rates are from America they were reflected across the globe, highlighting world recession. In 2012 the International Labour Office reported that of the 3.3 billion people in the global labour force, only 200 million are known to be employed (Office, 2012). Furthermore, they report that 900 million people are living on US$2 per day, which is below the poverty line. These recession and global labour force statistics evidence that there are a range of issues within labour markets. Not only are people unable to gain employment, but there is a group of people in the world who are not able to gain money to live at the threshold necessary to sustain basic living.

The World Trade Organization (WTO) (2011) evidenced that THE sectors have not only been a catalyst for global growth during the recession but have boosted investment and skill levels within each country. Furthermore, the hospitality sector is seen to offer quicker access to employment when in times of recession. The WTO (2011) also noted that employment in travel and tourism reached 98.6 million in 2006, with the largest increase seen in Asia.

From a review of Figure 3.1 you can see where employment for travel and tourism is in line with the country's gross domestic product. From this figure, Asia has a high GDP in comparison to the employment rates. In contrast, Europe has negative employment and GDP figures for T&T. This evidences patterns in employment and GDP within travel and tourism and can aid your consideration of working overseas within the THE sectors. Now consider Figure 3.2. This now evidences how America is the largest T&T economy and that Antigua and Barbuda are the most heavily dependent country on T&T for their GDP.

This WTO report on travel and tourism offers not only evidence of current employment and GDP for these sectors but also forecasts future growth. By 2012, Montenegro is suggested to be the largest growth country (12.4%) with Malawi taking 10th place at 6.9% growth. Thus, employment and labour market statistics can not only provide you with an understanding of current trends and job opportunities, but it can suggest future countries and places to start up a business within the THE sectors.

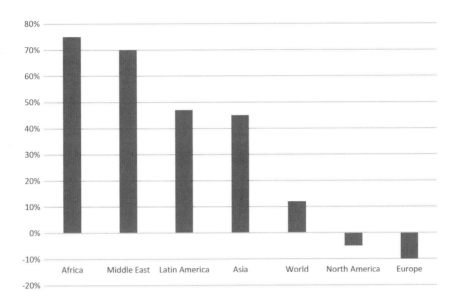

Figure 3.1 Travel and tourism employment related to global gross domestic product growth
Source: based on WTO, 2011: p.10

Figure 3.2 WTO gross domestic product and jobs
Source: based on WTO, 2011: p.19

More recently, a WTO (2019) study on youth support in employment noted the following:

- Tourism and travel businesses employ a significantly higher proportion of 15–24-year-old workers than other sectors.
- Within the ten countries studied (Canada, UK, Germany, France, Turkey, USA, Spain, Greece, Italy and Portugal) Canada was seen to employ the largest number of young

workers. Canada was seen to have a third of tourism workers as youth workers, compared to an eighth seen in the total economy.

- Retaining employers, an aging population and young people staying in education for longer has resulted in an overall decline in youth employment in tourism and travel.
- Employing younger people enables travel and tourism companies to contribute to inclusive employment, economic skills and knowledge growth, and poverty reduction.
- Competition for employment in travel and tourism is seen to advantage younger entrants due to their ability and knowledge in technology.

The summary points noted above from the WTO clarify that regardless of an aging population, youth employment is still a driving strategy for companies within these sectors. This means that the economic support for graduate employment and retaining these employees is maintaining pace within THE businesses.

ACTIVITY 3.3 WHAT IS THE LABOUR MARKET IN YOUR CLASS?

In your class work out the following:

1. Total number of students.
2. How many are working.
3. How many have part time work.
4. How many have temporary (zero hour) jobs.
5. How many hours a week they work.
6. What sector or roles they are all completing. Who is a chef/waiter etc.? Create clear roles so that you can create statistics for each type of role being completed.
7. What wages are being taken from these roles.
8. How many are female/male.
9. What qualifications they currently have. (Work out in classifications: school/college ones.)

With these figures work out the percentages for each. For this you will have to firstly organise clear categories for each question (for hours of work and role types you will need to separate them into equal categories). To work out the percentages, for example, if there are 26 people in your class and there are 14 males you would divide 14 by 26 (14/26 = 0.54 = 54% are male).

Now you have the statistics within your class you can start to analyse this labour market.

Consider:

- *If your class was a business within the THE sector are all jobs being completed? For example, if your class was a tourist resort do you have enough staff with enough qualifications and skills to make it run successfully? Pick a THE business* and write down the roles needed to run it. Do the people in your class currently have the skills and qualifications to complete these?

- *If your class was a country how wealthy would it be?* Think about the hours, wages and costs of living in your class. As a group do you currently have the ability to grow and sustain the living standards? What would happen if your parents, student loans or funding providers had to cease payments? How could you improve your incomes in the short term? How would your qualifications enable you to develop further?

Although you are currently a student of tourism, hospitality and events (and associated fields of study) your employment may take place in many other contexts and industries:

> The notion of an individual with one job is also changing; increasingly individuals will construct a career portfolio, or a series of jobs which encompass the working week (Hall, 1996). Herr (1992) emphasises that careers need to be construed as the creations of individuals; the word career can no longer be regarded as synonymous with job or occupation. Individuals need to 'regard themselves as being self-employed' (Collin and Watts, 1996, p.391), as they are expected to 'manage their own career' (Savickas, 1997, p.256).
>
> (Patton and Mcmahon, 2002, p.43)

This quotation from an Australian journal on vocational education evidences that your own career may not follow a fixed pattern of one employer for a number of years. In the THE sectors the work is often seasonal and fluctuating due to the demand levels from guests. This means that your own employment may fluctuate. In the leisure sector business demands may peak during summer or vacation periods. In events you may work within wedding planning and have a busy June–August and then be quieter for the rest of the year. If you become a supplier within the chain of companies supporting THE you may find yourself working for a range of companies throughout the year. This is why creating a 'career portfolio' is important for employment in THE. It is unlikely you will become a hotel/resort/event/airline manager and remain in that position until retirement. Instead, gaining experience in a range of positions will mean you can offer an employer evidence of a wide variety of skills, thus improving your bartering ability to gain the maximum wage and position available to you. In this way, your career may move in both horizontal and vertical directions within the sectors (O'Shannessy et al., 2002). Another benefit for creating a career portfolio and working for a range of employers is you start to build your own professional contacts, which will improve your success in gaining different employment (see Part 4 on developing your networking skills).

EMPLOYMENT IN TOURISM, HOSPITALITY AND EVENTS

Now we have reviewed employment markets supporting THE we will identify what opportunities are available for you in each THE area. This section considers THE employment opportunities in a range of business forms. As all THE companies exist as SMEs, MNCs and the self-employed, the following identifies the areas, major companies, roles and personal employment matches suitable. It is important to remember, however, that these are not your one and only career opportunity in THE. Therefore, the following can offer you an idea of various companies, jobs and roles to apply to for a life time of employment.

What type of company?

As shown in Table 3.3, the areas taught in THE areas correspond to the industry areas available to you. Tourism and events companies are located in the types of company shown in Table 3.5.

Tables 3.5 and 3.6 identify the types of companies you can work for. The self-employment list is by no means exhaustive as there are hundreds of potential supplier roles that can assist in these industries. For example, if you were to list the things needed for any tourist to go on holiday you could include businesses that build hotel/

Table 3.5 Employment companies for tourism and events

	Tourism	**Events**
SME	Travel agents Tourist information centres Outdoor pursuits companies	Festivals and outdoor events Museums Event venues (including sports, music, corporate, private and arts)
MNC	Holiday companies (including airlines, tour operators and subsidiaries of these) Transport supplies for holiday and tour companies	Olympics and major sporting events Event venues (including sports, music, corporate, private and arts)
Self-employment	Travel consultant Owning your own travel agents Creating a company to serve and supply another area of the industry	Event manager (all types) Staff manager Production manager Creating a company to serve and supply another area of the industry

Table 3.6 Employment companies in hospitality and leisure

	Hospitality	Leisure
SME	Hotels Restaurants Cafés/coffee shops Bars/public houses Nightclubs	Theme parks Fitness centres Sports coach Spas Cinema and entertainment complexes
MNC	Hotel chains Restaurant chains Cafés/coffee shop chains	Hospitality, tourism and events MNCs for leisure activities
Self-employment	Private event chef/manager Creating a company to serve and supply another area of the industry	Leisure consultant Creating a company to serve and supply another area of the industry

restaurants/roads/planes, medical provisions, local government councillors and even provisions for schools or universities to train the staff. THE is, therefore, a huge range of industries offering you an ever growing range of companies and locations in which to work.

What role?

The role and level you choose to enter will depend on your own competences, competency and comfort zone. Traditionally in THE there are four levels:

1. Floor/office staff.
2. Supervisors.
3. Managers.
4. Area managers.

Each of these roles are present within every different department of the company. For example, at a music festival you will see bar staff (1), supervisors of the bar (2), bar management on site (3) and then brewery managers who supply the alcohol (4). I often hear from students or graduates that they do not feel comfortable applying for management or area management roles until they have graduated or been in full-time employment for a number of years. My answer to this query and worry is always the same 'What have you got to lose?' If you want to work in a niche area of tourism (say a heritage site manager role in Malta, for example) you may be really interested in the role but feel that you are not good enough to be a manager yet. I would always advise to phone the company for an informal chat about the role before ruling it out entirely.

These informal chats you can have before applying for a role are extremely important. Firstly, it informs the employer that you are confident and driven to find out answers to questions. If you communicate well it can suffice to show that you are capable with communicating and dealing with others. Finally, it will leave an impression with the employer about you. Informal chats pre-application are 1000 times better than sending in lots of CVs. Just imagine, you are going to a restaurant to eat and you are presented with two options:

1. Read about the food available and order dishes after reading about them.
2. Taste test lots of different dishes to decide which one you want.

Option 1 is the usual way to order, but if you can taste the dish before ordering the whole dish you will have a much better idea of whether or not you will like it. This is the reason why pre-application informal chats are necessary. You may find out that even though the role says 'Manager' it actually only refers to supervisory duties that you have completed before. Alternatively, you could find out that the role is unsuitable but that they have alternative jobs available for you to apply for.

When considering a role in THE you need to feel comfortable and content that you can offer them the skills necessary to complete the main duties. There may also be points where you can use your skills to negotiate for a different role or role title.

What suits you best?

Part 2, Chapter 6 will enable you to specify your current and desired skill set. Prior to reviewing your current skills you need to consider what roles suit you at the moment. To assess this, some companies will ask you to complete a psychometric test. Psychometric testing shows an employer the match between your current ability, aptitude or personality and the standard and type of person the company currently wants. You can complete these tests any time and there are a number readily available online for you to complete. Cubiks (http://practicetests.cubiks.com/) offer a numerical and verbal test for business supporters, managers and graduates. Keirsey (www.keirsey.com) tests can be completed to show you your own temperament for certain roles. This said, these tests will only serve to offer a discrete insight into what type of employee you currently are (I am suspicious and reticent to say use them absolutely and base your own career direction on them). So, after having a bit of fun and personal discovery using these online tests I would suggest considering answers to the following questions:

1. Do you live to work or work to live?
2. Do you want to travel?
3. Do you want to develop or maintain your skills?

Answers to these questions will enable you to define your current suitable role. If you live to work then a role with lots of hours, responsibility and pressure will suit you. If you want to travel, consider an MNC so that you gain employee benefits and travel opportunities. If you want to maintain your skill set then look for work similar to the part-time work you completed whilst at college/university.

SUMMARY

1.   To understand what graduate employment means to students and employers.

The opening section clarified that graduate employment is being able to achieve a contract of employment or study after finishing your THE course. Four key areas from a job description were outlined to enable you to consider how these are perceived by employers and evident in your own experience. Completing qualifications and further travel after your studies were also noted as successful graduate routes that can be aligned to job specifications.

2.   To ascertain applicant skills graduate employers in tourism, hospitality and event management companies look for.

Chapter 6 of this part offers you a full skills appraisal exercise to identify your current skilling. This section outlined skills for employment through qualification criteria and competence and competencies for management.

3.   To evaluate company types to look for employment within (multi-national, small to medium, non-profit, public and self).

MNC, SME, public, non-profit and self-employment in THE businesses have been acknowledged for you to consider the form and function of business that you can apply to work within. These all differ in their support for your salary, responsibility, accountability and impact. As labour markets grow and shift, you will find that you will consider working in a range of these during your working life. The position and company you apply for will alter the impact and influence you will have within the company and needs consideration aligned to your current skills level (see the next chapter).

4.   To identify the form of business and role to apply for within THE.

The final area considered in this chapter was to enable you to consider which type and form of business and role you would like to apply for. This is important in planning for employment as you may not find the business or role available at the time of graduation. Identifying this early will enable you to set up notifications and networks with key THE businesses to support your employment. Larger businesses may have rigid roles and functions, but smaller businesses may even look to create a role to suit your expertise if they know you are interested, invested in them and planning for graduate employment.

Questions to support your learning and research

1. How is travelling after your studies seen to be a successful graduate route into employment?
2. What is the WTO?
3. What issues are seen to be contributing to a decrease in youth employment in THE sectors?
4. What types of companies will offer leisure employment?
5. How do the companies for employment differ for tourism, hospitality, events and leisure? How are they similar?

Websites in support of your learning from this chapter

World Travel and Tourism Council www.wttc.org/
WTO www.wto.org/

Chapter 4
Skills for tourism, hospitality and events employment

LEARNING OBJECTIVES

1. To identify what core, key and transferable skills are and how these are important for THE employment.
2. To complete activities in support of evidencing entrepreneurialism for THE employment and professional development.
3. To align and analyse skills in conjunction with job descriptions and job criteria.

INTRODUCTION

The terms 'employable' and 'employability' essentially mean do you have the suitable skills to gain employment or work? As a student you may already have a part-time job and so are able to gain temporary, flexible or casual work easily. However, when you graduate or look for more permanent, managerial roles, it is important that you evidence experience and ability in skills and knowledge to obtain a position of employment. This chapter will offer you further support in appraising your own employment and skills by considering forms of skills, entrepreneurialism and matching skills to job descriptions. These are equally important elements when considering skills for THE work. Part 2, Chapter 6 is a useful chapter to review in support of this chapter as it will allow you to appraise your own current skilling levels in conjunction.

CORE, KEY AND TRANSFERABLE SKILLS

As mentioned in the introduction to this chapter, a number of students hold part-time jobs whilst studying. This intermediate employment is important so that you can afford your weekly hobbies, attend social events, or purchase this textbook to help your employability! More importantly though, part-time or voluntary work during your studies allows you to experience and develop your skills in a less pressured and more supportive environment. Once you become a manager or team leader within work you will be seen as accountable and responsible for the targets and duties of your team and subordinate staff. A benefit to THE students is that they are often working within the business environment they are preparing for. This is advantageous as entry and access to work experience is relatively free of barriers. Conversely, for example, if you are training to become a medical doctor you will not be allowed access to patients or make decisions in patient care without a more significant employment contract. In this way, a number of the skills developed for THE are seen as generic and transferable, as they are developed in a range of service scenarios. Your work in a retail business or local sports team will naturally link to employment skills in THE as they require a similar set of abilities.

THINK POINT 4.1 YOUR PREVIOUS EMPLOYMENT AND EXPERIENCES

As a student, you will have completed either part-time, voluntary or hobby-related activities in support of your employment. Even if this was a singular event created at school or a family leisure activity, you will have already gained experience of transferable and generic skills for employment. This think point is to start your reflection on this and appraise your basic transferable and generic skills for THE employment.

1. Have you completed part-time work? If not, have you organised a leisure activity for a sports team, or for family or friends?
2. Thinking of this experience, what types of activity did you need to complete to make it a success?
3. Who did you need to liaise or communicate with?
4. What knowledge did you use and develop to complete this activity?

As you consider the answers to these questions you will be starting to appraise your general and transferable skills for THE employment.

Within THE it is relatively easy for students to gain part-time employment in local businesses (People 1st, 2011; Barclays, 2012). Whether it be working in a restaurant, café, theatre, leisure centre or tourist attraction there are usually a number of seasonal positions available. However, an important consideration is how well does this role fit with your own goals and employment direction? Is this job giving you the 'edge' over other future candidates who will be in competition with you for a graduate position? And ultimately, how employable is it making you?

Yorke (2006) confirmed that a person's employability requires core, key and transferable skills. The core and key skills are usually developed within school education and refer to literacy, numeracy and technology skills required for employment. These skills are transferable to any employment and show your capability in completing tasks on a daily basis. In the THE sectors it is often the transferable skills that are inspected at interview. Transferable skills can be general to any employment (as noted in the above think point), but also specific for the THE sectors.

Table 4.1 separates transferable skills to evidence specific ones required in THE. Any position in THE will require general transferable skills to complete daily tasks and duties. However, as THE often requires consistent guest interaction the specific transferable skills are vital to the success of the company. Therefore, becoming employable in THE requires clear evidence of these when applying for and attending an interview. Each of the specific transferable skills will now be discussed to outline their importance and suitable evidence of experience for employment in THE.

Understanding guest's needs is both an understanding of the operational procedures surrounding the guest's experience, and the metacognitive processes required in order to understand the guest and what they will expect. An example of understanding the guest's needs via the operations procedures is when a guest checks into a hotel. They will expect you to have their reservation and know how much they are to pay, and sometimes their preferences in room size and location. This is similar in tourism and leisure when guests check in to their flight or pick up their car hire, or in events when a guest arrives to collect their tickets or get them checked. By knowing these differences and the operations surrounding them you are able to check and anticipate the guest's needs prior to arrival. Other operational areas specific to THE and guests needs include dietary requirements, travel arrangements, billing and currency, type of guest (transient, business or leisure) and amenity use. In terms of employment in THE you will be required to show an understanding of these operational areas. The second component of understanding the guest's needs relates to empathy and your metacognition (discussed below).

Workplace awareness refers to your ability to show understanding and knowledge of workplace practices. This can sometimes be understood and seen as 'office politics.' Office politics is a colloquial term used to denote certain behaviour within a company. For example, staff breaks that are always taken at 11 o'clock and not half ten or half 11, or

Table 4.1 General and specific transferable skills for THE employment

General transferable skills	Specific transferable skills
Communication Problem-solving Teamwork Information technology Numeracy Literacy Intellectual	Understanding guests needs Workplace awareness Anticipating peoples requirements Self-efficacy Confidence Empathy

that one member of staff who always completes a certain task. Knowledge that there will be office politics within every company is important but not wholly representative of workplace awareness. Within THE you will be positioned within public areas. As you are in the public realm on a daily basis it is important you are professional at all times. As such, some companies in THE refer to your role as being on a theatre stage. Every action and reaction you have in work is seen not just by colleague but by guests paying the company, and also any member of the public passing through. In this way, workplace awareness in THE is about being aware of your role and your ability to consistently portray the company and brand when at work.

Anticipating peoples requirements. This relates to the employers requirements. If you work in the events industry you may be an external contractor rather than the event manager. In such an instance you will be expected to not only provide a service to suit the guests needs but also complete your role in accordance with your employer's requirements. This is also true in departments within tourism, hospitality and leisure sectors. Firth (2020) notes how service encounter theory omits the colleague, management and supplier interactions crucial for effective customer service. In this way, anticipating the needs of a range of people in employment is seen as a superior skill for THE employment.

Self-efficacy is the belief you have in your own ability. This can be evident in the structure and content of your CV or via competence tests at an interview. It must not be mistaken for confidence. An example of self-efficacy is shown in Case Study 4.1.

CASE STUDY 4.1 SINK OR SWIM: SELF EFFICACY IN THE

This example is from my own employment history. My first part-time position was within a restaurant in Sheffield when I was 17. On my first shift I was asked to work in the front of house. It was a 50-seat Italian restaurant with a full a-la-carte menu and service was not completed in sections, but as a whole. Each member of floor staff had one role to complete: either on the pass, or on the bar or on table service. I was asked to complete table service.

Specifically I had to:

- Speak to the customers when seated.
- Offer menus and menu advice.
- Take food and beverage orders.
- Deliver drinks.
- Clear plates.
- Deliver the bill.

When I started the shift I was not given any training or a staff handbook on the service standards or levels. Instead, I was given an apron, pen and pad, and serving cloths and let loose!

When the restaurant became busy I was struck with panic and confusion. There were so many tables being seated and other tables at differing points of service that I ended up spinning on the spot. I could not decide which table needed my assistance first and whether there was anyone I could ask for help or delegate the tasks to.

This situation will be very familiar to those of you who have had part-time roles in a restaurant, café or bar. As I was not given any training or guidance it is an example of 'sink or swim' as management were giving me a trial to see if I would work well within this pressure or crumble and make errors. On this occasion it is safe to say that I sank quick and fast. I felt panicked, scared and horrified that I had lost control of my role and did not know where to turn.

The next shift I was asked to work behind the bar and manage the drink orders. This time I worked through all of the orders in an efficient and timely manner.

This example evidences my self-efficacy in three ways:

1. At first I believed I could succeed in the situation because the manager had put me in the position and trusted me to perform well. This deteriorated after I panicked but was restored when given another role the following evening. It meant that the following time I was offered work on the floor I did not believe I could succeed. It was not until I was given sections of tables to manage that I felt comfortable running table service. This is referred to within social cognitive theory (see Bandura, 1989) and relates to how a person can view tasks. Tasks can either be seen as being too difficult to complete or as something to be mastered and completed.
2. When I panicked I could not see a way out. I was unable to view other staff around me who could help as this would be seen as failure. The ability to work within a team and learn through observations of others refers to social learning theory (see Rotter, 1954 and later articles). This requires self-perception and acceptance of others.
3. On the second shift at this restaurant I was asked to work behind the bar instead of on the floor. The managers joked saying I had literally made circles in the floor on the previous shift and had not been able to stay still. Their decision to put me on the bar was so that I was contained and also so that I had control and management of one thing. This clarified the failure I had felt in my first shift and taught me something about my own work habits: that I needed clear instructions and my own areas to control and manage. This is referred to as the self-concept theory (see works by Shavelson and Bolus, 1981).
4. Another consideration in this case was the attribution theory (see Zuckerman, 1979). I could have attributed my success in the bar and disregarded the failure of working on the floor. However, I was mainly concerned with doing any job well and continuing employment rather than consciously linking 'success' or 'failure' labels.

ACTIVITY 4.1

Think about an experience you have had in a part-time job where you feel you have failed. Consider the four components of self-efficacy described above and detail how you feel this has developed your own beliefs in your actions at work.

Confidence (not to be confused with self-efficacy or arrogance). Confidence is important for employment and guest service as it instils trust in you. Someone who is relaxed and confident will make a guest feel at ease and comfortable in their surroundings. As the majority of THE businesses have guests who arrive from different cities, or even continents, it is important you make guests feel at ease. In the case study above it was clear that my own confidence waned when working on the restaurant floor. When this happens it is evident to every guest around you, and as behaviour breeds behaviour, it is likely that guests will also feel the same way you are. Equally, when you are being interviewed it is important that your nerves are controlled and you show this quiet confidence. This will show your potential employers your ability to communicate and work effectively in new and pressured situations.

Empathy. Showing empathy with colleagues and guests will aid your ability to up sell and satisfy guests' needs. Empathy is referred to in the texts under the term 'emotional intelligence;'

> the management of feeling to create a publicly observable facial and bodily display.
> (Hoschschild, 1983: p.7 cited from Warhurst and Nickson, 2009)

The creation of your public and observable empathy is as important as your ability to actually empathise with the guests' needs.

This section has offered you an overview of some of the skills needed for employment in THE, clarifying what is needed to be employable in THE sectors. Please see Part 2 for more detail on skills for each of the THE sectors and Part 3 for how you can start to analyse your own specific THE transferable skills and develop them whilst studying.

BEING ENTREPRENEURIAL 24/7

Entrepreneurs are people who see unique ideas and create businesses around them. Steve Jobs of Apple and Richard Branson from Virgin are two famous entrepreneurs who have made fortunes from their own unique ideas and putting them into practice. Using entrepreneurialism in employment is seen as vital for business and strategy success as it enables companies to consider alternative and innovative methods of development. Being entrepreneurial not only requires you to evidence skills and knowledge but use initiative and self-motivation to drive the business forwards. Interns and graduates are consistently seen to be of benefit if they use these skills.

Upon graduating from a THE course you may work for yourself (sole trader/self-employed) or in a small business (SME) or a multinational (MNC). Within all of these business environments you will require an amount of initiative and creativity to complete the day-to-day duties. I am saying initiative and creativity instead of entrepreneurialism, but ultimately I mean the same thing.

- If you see a problem for a customer/supplier/stakeholder you may decide to solve it = initiative.
- How you solve the problem will depend on your own creativity.

The definition offered above is a very basic view of entrepreneurialism. This chapter will offer you definitions of being and becoming an entrepreneur, followed by entrepreneurialism within THE.

Definitions of 'the entrepreneur'

Richard Branson and Steve Jobs are two iconic entrepreneurs, but they do not conform to one clear definition of 'the entrepreneur.' Attempts to define 'entrepreneur' have been a subject of academic debate for many years:

> We never succeeded. Each of us had some notion of what he thought it was, for his purposes, a useful definition. And I don't think you're going to get farther than that.
>
> (Cole, 1969: p.17 cited in Gartner, 1989: p.47)

Cole's writings from 1969 show the length of debate over the idea of entrepreneurialism. This focus has come about as it has been apparent that entrepreneurs create profitable, unique and forward-thinking businesses. Unfortunately, the debates and problems on creating one clear definition are due to the fact that the essence of being entrepreneurial is different and changing in each person. There are various qualities of entrepreneurs in small businesses (noted in Table 4.2) and these qualities vary in each 'entrepreneur.'

The qualities noted in Table 4.2 can all be seen in differing amounts for each entrepreneur. That is to say, being an entrepreneur does not mean that you have to have every one of these. If you take 'vision and flair,' for example, this could refer to a great range of competences. Vision could mean that you are creative or forward thinking or informed on a specific area, thus are able to foresee potential gains. Flair is equally ambiguous. Does it mean you can dress well? Does it mean you can speak using a range of interesting words to communicate? This entirely depends on the industry and area you are working within.

Table 4.2 Qualities of entrepreneurs in small businesses

Qualities of entrepreneurs
Need for independence
Need for achievement
Internal locus of control
Ability to live with uncertainty
Takes measured risks
Ability to be opportunistic
Innovative
Self-confident
Proactive
Decisive
High energy
Self-motivated
Vision and flair

Source: Williams, 2008: p.1043

Entrepreneurial profit is the expression of the value of what the entrepreneur contributes to production in exactly the same sense that wages are the value expression of what the worker produces.

(Schrumpteter, 1934 cited from IBD, 1996: p.13)

Now we have considered the complexity of defining entrepreneurship, and reviewed its qualities for small businesses, it is salient to know that in large businesses entrepreneurship is called 'intrapreneurship.' This term was created by Gifford and Elizabeth Pinchot in their book on corporate entrepreneurship. This term is used to denote a whole organisation that evolves and embodies entrepreneurial spirit. Therefore, you may one day work for a company like this.

Becoming and being entrepreneurial in THE

Although the definition and levels of entrepreneurialism may be complex, developing entrepreneurial skills whilst studying is simple – via assessments, via your union or within your local community. There are also a range of textbooks supporting entrepreneurship for THE employment including Morrison et al. (2012), Page and Ateljevic (2009) and Lee-Ross and Lashley (2009). These books cover a range of theoretical considerations for entrepreneurialism including embedding the corporate, psychological and individual tenets into THE businesses and people. This section will focus specifically on three areas of development for entrepreneurialism in THE: gaining opportunities, innovating and being creative.

Opportunity knocks (see also Part 4, Chapter 20 on networking)

By opportunistic I mean that you need to take advantage of every potential opportunity. Whilst you are studying you have a great variety of resources available to you to create, develop and examine new ideas. Equally, you will meet and develop new networks from which opportunities can be created. To develop this consider the following actions:

- *ACTION 1 – Business cards – Order yourself some business cards through an online company (ones like Vistaprint www.vistaprint.co.uk are cheap and look professional).*
- *ACTION 2 – Network – Buy yourself a cheap business card holder or lever arch folder. Each time you meet someone new in THE ask for their business card and swap with your own one. Compile these and write yourself notes on the reverse of each card: what occasion did you meet them in? What rapport do you feel you had with them? Do they employ in the THE industries? Do they train? What would you like from them? Follow up each meeting and business card with a phone call and email asking if they have any employment or experience opportunities available. If they do not have anything at present, ask them to keep your CV and records on file for future use.*
- *ACTION 3 – Guest lecturers – Within your course you may be offered guest lectures from key managers and academics in specific fields of study. Attend every one of these offered. I repeat. ATTEND EVERY ONE OF THESE OFFERED! The reason for this is that these people will not usually be presented in front of you. If you get a chance for a personal chat after these I would repeat instructions from action 2 above.*
- *ACTION 4 – Current markets – You may be required to compile a report on the markets or current industry scope in THE whilst studying. This is vital if you want to take advantage of employment opportunities within THE. In order to know the industry you need to also know the current products and direction of the markets. For example, in events there is a lot of innovation and new companies creating ticket and registration technology (like Eventbrite and iZettle). Knowing these developing areas will allow you an insight into current companies who are entrepreneurial. Contact these companies and ask if they have any work experience or internships available for you.*
- *ACTION 5 – Be studious – Each and every piece of assessment you complete at university or college offers you a new occasion to investigate something. Each of these are an opportunity to learn and develop understanding in new areas. An entrepreneurial student will not just follow a simple or easy path in completing these. Instead, consider how to 'push' the assessment further. For example, if you are asked to write an essay on staff management*

in a THE company, do not just consider the staff present in the company. You could con-
sider the suppliers and other stakeholder who are also managed. The point in this action is
that you should always ask 'So what?' and 'What else is there to know around this topic?'
By pushing the boundaries and questioning the assessment parameters, you will create
new opportunities to learn around a subject area. This will offer you a unique edge in terms
of the knowledge you can offer employers in the future.

These action points will enable you to create and experience new opportunities whilst
studying. Joining student union societies, attending local business networking events, seeing
guest lectures in your faculty and around other campuses will give you access to these
opportunities. Ultimately, you need to act. The sooner you start this, the more opportunities
and better options you will be offered.

Ah, push it – push it good. Ah, push it – p-push it real good

What I am evoking here is that you need to always think on your feet and suggest new and
different ways to complete tasks. Innovate, offer suggestions and never rely on
standardised processes or facts.

- *ACTION 1 – Part-time jobs – If you are currently working in a part-time job in a THE*
  company you have a perfect opportunity to be innovative. For example, in a restaurant
  you may notice there are certain 'norms' to the service offered to customers. There
  may be stations used or specific roles assigned to other staff within the working envir-
  onment. If you witness any problems in this service (from staff or customers) use this
  to innovate a new idea. Speak with your managers and ask if they also perceive this
  problem and if you can help identify a solution.
- *ACTION 2 – Research – Most THE students will complete a research project whilst*
  studying. This may comprise of a dissertation or small report. Regardless of the size
  of this assessment, this is a prime opportunity for innovation. Whether you innovate
  in methodology or topic, you have the power and option to investigate something
  unique. In my own experience, students will often hone in on staff or marketing
  issues when offered the choice of research topic. This is because they are both
  something easy to relate to. We are all marketed to and we are all staff. However,
  when considering options available, review potential future areas of development.
  In hospitality you could consider future culinary arts techniques (like molecular gas-
  tronomy). For tourism you could explore innovative sustainability and community
  strategies (like the debates on paying to reduce carbon footprints or corporate citi-
  zenship). In events and leisure there is a need for sustainable projects and events
  as the standard markets become increasingly filled (for example new forms of
  a 'festival' or 'museum').
- *ACTION 3 – Community engagement – As a student you will be located in many com-*
  munities. Your campus, class, accommodation and work communities all need you to
  be an active citizen to maintain their development. Within each of these consider your

current role. Do you vote? Do you attend every class? Do you do your share of the cleaning? Each one of these communities offers you experiences and areas to change. You could create a new society within your student accommodation to help other students with budgeting/knitting/movie knowledge/games etc. Or you could meet with local residents and find out what is missing in that area for THE support. Do they want more leisure outlets? Do they like the restaurant provisions? Each of these are ways of engaging and developing your community further.

Turn on the light!

Creativity is an area some of you may want to avoid and scream and run from with flailing arms. However, I would argue that every person has an element of creativity. You just need to develop it (or even turn it on!). By completing the following actions each and every one of you can offer creativity evidence to potential employers.

- *ACTION 1 – Your own room – As a first action I want you to consider your own bedroom. Look around at your walls, furniture and study space. What does it look like? Do you have bare walls or lots of posters? Do you live in organised chaos? Whatever the status quo, I want you to change it to the opposite version. So, if you have lots of posters, take them down. If you are allowed to do so, paint the walls (this can be as simple as using a new single colour, stencilling, or painting a whole wall with a picture). By making changes in your own environment you can create your own personal creative space. Once you have done this you can proudly say 'I created this.' Feels good hey? Then let's move on to the next level.*
- *ACTION 2 – Part-time work – Each of your part-time jobs will use 'points of display' to market certain products or tickets or services. These may be for certain seasonally promoted items or discounted products. In this part-time job I want you to offer to come in on your day off (yes, without pay). On this day off you should ask the manager if you can create a new display for these products/services. Ask management for tools available to do this and start to plan what you can do to change this. Like Action 1, try reversing the current state. So, if there are currently menus or posters being used, use the opposite. You could serve as a human point of sale and decorate your clothes with the flyers? Or you could write a new blurb to attach to menus or bills?*
- *ACTION 3 – Creative assignments – Similar to Action 2 in the previous section, you need to use your creativity when writing or researching for your course. Any group project or live assignment will require you to develop logos.*

MATCHING SKILLS TO JOB DESCRIPTIONS IN THE SERVICE SECTORS

So far we have analysed what it is to be employable for THE, considered core, key and transferable skills for the sectors, and outlined entrepreneurialism as a core skill to evidence initiative and creativity in employment. Now, to consider matching skills to job descriptions, this section will offer examples of how you can use the job descriptions to appraise and develop your skills for THE employment.

A job description is usually created and posted for each position that needs filling in a company. So for every role – housekeeper, steward, kitchen porter, security officer and so on, there should be a job description in place. This document will offer clarity on the specific duties and tasks required within the position. To begin the job description a summary of the role is usually offered:

> Assistant Manager – Catering Sales – Marriott International Assists the property's Banquets/ Catering Department in the property's reactive and proactive sales efforts with a focus on group and catering accounts. The position contributes to achieving revenue goals and the financial performance of the department. Assists in implementing the brand's service strategy and applicable brand initiatives in all aspects of the sales process. Position supports the administrative processes associated with the pre-event and post-event phases of an event and the associated transitions between all event phases. Assists the seamless turnover from sales to operations and back to sales while consistently delivering a high level of service. Ensures the team maximizes revenue opportunities by up-selling and accurately forecasting (catering and group rooms) all events.
>
> (International, 2012)

This example of a job summary within a job description from Marriott International clarifies the length and scope of a summary. It is the first point of reference available to you to explain what types of things you are expected to do. In order to evidence your competence in this role you would firstly need to evidence awareness of reactive and proactive sales. Reactive is reacting to customer enquiries for business and proactive is going out and sourcing new business. Thus, your application would need to evidence experience of completing both. An example of reactive sales from your own curriculum vitae (CV) may be upselling services to customers or understanding what products they need and offering them one tailored to their requirements. Proactive sales would entail gathering and keeping new customers. It is vital that you consider the contents of the job summary and change your CV to reflect what the company need. Your CV needs to reflect each and every component within the job summary, and the subsequent duties and responsibilities. If you write and submit a generic CV when applying for a THE job you have wasted an employment opportunity and it is unlikely you will be invited for interview.

The duties and responsibilities of a role will usually be noted within the job description. These will outline the specific daily and frequent duties expected within the job. Again, you need to consider if you already have experience and evidence to complete these tasks. However, when gaining or moving employment it may be that you have some but not all competences for the role. You may want the position to develop skills in the new areas. In this situation you must clarify that although you have no prior experience in one component of the role, you are interested in developing these skills further.

Another aspect of the job description often used within THE is the person specification:

- German speaker, fluent in English.
- An experienced sales professional with a proven track record in high ticket products, preferably in the marine industry.
- One with good interpersonal skills and must have the ability to negotiate and communicate effectively at all levels.
- One with a flexible approach to the job and adaptable attitude.
- One preferably with the ability to converse in other languages i.e. Dutch, French, but not required.
- Highly organized with an entrepreneurial approach. To his or her job.
- One with the ability to understand and explain financial evaluations and presentations.
- Self-motivated, exhibit perseverance and a strong work ethic.
- Able to quickly gain credibility and confidently close sales.
- A highly skilled negotiator and communicator.
- Confident when making presentations to clients face to face, over the phone or in writing.
- PC literate with advanced use of Microsoft Office (knowledge of Goldmine® a plus).

(TUI, 2012)

The example above is from a large tourism organisation, TUI, offering a job description for a Boat Sales representative in TUI Marine. You will note that these bullet points refer to a number of general transferable skills like literacy and numeracy. This specification can be evidenced within both your CV and interview. For example, you can write how many languages you speak and to the level of qualification gained as evidence in the CV, however, in order to fully show your ability for the communication and motivational aspects they would have to meet and interview you. This means that the CV should also offer references to offer evidence that you have these. An employment reference does not need to be general for any job. You can ask previous employers to review the new position and ask for their recommendation of your abilities in certain areas. This is beneficial when applying for new jobs as the reference will speak directly to the new employer. However, caution is needed if you want a reference from your current employer as you may need privacy when applying for new roles. In such an instance you can refer to previous employers.

Thus, matching your skills to a job description is an important first step to gaining new employment in THE. However, it is not the only route to gaining employment. Other routes include social networking, employment agencies and blogs.

You may have already been asked to create a profile on a website called LinkedIn. LinkedIn is a professional social network site where you can connect with other professionals and list your current experience or abilities. This is used by companies who want to recruit as they can see where current professionals are employed and what skills and abilities they can offer them. Your LinkedIn profile can be seen as an online CV. However, this also means that it has to be up to date and reflect the skills and abilities you want to promote to gain any new employment. If you are currently at a supervisory level and are aiming for a management role, it is good practice to write on your LinkedIn profile that you are interested in management roles due to your current ability at a supervisory level. Another benefit of LinkedIn is that you can join groups within the network. Examples of these are numerous, but to offer you an initial review have a look at 'Executive Hospitality Jobs,' 'Stage Management,' or even in specific geographic locations like the 'China Leisure, Travel and Tourism Jobs' group. Membership to these groups is free and they will offer you up to date jobs and insights into employment for specific THE roles. Your current THE course may also offer you a LinkedIn group showcasing new opportunities found by your teachers (for example 'MMU BA (hons) Events Management Alumni').

Agencies are another avenue to explore when seeking employment in THE. Live recruitment (see www.live-recruitment.co.uk) are a UK agency offering specialist help securing employment in events. You can register as one of their candidates and they will complete the job description analysis and compare to your current CV on your behalf. This is a good option if you are not urgently seeking employment but are interested in other opportunities available. However, the agency will take a commission if they put you forward and you are awarded the position. In this way you may not get the same benefits and wages as you would if you found the position yourself.

An online blog may be beneficial to develop your online professional presence further. It is now common practice for employers to Google candidates. If you currently only have a personal Facebook and Twitter page, now is the time to review this online content and security. Google you own name. If social pictures and content appears then your potential employers are not seeing the 'professional you.' Ensure the security of your personal online content is restricted so that only authorised contacts or friends can view it. Then create a LinkedIn profile and consider creating a blog. A blog is an online diary. If an employer in your area is looking for a temporary employee to work within their resort, event, spa or café they may well Google the role name, for example 'lighting technician in Kyoto.' If you have a blog entitled with your current role or the role you are aspiring for you can evidence to the online community your passion, interest and competences in this area.

CASE STUDY 4.2 IS IT WHO YOU KNOW NOT WHAT YOU KNOW?

From teaching hospitality, tourism and events I have encountered a number of students and graduates who want to work in niche areas of THE. Read the following case example and consider the key actions taken to gain employment:

Samantha Keeper came to study Events Management due to her keen interest in music festivals. She was informed by academics that employment in this field is

tricky as the events are seasonal and managed by a number of different profes-
sionals. Gaining access to the managers and being offered paid work within festi-
vals requires tenacity and direct involvement. This did not put Samantha off her
desired career and she set about finding opportunities in the summer after her
first year. She gained a voluntary role at a small student festival as a steward.
From this she met and worked with the managers and a variety of suppliers in the
area. The subsequent year she was requested to work again, still as a volunteer
but with more responsibility. On the third year she was offered pay to work
another three festivals. This was due to her personal contacts in the festivals and
improved knowledge of their requirements. When she graduated she decided that
she wanted to have consistent employment and set up her own business providing
supplies to the events. As she already knew the people in the sector she was
a preferred supplier as she was trusted and known by the managers. Receiving
a 2.1 classification also meant that they could see that she was a focussed and
diligent worker.

The case study offered above evidences the importance of being known by potential employers. Although volunteer work was completed to gain employers trust and acquaintance, any person can achieve this familiarity very easily. For example, when you next find a job description go to the place of business and speak directly to employees and managers to see what the job entails. If this is not possible, phone them directly. This is a crucial step for employment in THE. Students will all too often send out a generic CV without speaking to the employers or chasing their application. Do not rely on electronic communication alone. Phone or visit the employer directly and refer to your application or intent to apply. This will mean that the employers will remember your name when it appears on an application. It also means that they have a sense of you as a real person and potential employee.

SUMMARY

1. To identify what core, key and transferable skills are and how these are important for THE employment.

Core and key skills were defined as job specific-skills which require evidence and experience to communicate on your CV. Transferable skills were outlined to clarify that in addition to language, numeracy and technology, THE roles require specific transferable skills to meet the demands and needs of a range of people working within these sectors.

2. To complete activities in support of evidencing entrepreneurialism for THE employment and professional development.

Linking entrepreneurialism to initiative and creativity, this chapter allowed you to complete a number of actions to evidence and start working entrepreneurially. This is seen as an important element of employment as it uses your knowledge and self-motivation to create new operations and positions of thought. Being entrepreneurial can be linked to critical thinking and critical analysis (covered in Part 3) as it requires you to think outside of the box and approach tasks in alternative ways.

3. To align and analyse skills in conjunction with job descriptions and job criteria.

Examples of a job summary and job description were offered to allow you to outline skills necessary to apply for an employment position. Within each application, you are advised to tailor your CV to suit these specific roles to maximise the potential for shortlisting to an interview for the post. Part 2 Chapter 6 can be used to outline your current skills in support of this and Part 4 for outlining methods of communicating your skills most effectively on a CV.

Questions to support your learning and research

1. Where are key skills usually developed in THE studies?
2. How is self-efficacy a specific transferable skill for THE?
3. Are you a natural entrepreneur or can you develop as an entrepreneur?
4. When reviewing a job advert, what steps do you need to take to consider your application?

Websites in support of your learning from this chapter

Global Employment Trends published by the International Labour Office. Report published in January 2012 and is available via www.ilo.org

Linked In – UK Site – uk.linked.com

Chapter 5
Text structure

INTRODUCTION

This chapter offers readers an overview of how to use this publication. As this textbook aims to support students and new entrants into successful employment in tourism, hospitality and events (THE) management positions its structure is sympathetic to enabling reflective and reflexive, professional and personal development. This chapter is descriptive and does not refer to academic or industry sources. Refer to this chapter if you are interested in using this textbook and want to know what key component parts are there for!

STRUCTURE OF THE TEXTBOOK PARTS

This textbook offers four parts which support personal, academic and professional development to gain employment in THE. Each part overview is presented below for clarification on its purpose and content:

Part 1 – the current part

The current part will introduce the text and situate the sectors of tourism, hospitality and events management. An overview of each of the industries will clarify their specific context within global economies. This context will lead to an explanation of the specific types of business within which tourism, hospitality and events management students can obtain employment. As the majority of these industries rely on small- to medium-sized businesses (SMEs) the skills are also identified as specific to the industries. Theory on communication, society and entrepreneurial skills will be described to clarify some of the industry specific skills needed to obtain employment in tourism, hospitality and events management. The structure and content of the following three parts is then identified.

Part 2

Personal development is crucial in tourism, hospitality and events management as students will manage and work with a wide range of guests and colleagues. The interpersonal dimension to their graduate work means that their own personal development is more important than work in other sectors. This will be clarified in Chapter 6 using soft skill and interpersonal skill theory situated in tourism, hospitality and events management research contexts. From this, four areas of personal development are identified using tourism, hospitality and events management contexts and research to clarify how these are unique and specific to these sectors. For example, relationship skills are vital in hospitality employment as students will be serving guests in private and personal events.

Part 3

This part identifies academic development strategies and processes to support tourism, hospitality and events management students. Although the premise of this part could support a wide range of students I will offer specific examples for tourism, hospitality and events management students and link to the academic work they will be required to complete in industry. For example, group work is not only a usual assessment method for these students; it is a core component of their graduate work. Each of the sub-sections will therefore identify what students need to do in their studies and then link this to graduate roles in the leisure sectors.

Part 4

This part will define and examine four types of work experience for tourism, hospitality and events management students. The benefits and challenges associated with these experiences will also be explained to allow students to choose their work placements carefully. Career mapping will be used as a guide to explore how a range of experiences can aid students targeting a specific career path within these industries.

Within each part there are chapters to support knowledge development over the overarching theme. There are 5 to 7 chapters within each part. These can be viewed within the contents pages at the beginning of the textbook for clarification on title. You can also use the index to find specific areas of content.

ADDED SUPPORT: CASE STUDIES, ACTIVITIES AND THINK POINTS

Within each chapter, you are presented with case studies, activities and think points within the discussion of key theories and current knowledge. These were created to offer readers the opportunity to reflect, apply and consider content within the chapter.

Instructions on how to use these are noted below:

 Case studies situate and apply theory within working THE contexts. They illuminate real life situations within which chapter information can be seen in a reflexive approach to personal, academic and professional development.

 Activities are written for you to answer and apply learnt knowledge within key areas discussed in chapters. These enable to you respond and consider how knowledge and action in THE employment is applied.

 Think points are offered to readers to enable you to reflect upon content offered within the chapter. This could be to apply your knowledge to your own situation or context, or to empathise with workers or management with THE management.

Tables, figures and photos are also offered throughout this textbook. These are either taken from existing publications or created to illustrate links or relationships within key areas discussed. Again, these allow readers to observe how knowledge is applied within employability and skills for THE.

REVISION QUESTIONS, ADDITIONAL SOURCES AND REFERENCE LISTS

At the end of each chapter there are revision questions, additional sources and reference lists. The following identifies how these should be used:

- Revision questions should be used after reading whole chapters. They are to check and ascertain knowledge learnt from reading the chapter. If you are unable to answer some of these, go back within the chapter and read through again to ascertain this information.

- Additional sources can be used to support and enhance knowledge discussed within each chapter. These can be used for wider reading and research within the topic area. These are not exhaustive and should be used only as a starting point to research within these topic areas.
- Reference lists are presented to establish where knowledge discussed is taken from. In writing this textbook a range a sources have been used to offer information on employability and skills for THE. As this textbook is written in English, all sources are from English language publications available at the time of writing.

As a student or new entrant into THE, the revision questions, additional sources and reference lists are important for you to learn and establish where current published research comes from and how it is positioned.

LEARNING GAINS FROM LEARNING OUTCOMES

You will note that each chapter begins with a set of learning outcomes. These are then clarified as complete through the summary at the end of each chapter. Learning outcomes are used to frame the structure and content of each chapter. However, they also clarify the learning potential from completing each chapter. Readers can use these to consider the content of each chapter and how they can aid knowledge development in key employability and skills for employment.

A NOTE FOR ACADEMICS AND TEACHERS

Although this textbook is aimed at students and new entrants into employment within THE, it is anticipated that this textbook can be used in conjunction with courses and sessions delivered in education institutions. Teachers of full-time, part-time, distance learning and short courses in THE can utilise this handbook in classes and modules relating to employment, skills and knowledge.

Chapters within each part can be used to aid creation of classes or courses for employability and skills in THE. Use chapters to plan focussed classes and test the learning outcomes using the revision questions. Alternatively, the case studies, activities and revision questions can be used independently to support the delivery of courses for employability and skills.

Programmes of study particularly suited for using this textbook are noted below:

- Tourism management.
- Hospitality management.
- Events management.
- Sports management.
- Arts management.

- Services management.
- Culinary arts management.
- Hotel and restaurant management.
- Tour guide management.
- Leisure management.
- Recreation management.
- Outdoor activity management.
- Theatre and stage management.

In addition to the overall degree programme name which links to this publication, a number of units or courses would also benefit from key chapters. Specifically, units/courses linked to anthropology, economics, business management, history, sociology, leisure, recreation, geography, development studies, political science, international studies, architecture, urban studies, rural development, language and culture studies, will all find elements of this textbook of use also.

SUMMARY

1. To understand the structure of the textbook: parts, chapters and sub-sections.

This textbook is structured with four large parts to enable personal and professional development for employment in tourism, hospitality and events management.

2. To identify how to use the think points, activities and case studies presented.

Chapters within each part include think points, activities and case studies to enable readers to reflect and apply knowledge learnt in the chapter and appraise their knowledge development.

3. To outline how the revision questions, additional sources and reference lists can be used.

Readers can use lists offered at the end of each chapter for testing knowledge learnt and wider academic and industry reading. Academics and teachers creating courses in support of employability and skills for THE can also use and refer to these in course creation.

4. To facilitate the use of learning outcomes offered for each chapter.

The learning outcomes are offered to clarify the content of each chapter. These are summarised at the end of each chapter to identify how these should have been met. Again, readers can use these to test and confirm their own understanding of the chapter contents.

Part 2

Personal development

Personal development is crucial in tourism, hospitality and events management as students will manage and work with a wide range of guests and colleagues. The interpersonal dimension to their graduate work means that their own personal development is more important than work in other sectors. This will be clarified in the opening section using soft skill and interpersonal skill theory situated in tourism, hospitality and events management research contexts. From this, four areas of personal development are identified using tourism, hospitality and events management contexts and research to clarify how these are unique and specific to these sectors. For example, relationship skills are vital in hospitality employment as students will be serving guests in private and personal events.

Chapter 6
Personal development in tourism, hospitality and events

LEARNING OBJECTIVES

1. To identify what personal development is.
2. To outline your current skilling abilities.
3. To create a SWOT analysis of your skills.
4. To start your skills journey by assessing, appraising and prioritising skills for personal development.

INTRODUCTION

Part 1 offered an overview of the sectors, businesses and roles of employment this text seeks to support. This part is now moving to consider your own personal development in support of employment and skills for tourism, hospitality and events (THE) management contexts. This chapter will enable you to identify your current and projected skills to outline where improvements and experience is required. This part should be followed step by step so that you systematically create your own skill map based on a staged process. You need to appraise your skills, place them in a SWOT box and finally map them out so that you are clear on your current and projected route to employment in THE.

A PERSONAL SKILLS APPRAISAL

To reflect upon your skills and career path this chapter will begin by getting you to appraise your current skills. Skill gaps in THE areas are larger than other industries. People 1st (2013) estimate that in the UK there are 21% of employees in the industry with skill gaps in comparison to 13% in other industries. Therefore, this skills appraisal is essential for you to identify where your own gaps are. Sometimes this is called an audit or a personal development plan. I have chosen to use the term appraisal as you will continue to complete these in the workplace upon graduation. Usually performance appraisals happen each year within employment and will be a meeting between you and your employer where you agree to certain goals and targets in the coming year (see Chapter 12 in Part 3 for creating goals and targets also). Therefore, the appraisal you start now can be built upon within any future employment.

An appraisal is about considering and discussing your current situation and identifying what learning or experience you need to complete to achieve certain goals (CIPD, 2012). Even if you have not decided on a career path yet, this skills appraisal will help you to identify your current position in order to identify employment opportunities.

From the previous chapters you now have an understanding of what employability and skills are needed for THE. You know about the difference and importance of both competences and competency and how these can be matched to job descriptions and person specifications. Therefore, the first action to complete in your skills appraisal is to identify your current skill set. In order to identify these, Table 6.1 outlines key skills for THE employment.

Part 1 Chapter 4 offered a range of skills to support employment in THE. However, Table 6.1 clarifies specific skills relevant for any employment in THE in order to appraise personal development. These are present in private and professional contexts. The list of 24 skills are not all required for every situation, but evidence of all of these will ensure interviews and personal development is completed effectively. Evidently the skills noted in the table all require business and industry knowledge in order to complete them. One particular area of knowledge key to this is commercial awareness.

ACTIVITY 6.1 SWOTING YOUR SKILLS

Use Table 6.1 on skills for THE employment for this activity to clarify the strengths, weaknesses, opportunities and threats (SWOT) in your current skill levels.

1. For each of the 24 skills identify an example of linked experience.
2. Going back to your evidence from each of these identify which ones are strengths, weaknesses, opportunities or threats.

a) Using the strengths – how is your current personal development evident?
b) Using the weaknesses – are these due to personality traits or lack of experience? Can you plan to develop and improve these?
c) Using the opportunities – which skills do you need to practice more of? Can you do this in current employment or personal time?
d) Using the threats – question whether these are threats in every context. Could they be seen as a strength in other situations?

Please note that all weaknesses can turn into threats if not developed and improved.

Table 6.1 Table of skills for THE employment

	Skill	Detail (linked parts and chapters in this book)
1	Communication (verbal, written and non-verbal)	Evidence of ability to express your ideas and intentions clearly and succinctly in a variety of modes. Using contexts like face to face, virtual and published content (see Chapter 11).
2	Groupwork	Can work as amember of ateam effectively and coherently with in the group structure (see Chapter 18).
3	Analysis	Able to gather, understand and critique information from a range of sources. Your analysis leads to the resolution of business problems (see Chapters 14 and 15 for this in academic practice).
4	Initiative (linked to self-motivation)	Activity completed based on your gut instinct (initiative). Evidence of using your motivation in work to support the business's goals using personal initiative (see Chapter 17).
5	Drive	Showing a determination to get things done. Evidence of actioning things and consistently looking for improved practices (see Chapter 17).
6	Organisation	Evidence of planning work and operating in an organised way. (Parts 3 and 4 clarify how to be organised in academic and professional practice).
7	Flexibility	Evidence of adjusting your work or approach to tasks in support of customers and colleagues. Adjustments made in light of changing business contexts.
8	Time management	Manage personal and professional time efficiently, prioritising and completing tasks to set deadlines (see Chapter 9).
9	Global skills	Linguistic knowledge and ability to communicate to a range of people (see Chapter 8).
10	Negotiating and persuading	Knowledge of how influence can be used to improv processes and practices in working contexts. Ability to agree to new ideas or ways of doing things (see Chapters 21 and 22).
11	Leadership	Directing and motivating others. Being an expert innovator and manager (see Part 4).
12	Numeracy	Effectively using numbers to communicate current business situations and goals to support business growth (see Chapters 14 and 16).
13	Computing	Competent use of computer programmes and software to communicate with internal and external stakeholders (see Chapter 15).
14	Self-awareness	Awareness of ability, weaknesses, aims and goals for personal and professional development (see Chapter 7).

(Continued)

Table 6.1 (Cont.)

	Skill	**Detail (linked parts and chapters in this book)**
15	Personal impact and confidence	Presentation of clear professional confidence and impact within a business. Commanding and eliciting respect from others (see Chapter 7).
16	Lifelong learning	Evidence of a portfolio of courses and training which supports continuous learning (see Chapter 12).
17	Stress tolerance	An ability to manage emotional stress within organisational contexts (see Chapter 18).
18	Integrity	A personality trait which is evident within working to organisational procedures, confidentiality maintenance and using appropriate behaviour. Also challenges inappropriate behaviour of others (see Part 4).
19	Independence	Ability to complete tasks and duties with individual attention and drive. Initiative and self-motivation evident (see Chapters 7 and 17).
20	Developing professionalism	Working in a professional way will be evident from customer and management feedback. Again it is within the individual ways in which you respond to situations (see Part 4).
21	Action planning	Linked to organisation, this is evidence of identifying goals and creating plans to achieve these (see Chapter 12).
22	Decision-making	Actions completed as a result of making decisions in support of organisational goals (see Part 4).
23	Interpersonal sensitivity	Awareness of individual differences present within communication to others. Responses and actions are sympathetic to differences in opinion and expectations (see Chapter 8).
24	Creativity	An ability to consider positions and actions in other ways. Applying creative solutions to complex problems (see Chapter 19).

By completing a SWOT on your skilling level you have started to appraise your current level of ability. Using evidence of experiences is vital for reflection on your personal development but these can also be used in interview scenarios. Interviews for employment often require you to offer scenario examples in support of the role duties. For example, an interviewer may ask you 'Can you offer me an example of a time when you demonstrated initiative?' In this way, the SWOT activity not only reflects on your current position but also prepares you to communicate examples of personal development and professional practice for employment.

ACTIVITY 6.2 COMPETENCE AND COMPETENCY FOR PERSONAL DEVELOPMENT

Part 1, Chapter 3 outlined what competence and competencies are. After completing a SWOT on your skills for employment in THE, this activity now requires you to reflect on your particular competence and competencies.

Competence is seen in using skills and knowledge in an experience or activity you have completed.

Competency is whereby you have completed a course, qualification or training within a specific skill or area of knowledge.

Write a list of competences below:

1.   Which skills have been identified in these lists in addition to the SWOT analysis?
2.   Do all competencies confirm your competence to complete these skills? If not, what additional training can you do to support these?

ACTIVITY 6.3 SKILLING QUESTIONS FOR THE EMPLOYMENT

From completing a SWOT of your skills and aligning these to competence and competencies, this activity will now offer extensive questions to consider in your personal development. Work through these with a colleague or friend. Discussion of these will enable you to reflect on your own perceptions on skills for THE employment.

1.   What do you consider to be your top three skills?
2.   Pick two friends at university/college/work. What skills do they have that you do not?
3.   What do you consider to be unique about your skills and work ethos? For example are you always early? Do you enjoy working late?
4.   What do you consider to be your top three skills to improve?
5.   What subjects are you studying next year? If you are in final year or are a graduate, what area do you want to learn about next?
6.   When you complete part/full-time work, what compliments have managers given you about your work input?
7.   Are there any activities that you frequently try to avoid? This can include assignment writing as well as the washing up at home.
8.   What compliments have customers given you on your service?
9.   Are you confident about your skill set and ability?

10. What do you pride yourself on when working?
11. Can you see any gaps in the service offered in your THE area?
12. What problems occur at work from serving customers? Are these frequent or infrequent problems?
13. What do you do at work that is better than anyone else?
14. Are you always on time when attending class?
15. What trends are you aware of in THE? Which of these are you most interested in?
16. What aspects of work do you enjoy most?
17. What obstacles do you have for developing and using your skills?
18. What values do you think are important for working in THE?
19. What skills are needed in the labour market you currently work in?
20. Do you have any skills that no one else in your class/work has?
21. Think about your friend and work network, what access do they have to different employers and training?
22. What languages do you speak?
23. Are you always on time when meeting someone?
24. What qualifications do you have?
25. Does your job change frequently?
26. What certificates do you have from any extra curricula hobby?
27. What grades are you getting at university/college? Can these be improved?
28. Would you say you are enthusiastic/dedicated/driven?
29. When you complete part/full-time work, what areas of operation are you not confident in?
30. Can you see any problems in the company you are working in?

Some of the above questions are dependent on prior work experience. If you have not completed work within an organisation previously, apply these instead to family life, groups or clubs which you have been a part of.

This section has provided activities to enable you to appraise, identify and action development of your skills for THE. Personal and professional development is never complete and these activities can be used at the beginning and end of a course to allow you to track improvements. Within work, you can also use these to signal skills to improve in coming years.

SKILL MAPPING FOR TOURISM, HOSPITALITY AND EVENTS

From identifying evidence and experience of using skills, it is now important to strategise your personal development. You will already have a number of skills to communicate to a future employer, but it is also appropriate to clarify skills which you wish to improve or seek training on. This not only shows drive and ambition but self-effacing reflection on your skills. Figure 6.1 clarifies three stages in analysis of your skills.

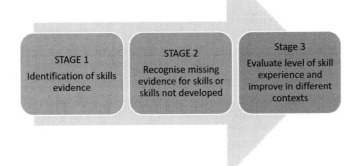

Figure 6.1 Appraising skills in three stages

You have already completed stages 1 and 2 in Figure 6.1 by outlining your skills proficiencies and shortages. In order to evaluate and develop skills for THE employment you can use SMART goals (see Part 3 Chapter 12 also). SMART refers to the following areas:

- Specific.
- Measurable.
- Achievable.
- Realistic.
- Timely.

An example of using SMART within skill development is offered as follows:

Specific	To evidence creativity in employment.
Measurement	No evidence to begin with. Evidence of action is therefore measured as an improvement.
Achievable	Opportunities are available for you to compete tasks in a creative way. You would require employment and management who support this.
Realistic	Employment contexts allow you to choose ways of operating and thinking about the services offered.
Timely	Are you in a position in personal development where you have the confidence, initiative and influence to offer creative ideas and actions?

Using SMART goals you can evaluate your own skills in a measured and efficient manner. This not only evidences excellent organisation and drive in personal development but allows you to focus skill development in an efficient manner.

Figure 6.2 Goals for skill development

The figure above offers insight into how your career, competence and competency are linked in skill development. If you consider each of these as goals for skill development, you can action and plan improvements within each. Goals linking to these could include:

Competence	To prove my reliability in work within a month.
	To take more initiative in work within 6 months.
	To learn and use (insert software) in the next 2 weeks.
Competency	To gain my personal licence (alcohol) within 12 months.
	To gain marks of over (insert number) in (specified subject) by (insert date).
	To pass my NVQ level 3 before (insert date).
Career	To gain a graduate job of at least £19,000 per annum.
	To get volunteer experience at music festivals over the summer.
	To achieve a management role by the time I am (insert age).

As you will notice with the above goals there is an easy formula to follow when creating these. Start with 'To,' then follow this with a verb (action word), then the thing you want to do, and finally a deadline to complete the goal by. After writing them, double check that they are address of the weaknesses noted from your SWOT box. You can also check if these match requirements in the essential duties or experience suggested in a job advert.

If you create these goals in support of your skill development, you must follow up with deadlines, actions and evaluation.

By completing the three stages in Figure 6.3, you will have completed a successful skills journey. This chapter has enabled you to complete stage 1. Part 2, Chapter 6 enables you to consider actions and goals and Part 4, Chapter 23 will enable you to complete reflections and evaluations of these.

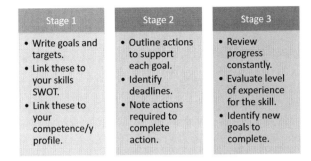

Figure 6.3 Stages of skill development

To effectively move from stage 1 to stage 2 in skills development you can prioritise these skills in support of career development. For example, if you have identified that global skills need improvement, you can use job adverts to assess the importance of this for employment.

ACTIVITY 6.4 ASSESSING AND PRIORITISING SKILLS FOR THE

To complete this activity it is advisable that you have completed the SWOT and competency activities in this chapter.

In order to complete stage 2 of in skills development you should have a list of skills to improve and develop. Moving forwards with actions for these requires further reflection on their importance and relation to specific THE roles.

1. Find a job advert for a role you wish to apply for or find the promotion requirements for the career track you are in to ascertain the next level of work.
2. List the skills, competences and competencies needed for these roles.
3. Match these against your list of skill improvements.
4. List these skills in order of importance according to the job description.

If there is no job description available for your role, or you are wanting to set up your own company, use your professional networks (see Part 4, Chapter 22) and ask colleagues which skills they would identify as important. Equally important in the assessment of skills is using a professional mentor to discuss the level to which these skills are deemed necessary (again see Part 4, Chapter 23).

Prioritising and assessing your skills is an organisational activity which can be completed easily. Self-motivation, checking and changing these when problems occur is the more difficult part of maintaining pace to achieve them. If your goals are to remain SMART, you have to make sure you keep abreast of each goal and action. I would advise that within each skilling goal you discuss your progress with an industry mentor (see Part 4, Chapter 23).

THINK POINT 6.1 'I TRIED TO BE PATIENT, BUT IT TOOK TOO LONG!'

Within the skills list offered in this chapter I purposely kept personality traits (like enthusiasm and patience) out. This is due to them being seen as linked to individual personalities rather than skills required by employers. However, it is important to consider how these affect your actions and behaviour in your use of skills. If you are an impatient person, how does this affect your skill development and depth of experience in skill use? If you are not enthusiastic about a role, how do you perceive opportunities to develop or show your skills?

The final stage for these goals on your skills development is to review and evaluate the skills you have developed. As each goal should be written with times and dates in mind (SMART), you can use the following questions to start evaluating your skills journey:

1. Did I complete the development in time?
2. What additional skills and knowledge were developed in conjunction with this skill?
3. What new networks and contacts have I developed in tandem?
4. Was my work hindered in the process of gaining skill development? If so, how can I manage the potential of this in the future?
5. Am I aware of new strengths in skills and knowledge for THE?

SUMMARY

1. To identify what personal development is.

This chapter has evidenced personal development by aligning professional and personal the skills to employment for THE. Skill development, targets, goals and actions have all been discussed to offer a strategy for personal development. Personal development requires self-awareness, relationship skills, time management and effective communication. All of these will be discussed in the following chapters.

2. To outline your current skilling abilities.

Completing the activities in this chapter will have enabled you to identify your current skills, competences and competencies for THE employment. These will be present regardless of your employment history as each education and training programme completed will have enabled the development and experience of some of these. Reflection is needed in skilling ability in mind of your own personality traits. Acknowledgement of identity and personality traits is vital in personal development as it will enable you to understand why some skills are easier to evidence and improve than others.

3.   To create a SWOT analysis of your skills.

Using the skills list offered you will have noted the strengths, weaknesses, opportunities and threats seen in your current skills. This allows you to highlight skills to improve, and knowledge to develop, to enhance your use of certain skills. This framework is useful in enabling you to clarify potential threats in your current ability. Weak skills need to be identified and experience linked to enable you to improve these. Opportunities seen in skills underdeveloped can enable you to action new experiences or duties in support of these skills. The skills noted as strong will have been aligned to specific incidents of experience. These can be used in interviews when you are asked for situational examples.

4.   To start your skills journey by assessing, appraising and prioritising skills for personal development.

Appraising your skills, setting goals and assessing your current skills portfolio has been discussed. These will enable you to identify how to prioritise your skills for personal development. This is an important starting point for self-awareness, relationship skills, time management and effective communication. Parts 3 and 4 can be used to develop this further within academic and professional development.

Questions to support your learning and research

1.   How does experience evidence skill proficiency?
2.   What global skills do you have?
3.   How does evidence of your skills from experience support interviews?
4.   Why does personality affect skill use and development?
5.   Which are your top three skills to improve?
6.   Which section can you use to help meet goals and targets for skills improvement?

Websites in support of your learning from this chapter

Figure out your skills – New Zealand Government www.careers.govt.nz/plan-your-career/not-sure-what-to-do/figure-out-your-skills/
What are skills? www.myworldofwork.co.uk/what-are-my-skills-0
Types of skills for employment www.careerkey.org/identify-your-skills/index.html

Chapter 7
Self-awareness

LEARNING OBJECTIVES

1. To understand definitions of self-awareness in support of personal development.
2. To link critical thinking and neuro-linguistic programming to self-awareness.
3. To outline how personal performance and presentation is evidence of self-awareness.

INTRODUCTION

Self-awareness is an important element of personal development as it enables you to reflect and consider your own position within different contexts. This chapter will enable you to learn about current definitions of self-awareness in review of consciousness, professional self-awareness, self-concept and reputation management. Following this, discussion on critical thinking will be offered to outline how self-awareness and self-concept enable critical thinking for personal and professional practice. Finally, personal performance is identified as outcomes of effective self-awareness.

DEFINITIONS OF SELF-AWARENESS

Self-awareness is linked to a range of academic disciplines. Psychology, philosophy, sociology and arts researchers have considered self-awareness as it enables a person to achieve the most in life. This chapter will offer an overview of common positions on self-awareness to enable you to critique and understand your own self-awareness. This is seen as essential for personal development as you need to appraise and know your own strengths and weaknesses in order to develop your skills and knowledge for employment.

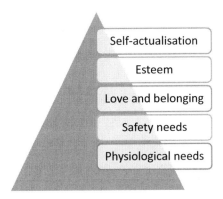

Figure 7.1 Maslow's (1943) hierarchy of needs to be applied to self-awareness
Source: Maslow, 1943

Within business literature, self-actualisation (Maslow, 1943) is often linked to self-awareness or personal development. Maslow's stages of self-actualisation are a useful position to start a review of self-awareness as it enables you to consider the levels and areas of support needed to maximise your potential.

Maslow's hierarchy of needs for self-actualisation (Figure 7.1) clarifies levels from which a person can become the best they can be. To link this to self-awareness the following clarifies points that should be considered within each level:

- Psychological needs – having access to air, food, water, shelter, sleep, clothing and relationships. These are the basis of the pyramid. Acknowledgement of these for your-self, and others, enables self-analysis on what you have access and support with. For example, some people require access to money to afford clothes as a basic physio-logical need. The level of money required to fulfil this specific physiological need will depend on the person and their passion and interests.
- Safety needs – linked directly to employment, this need outlines your access to and ability to use safety mechanisms. Health, property, personal and employment safety are all seen as important elements of this level. For example, having your own room which feels safe and secure to store your personal belongings is seen as more or less important to different people.
- Love and belonging – similar to the basic need for access to relationships, knowing and feeling that you belong and are regarded and loved by others is the following level in the pyramid. For example, friends who inform you of how they feel about you and how you benefit their own self-esteem will aid reflection on this level.
- Esteem – having self-respect, recognition of your abilities, using freedom and showing strength and resilience. For example, when someone does not treat you in a way which is appropriate or reflective of your ability you may show self-esteem by confronting others.
- Self-actualisation – this level is what this textbook addresses and aims to support. A desire to become the best that you can be. This can be difficult if you are insecure

about your personal ability, or unaware of over confidence in areas which you are not an expert. Self-awareness is crucial to evidence self-actualisation as you need to be humble and considered in your abilities and areas for growth and development. For example, you may feel competent within a sports team or music group but you will be aware of improvements you can make. This desire to become better and support a group is a good example of working towards self-actualisation.

The five levels towards self-actualisation discussed previosuly can be used in reflection on your self-awareness of the basic and intricate elements that support your personal development.

In order to complete reflection on Maslow's hierarchy of needs, and so to outline your self-awareness, it is important to understand the causes of your understanding and the validity of your perceptions. For example, you may feel that you are confident within interview situations and enjoy them, but then do not obtain employment after completing a number of interviews. This suggests there is an issue in your reflection of your ability and confidence within a situation. Subjectivity is seen in this example and it is important to be objective when reflecting on yourself. Fenigstein et al. (1975) clarified that self-awareness discussion stemmed from psychology research into how the mind processes conscious and unconscious reflection. A person's ability to recognise thoughts, motivations and defence mechanisms, therefore, outlines how a person can recognise their self. This is crucial when completing self-reflection (linked to counselling in their article) as it enables a person to address their own reactions and thoughts around certain situations. For personal development, recognition of how you think and process is equally important in order to show reflexive and flexible approaches to situations.

Research on self-awareness linked to a person's psychology requires an understanding on attribution theory and causal relations in thought processes (Kelley and Angeles, 1973). Attribution theory is noted by Weiner (2010) as a person's ability to identify the cause of success and failure. When you consider your own personal abilities you will naturally self-reflect and gauge how well you completed something. If there are clear levels or marks associated with a task then the answer to this success or failure will be made clear. However, if you have noted a successful relationship with friends, the elements contributing and attributed to this success will be varied. For self-awareness you require an understanding of the attributes supporting the outcome and causes surrounding this.

It is noted that causal understanding can be linked to three areas: location, endurance and controllability (Weiner, 2010). The location of causality can be either internal or external. Internally you may feel confident and capable of completing an activity, however, externally you may appear nervous or even incompetent. This dichotomy is important for defining self-awareness as it enables a person to accept that you may have a different perspective of yourself than others. How this is manifested and perceived is dependent on the others present in the context. Endurance in causality of attribution refers to the length of time within which you are subjecting a cause or reason for something. For example, if you are feeling unconfident about completing a task you can tell yourself mentally three times that you can do it. Repeating assertive phrases, or repeating behaviour, will lead you to unconsciously perceive this as being correct. Issues arise when this is not correct and you require additional personal development in order to improve or change your ways of doing or processing things. In comparison to Weiner (2010), Tobin (2012) suggested that causal attribution links to two attributions:

1. Dispositional attribution – a person thinks, behaves or acts in a specific way in order to cause an event.
2. Situational attribution – the environment in which the event is located caused the thought, behaviour or action.

These two papers by Weiner (2010) and Tobin (2012) clarify that there are a range of positions and perspectives on how a person can explain their self-awareness and reactions within a situation. Within personal development it is crucial that you reflect on your thoughts, behaviour and actions in various situations in order to improve your understanding of yourself and be flexible and adaptable in a range of future situations. Complete Activity 7.1 to appraise your understanding of yourself in private, public and social contexts.

It is important to analyse causality of self-awareness as this will enable you to understand the motivations and reasons for why you feel or act in a certain way. This is an interesting position as Duval and Silvia (2002) also note that it is imperative for a person to understand when they may have a self-serving bias. This is whereby a person may perceive something as a failure internally when it is actually perceived as a success externally. For example, you may feel that you are not good at doing something and yet friends or relatives may have an opposite perspective. This can be difficult to understand as your self-awareness is contradicted due to internal bias. This is why Silvia and Duval (2001) suggest that objectivity within self-awareness is crucial in order to ensure the thoughts and perceptions of yourself are accurate and measured appropriately.

ACTIVITY 7.1 PRIVATE, PUBLIC AND SOCIAL SELF-AWARENESS

For each of the following statements, tick which ones apply to you:

Public

I am worried about the way I present myself.

I am nervous about making a good impression to others.

I often feel self-conscious on how I look.

I feel conscious about my style not being the same as others.

Private

I keep trying to figure myself out.

I reflect a lot about myself.

I am alert to changes in my mood.

I know how to work through a problem in my mind.

Social

I am easily embarrassed.

Large groups make me feel nervous.

I find it difficult to talk to strangers.

I cannot work if someone is watching me.

Once you have ticked the statements that you feel apply to you, count the number of ticks noted for each area of social awareness. Which area do you score highest in? Do you feel you have more social awareness in this area? If not, where are the differences? Would your friends and family agree with the statements you have ticked?

Self-bias and causal attribution is seen to be due to a need to protect and manage self-esteem (Zuckerman, 1979). From completing the activity above you will note that you may have a range of negative and positive perceptions on your ability in public, private and social areas. These perceptions are seen as important in protecting the fourth level of Maslow's hierarchy: self-esteem. Self-esteem is seen as self-serving in developing confidence in behaviour, thought and task. In order to feel comfortable in situations you need a level of self-esteem to enable you to complete the task and behave appropriately. Issues arise in self-esteem when self-bias is developed incorrectly.

THINK POINT 7.1 SELF-BIAS IN SELF-ESTEEM

Have you encountered a situation when you have felt that you were able and capable of something, only to discover that others have a different perspective? This is where self-bias is evident due to incorrect self-esteem. How do you feel if this happens? How do you overcome this and address self-bias to develop and improve?

Self-awareness has been defined through discussion of your thoughts, behaviour and actions. Understanding your own abilities and critiquing self-bias compared to external opinion will enable you to critique and reflect on your abilities and improve your personal development. Two other areas in which this can be analysed is with face recognition and dream analysis. Have you ever yawned because someone else has just yawned? This is an example of self-awareness through face recognition (Platek et al., 2003), whereby you unconsciously mirror someone else. This is important within personal development. In order to self-appraise and be aware of yourself you need an understanding of others. Yawning after someone else has just yawned can be noted as an example of your ability to perceive others and copy their behaviour due to the context within which you are located. Voss et al. (2014) offer an interesting perspective on how your dreams can elude to your unconscious understanding of self-awareness and ability. Usually when you dream you do not have conscious awareness or ability to control elements of the dream. Voss et al.'s (2014) research clarified how self-awareness can be created for dreaming.

Consideration of contagious yawning and using self-awareness in dreams are two examples of how self-awareness can also be unconscious reactions. Have you ever woken up and wondered why you acted in a particular way within a dream? Have you ever felt embarrassed that you yawned after someone else? These examples allow you to accept that self-awareness is not simply a conscious state where you can specify the thought and motivation for your behaviours.

So far, we have discussed self-awareness within personal psychology and reflection on your ability to adapt and reflect on your natural and context-based behaviours. It is important now to ascertain professional self-awareness in management of your personal reputation. Conscious, reflective and reflexive awareness are discussed below and aligned to examples of how these are completed within personal, academic and professional contexts.

Conscious awareness

Being in an active or alert state to what you are thinking, doing or feeling. This links to being present within a situation. You need to be awake and alert to a situation in order to be seen in conscious awareness. When completing assignments or duties in work, conscious awareness may be difficult as you try to multi-task and satisfy a range of other people. For example, you will have a range of thoughts during your day. How you allow these thoughts to penetrate your consciousness and affect your mood and behaviour will depend on how conscious you are of the situation. Have you ever driven somewhere and not been conscious about the route and methods taken to navigate traffic on your route? This is due to you not being consciously aware and having allowed your thoughts to wander. Within THE employment conscious awareness may be limited if you are required to use a script when liaising with customers. Using scripted service in THE business is frequent as it enables a company to manage their brand and customer perceptions of the service offered. However, using standardised service will lead to a lack of conscious awareness and thus might lead to misunderstandings if the person is not present within the situation.

Reflective awareness

Reflecting on yourself is the key to this element of self-awareness and requires you to step to one side and be critical of yourself and examine the way in which you completed an action or behaviour. If you know yourself and address how you think, react and behave, you are evidencing reflective awareness. You may have had a parent or teacher ask you to think about something you have just done. This is an example of supported reflective awareness. It does not mean that future thoughts and behaviour will change, but it can evidence your ability to consider who you are and what you do within a situation. Reflective awareness needs to be completed individually and with self-motivation. It is unusual for employers or teachers to require you to complete this self-assessment but is imperative for you to understand who you are. Complete the activities in this chapter to enable you to consider reflective awareness.

Reflexive awareness

This element links to the ability to understand how others can have a counter view to yourself. The inner beliefs and external opinions on yourself can be contradictory or supplementary. Knowledge of external and internal awareness of one's self is the core to reflexive awareness. Assignment or exam feedback and professional development reviews (PDRs) enable you to complete reflective awareness for THE. For example, the feedback written and marks awarded on a piece of academic work will enable you to reflect upon what you wanted to convey and what was perceived in the submission. In PDRs your line manager will assess your current ability and work completed in discussion with your career goals and targets. Both assignments and PDRs offer a situation within which you can understand external perspectives on your own abilities.

Reputation

Your reputation and distinctiveness is important so that people remember you for good reasons and are clear on what you can offer. This requires you to have reflexive awareness of yourself and maintain control of your abilities. Just like a THE business, you have a competitive advantage over others due to your unique personality and skill set (see Chapter 6 of this part to appraise these).

Self-interest

Linked to reputation is the perception of your own self-interest. This is visible in your social media pages, branding (aesthetics) and positions taken in different situations. Self-interest, similarly to self-esteem, is a protective element of self-awareness as it enables you to focus on your thoughts and behaviours, which supports the development of your 'self.'

ACTIVITY 7.2 YOUR 'SELF' AS A THE BUSINESS: REPUTATION DEVELOPMENT

From a review of reputation and self-interest, answer the following questions to enable a conscious, reflective and reflexive self-awareness evaluation:

1.   What photos are there of you on social media?
2.   What do your friends think of your social media photos?
3.   What would your teachers or management think about your photos on social media?
4.   How do you alter your appearance in different contexts?
5.   How does your behaviour and attitude change in different contexts?
6.   If your parents saw you working, would they be shocked at the difference in your behaviour and language?
7.   Are you aware of specific benefits your personality and 'self' has over others?
8.   What do you think your strengths are?
9.   What would your family say your strengths are?
10.   What would your teachers say your strengths are?
11.   Do you maintain your 'self' or alter it dependent on the situation?

By applying business and organisation positions to understanding your own self-awareness through reputation and self-interest management, the activity above will have enabled you to complete reflective and reflexive thinking for self-awareness. Reputation and self-interest are crucial to self-awareness as you must be aware of how others perceive you in order to manage and control your personal development.

The final area for discussion in self-awareness definitions is to accept and acknowledge that concepts of your 'self' are not static nor limited. Your thoughts, abilities and development are controlled and driven by yourself. If you want to achieve more and do better to become the best version of yourself (self-actualisation) you need to understand what you are capable of and how to work with your individual ability. Self-concept is based upon what others say about us and what we tell ourselves (Moua, 2010). It is, therefore, learnt and yet dynamic. Self-concepts can enable us to be our most brilliant self but also inhibit our abilities. For example, if I told myself I could not write this textbook, then I perhaps would not find the motivation to do so. If, instead, I acknowledge that students will benefit from this textbook, then I will be motivated to write and complete it in order to support others. Self-concept, therefore, naturally relates to self-efficacy (discussed in Part 1). Your self-belief and self-confidence is inherently linked to your ability to become the best version of yourself.

CRITICAL THINKING AND NEURO-LINGUISTIC PROGRAMMING FOR SELF-AWARENESS

Having defined self-awareness, this section will now look to link this to critical thinking in order to communicate your ability and strengths. Part 3 considers academic critical analysis and writing, but in order to complete this you need to use self-awareness in order to take positions and convey arguments from your own opinions.

Being critical is the ability to clarify patterns seen and counter positions taken. Personality traits like being opinionated, bitchy, single-minded or narrow-minded are seen as the adverse elements to being critical. All are necessary in order to perceive patterns and counter positions. For example, you will have an opinion on how you should greet someone. This may be based on your experience within a country and following and repeating the usual social norms seen (similar to face recognition and contagious behaviours). However, you may not like the social norms in greeting people seen around you and so may not act in this way due to your personal feelings. In France, it is usual to greet people with a kiss on either cheek. If you do not like getting close to strangers you will be critical of this approach and may offer an alternative (like a hand outstretched to shake). This example clarifies how a cultural norm can be accepted if liked by someone, or rejected in the knowledge of alternative greeting forms. Critical thinking is evident as patterns of behaviour are acknowledged and alternative forms are offered or considered.

To develop and evidence critical thinking for self-awareness, neuro-linguistic programming (NLP) will be used as a framework for discussion. This was developed by Bandler and Grinder (1979) in order to allow people to accept their usual personal reactions and thoughts and change these to succeed in any situation. In order to use NLP you require critical conscious awareness to adapt and change natural behaviours and reactions efficiently. Emotional state, situational language and behaviour, building rapport, setting goals and achieving targets, achieving success through model behaviour and reprogramming subjective experiences (Smale and Fowlie, 2009) are now discussed to outline how NLP can support self-awareness for personal development.

Emotional state

Acknowledgement of your emotional state enables you to accept and then address any changes required. If you have a satisfactory physiological basis (see Maslow's hierarchy at the start of this chapter) then you are likely to have a stable emotional state. However, if you have not slept well or have eaten incorrectly, your emotions may be imbalanced. This is a basic example of altered emotional states but clarifies how self-awareness of physiological needs are crucial to critical thinking for self-awareness. You may want to stay up late to watch a movie, but in reflection, you may understand that a lack of sleep will lead to reduced energy the following day. This evidences critical thinking as you are aware of potential actions and behaviour which will lead to altered emotional states. Furthermore, if you are in a negative emotional state, you may find you are unable to perform to your optimum level. Examples of the types of emotional states present at any time are listed as follows:

Table 7.1 Positive and negative emotions

Positive emotions	Negative emotions
Adoration Awe Calmness Craving Entrancement Excitement Interest Joy Nostalgia Romance Satisfaction Sexual desire Sympathy Triumph	Amusement at other's misfortune Anxiety Awkwardness Boredom Confusion Disgust Empathetic pain Envy Fear Horror Sadness

The lists of emotions in Table 7.1 are indicative only and not accurate for every situation. As noted, your emotional state will be influenced by a range of emotions, not simply one. If you are feeling empathetic pain you may also be interested in someone. In this way the combination of emotions may result in either positive or negative outcomes. Being aware of these and how to change them is essential in developing self-awareness.

From the discussion on emotional states it is also important to consider how these are present in your personality and how they influence your personal development. McShane and Travaglione (2003) suggest a useful mnemonic in behavioural prompts, which can be linked to your personality and management of emotions:

M   Motivation
A   Ability
R   Role perceptions
S   Situation

Using the above mnemonic can enable you to reflect on your emotional states and natural emotional reactions within your unique personality. Consider what motivations you had for feeling and reacting in certain ways. What are your abilities and how do emotions naturally come out due to these? For example, if you are naturally an enthusiastic person, how do you manage this ability to enthuse? Within each situation you will place yourself in a role (friend, colleague, student) and others in the same way (friend, colleague, teacher). These perceptions will influence your behaviour and alter your emotional states and reactions. Finally, the situation within which you are present will also impact upon your decisions in behaviour and emotion.

Situational language and behaviour

Within different situations you will be aware of alternative ways of communicating and expressing yourself. Using conscious awareness, you will be able to control and adapt your language and interpretation of others language effectively. This is often difficult when your emotional state is imbalanced or you are in a busy situation completing a number of tasks. 'Speaking before thinking' is often referred to when you realise your reaction was inappropriate for the situation present. NLP advocates for conscious alert attention in language and behaviour to ensure you reflect on the choices for communication before acting instinctively.

Building rapport

This is covered in depth in Chapter 8 of this part within relationship skill development. However, your ability to control, manage and maintain relationships is crucial for self-esteem and management of self-efficacy. Developing rapport through complex interpersonal skill use is essential in personal development for employment.

Setting goals and achieving targets

Covered in Part 3 in more depth, having clear goals and targets to achieve will enable you to evidence critical thinking in self-awareness development. For example, you may be aware of a personality trait which inhibits your ability to succeed. Using goals and targets to manage this will allow you to control this more easily. A personal example of this is my lack of patience in situations. I can often see the ultimate outcome of a discussion or activity and want to fast track to that end before the natural sequence of events lead to that point. This means I am disadvantaged in some situations as my patience overtakes my ability to consider and approach activities in a measured and steady way. In reflection of my own self-awareness here, I set myself targets which support patience development (like using stages in processes to check and monitor process and thoughts).

Achieving success through model behaviour

In order to become successful you must review how others have completed similar tasks, model this behaviour and seek to improve the outcome. In this way you need to identify patterns in behaviour usual to success and copy them. A simple example of this, seen from studying and teaching experience, is when students start their assignments in good time and plan to complete the work in set stages without the pressure of the deadline looming. Using time management for assignments is often a condition for the resulting success of the submission as you have more time to consider, edit and reflect on elements of the work. However, it is accepted that some students will prefer to work at the last minute due to a perception that they work better under pressure. If students working last minute modelled their behaviour on others who use time management efficiently, they may see increases in their marks and standard of work submitted. This example requires you to understand your natural management of academic work around other work and life tasks, as well as appraising other student's behaviour as being better or more beneficial.

Reprogramming subjective experiences

The final, but possibly most important element in NLP to consider for critical thinking in self-awareness is how you can change and re-programme your own subjectivity of previous experiences. As humans, we naturally learn through copying behaviour. However, this can lead to repeated behaviour, thought and action which influences a negative outcome. Reflective reflexive thinking is needed when you address and encounter a repeated experience in order to develop and improve outcomes. This form of NLP is applied in combat of phobias or addictions like smoking or over eating.

The six central elements of NLP have been discussed in this section to enable you to perceive how this can be used with critical thinking to analyse your own self-awareness in personal development. Perceiving patterns of thought, experience and emotion and acknowledging alternative positions will support your personal development and allow you to approach tasks in different, more effective ways.

PERSONAL PERFORMANCE AND PRESENTATION

This final section will enable you to consider how your personal performance and presentation is known by you and perceived by others in successfully completing tasks. The impact of this is varied but is essential in evaluating your personal development within self-awareness. Here, we are also considering the material and visual elements of others perceptions of our self. This was noted as vital for reflexive awareness and subjective to critical thinking to change your usual ways of thinking and doing.

To begin, activities and discussion in self-awareness has required you to interpret your own understanding of your 'self.' This is due to your own knowledge and reflection on how you feel and think of yourself. We often use metaphors and stories in order to complete this. For personal development we will use the metaphor of your self-awareness journey. Journeys are a frequent metaphor used in talent show competitions to evidence how a person has grown and developed during the contes – this is also true of your own education and employment experiences.

ACTIVITY 7.3 YOUR PERSONAL DEVELOPMENT JOURNEY TO ENHANCED SELF-AWARENESS

Your current situation:

1. How do you feel about yourself?
2. When you approach a task how do you plan and organise your time?
3. Do you compare yourself to others in order to feel better about yourself?
4. What feelings do you have when completing education assignments?
5. What goals and targets do you set to complete tasks?

Actors influencing your journey who are present and influential:

E.g. parents, friends, class mates, significant romantic partner/s, neighbours, siblings, work colleagues, managers, professionals like medical practitioners.

Using the list of influencers above, identify how they each react and support your self-awareness journey.

Link the influencer's reactions and support to the answers to your current situation. How much do you apply their perspectives in consideration of your current situation? Which elements do you use for your own self-esteem and self-efficacy?

When completing a journey you will encounter problems along the way. Wrong turns, bad direction and time spent on unnecessary tasks will undoubtedly occur. Your personal performance evidencing self-awareness will be the same. Self-development is emergent, fluid and dependent on reflection of how you think and behave in situations. It is often difficult to reflect on how you work in a productive and successful manner and the failures are easier to champion. Use Think Point 7.2 to outline a memorable personal performance failure and how this was perceived and presented to others.

THINK POINT 7.2 MY GREATEST FAILURE IN PERSONAL PRESENTATION

Establish a memory of a situation in which you realised your personal performance was unsatisfactory. How did others react? Did they alert you to the issue or did you perceive this due to their reactions? What led to this situation and how have you changed your decisions for this in the future?

ACTIVITY 7.4 SELF-AWARENESS OF STRUCTURE FOR PERSONAL PERFORMANCE

Use the following statements to align your usual approach to tasks in consideration of the structures you use for personal performance.

Statement	Strongly agree (1)	Agree (2)	Neutral (3)	Disagree (4)	Strongly disagree (5)
I always meet deadlines.					
I write lists to support meeting goals.					
I like being organised.					
I work in set time periods according to a shift of work.					
I only take breaks when I have completed certain tasks.					
I do not finish working until the tasks are finished in line with the deadlines.					

Look at the boxes you have ticked and add up the numbers aligned to each response. Lower scores (under 12) show you prefer a more structured approach to personal performance. Higher scores (above 24) suggest you use a less structured approach. In consideration of these results, how can you adapt your performance in a structured way to enhance your personal performance?

A further consideration in personal performance is the extent to which you structure and organise activities (Cottrell, 2010). Activity 7.4 enables you to reflect on your usual approach to activities and evaluate if you usually work using structured support for these. This consideration of personal performance is essential in self-awareness as you can only develop and improve if you are aware of and address outcomes of your performance and seek to make improvements in the future.

By reviewing your personal performance in tasks you will have identified how you usually address tasks and consider your 'self.' This performance is evident within your personal presentation. O'Shannessy et al. (2002) offered an overview of personal presentation to aid employment in tourism. Similarly to the work on aesthetic labour (discussed in Chapter 8 of this part) personal presentation is how you appear to others. This may be prescribed by your employers or education establishment but is always dependent on your own time and ability in maintaining presentation to a set standard.

> When people look at us, they immediately begin to form an opinion about us. This is their perception of who and what we are.
>
> (O'Shannessy et al., 2002: p.43)

This position is important in self-awareness as we have discussed how reflexivity of others perception's is important in changing, challenging and adapting your usual behaviour. Self-awareness of personal presentation is also a core employment skill needed for interviews and professional meetings. You may also be required to use your usual presentation skills in order to meet the needs of a new employer.

There are two types of personal presentation noted in THE employment: industry and enterprise (O'Shannessy et al., 2002). Industry presentation is whereby there may be personal presentation standards for a role or function. Examples of these for THE include being clean shaven or having neat haircuts and no piercings when working with food. Enterprise standards for personal presentation are then seen in specific organisations and can be noted in make-up standards and the colour and style of uniform. Both industry and enterprise personal presentation standards need to conform to regulation and brand standards. Working with food in hospitality businesses necessitates some staff to wear hair nets and remove certain jewellery in support of the hygiene and safety of cooking areas. Having an awareness of this and how it can affect your own self-awareness is important here.

CASE STUDY 7.1 PERSONAL PRESENTATION IN THE

The photos in the above case study are offered to outline the variance in appearance through uniform standards in different THE roles. Finally, in consideration of personal presentation, elements of your personal grooming will now be outlined to clarify how these affect others perceptions of you.

Hair

As noted above, your hair and hair style will portray who you are. If you choose a conventional and neat hair cut this may go un noticed. However, if you like hair-cuts that are contemporary and innovative, you may have more attention paid to you. This attention can be positive or negative and will come with connotations. For example, if a woman has a shaved head this can lead to you being perceived as being harsh, hard or unconventional. Being resilient to comments made on your hair, and knowledge of how this can be perceived by others, is important to ensure you are reflexive on others perceptions of you.

Clothing

When in work and education you may be required to wear a uniform. A uniform maintains the brand image of the company and allows you to be seen as similar to others working there and blend in. However, if you are in situations where you can choose your own attire it is important to reflect on how this will be perceived by others. An example of how this can be used in contemporary media is to consider Lady Gaga. As a music artist, Lady Gaga could wear conventional or designer clothing. However, whenever this artist is on stage or attending galas and dinners, she chooses to use her clothing to express her personality. In this way it is clear that clothing can both reflect our personality, affect our emotions and be perceived by others as a reflection of your personality. Fashion trends constantly change and some people choose to follow these (therefore appearing as a trend follower). However, if you choose to wear usual clothes, this can make you appear as someone who wants to fit in, not stand out and is conventional. Equally, if you choose to wear clothes which appear damaged (rips in jeans being the obvious example here) this can make you appear as messy and un-kempt. Clothing is a personal choice and can enable you to showcase your personality in a positive way. If you enjoy wearing certain clothes this can also enable you to feel more confident. It is important for you to reflect on how these are perceived by others in the contexts within which you are present to ensure there is some homogeny with this context. If you were to go bathing in a Muslim country and you wore a bikini or small swimwear this could be perceived as offensive to others due to their religion. You may not have intended to offend others, and so knowledge of appropriate dress is also important for cohesion in the local community.

Hygiene

When working in THE businesses you will find that you may work long shifts (10 hrs or more). Working for long periods of time in one outfit may lead to you creating more sweat than you usually would. In this example it is important for you to consider your personal hygiene. Similar to hair and clothing, people perceive sweat, body odour and oral hygiene as a factor attributed to being a clean, healthy and nice person. Rightly or wrongly, others will make assumptions on you due to your personal hygiene. When you are aware you will complete long shifts for a long period of time within an activity it is important that you take deodorant, mouthwash and perhaps spare sets of clothes to change into. This will not only make you feel more comfortable but will ensure your personal hygiene standards are maintained.

Personal grooming in hair, clothing and hygiene has been discussed here to evidence the requirement for your self-awareness on how your image will affect both your feelings and others perceptions of you. Self-awareness here is, again, not simply about your awareness of how you feel (reflective and conscious), but how this leads to others making judgements and opinions on your personality, behaviour and even capability. Within THE roles and employment you need to also be aware of how staff 'look' in certain roles. Review Chapter 8, which includes details on aesthetic labour, to consider differences in appearance for THE roles.

SUMMARY

1.   To understand definitions of self-awareness in support of personal development.

Definitions of self-awareness have been linked to psychology research. Understanding how your thoughts, actions and behaviour are internally and externally perceived are integral to self-awareness. Self-bias and self-efficacy can negatively affect your self-awareness. Appraising and understanding your 'self' is important in personal development in order to identify areas in which you are competent or require further development.

2.   To link critical thinking and neuro-linguistic programming to self-awareness.

Critical thinking was defined as an ability to perceive patterns and choose alternative positions to a task, thought or behaviour. Using the six components of NLP you will be able to consider a variety of potential behaviours in a variety of contexts.

3.   To outline how personal performance and presentation is evidence of self-awareness.

This chapter clarified how your self-awareness of performance and presentation will affect your ability to complete tasks effectively. These elements are mostly within your own control (except where business or education demands alternative methods like uniform or grooming standards). These were discussed in order to apply your knowledge of self-awareness in the personal creation of yourself to others. Whether this is within personal, social, public or employment contexts, these will be evident to others and will lead to perceptions on your ability and capability.

Questions to support your learning and research

1. How can you use the hierarchy of self-actualisation to start an appraisal of your own self-awareness?
2. What is self-bias?
3. Why do you need to reflect on others perceptions on yourself in order to appraise self-awareness?
4. How do dreams and contagious yawning help you to understand self-awareness?
5. What is NLP?
6. How does critical thinking enable effective self-awareness?
7. What emotions are seen as negative when completing tasks?
8. What are industry and enterprise personal presentation standards and how do these differ?
9. How does personal grooming affect others perceptions of you?

Further reading in support of your learning from this chapter

Alvesson, M. (2010). Self-doubters, strugglers, storytellers, surfers and others: Images of self-identities in organization studies. *Human Relations*, 63(2), pp. 193–217.

Asendorpf, J. and Baudonniere, P.-M. (1993). Self-awareness and other-awareness: Mirror self-recognition and synchronic imitation among unfamiliar peers. *Development Psychology*, 29(1), pp. 88–95.

Beitel, M., Ferrer, E. and Cecero, J.J. (2005). Psychological mindedness and awareness of self and others. *Journal of Clinical Psychology*, 61(6), pp. 739–50. [online]. Available from: www.ncbi.nlm.nih.gov/pubmed/15546143 [Accessed September 19, 2011].

Kondrat, M. (1999). Who is the 'self' in self-aware: Professional self-awareness from a critical theory perspective. *Social Service Review*, 73(4), pp. 451–477. [online]. Available from: www.journals.uchicago.edu/doi/10.1086/514441.

McEwan, T. (2001). *Managing Values and Beliefs in Organisations*. London, England: Pearson.

Milde, M. (2010). Who am I? The reflexivity of self-identity through tourism. San Jose State University.

Shavelson, R. and Bolus, R. (1981). *Self-concept: The Interplay of Theory and Methods*. p. 43.

Yeh, R. et al. (2013). Hotel employees' uniform and their self-perceptions in Southern California. *Tourism Management Perspectives*, 6, pp. 79–81. [online]. Available from: http://linkinghub.elsevier.com/retrieve/pii/S2211973612000840 [Accessed October 11, 2013].

Chapter 8

Relationship skills

LEARNING OBJECTIVES

- -

1. To understand how to make connections and develop personal relationships.
2. To identify how soft and interpersonal skills are necessary for successful professional relationships.
3. To analyse how culture and cross cultural and intercultural elements of communication can support effective relationships.
4. To evaluate personal emotions, aesthetics and sexualisation present in relationships.
5. To outline how being perceived as a citizen of the world is important for effective relationships.

INTRODUCTION

So far in this part, we have outlined skills appraisal and reflections on your own self-awareness. These are important critical evaluation exercises to enable you to define and outline your current personal development. This chapter will now identify how to develop and maintain successful relationships. This is central for effective business networking (see Part 4, Chapter 22) but also for personal and academic development. Within your personal, professional and academic life you will need to develop and maintain relationships in order to feel valued as a person and linked to others who have common beliefs. This is important not only for success in these contexts, but also for your own sense of self-worth and self-esteem.

In addition to noting skills for creating relationships (interpersonal, soft and aesthetic), this part offers links to cross-cultural relationship development and social responsibility used in relationship development. These two areas are outlined as contemporary employability skills needed for THE employment.

PERSONAL RELATIONSHIPS

Personal relationships are acknowledged firstly as these are the primary form of relationship developed in your life. In order to build personal relationships you will have used a range of skills to develop and maintain your connections with others. Communication, empathy and awareness are three key skills needed for personal relationship development and are present in every successful relationship. In order to start personal relationships you need to firstly get to know another person. Figure 8.1 outlines elements of this for discussion.

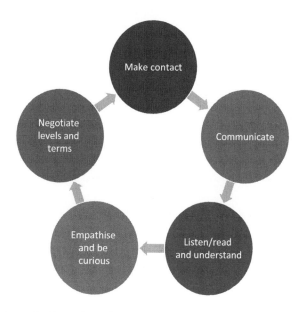

Figure 8.1 Elements required in getting to know someone

Beginning with making contact, the above figure evidences a cycle of relationship development to aid reflection. Every personal relationship begins with contact with another person. Whether this is face to face, written or virtual, contact is required to lead to communication. Dependent on the contact form, communication can then take place between people. This can be with one or more people and the communication form and style will vary according to the context and roles within which the contact was made. For example, if you meet someone in a sports activity, you may be in casual dress, considered a team mate and already have similar interests. Conversely, if you meet someone in a waiting room for a job interview, or a doctor's surgery, you will be dressed differently and your emotional state will be altered. Review Chapter 10 of this part to identify how to complete effective communication in a range of contexts.

The next step on this figure refers to listening/reading and understanding. Active listening, and confirmed communicated understanding of this, is also covered in Chapter 10 of this part. This is crucial in relationship development as you need to be clear in your understanding of others as well as direct in your own communication. Conveying information to the other person is essential in the forming stages of personal relationships. How this is completed and how clear you are will also influence the effectiveness of the relationship. Getting to know someone also necessitates you to be empathetic and curious. Understanding communication and information from another person's perspective allows you to see patterns and similarities between you and others. This is often referred to as being empathetic (covered in the next chapter) and shows you care and have an interest in another person. Being curious means you need to ask appropriate questions and learn about the other person.

The final element in Figure 8.1 is based on negotiating the terms and levels of the relationship. Examples of this include:

- How often you communicate.
- What the basis of the relationship is (hobbies, interests, common friends).
- In which situations you meet in person.
- Humour use appropriate within the relationship.
- Amount of personal detail and information offered.
- Motivations for continuing and maintaining the relationship.

The six elements within personal relationships listed above are not always explicitly discussed, but they are always present. Knowledge on these is important in effective personal relationships and reflection on what you bring to the relationship. Issues arise when these change or are disharmonious to the others in the relationship. For example, if you have a certain form of humour and this is not clear in the forming stages of the relationship this may cause problems in the developing relationship when communicated at a later date. Being self-aware of this and clarifying that you have awareness of this will enable a negotiation of how you and the other person are happy to continue getting to know each other.

As personal relationships require consistent review and improvement, the figure offered works in a circular flow to ensure you are aware of the constant need for communication, empathy and understanding of the other person. An underlying element of developing relationships and getting to know someone is whether or not you like them and the motivation for the relationship. Sometimes you will not like someone but will still maintain an effective personal relationship due to the social contexts within which you need to meet and communicate. In this way, developing effective personal relationships also requires you to be aware of your likes and dislikes about someone and the context within which the relationship is developed.

ACTIVITY 8.1 HOW TO MAKE CONNECTIONS IN RELATIONSHIP DEVELOPMENT

Next time you meet a new person and begin the development of a personal relationship, consider the following elements:

1. How does the person's personality appear to you?
2. How does their clothing or writing style affect your interpretation of them?
3. Do they smile when communicating?
4. Are they polite? What form of politeness do they use? Familiar or professional?
5. Are they inquisitive about you?
6. Do they use humour?
7. Do they appear genuine in their communication?
8. What motivation do you think they have in developing a personal relationship with you? How do you know this?

Within all personal relationship development you need to use self-confidence. This does not mean being confident or assertive but being aware of yourself, showing confidence and assuring the other person that you are clear on your own motivations and information to communicate. Lack of self-confidence is often seen as a barrier to effective personal relationship development. This can be due to someone not feeling comfortable or capable of offering something to another person. In order to feel self-confident in personal relationship development complete the following activity to appraise your own personality and positive aspects you bring to relationships.

ACTIVITY 8.2 EVALUATING YOURSELF FOR CONFIDENCE IN PERSONAL RELATIONSHIPS

As it is often difficult to note good aspects of yourself (usually due to this being seen as bragging or being arrogant) this activity requires you to talk to others in ascertaining feedback on yourself.

1. Pick a family member or friend who has known you for a long period of time (usually best done with someone who has known you for 3+ years).
2. Inform them that you are completing an evaluation of yourself in development and appraisal of self-confidence for personal relationship development. Note to them that this is important for you to improve in relationship development for personal and professional situations.

3. Ask the person to write down or tell you what aspects of your personality they admire and like most.

4. Ask them what positive elements you bring to their life through your personal relationship with them.

5. If you are aware you lack self-confidence, ask them if they perceive this also and how this affects your relationship (positively or negatively).

By completing these tasks in communicating with a person in an established personal relationship you will be able to evaluate how you appear and support this relationship. This external, although subjective, feedback will enable you to understand more clearly how you are perceived within personal relationships.

SOFT AND INTERPERSONAL SKILLS FOR PROFESSIONAL RELATIONSHIPS

Relationships are developed and maintained by successful use of your inter- and intrapersonal skills. This section considers soft and interpersonal skills in order to enable reflection and practice on your skills for effective professional relationships. Self-awareness of these, and improvement, is core to both personal and professional development. Discussion on the types of soft and interpersonal skills are offered (included as skills in Chapter 6 of this part) and issues from THE literature on soft skills are offered as an industry perspective on requirements of these in applicants to employment in THE.

Within published academic literature for THE, interpersonal and soft skills are often used in tandem and relate to similar abilities. Hinchliffe (2013) noted that interpersonal skills were the most important skill needed by employers from their applicants to new roles. Interpersonal skills are therefore not just important for relationship development but successful employment. THE researchers, such as Nickson et al. (2007), use soft skills to refer to interpersonal and intrapersonal skills, Bailly and Lene (2013) and Nickson (2007) use soft skills to infer social and interpersonal skills, and Baum's research (Baum, 1996, 2002, 2006b, 2007; Baum and Nickson, 1998) focuses on soft skills, which are seen to be the same as interpersonal skills. As a number of THE academics have considered soft and interpersonal skills it is clear these are important for employment. However, this chapter is outlining them for your own personal development and self-awareness in order to improve in these. Naturally, this should lead to improved employability, but it should be noted that this chapter seeks to consider it for your self-awareness of these skills firstly. To illustrate the similarities in soft and interpersonal skills, Table 8.1 uses two sources of research to align skills for both.

Table 8.1 outlines elements of interpersonal and soft skills to clarify how these overlap and use similar skilling types. Since early articles from Burns and Sparks and Callan (see Table 8.1), THE research has primarily focused on soft skills as the term with which to explain the

Table 8.1 Interpersonal and soft skill attributes

Sparks and Callan (1992) – Interpersonal	Burns (1997) – Soft
Verbal and non-verbal communication Eye contact Attitude Behaviour Perceptions of people Motivation Social competence	Verbal and non-verbal communication Emotional behaviour Attitude Empathy

Source: Sparks and Callan, 1992; Burns, 1997

types of skills needed in leisure education and training. Furthermore, it is accepted that in support of service sector economic development, governments also refer to soft skills as being a gap in applicants to leisure based roles (for example, see UK government reports from The Dearing Report, 1997; Leitch, 2006).

In terms of the context in which current literature positions use of these soft skills from graduates entering industry THE roles, it is evident that these skills are needed in customer service encounters to deliver effective customer service and produce what Burns (1997: p.240) calls the production of *'unreality.'* Soft skills are needed when communicating and interacting with customers in industry to create, perform and deliver leisure experiences. Burns (1997) calls a customer service encounter in THE *'unreality'* because customers are receiving a service, part of which is intangible and unquantifiable, from graduates/staff. This ephemeral characteristic is perceived and experienced differently by each guest. Considering soft skills from a customer satisfaction perspective in THE research does not allow for a thorough account of how these affect all relationships though.

Hassanien et al. (2010), Smith and Warburton (2012) and Chon and Maier (2009) suggest that hospitality businesses segment their customer markets in order to understand their reason for visiting the business (business or leisure, for example). Similarly, soft skills are offered dependent on the context and person you are communicating with.

ACTIVITY 8.3 **APPLYING SOFT SKILLS IN DIFFERENT RELATIONSHIP CONTEXTS**

Using the following list of soft skills, identify how these are different in personal, professional and private contexts:

- Communication.
- Empathy.
- Listening.

- Awareness.
- Body language.
- Attitude.
- Behaviour.
- Motivation.

From the above activity you will have outlines of how soft skills vary dependent on the context and person you are relating to. Some of these examples will require you to perform these, rather than create them as genuine reactions. This relates to what Burns (1997) notes as being *'unreality.'* You will not simply offer soft skills in a consistently genuine and real way due to the social norms and expectations known within the differing contexts. Performance of soft skills means that soft skills are often offered within an *'unreal'* space, and that the skills are demanded by a range of people who each have a variety of requirements and preconceptions. This context suggests that soft skills are neither general nor robotic but need to be adaptable, flexible and reflexive for each relationship. You therefore need an ability to assess and analyse consistently what soft skills are used and effective in relationship development.

To examine the soft skilling literature and issues within this research further, Professor Tom Baum's work will now be reviewed. Baum's work focuses on THE education and employee training both in the UK and internationally. His research spans the last 20 years on soft skilling and has followed the progress of issues and debates in this field. Discussion here will focus upon the general perceptions and importance of soft skills in THE, the viewpoint from which these skills are analysed and, finally, industry problems in maintaining a workforce with adequate soft skills. Although Baum does not explicitly link these to successful relationship development, it is clear there is parity in soft skill use and successful relationships as they are used to meet and exceed expectations of others.

Issues identified by Baum include how hospitality roles were deemed to be low- or semi-skilled, which was seen as an incorrect assumption of the skills used (Baum, 1996). Leisure work being deemed as low or unskilled was noted as an inappropriate portrayal of the roles due to the inherent international dimension of the industry and multiple soft skills needed (Baum, 1996). This historic denigrating perception of THE work is also highlighted by People 1st (2011), which suggest that this perception is still felt throughout the sectors and, therefore, can lead to recruitment problems. Perceiving skills for leisure work to be low or unskilled means that there has been a consistent *'myth that undermines their (staff) contribution'* (Lucas, 2004: p.31). Undermining the work and employee contribution to service due to a poor perception of soft skills is an issue in the literature, as it suggests that the work is easy and menial. Baum's argument in 1996 was that this inadequate perception of soft skills needed addressing to support managers and staff in leisure businesses. Later, research by Bailly and Lene (2012: p.87) noted that, actually, most employers still do not *'fully understand'* how these skills are demanded. This textbook advocates for effective soft skills to be used in relationship development and successful encounters with colleagues and management in employment.

The next issue to be noted from Baum's work on soft skilling is the perspective from which these soft skills are analysed. THE workers interact and serve guests who derive from a range of backgrounds and requirements. This means that the soft skills used are complex (Baum, 2002). Baum and Nickson (1998) identify that the weakness in this position is that soft skill research only focuses on service quality from the customers' perspective, when it should consider both employer and staff perspectives. THE industry employers are consistently reporting a lack of soft skills (from People 1st, 2011 and 2013) in their applicants and, by judging these skills in relation to customer service quality, current research appears not to engage fully with the variety of perspectives available (including yours as a THE student developing professional and personal competence). Hassanien et al. (2010: p.95) offered a partial response to this by noting that staff should be treated as *'internal customers'* and served by their managers, but there is no clear definition or account of the service encounters and customer demands which require these skills. Although you may be trained on soft skill use for employment in meeting customer demands, it is salient you also champion your soft skill use in all relationships.

Baum's early work clearly sought to dispel the belief that THE skills are low or unskilled, and identified this through examination of customer service encounters with international guests. This initial research on skilling for THE was in response to the negative connotations given to THE workers' skills, and identifies that there is a historical issue surrounding the importance of soft skilling and the perspective from which it is interrogated (addressed in the emergent professionalisation of THE in Part 1).

As noted in Part 1, THE training and education has only been deemed as a professional strand in the last 20 years. Obtaining employment in THE does not require students to complete postgraduate courses in order to become fully employer-ready for their role in industry. Unlike medical and teaching education, THE students move directly into industry. Baum (2002) noted that employee training is largely completed on the job rather than in a structured and assessed framework. Bailly and Lene (2012: p.88) confirm this and note that businesses pay *'scant attention in training programmes.'* This poor attention to employee training is mainly due to sector composition. Within the leisure industry, the majority of businesses are private small and medium-sized businesses rather than public or large multi-national companies (46% employ fewer than five staff and only 1% employ more than 100; People 1st, 2013). This suggests a reason as to why employers require new staff who already possess adequate soft skills to deal with their customers: they may not have the resources with which to train them on the job as there is no nationally nor internationally available accreditation. If it is accepted that THE businesses need soft skills from their applicants and are unable to train them on these within their roles, then it stands to reason that students on THE courses require reflection on these to enhance them further. The skills appraisal in Chapter 6 of this part enables you to complete this.

From Baum's research on soft skills it is apparent that they are vitally important in THE businesses. Baum's research spans the developments in soft skills research in THE industry and education and identifies how diversification in labour markets, international travel and education have all affected the way in which soft skills are now prioritised. This is a shift from the 1980s and 1990s, when technical skills were prioritised by educators and industry, until now, when soft skills are seen as a priority. The poor perception of these skills has meant that there has been a negative perception of the skills needed to work in THE. Despite this perception, it is evident that soft skills are needed in staff working in industry for successful relationships and customer service.

In discussion of the definitions for soft and interpersonal skills it is evident these are used in communication and in the development of relationships. These are also a core employment skill seen as missing in applicants for THE roles and current workers:

> The big challenge hiring – getting the right sort of people. It's a whole package and you need people with interpersonal skills who are motivated, who want to be engaged, and who want to work in a team – people who like people. And then in a sense you can teach the skills.
>
> (People 1st, 2013: p.48)

Linked to soft skills in this quotation is the ability to show self-motivation (see Chapter 17 in Part 3), influence others (Chapter 19 in Part 4), and network with others (see Chapter 22 in Part 4). The dynamism seen in soft and interpersonal skill use is dependent on the people and context within which they are used.

CULTURAL, CROSS-CULTURAL AND INTERCULTURAL TENETS OF RELATIONSHIPS

Acknowledgement of successful relationship development and soft/interpersonal skill use for relationships has outlined a range of skills to evaluate in personal development. This section now considers the cultural and intercultural elements present in relationships. Your individual and grouped culture is present and visible in your attitude and behaviour. Reflecting on your culture will enable you to be self-aware of how culture affects relationships.

To begin, cross-cultural dimensions are present in every conversation and encounter you have with another person. Whether this is in verbal, non-verbal or written communication, there will be elements of culture affecting your relationship development (positively and negatively). Knowledge of different cultures is vital in THE employment as visitors and tourists will not necessarily be from the local area. Their understanding, attitudes towards and behaviours within tourist experiences may, therefore, be incongruent to the usual social norms present. Culture is noted as different due to the following areas:

- A country in which a person is born (national culture).
- A family you are raised within.

- Religious beliefs.
- Languages spoken.
- Experiences of other nationalities.
- An understanding differences in people as individuals.
- Flexibility and adaptability to difference.
- Perceptions of difference as a positive or negative element.

Each of the above are perceived as 'differences' between you and another person. This is crucial in defining culture and cross-culture as it is based on an alternative perception or acknowledgement of difference which eludes to cultural comparison. It is not simply different nationality or language but is linked to individual personality and experiences. In this way, I am requiring you to consider culture with a small culture position. Hofstede (2006) is often cited within cultural definition and dimensions of, however, this only allows for a large and nationalistic view of culture. Holliday's (1999) definition of culture being small (individual) and large (national) enables you to apply cross-cultural understanding to each relationship and appraise this for personal development.

To discuss culture within relationship development this section will outline issues from cross-cultural conflict and competence development for intercultural communication.

O'Shannessy et al. (2002) identified cross-cultural conflict evident within work ethics, national holidays and discrimination. These will be outlined to evidence cross-cultural conflict in relationships from a large and small culture perspective (Holliday, 1999).

Work ethics

Within each country there are social and professional norms in how work should be completed. For example, in Japan, workers will have limited days per year for holidays and will work long hours in order to retire early. In the UK, it is usual to have a tea break in the morning (not necessarily to drink tea but for a break from work). In America they have at will working contracts, meaning they can choose how much to work. These large cultural differences in work mean that newcomers may be surprised at differences in working practices. Similarly, in a small culture perspective, some people prefer to work early in the day and others work into the night. These individual work ethics will affect how others see your work and how you work. Cross-cultural conflict arises when these are unclear, not communicated, or implicit rather than explicit.

National holidays

These can only be viewed in a large culture dimension. Each country will have a variety of national holidays based on their traditions, religions and celebrations of historic events.

Table 8.2 Independence days around the world

Country	Date	Country	Date
Jamaica	6th August	Maldives	26th July
Jordan	25th May	Mexico	16th September
Kuwait	25th February	Qatar	3rd September
Indonesia	17th August	Peru	28th July
Iceland	17th June	Sierra Leone	27th April
Guatemala	15th September	Vietnam	2nd September
Greece	25th March	USA	4th July

Table 8.2 lists one particular national holiday, Independence Day, across 14 different countries. Not only do the dates differ for these but the unique traditions and events occurring within each will also vary. If you are a tourist or worker moving to these countries or developing networks and relationships with them, knowledge on this variance is important as you may request meetings or work to be completed on these significant national days. Cross-cultural conflict arises when a person does not ascertain national holidays and support the celebration of these. Exceptional management in THE businesses not only acknowledge these in the local community, but can also offer paid leave for workers from these countries in support of their large national cultural celebrations.

Discrimination

Discrimination is often due to a prejudice or judgement made on another person and how this affects your treatment of them. Discrimination is most notably seen via a persons altered treatment of others due to their gender, disability, race, age, ethnicity and sexual preference. In some countries these classifications associated with a person may be protected within equality and diversity legislation (Daniels and MacDonald, 2005). If they are protected via legal bills or legislation then an employer or worker could be reprimanded or face legal action if they are proven as acting in a discriminatory way. Discriminatory actions can be seen and linked in the following actions:

- Not offering someone a job.
- Not supporting their professional development.
- Treating them less favourably than others.
- Changing the way you communicate with them.
- Omitting important information for them to carry out their job.

If the above actions are seen, they can all be noted as discriminatory actions. However, if the person is grouped within the listed characteristics, such as gender, then they are seen as targeted discrimination.

The three areas discussed above all outline small and large cultural differences in working environments. Your knowledge on these is important in cross-cultural relationships with colleagues, friends and customers. In addition to these three areas of cross-cultural conflict offered by O'Shannessy et al. (2002) – work ethics, national holidays and discrimination – context, emotional state and experience are now discussed in addition, and seen as equally present and important when resolving any perceived cross-cultural conflict.

Context

Cross-cultural dimensions of relationships will vary according to the context within which they are manifest. If you are communicating with a friend over a social media chat group then the written communication will be affected by your written language. Abbreviations, acronyms and colloquial phrases in written communication may lead to cross-cultural conflict here. If you bump into a teacher, customer or manager in a social environment (like a restaurant) you may find cross-cultural conflict arises as you have to adapt and alter your usual communication. This can also alter your judgement on a person.

Emotional state

As noted in Chapter 7 of this part, your emotional state can enable self-awareness but is also a condition from which you react and behave. Tiredness can lead to irritability, which in turn will mean your usual reactions to cultural difference may be exacerbated.

Prior experiences

Although it is noted that we live in societies with transnational flows of people, your own prior experience in cultural difference will affect your ability to manage cross-cultural conflict. If you have developed relationships with a range of different people then you will have developed an ability to perceive, understand and reflect on difference appropriately. Without experience, cultural differences will be more stark and confusing and may lead to cross-cultural conflict.

In addition to experiencing cultural differences as a tourist in different cities and countries, cultural difference can be experienced within your classroom. Using a small culture approach (Holliday, 1999) you can consider each classmate as having a different culture.

ACTIVITY 8.4 CULTURAL DIFFERENCES IN THE CLASSROOM

Using a classroom you participate in, note the following information from each person:

- Gender.
- Age.
- Nationality.
- Country and cities lived in.
- Languages spoken.
- Religion.
- Sexuality.
- Family size.
- Hobbies.
- Favourite music artist or book author.
- Perceptions on, and understanding of, cultural difference.

The above information gathered on members of your class will describe them and outline their unique and individual cultural differences. Using grouped and subjective elements of these people will allow you to identify your experience of cultural difference within usual contexts. In this way it is possible to ascertain cross-cultural difference from an individual, local position.

Moving on to consider the term intercultural competence (IC), this refers to the competences (skills learnt via experience) required for intercultural communication. Intercultural communication is discussed in Chapter 10 of this part. Definitions of IC are varied and refer to either macro of micro cultures (large or small like Holliday's definition). Deardorff's (2009) text offers the most recent account of IC history and approaches. Spitzberg and Changnon (2009) suggest that IC is needed for any business person to compete globally and successfully. These authors take a macro view of the term. IC, according to Spitzberg and Changnon (2009), is about having knowledge of cultural diversity and skills in relating to people of different ethnic backgrounds. From their review of literature on IC they identify overarching models of IC present today (see Table 8.3).

Table 8.3 refers to ethnocentric and ethnorelative positions on culture. Bennett's (1986) model on intercultural sensitivity clarifies that ethnocentricity means a person views culture from their own position as a large grouping of national difference. This is different to ethnorelativity, which is whereby individual differences are accepted and seen as unique components of cultural difference. The ideal position is seen in moving from an ethnocentric to ethnorelative position.

Table 8.3 Models of intercultural competence (in communication)

Model	Authors	Component
Compositional	(Deardorff, 2006)	Lists of IC behaviours, knowledge and skills used to identify a pyramid of effective IC communication.
Co-orientational	(Fantini, 2001) (Byram, 1997)	Linguistic processes and skills to achieve effective IC.
Developmental	(King and Baxter Magolda, 2005) (INCA, 2004) (Bennett, 1986)	Competence evolves and develops over time. Moving from ethnocentric to ethnorelative communication. Intercultural sensitivity.
Adaptational	(Kim, 2008)	Refers to intercultural communicative competence development via encounter and adaptation. It is something that develops through stages and where each person adapts to suit the interlocutor.
Causal path	(Arasaratnam and Doerfel, 2005)	A linear process in which communication variables are examined individually.

Source: created from information in Spitzberg and Changnon, 2009

Compositional models of IC list what component skills are required to show competency in intercultural communication. The competency headings frequently used are behaviour, knowledge and skills, and may have the following outcome statements. For example 'To have the ability to articulate cultural similarities and differences' can be something stated from which to assess and evaluate your IC. Behaviour, knowledge and skills are all required in development of relationships with a range of people with varied cultural difference and experience. In mind of the compositional models of IC, Table 8.4 identifies knowledge, skills and attitudes that may be necessary for relationship development in support of THE employment.

Table 8.4 reflects on compositional elements of IC which can be used to list your own attitudes, skills and knowledge on cultural difference to gauge your current position. As all of the linked areas require you to consider others and how you react and communicate with others, it is a useful guideline to examine your own cross-cultural awareness.

EMOTION, AESTHETICS AND SEXUALISATION IN RELATIONSHIPS

Consideration of personal relationships earlier in this chapter outlined how your emotions and personal appearance affect your ability to communicate effectively. Emotions and appearance were also confirmed as being perceived by others and led to alternative perspectives on you (reflexive positions). Here, literature on emotional, aesthetic and sexualised labour is considered for you to apply and value within personal development.

Table 8.4 Attitudes, skills and knowledge for intercultural competence in relationship development

Type of competence	Area	Example
Attitude	Personal awareness	Understanding you are different to others in individual ways.
	Group awareness	Being aware that you are part of a group that is different to the group that the other person is a part of.
	Discrimination	An understanding that discrimination can occur when communicating with another person (accidental and on purpose). Knowledge of how to manage this.
	Ethnocentric assumptions	Knowledge of ethnocentric, large culture opinions and how these can be used to define people.
	Taking risks	An appreciation of the risks associated in communicating with another person and that in communication there may be a realisation of difference between the two parties.
	Cross cultural interactions	Acknowledgement of cross cultural interactions present in daily encounters.
Skill	Self-reflection	Showing an ability to self-reflect on your own position when communicating with another.
	Communicate similarities or differences	An ability to articulate your similarity or difference to another person.
	Multiple perspectives	Identification of a range of perspectives when communicating with another.
	Multiple contexts	Understanding that each person communicates from a range of contexts and this will inform their current position.
	Challenge discrimination	An ability to identify someone who discriminates and challenges this via communication (verbal or nonverbal).
	Cross cultural communication	Communicating with people of different cultures.
Knowledge	Cultural identity	Knowledge of your own cultural identity.
	Similarities and difference	Knowledge of similarities and differences across cultures.
	Oppression	Knowledge of people's oppression due to their culture.
	Intersecting oppressions	Differentiation of oppressions from culture (like race, age and gender).
	Social change	Knowledge of how social change happens.
	How cultural difference effects communication	Knowledge that communication can differ according to cultural differences and not just linguistic differences.

Source: adapted from Hamilton et al.'s 1998 model of intercultural competence components cited from Spitzberg and Changnon, 2009: p.11

Beginning with emotional labour, Arlie Hochschild's book is notable in defining and using the term within THE contexts. She documented her experiences in airline training sessions where employees were asked to smile and convey emotions in order to satisfy and appease customers on flights. Her work is seminal in emotional labour and has been widely cited within leisure, business, sociology, psychology and gender research since the first edition in 1983. The premise of this type of labour originated in the known training phrase 'service with a smile.' Surprenant et al.'s (1987) paper also noted how smiling was a necessary skill and part of a customer service encounter (Firth, 2020). It was not until Hochschild's work that this became a theorised skill for all THE and service staff. Hochschild identified how staff were told to use their smile – their greatest asset – to ensure that airline guests were happy and satisfied. However, this facial display was not to be a performance but rather a *travel experience of real happiness and calm*' (Hochschild, 2012: p.5). The notion that staff should not only appear happy but also be happy is a powerful concept when dealing with customers, who each have their own background, history and personal experiences. This smile, or positive emotional display, exemplifies a brand message ensuring that customers receive the appropriate level of service and satisfaction with their experience. Thus, emotional labour was seen by Hochschild as a commodity rather than a personal choice of feeling. Since this initial study of an American airline, other researchers in the UK have sought to analyse emotional labour in different forms of THE business and in different geographical locations.

THINK POINT 8.1 CONTROLLING AND USING YOUR EMOTIONS

When you are communicating with friends, family, colleagues and teachers do you use facial displays of emotion? Which situations make you smile, frown, sulk and laugh? Are these automatic expressions or do you ever consciously think about smiling or showing emotion?

Discussion on emotional labour (EL) will be offered using research papers that applied the term in THE working contexts. These considered EL as a key employment skill for service sector roles, but here you will be required to apply knowledge of this term within relationship development.

Firstly, Seymour (2000) considered EL through comparisons between fast food and traditional hospitality outlets. Here EL was linked to whether uniform (aesthetic labour) and service scripts (communication standards) affected EL. Uniforms are considered to be within aesthetic labour and are discussed later in this chapter. Scripted service is a service and training tool used by numerous chain leisure businesses. *'Have a good day,' 'How can I be of service?' 'Can I assist you with anything today?'* and *'Is everything to your satisfaction?'* are examples of scripted lines that staff are required to say to their customers to maintain customer satisfaction (discussed in Chapter 10 of this part). It is important here to note that there is no research suggesting that these phrases could also annoy customers. Seymour (2000) analysed where staff deviated from these scripted lines in order to ascertain employee motivation to personalise the service:

> If you sell yourself all the time you end up losing your identity. You must hold a part of you back. You don't want to end up being just part of the meal experience. You need to learn to keep respect for yourself.
>
> (Seymour, 2000: p.167)

Like Hochschild's work with airline crew, Seymour's participants felt that the emotion communicated in conversation needed to be limited in order to ensure that their personality and identity were protected. This is an important consideration when evaluating teh use of emotions in relationships. Personal and professional relationships are different in terms of the people you develop them with and the motivations for maintaining them. You may find that you are less careful with emotional displays when with personal relations. Comparatively, you may feel more 'guarded' when around professional relations (like management, customers or colleagues). Holding back emotion, feeling protective of your emotions and controlling these are all examples of self-reflection and management of emotion. Your pre-existing emotional state and basic physiological needs will affect your ability to control these. For example, have you heard of the expression when someone is 'hangry'? This refers to when someone is emotionally distressed and upset due to being hungry. In this way, irrespective of your need to control and express emotions, a basic need overrides your ability to act logically and rationally.

From these observations it appears that EL has two axes of conflict. Vertically, EL is a commodity that is produced and consumed, intangible and changing according to the interaction with and demands from a guest. Horizontally, staff have to be both robotic in communicating set scripts and individual in offering personality and flair to their service. The skills for displaying and creating EL are what Stinchcombe (1990, as cited in Seymour, 2000) calls *'ethnomethodological competence.'* This type of competence is seen as a core occupational skill for THE staff because they need to control interactions, which are dependent on guest requirements and organisational duties.

> Employees are expected to give the appearance of enjoying their work as much as visitors are enjoying their time.
>
> (Baum, 2006a: p.135)

> Emotional demands are made of employees to constantly be in a positive, joyful and even playful mood. An ability to cope with such demands must be recognised as a real skill.
>
> (Baum, 2002: p.79)

Within Baum's soft skilling research he reflects on EL as an important soft skill needed by workers in THE, wherein they have to show positivity and enjoyment when serving guests in order to maintain customer satisfaction. Hochschild's seminal work in EL, followed by that of Seymour and Baum, identifies that EL is a soft skill embedded in customer service encounters throughout the THE industries. Giving an impression that you are happy will enable you to appear as a content and capable person. This is important in relationship development as it will enable the other person to perceive you as an emotionally stable person.

THINK POINT 8.2 PERCEPTIONS OF EMOTIONS LINKED TO PERSONALITY

Have you met someone who always seems to whinge or moan about things? Or perhaps someone who is critical of their life and ways of doing things? How does this make you feel about spending time with them? How does this affect your perception of their personality?

EL necessitated in THE working contexts is seen to conflict with the identity and personality of a person, whereby robotic effigies of the brand are created in the staff to represent the company they work for. Emotional displays are noted as important in relationship development as it signals your feelings, desires and opinions. Effective use of these will enable you to develop and maintain effective relationships. The level to which you portray and use these need reflection to ensure you do not over emote.

ACTIVITY 8.5 EMOTING IN RELATIONSHIPS

Showing and using emotions has been noted as important to convey happiness and service, which is enjoyed by staff and customers in THE. However, emotions are not simply on or off. The levels to which you use and portray your emotions can be effective and detrimental in relationships. Review the following list of emotions:

Adoration
Amusement
Anxiety
Awe
Awkwardness
Boredom
Calmness
Confusion
Craving
Disgust
Entrancement
Envy

Excitement

Fear

Horror

Interest

Joy

Sadness

Satisfaction

Sexual desire

Sympathy

Using the above list:

1. Try and convey these using facial expression only (without talking).
2. Classify them as being positive or detrimental to relationships.
3. From the list of emotions that could be detrimental, which ones are necessary for genuine and long - lasting relationships?
4. Which people is it imperative you show genuine emotions with? What does this enable you to develop and maintain?

The activity on using your emotions can be used to evaluate your ability to express and reflect on emotions. These will result in furthering trust developed within the relationship. Trust is naturally linked to emotion as emotions can be performed and displayed in order to manipulate perspectives others have on you. If you always smile and appear happy, people will presume you are ok. However, if you do this to avoid opening up to others, they may feel distrust in you not appearing as a genuine or normal person. Social norms are also linked to emotional display and it is important to reflect on your understanding of emotions as being anchored in your own cultural and societal experiences. For example, if you are not asked to smile when posing for a camera then you will not feel this is an appropriate context to display emotion. Control of emotions was defined as being either surface or deep acting by Hochschild.

THINK POINT 8.3 SURFACE AND DEEP EMOTIONAL DISPLAYS

Reflective and reflexive evaluation of yourself in this chapter (and Chapter 7) has eluded to your ability to portray emotions in a controlled manner. Surface acting is seen as a performance of emotions that may not be genuine. Deep acting of emotions are noted as genuine and real.

- Is it possible to manage deeply felt emotions in all situations?
- In which situations do you need to use more internal strength to manage deeply felt emotions?

> - In what types of relationships do you notice consistent use of your surface and performed emotions?
> - If you perform your emotions consistently, how does this make you feel?
> - Do you talk about your emotional use and displays with others?

From the work completed on EL, aesthetic labour (AL) emerged as a term with which to describe how THE staff need to present themselves physically (also covered in personal grooming in Chapter 8). Seymour's (2000) research on EL also considered uniform and appearance, as it enables '*surface acting*' to portray their role in the company (p.164). AL was conceptualised by Witz et al. (2003) as follows:

> we feel that the concept of emotional labour foregrounds the worker as a mindful, fee-lingful self, but loses a secure conceptual grip on the worker as an embodied self.
>
> (p.36)

Witz et al. critiqued Hochschild's text, as they felt that the separation of surface and deep acting diminished the visible and innate bodily functions surrounding EL. For example, a person's body is tall, short, fat, thin, etc., regardless of their own personal feelings and performance of emotions. The following list outlines elements of your physical appearance within which emotions are portrayed:

- Height.
- Weight.
- Skin colour.
- Hair (facial and body).
- Feature sizes (nose, eyes, ears).
- Muscular composition.
- Disability (visible physical ones).

The list of physical features is offered for you to consider the complexity of human appearance. These are seen in the AL literature as being mobilised and commodified in support of brand recognition and repeat custom.

ACTIVITY 8.6 STAFF LOOKING THE PART

Clothing retail stores often employ staff who look good wearing their clothes. This is a form of aesthetic labour as they appear to recruit good looking and attractive people. Clothes looking good on good looking staff aid purchases as the items are perceived as attractive due to the people wearing them. Next time you are shopping for clothes take note of the shape, age and gender of the employees and consider if they match the brand. Does the clothing retailer appear to employ anyone who would not look good wearing their clothes? Is this appropriate?

As noted in the case study on AL a company makes use of these *'embodied capacities'* (Witz et al., 2003: p.37) in recruitment and training to transfer staff appearance so as to portray their brand and style within service. Their conceptualisation of AL refers to the control that managers have over employee hair, makeup, uniform and weight, and how this is controlled to create high service levels and aid employee EL.

THINK POINT 8.4 AESTHETIC CHOICES IN DIFFERENT RELATIONSHIPS

When you are going to meet a friend, classmate or sexual partner how do you alter your appearance? Do you change your standard of grooming? Do you alter your clothing style? Why do you do this?

Witz et al. (2003) suggest that AL in organisations seeks to diminish an employee's personal feelings when made to look part of a business (ultimately an intangible and corporate thing). However, they highlight an important aspect of business priority in creating a styled labour force to portray a brand and offer a specific level of service to guests. This is similar to your reflection on how you will change you appearance when meeting with personal relations (friends and partners). Furthermore, they suggested that uniform and staff appearance offer customers a *'distinctive mode of exchange beyond contract'* (p.35). This suggests that uniform/attire is a mandatory practice, even if it is not within the employment contract. It is important to accept this within professional relationships as your appearance will be perceived (taken) as a part of the service. This was discussed in grooming, as others perceptions of your look will infer elements of your personality (using flare or unconventional dress as signals of confidence or assertiveness). If AL is seen as exchanged by people, then it is clear that appearance is taken and received in support of relationship development. In acknowledgement of AL as being the visual aspect within which EL is present, it is recognised as a skill necessary for employment and successful relationship development and maintenance. Current literature in THE fails to fully evaluate the incompatibility the uniform may have between a person's identity and feelings and being made to look a certain way.

CASE STUDY 8.1 UNIFORM AND GROOMING STANDARDS JARRING WITH YOUR IDENTITY AND FEELINGS

The following are examples of uniform and grooming standards required in different THE roles:

- Being clean shaven (no facial hair).
- Shoes with a heel of at least 1.5 inches.

- Black trousers.
- Synthetic materials used in uniforms supplied.
- Applying a minimum cover of make-up products.
- Tying or cutting hair in specific styles.

The list of uniform and grooming standards are known to be applied in a number of THE roles. These will vary according to the brand and level of quality a company works within. Using one of these, hair style, how would this affect your personal relationships and self-esteem? How would this change your ability to act with initiative and as an individual within professional contexts?

THINK POINT 8.5 THE RISE OF THE HIPSTER: CONFLICT IN PROFESSIONAL APPEARANCE

Contemporary fashion and styles of clothing and hair-cuts will consistently change. More recently there has been an evident rise in the hipster look. Hipsters are said to have an informal look that goes against the local norms and they are seen as trendsetting and unconventional. Long beards, passion for real ale and hoppy lager are subjective elements usually linked to being a hipster. If you conform to this style and want to work in THE where there are strict grooming and uniform standards are you discriminated against due to your choice in style and look? Does this mean that hipsters can only apply for work that allows for this personal flair in clothing and grooming? How have local THE companies embraced this to employ staff who conform to this look?

Warhurst and Nickson's (2007) research in hospitality and retail noted that employers prioritise attitude and appearance as vital aspects of their staff but that on-the-job training focused on hard and technical skills and expected the recruitment process to control for appropriate appearance and attitude skills in new staff:

> For those staff who had received appearance related training 62 percent had training in dress sense and style, 60 percent in body language and nearly a third in make-up and grooming (29%).

> (Warhurst and Nickson, 2007: p.114)

This confirms that appearance (as soft skills) are pre-eminent, and these are developed in recruitment and followed up with on-the-job training. Development of your own personal style and appearance will only occur if you are interested in how you look. Enjoyment of trying different appearance styles and changing these is also seen as a personal personality trait that varies in individuals. Again, Warhurst and Nickson (2007) are seen to omit employee feelings when being trained in style, uniform and appearance. They do not consider how effectively AL is implanted and how the rigidity of appearance and grooming standards can either positively or negatively affect staff.

From the discussion of AL emerging from EL literature, it is evident that grooming and appearance standards are not simply chosen by individuals but may be prescribed in employment. You may have feelings about this appearance and it will naturally affect your emotional state. Certain clothes and styles naturally suit and look good on specific bodies. As we are all different, there is an issue noted here in how you manage your emotions when being asked to wear or present yourself in a specific way. Your flexibility and openness to look differently to others, or conform to a standard appearance, will convey a brand but also reflect your own personality. In this way, appearance is linked to how you are perceived by others in the development of successful relationships.

ACTIVITY 8.7 DRESS AND GROOMING IN DIFFERENT SITUATIONS

Using the following situations, outline your usual choice in grooming and clothing:

1. Attending a job interview.
2. Meeting a friend for dinner.
3. Going shopping with family.
4. Grocery shopping.
5. A leisure activity with family (theme park or museum).
6. Going on a romantic date at the cinema.
7. Attending a sports team practice.
8. Watching a TV series at home.
9. Taking a flight for leisure purposes.
10. Using public transport to attend class.

Compare your answers with a partner to identify similarities and differences. Are these influenced by cultural/individual/social elements?

If you were asked to have the same clothing attire and grooming standard for all of these situations, how would you feel?

Warhurst and Nickson (2009) later considered sexuality and sexualised labour (SL) to be components of AL. Employee appearance, including flirting and sex appeal, is seen as a core aspect of serving guests in THE employment. This is due to the need for employees to develop effective relationships with customers and for customers to enjoy their experience.

Making connections quickly with good rapport, having 'banter' and being liked by customers in THE will usually lead to some form of personal communication. Personal communication is seen to lead to flirtation or personal discussion due to the usual services offered. This will be different dependent on the context within which the THE business is located. If the company operates in a country which is predominantly Muslim, for example, female employees may not be welcome to talk or address male customers. SL is therefore dependent on the religion and cultural norms present around the THE business. Furthermore, if staff from a culture that limits appearance and communication between genders are employed in a culture that has more freedom and flexibility, the employee may need support and training to feel comfortable and understand how their appearance is used.

CASE STUDY 8.2 SEXUALISATION: I NEVER THOUGHT IT WOULD HAPPEN TO ME

Sally worked in a 5 star hotel part time during her studies in tourism management. She had chosen to work in a hotel to develop her employment skills and earn money to support her welfare.

During a night shift on the hotel bar a customer grabbed her hand and asked if instead of paying the bill he could take her to his room.

Sally was shocked by this incident but was aware of the sexualisation and flirting culture of work in hospitality. She was unaware of how to deal with this incident. Her manager saw the incident and came to support her and talk to the customer.

On reflection, Sally was not shocked by the customer's request and approach but that it happened to her. Without prior reflection on sexualisation in work she was unprepared to deal with this customer. As a result, she also decided she did not want to work late shifts on the bar again.

Source: Firth, 2020

Case Study 8.3 clarifies how employees may be aware of sexualisation, but if they do not appraise or reflect on how they would deal with this they may struggle to respond professionally. It also had a negative effect on the company's retention of staff for the bar as she refused to work late nights after this incident. Here, dealing with sexualisation in professional contexts requires you to not only have a knowledge of this element of work in THE, but practice and the ability to deal with it.

ACTIVITY 8.8 DEALING WITH SEXUALISATION APPROPRIATELY

This activity will offer you tools to develop your ability to deal with sexualisation as well as outline situations within which you can identify sexualisation present.

Examples of sexualisation:

- Verbal comments on your attractive appearance.
- Using sexual innuendos in conversation.
- Clicking fingers or whistling to gain attention.
- Physical touch which feels inappropriate.
- Offering a phone number or asking to meet in a personal nature.
- Asking for sexual services.
- Inebriation leading to inappropriate sexual behaviour.

Possible responses:

- Walking away to a safe area (back of house or toilets).
- Moving to be with someone else (colleague or friend).
- Saying 'I do not find that appropriate in this situation.'
- Saying 'Thank you for your kind comment, but I do not think it is appropriate for you to note this at this time.'
- Informing colleagues and management that you suspect someone is being sexually inappropriate.
- Asking for assistance from friends or colleagues to deal with others who are seen to be sexually inappropriate.
- Ignoring the behaviour and continuing in work.

The above examples of sexualisation and potential ways to react to these should be discussed with others to ascertain previous experience of and ability to use these in personal and professional contexts. You will not be able to control how others act in situations but reflecting on ways to handle and deal with them is essential in maintaining professionalism and self-esteem.

Activity 8.7 on dealing with sexualisation will aid your ability to react in potentially difficult situations. As THE employment customer relations and personal relationships may include sexualisation it is important to address this aspect in development of your interpersonal skills. Equally, if your uniform (AL) or clothing enhances your attractiveness you need awareness strategies to deal with sexualisation, as this attire may naturally lead to an increase in incidents of sexualisation.

Warhurst and Nickson (2009) note three levels of SL in THE businesses. These range from being sanctioned by management to being a specific strategic element of the business. Hooters bars in America are an example of strategic sexualised labour, as their uniform consists of:

> short shorts and a choice of a tight tank top or crop or a tight T-shirt to deliberately make up female employees as sexy waitresses.

> (p.396)

Warhurst and Nickson do not explore how being sexy or sex appeal is defined, understood or consumed. Instead, they critique how it is seen and trained through AL. Specifically, they identify how staff use this sex appeal between colleagues to improve their working environment:

> As such, appealing to the senses of other staff, through flirting, for example, is behaviour used to create less boring and less bureaucratic, more exciting and more personal workplaces.

> (pp.391–393)

Sexual harassment and unwanted sexual advances must be a concern to managers and employees using this form of AL. Flirting conversation is understood and produced with a range of intentions. If people are not aware of the motivation behind this behaviour, then it could be misconstrued and lead to problems between staff and customers. Equally, with the perception of a lower professionalisation of work in THE (discussed in Part 1) and retention issues present across THE sectors, sexual harassment could be a defining factor to improve customer and staff relationships. Instead of accepting or ignoring this element in industry, management can use activities on dealing with sexualisation to improve staff skills.

Inebriation due to alcohol consumption was noted as a potential reason for sexualisation in the workplace. Conversely to 'others' inebriation, Warhurst and Nickson (2009) suggest that some staff working as tour reps in holiday destinations use alcohol to increase SL. Tour reps are seen to consume alcohol to feel and behave in a more flirtatious manner. The danger of SL here is made clear by Warhurst and Nickson, who note how female workers choose to drink less alcohol to ensure that they *remain in control* (p.400). Specifying that female workers may have increased sexualisation if they consume alcohol is a gendered statement but is based on the lower body mass of women compared to men. Equally, if you do not consume alcohol regularly you are more susceptible to adverse effects.

THINK POINT 8.6 VARYING EFFECTS OF ALCOHOL

Consider if you have consumed alcohol before.* How did this affect you? How were your emotions altered? Did you act differently? If an inebriated friend or customer acts in a similar way do you empathise and change your reaction due to the know-ledge of their inebriation?

*If you have not consumed alcohol you can also apply this think point to when you have had excess amounts of caffeine (tea or coffee) or if you have not eaten or eaten too much.

SL is seen to negatively affect employment as it can lead to employee harassment, discrimination and illegal behaviour. However, it is accepted as a part of personal and professional relationships as you may enhance your attractiveness to maintain these relationships. Currently, research on SL in THE mainly outlines issues felt by female staff from male customers. More research and consideration is needed for male staff and homo-sexualisation.

This section has sought to offer definitions of emotional, aesthetic and sexualised labour as these relate to your appearance in personal and professional relationships. Each of these enable you to evaluate and develop soft skills. If you are to gain and maintain successful graduate employment, these need reflection and consideration in order for you to feel comfortable and confident in a range of contexts.

BEING A CITIZEN OF THE WORLD

The final section in this chapter is to consider how you, acting as a good citizen, will develop relationships due to social responsibility and ethical actions and behaviour. This links to perceptions of you being a good citizen and being aware of your position and influence in the world. Being a global citizen is seen as an important skill for THE employment and also allows you to evaluate your awareness of your social responsibility and ethical choices in relationships.

You can evidence being a good citizen in a range of actions and behaviour. For example, you may take old clothes to a charity shop. This could be seen as indirect support for your local community but shows an awareness of how you can support local causes in additional income raised. Being a good citizen is important to support your local community but will also enable connections within society. Altruism is often a precondition to completing good citizen actions.

THINK POINT 8.7 ALTRUISM IN RELATIONSHIPS

Altruism is whereby you are selfless in your actions, which are directly offered in sup-port of others. Think about incidents in which you have done something selflessly. Why did you do this? How did it make you feel? What new connections or relation-ships did you develop?

Completing altruistic actions or having altruistic motivations enables you to show social responsibility. Helping a friend, community or colleagues for selfless reasons leads to a perception that you are interested in supporting others. Druckman (2001) and Arnstein (2019) both clarified that citizenship has a range of levels, forms and competences. As such, evidence of this will be emergent in a range of actions, rather than being a consistent personality trait. Recreation businesses noted in Part 1 rely on good citizenship from employees and customers so that natural environments are protected and maintained. Acknowledgement of good citizenship action and behaviour will enable you to ascertain how your actions affect others and how you are a component part of a wider, global society.

CASE STUDY 8.3 **FOOD MILES AND ETHICAL PRODUCTS**

Ethically aware companies, such as Global Source Kitchen, have grown in the last decade due to consumer pressure to access food consumables that are supportive rather than detrimental to society.

Global Source Kitchen operates as a vegan food company with an ethical and socially responsible strategy:

Global Source Kitchen is an up-and-coming vegan street food project set up by a pair of fun-loving lads from North Yorkshire, providing dishes which draw inspiration from a wide range of cuisines from around the world. Drawing on a passion for authentic, high-quality food, as well as an adventurous culinary style that reworks classic recipes without losing sight of what defines them, expect a carefully crafted selection of dishes full of flavour and attitude.

We also run Manchester's first and only hummus delivery service; an independent alternative to nasty exploitative companies like Deliveroo and Uber Eats. In addition to hummus, we offer a rotating menu of takeaway options, with a different dish available every Friday night.

We aim to promote vegan living through sharing delicious food and encouraging our customers to try cooking vegan themselves. We are happy to serve anyone, however – we're not going to turn you away if you enjoy a sausage sandwich once in a while. As far as we're concerned, every black bean burrito or tofu katsu curry that we sell means another Big Mac that doesn't get bought. We also work in partnership with charities and non-profit organisations, promoting and raising money for worthy causes that benefit vulnerable people.

Source: www.facebook.com/globalsourcekitchen/

Case Study 8.4 depicts a company who not only strives to reduce food miles (carbon footprint) but also gives back to the local community. They strive to combat MNCs who appear to operate unethically (McDonald's noted). This form of business appeals to customers as they perceive that the company is not simply created for profit but is also supportive of the planet.

Figure 8.2 on people, profit and planet is a useful structure to consider how a company not only supports employees and profit margins, but the local community also. Use this to ascertain how you also impact people, organise your financial management and positively affect your local community.

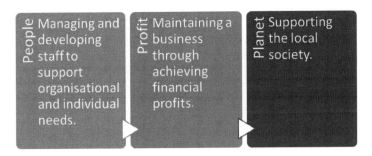

Figure 8.2 Triple bottom line: people, profit and planet

In terms of skills for good citizenship the following is noted:

- Integrity.
- Trustworthiness.
- Fairness.
- Loyalty.
- Reputation.
- Respect for others.
- Honesty.

Evaluation of these skills will evidence your reflexivity in your impact on the local and global community. Whether this is in your ability to understand difference (intercultural noted earlier) or decisions that reduce the impact on global issues and support the local population, you will be able to show good citizenship.

To understand areas of good citizenship, use the following areas and questions to evaluate and consider your current actions and behaviour:

Food

1. Where do you purchase your food from?
2. Do you check the origin of the food purchased?

3. Are you aware of the portion of the product price going to the manufacturers and owners?

Travel

1. What forms of transport do you use?
2. What is most important in your travel decisions: cost or carbon footprint?
3. Do you think your travel decisions will change as you increase in income? Why?

Clothes

1. How often do you purchase new clothes?
2. Do you purchase fast fashion (cheap contemporary), classic fashion (middle prize basic clothing), charity shop or designer clothes?
3. Do you research where the clothes are made and how much is offered to the workers making them?

Waste

1. Do you recycle waste at home? If so, which products?
2. Do you use plastic packaging when purchasing food items?
3. Do you search for local farms to purchase meat and vegetables from?

Leisure activity

1. Do you research the social and environmental support a leisure company offers?
2. Do you care how a leisure activity operates within the local society?
3. Is it clear when a company involves and supports the local population?

The questions listed above will enable you to consider your usual behaviour and actions. If you consider the local society and ethical behaviour of the companies you purchase from, this will evidence good citizenship. However, cost is often attributed as a de-motivator to these good citizenship actions. Local products may yield higher costs as the employees and infrastructure is at a higher standard and lower production quantity. As you increase in disposable income it is important you reconsider these and aid others to make ethical purchasing decisions.

CASE STUDY 8.4 INTERVIEW QUESTIONS ON YOUR SOCIAL RESPONSIBILITY

Students studying at undergraduate level have noted how interviews can include questioning their support and work in local charities. When preparing for an interview it is important you consider your own work with local charity and environmental protection. This is increasingly seen as an important employment skill for THE as corporate citizenship requires employees to participate in societal development actions.

This section has outlined how you can be seen as a good citizen. Although it is primarily aligned to action and participation, it denotes altruistic motivations in support of your local community. If you act locally and think globally, you will develop and support a number of personal and professional relationships as a citizen of the world.

SUMMARY

1. To understand how to make connections and develop personal relationships.

Making connections with people is vital to start and develop effective personal relationships. Awareness of the cyclical and reflexive elements of personal relationship is important for you to be able to sustain and manage these effectively.

2. To identify how soft and interpersonal skills are necessary for successful professional relationships.

Literature from THE authors consistently note how soft and interpersonal skills are an important skill for employment. In this chapter we outlined what these were and evidenced how they are needed for relationship development with friends, family, teachers, colleagues and management. Your ability to perform and recreate these when required will ensure you maintain successful personal and professional relationships.

3. To analyse how culture and cross-cultural and intercultural elements of communication can support effective relationships.

Culture was defined as a noted difference between one person and another. Culture is seen in large and small categories allowing a person to be grouped or seen as unique. This chapter advocated for a small and ethnorelative position on culture to enable you to perceive cultural difference as positive, emergent and flexible. Intercultural competence models were outlined in order for you to understand how these specify skills, attitude and knowledge for effective relationships.

4. To evaluate personal emotions, aesthetics and sexualisation present in relationships.

Hochschild and Seymour's work on emotional labour identifies how emotions are acted and performed to maintain a company's brand image. In order to use EL, you need to be ethnomethodologically competent to understand what others want in your emotional displays. Warhurst, Witz and Nickson's critique of EL speculated that emotions cannot be devoid of the bodies in which employees portray and complete their duties. Their creation of aesthetic labour allows you to consider appearance as a soft skill and how this can be used in the development and maintenance of successful relationships. From AL, sexualised labour was defined to outline how sex appeal is present in your appearance and used to sell and maintain guest satisfaction in THE businesses. Although EL, AL and SL are all noted as soft skills, current literature focuses on how this serves to make a THE business successful and not how staff or students learn these skills and manage their feelings in situations. Use activities and case studies offered here to appraise your own opinions on emotion, appearance and sexualisation in personal and professional relationships.

5.   To outline how being perceived as a citizen of the world is important for effective relationships.

Businesses are now focussed on how they not only support their staff and profit margins but also the surrounding communities in which they operate. In addition, ethical and environmentally responsible THE businesses are growing due to consumer pressure. Being socially responsible is identified as important for acknowledgement of your impact in the world, but also as a skill for employment in THE. By stating your usual behaviour and actions in travel, food, clothing and leisure experiences you can consider if you behave ethically and with social responsibility. Relationships will require you to act altruistically in order to give back to others, but being a good citizen will mean you can evidence a larger positive impact in your local community.

Questions to support your learning and research

1.   How many steps are noted in the 'getting to know you' figure (Figure 8.1)?
2.   Are soft and interpersonal skills similar?
3.   List five examples of soft skills.
4.   What does IC stand for?
5.   What types of IC models were outlined?
6.   Is being ethnocentric seen to be a positive position in developing relationships?
7.   How are emotions evident in facial expression?
8.   How do your clothes portray your personality and individuality?
9.   How can you combat sexualisation?
10. How can purchasing decisions evidence good citizenship?
11. Why do companies want to know how you support local charities?

References in support of your learning from this chapter

Green, A. (1998). Core skills, key skills and general culture: In search of the common foundation in vocational education. *Evaluation and Research in Education*, 12(1), pp. 23–43.

Holland, D., Skinner, D., Lachicotte, W. and Cain, C. (2003). *Identity and Agency in Cultured Worlds*. USA: Harvard University Press.

Hoskins, B. (2006). *Draft framework on Indicators for Active Citizenship*. Ispra: CRELL.

Hoskins, B. and Mascherini, M. (2009). Measuring Active Citizenship through the development of a composite indicator. *Social Research Indicators*, 90, pp. 459–488.

Jansen, T., Chioncel, N. and Dekkers, H. (2006). Social cohesion and integration: Learning active citizenship. *British Journal of Sociology of Education*, 27(2), pp. 189–205.

Joseph, H. and Veldhuis, R. (2006). Indicators on Active Citizenship for Democracy – The social, cultural and economic domain, published by CRELL, accessed on 8th June 2010, available at http://crell.jrc.ec.europa.eu/ActiveCitizenship/Conference/03_AbsVeldhuis.pdf

Marshall, T. H. (1950). *Citizenship and Social Class and Other Essays*. UK: Cambridge University Press.

Mascherini, M. (2009). Measuring Active Citizenship through A composite indicator, Presented in Firenze, November 2009 for the European Commission Joint Research Centre. Accessed on 8th June 2010, available at http://eprints.unifi.it/archive/00001973/01/Mascherini_161109.pdf.

Organ, D. (1988). *Organizational Citizenship Behavior*. Lexington, MA: Lexington Books.

Chapter 9
Time management

LEARNING OBJECTIVES

1. To understand what time management is, how this is part of your own personal ability and how it affects your academic and professional development.
2. To identify strategies for time management.

INTRODUCTION

Managing your time effectively is crucial for academic and professional development. For THE employment it is even more important as you may be required to complete a number of tasks or duties in support of a range of stakeholders (customers, management, suppliers and colleagues). This chapter will outline what time management is, how it is organised and categorised, and how you can become more effective at using it to support your academic and professional development.

TIME MANAGEMENT AS A PERSONAL ABILITY

Using your time efficiently is a skill. It links to your ability to be organised and considerate of tasks to complete. One caveat within this is that although it is a skill that can be taught or developed, some people are naturally better at this than others. This can be quite frustrating if you are in a class or team and other people are seemingly better at using their time to complete the work or duties faster or to a higher standard. This chapter's activities can be used to help you assess and develop better time management skills in support of your academic and professional development.

ACTIVITY 9.1 HOW DO YOU APPROACH TASKS?

When you are given a piece of work to complete (academic or work related) consider the following questions and note your answers:

1. Do you put the work to one side and plan to review its requirements at a later time?
2. Do you review the work immediately and put in deadlines for key tasks in support of the work?

The answers to the above questions will depend on the task and context within which the task was offered. However, if you plan to approach every task in the same way, you can control your time most effectively.

1. Do you use a diary?
2. Do you use your phone calendar to input tasks on dates?
3. Do you use one email account (education/personal/work)?

These questions will require you to consider how you go about managing your time via calendar or diaries. The more places you note tasks or manage responses to tasks, the less likely you are to be able to manage these tasks within the time. For example, if you use three email accounts (work, education and personal) you will have to use more time to manage and ascertain when work is required and when to reply to people requiring your assistance.

1. Ascertain if you can direct your emails to one account.
2. Link this one account to your mobile phone or laptop.
3. Check this account once per day to check on work required or responses needed.
4. Use folders and the calendar to make note of work coming up.

Another element of time management is that it is not divorced from the context and people surrounding you. Consider the areas given in Figure 9.1, which may affect management of this.

All the areas given in the figure are barriers to effective time management. How you identify and manage these is a personal choice. It is also noted that some are personality traits and that some people embrace or ignore these, which again will lead to poor time management. Lacking the skills or knowledge and unclear directions on a task will mean more time is needed to complete the work. Acknowledgement of this is important so that you can plan to increase your knowledge and skills.

When completing academic and professional work it is important you maintain motivation (see Part 3, Chapter 17) for the task. This will require you to have the basic physiological

Figure 9.1 Six areas affecting time management

needs outlined by Maslow (Chapter 6 of this part). In order for tasks to be completed effectively you need to identify times when you will eat, break, have leisure time, have personal time and reflect on your progress.

Social time and breaks from work are separated in Figure 9.2, which shows supporting elements for time management. This is because social media can be completed quickly using your phone and could be perceived as social time. Instead, here I am noting how you need to talk or meet with others in a social situation. Breaks from work can be a walk around the local supermarket and, therefore, not social time. Allowing for private, reflection and reviewing time will ensure that the task is being completed to the correct standard. Within these you may identify more time is needed on certain elements of a task and so you will need both reflective and reflexive thinking here (Part 4, Chapter 23).

All of the elements noted in Figure 9.2 are crucial to effective task completion and time management. However, you need self-awareness on how you usually work in order to identify deadlines and targets for task completion. Are you a present or absent person? Do you attend every class scheduled or do you look to catch up with notes at a later time? The variety to which you engage and attend education and work will evidence your time management ability (a skill vital for employment).

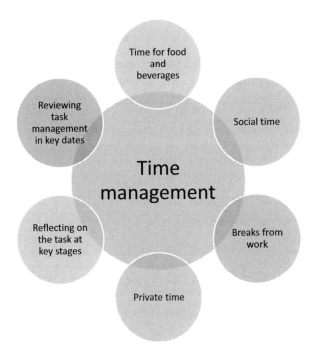

Figure 9.2 Supporting elements for time management

CASE STUDY 9.1 BURNOUT FROM PRESENTEISM

Matthew is a student completing a course in culinary arts management and he wants to open his own business in the future. During a usual week his time is managed as follows:

	Mon day	Tuesday	Wednes day	Thurs day	Friday	Satur day	Sunday
AM	E	E	E	E	E	W	W
PM	E	FT	E	E	E	W	W
EVE	FT	E	S	FT	S	W	W

E = Education (class and study time)

W = Work

S = Social time

FT = Free time

After three months working to this schedule Matthew became unwell and was not able to complete any of the work, education or social activities. Matthew was seen as being a present worker: someone who will work late and work consistently hard regardless of their own physiological needs for time off from the pressures of work and education.

Use the following table to identify your own pattern of time management:

	Mon day	Tues day	Wednes day	Thurs day	Friday	Saturday	Sunday
AM							
PM							
EVE							

How does your table compare to Matthew's? It is usual to ensure you have free time every day in order to maintain a good work/life balance and avoid burnout. If you are working around your studies, try to keep the shift lower than 10 hours or if you do a 12 hour shift, only do this once per week.

Before moving on to outline strategies you can use for effective time management, the following activity allows you to reflect on your usual procrastination around tasks, which can lead to poor time management.

ACTIVITY 9.2 PROCRASTINATING AND POOR TIME MANAGEMENT

Consider the following statements and give them a number from 1–10 based on the strength of agreement you feel (1 being strongly disagree and 10 being strongly agree).

1. I need pressure from a lack of time in order to complete tasks.
2. I ignore important tasks.
3. I often have important interruptions to my tasks.
4. I often find excuses for not completing tasks.
5. I start new tasks in the middle of completing others.
6. I often feel tired and this stops me completing tasks planned.

Add up your scores for the statements above. Compare these with a partner and discuss reasons why you feel you work in this way. How does procrastination aid or inhibit your time management? If you accept your usual ways of feeling and acting around tasks can you identify alternative ways of working to develop better methods of work?

From noting the elements supporting and affecting time management, this section has defined time management as an individual and context-based issue for personal development. Issues arise in time management when you do not consider your usual ways of approaching tasks. Reflecting on these will allow you to improve on your time management and you will also need to use further strategies in support of this.

STRATEGIES FOR TIME MANAGEMENT

This section will offer you a variety of strategies in support of effective time management. It is important you try a variety of these and apply them to different tasks in order to use your time most effectively. Some tasks will require specific strategies due to the work to be completed. For example, when completing a shift at work you are managed and have to complete the duties required. Comparatively, if you timetable a day in the library but then wake up late, you are not as easily reprimanded and need to use self-discipline in order to complete the work. In this way, self-motivation is crucial for academic development (discussed in Part 3). Using a diary, gantt charts, negotiated targets for tasks with others and supporting actions for usual procrastination is offered to enable you to strategise your time management.

Diaries

As we work within set days and time zones, using a diary is a basic foundation to time management. The form of diary and how this is used will affect your ability to manage your time. Again, this needs to fit your personal preference and ways of working rather than be seen as an additional task set up for failure.

Examples of diaries are noted as follows:

1. Timetables (education and work rotas).
2. Physical, personal or academic diaries.
3. Gantt charts for tasks (task-based diary).
4. Social diaries (on social media or physical diaries).
5. Wall calendars (family or home activities).

From working in education and industry over a number of years I would advise that you keep one form of personal diary, which includes all education, employment and social activities. You will naturally use a range of diaries, but identifying which single one you will use for all of your tasks is important for managing your time. Using an online diary will ensure you can access this from any location where there is a computer, however, some people prefer the physicality of a paper diary to write in. Pick a form of diary you will continue to use and only use this for noting activities coming up.

Within your diary it is important that you note the time at which activities start and finish. This will enable you to clarify where your social and personal time is available around academic and professional tasks. You can also use pictures or highlighting to classify the type of activity you will complete. The ways in which you use your diary will depend on your learning style (see Chapter 23 of this part) and this is individual to your approach and needs from using the diary.

Within your diary you need to consider how you prioritise tasks. There will be occasions when someone asks you to do something which is within a time you may have already attributed a task. At this point you immediately begin to weigh up the importance of both tasks. This is also where your determination and self-motivation comes into play. If you have a task in your diary that you are not looking forward to it is easy to swap it for another, more enjoyable task. In prioritising it is crucial you have an overview of the elements needed for the task and if you can move individual tasks to a later date. Never simply cancel a task, always look to when this can be completed later and whether this is feasible.

ACTIVITY 9.3 PRIORITISING FOR DIARY MANAGEMENT

1. Pick an academic task you need to complete, which does not need to be completed for at least a month.
2. Clarify if you have set appropriate tasks to complete this to a high standard in the time leading up to the deadline.
3. Have you spread out the tasks over this time?
4. Which stages have you identified?
5. How much time have you denoted for each task?
6. Is it possible for you to change the time according to your own ability?
7. Do you need contingency time for this task in case other tasks come up?

In the activity above you will have reflected on your usual ability to outline tasks in support of academic work submission. Adding in time for contingency purposes (if other things come up) is essential in diary management as this will enable you flexibility for completing the assignment. If you complete the work earlier than planned, this will also mean you have further time for editing and proof reading (which will undoubtedly lead to a higher standard of work).

Gantt charts

Gantt charts are often used in events management planning. A large event requires a series of tasks to plan, build, produce (perform) and remove the event from a venue.

CASE STUDY 9.2 TASKS NEEDED FOR DIFFERENT EVENTS

The following table outlines the tasks to complete as an event manager for three events.

50th birthday party for 60 guests	Community festival in local park	Conference on student dissertation research
• Find venue. • Ascertain contractual requirements. • Clarify menu. • Invite guests. • Confirm attendees. • Organise entertainment. • Check legal elements associated with the event. • Liaise with customers and venue on dietary requirements. • Obtain decorations for theming the event. • Run the event. • Evaluate the success of the event and plan to make changes in future events.	• Establish the target market for the event (families, youth, working professionals). • Find local park to host event and ascertain their contractual requirements. • Establish event committee to support. • Outline financial costs associated. • Confirm entertainment. • Social media and ticketing channels. • Food and beverage stalls to operate at the event. • Create marketing channels to support. • Run the event. • Remove all elements from the park. • Evaluate the success of the event and plan to make changes in future events.	• Identify how many students will present and how they will present their research. • Find a venue for the conference. • Outline financial costs associated. • Create ticketing site. • Create marketing channels and platforms. • Support ticket registrations. • Liaise with venue and customers on dietary requirements. • Run the event. • Evaluate the success of the event and plan to make changes in future events.

Case Study 9.2 on the tasks associated with different events enables you to consider the range of tasks associated with event management. These will differ according to the type of event (private, sports, professional) to be created. Similarly, academic work will require the following stages:

1.   Obtaining instructions for assessment.
2.   Reading and understanding what the assignment requires in content, structure and knowledge.
3.   Reading and conducting research for the assignment.
4.   Writing or creating the assignment.
5.   Having a break to leave the work.
6.   Editing the assignment.
7.   Proof reading and checking the assignment.

The seven stages outlined for academic assignment creation include an important stage: breaking to leave the work. This is important in academic work as you will find that when writing an assignment you will be thinking and writing in tandem. Having a break before completing edits and proof reading will mean you have a clearer and more objective approach to the work.

Table 9.1 clarifies the first three stages in organising your time for academic assignment work. The time allocated to each task will depend on the assessment requirements (word length and research required). Gantt charts allow you a visual example of how you will organise your time for specific tasks. They should be used in conjunction with your diary to ensure you have allocated time around other activities (social, professional and private). Within your education studies I would advise you use a gantt chart for each submission you need to complete. Print these and put them on your wall and tick off each task as it is completed. This will enable you to develop self-esteem in your academic work and improve motivation for later stages.

Targets negotiated with others

One strategy that will aid your own motivation and sense of accomplishment is if you work with others or negotiate targets. This is whereby group work is seen as beneficial to task

Table 9.1 Gantt chart for assignment work

Task	Monday	Tuesday	Wednesday	Thursday	Friday
Obtaining instructions.	Class 12–2				
Understand the assessment requirements.	5–6 in library				
Reading for the assignment.			12–4		10–2

standards (discussed in Part 3, Chapter 18) but is also noted here to make you more accountable for the deadlines and tasks in term sof for time management.

When you have noted a task needing significant work (academic or professional) liaise with other stakeholders or class mates on the stages you will complete in support of this. Stakeholders who can work with you in this negotiation are clarified as follows:

- Friend.
- Class mate.
- Family member.
- Flat mate.
- Teacher.
- Manager.
- Colleague.
- Supplier.
- Consultant or mentor (external to the company, private or education contexts).

The list of stakeholders noted above can be used in your negotiation of deadlines and tasks. How you choose to involve these people is your own choice.

By outlining stakeholders who can support your task deadlines by discussion and negotiation, Table 9.2 clarifies how these can be used for self-motivation. This motivation comes from you not only being accountable for your own work and actions, but the fact that others are also expecting you to meet these.

Table 9.2 Stakeholders used in negotiation of time management

Stakeholder	How they may be used in task planning	Outcome
Class mate	Both working to similar deadlines for an academic assignment.	Both feel competent and able to complete the assignment in time and to a high standard.
Family member	Clarify the deadline you are working to and that once complete you will send evidence of the work.	Reward (monetary, experience or gift).
Mentor or consultant	Outlines additional tasks to support academic or professional development.	Academic work is at a higher standard. Promotion and work is known and could be promoted to others.
Colleague	Share duties in work to support customer satisfaction.	Work is less pressured and customers are satisfied.
Supplier	Deadlines confirmed to fit in line with supplier work.	Efficient use of your time in support of external suppliers for the task.

Actions for procrastination

From Activity 9.2, completed earlier in this chapter, you will have outlined your agreements in procrastination statements. Use Case Study 9.3 to understand thoughts and actions you can address in support of these. The aim is that if you recognise your procrastination, you can alter your usual thoughts and actions to these in a more positive direction for effective time management.

CASE STUDY 9.3 CHANGING THOUGHTS AND ACTIONS IN PROCRASTINATION

I need pressure from a lack of time in order to complete tasks.

- Use a diary and gantt chart to plan in time to complete tasks in advance of the deadline.
- Acknowledge that if you leave work until the last minute the work will not be the highest standard possible.
- Negotiate tasks with other stakeholders so that others will check on your progress.

I ignore important tasks.

- Identify levels of priority to your weekly tasks.
- Important repeated tasks (such as financial budgeting or reading) need to be aligned to rewards on completing them.
- Acknowledge that ignoring a task does not mean it disappears and that important tasks lead to rewards.

I often have important interruptions to my tasks.

- Plan to complete tasks in locations where you have minimal interruption.
- Turn your phone on silent.
- Do not check social media during time when you are meant to complete tasks.

I often find excuses for not completing tasks.

- Identify the punishment for not completing a task.
- Use a stakeholder to negotiate or discuss how to complete tasks you often ignore.

I start new tasks in the middle of completing others.

- Work in an environment where you cannot complete other tasks (such as washing or reorganising your sock drawer).
- Inform others around you of the task you need to complete and ask them to remind you to not interrupt this task.
- Work alongside another person completing a similar task so that you have a sense of competition and accountability in completing the task.

I often feel tired and this stops me completing tasks planned.

- Maintain regular sleep patterns.
- Have social, private and personal time in your diary to avoid burnout.
- Eat and drink an appropriate amount to support normal bodily function.
- If you feel you have a mental health issue (anxiety, depression or similar), speak to a professional about this.

This case study of potential actions and thoughts to counteract procrastination is not feasible nor possible for everyone in every context. Use these examples to consider how you might combat procrastination and negative actions for effective time management. Ultimately, the levels of self-determination and self-motivation you have for different tasks will define your ability to complete work within the set time allocated. Your emotional state, amount of sleep, diet, personal relations and mental health are all present here. In this way, you should also use reflexivity in ensuring that when you miss a deadline or do not complete a task in time, you are able to identify the reason why and use determination to complete the task when possible.

Another area considered in Case Study 9.3 is within punishment and reward for completing tasks on time. If you use the strategies in this chapter to organise your time effectively, you also need to consider where reward and punishment will emerge. If the punishment is not deemed severe, then it is more likely you will not stick to the task in the allotted time. Equally, if there is a perceived higher reward for a task, you may complete this quickly. This links to forms of motivation (covered in Part 3, Chapter 17).

SUMMARY

1. To understand what time management is, how this is part of your own personal ability and how it affects your academic and professional development.

Time management was defined in supporting and affecting your use of time. These need consideration in order to ensure you are in good physical and mental health to complete tasks required. Analysis of your usual procrastination in task completion will enable you to discuss and appraise your usual approach to tasks (reflective). Self-motivation is seen as linked and important in time management as this can inhibit your ability to complete work planned.

2.   To identify strategies for time management.

Diary management, gantt charts, negotiation with stakeholders and combating procrastination were offered as strategies for effective time management. Use a combination of these in your academic and professional tasks in order to organise and manage your time. Your individual and usual patterns in time management may need further work in order to get used to using these. Using self-determination and self-motivation for these tasks will ensure you stick to schedules and use your time effectively.

Questions to support your learning and research

1.   Which physiological elements are needed for effective time management?
2.   Is everyone good at time management? Why?
3.   How is social time defined?
4.   What is burnout?
5.   What form of diary do you use?
6.   How should you use your diary?
7.   How is colour used in a gantt chart?
8.   How can you change your usual ways of managing your time?
9.   How can a mentor support your time management?
10.   What can flat mates do to help your time management? How can you support theirs?

Chapter 10
Learning styles

LEARNING OBJECTIVES

1. To understand different approaches to learning.
2. To identify different learning styles.
3. To evaluate different learning forms and styles used in your academic and professional development.

INTRODUCTION

This chapter addresses knowledge and research on learning styles. Each individual is seen to prefer and use a different learning style for each task completed. Knowledge and reflection on this will enable readers to appraise their learning style and alter ways of completing work in support of this. It should be acknowledged that in addition to different learning styles being present in different contexts, these can also change over time due to increased experience in task completion. Forms of knowledge (explicit and implicit – noted in Part 1, Chapter 1) and skills (Part 2, Chapter 6) will only be developed if effective learning has taken place. Awareness of this is important so that you can adapt your learning environment to suit the desired learning outcomes.

APPROACHES TO LEARNING

Learning is said to be completed in mind of a number of positions and approaches. It is important to understand these approaches as they affect your ability to learn and the level to which you process learning. This chapter will consider behaviourist, cognitivist, positivist and social constructivist.

Behaviourist learning

Pavlov's (1927) research and publications on how people learn via prompted behaviour is seminal in behaviourist learning. In order to understand this form of learning there are stages present in supporting the learning style:

1. Drive.
2. Stimulation.
3. Response.
4. Reinforcement.

Drive links to your motivation and self-determination to complete something. If you have no drive, then the following actions cannot take place. Stimulation is whereby something triggers your motivation or desire to complete an action. Learning is then seen in the response offered to the stimulation. This should evidence a new set of behaviours emergent from the drive and stimulation. Reinforcement is then essential to improve learning and ensure bad habits are not repeated.

THINK POINT 10.1 HOW ARE YOU DRIVEN?

Behaviourist learning has identified how your drive is essential in gaining and retaining new information. What drives you? Does this differ according to the task being completed? Have you perhaps maintained poor behaviour due to a lack of drive in addressing or changing your behaviour?

Cognitivist learning

Cognitive psychology is whereby learning is seen as a process of increasing knowledge and using this to solve problems (Harrison, 2009). Three elements are seen in this form of learning:

1. Assimilation.
2. Accommodation.
3. Rejection.

The classification of cognitive psychology in learning is from Piaget's (1950) work in child psychology. Assimilation is whereby you accept new information as it fits with your current cognitive frameworks of information. Accommodating new information must then occur, irrespective of tension felt in the new knowledge fitting with previous positions. For example, if we are faced with a fact that appears to contradict our prior knowledge, we need to reflect on this and accommodate it in logical connection to current knowledge. Rejection is then where new contradictory information is not accepted and not learnt.

ACTIVITY 10.1 SOLVING PROBLEMS VIA KNOWLEDGE DEVELOPMENT

1. Identify a new dish that you wish to make for a dinner party with friends.
2. Find a recipe that you can follow to create the dish.
3. Outline the ingredients or methods in the recipe that you are unfamiliar with.
4. What new knowledge and skills do you need to create this dish?
5. How will you find and develop your knowledge and skills further?

Positivist learning

A positivistic approach is seen as a form of research position (see Part 3, Chapter 12 where research philosophies are considered). Here, the role of the trainer is outlined as pre-eminent in knowledge development. It is not simply that a learner is an empty vessel that needs to consume and retain knowledge, but that the trainer is connected in the learning and, therefore, has a significant part in the process. Trainers need to design a curriculum, clarify objectives for learning, reinforce accurate knowledge developed and challenge incorrect knowledge before it becomes a bad habit.

CASE STUDY 10.1 DOING AS ACADEMICS DO, NOT AS ACADEMICS SAY

An academic (or teacher) informs their students that they are going to learn about employability and skills for tourism, hospitality and events management. Specifically, they want students to develop an understanding of learning styles in support of their personal development.

In order to teach this topic area the academic has a number of methods they use:

1. Distribute reading.
2. Present their (academic's) research completed in learning styles.
3. Enquire what knowledge students currently have on learning styles.
4. Talk at students about knowledge on learning styles form a range of sources.
5. Ask students to talk about their opinions on learning styles.
6. Watch a video on learning styles.

Methods 3 and 5 enable the academic to understand the position in which student's current knowledge stands. These reflect a positivistic view of learning as they acknowledge that students will have a basis of understanding already. From this, a range of tasks can be completed to scaffold the learning.

Social constructivist learning

Knowles (1980) is seen as a core author in social constructivist learning and this is seen as 'humanist' type of learning (Harrison, 2009). This refers to our own perceptions and views of the world (epistemology) and how this affects our ability to learn. Like other forms of learning, a person has a basis of knowledge that is used as a framework to accept or reject new information. However, this is not divorced from the context and situation within which this is processed. We have beliefs and emotions present in every situation and these will affect our ability to learn and the type of information we choose to accept or reject. In this way social constructivist learning is seen as situated learning.

ACTIVITY 10.2 FORMS OF LEARNING EXPERIENCED SO FAR

From your work completed using this textbook for employment and skills for THE, identify the information learnt and how this has been applied using the four forms of learning:

Learning	Knowledge	How learnt (list actions or thought)
Behaviourist		
Cognitivist		
Positivist		
Social constructivist		

LEARNING STYLES

From outlining the forms of learning it is clear that the context and processes needed for learning will vary. The type of learning style present for learning will also vary. Acknowledgement and identification of this is important for your personal, academic and professional development. Learning will not simply take place within a class or training room. You will be required to learn in your own private study time. This time needs to be used effectively and so addressing your learning style will make sure this time is used most efficiently. Learning styles addressed here include visual, auditory, kinaesthetic, work based and Honey and Mumford's (1992).

Visual

Visual learners require viewing information in order to process and acquire knowledge (Horn, 2009). You will perceive this if you need to draw figures or diagrams to clarify information. Examples of how visual learners learn are noted as follows:

- Detailed notes when reading or processing new information.
- Using colourful figures or pictures to understand information.
- Memory of information is often in pictorial form.

Auditory

Talking and listening to others in discussion of information is key in this learning style. Instead of sitting in the quiet, these learners will need to verbalise their learning or listen to recordings of information in order to process this.

Kinaesthetic

Hands-on learners are seen to need to do things in order to learn. Operational skills are examples of this in THE employment. A chef's ability to cut quickly and precisely is an example of this as the consistent tactile practice enables them to learn the best ways for completing the task. When completing written work, you may also find that you need to take regular breaks to walk or move around. This is also a form of kinaesthetic learning as you need to move in order to learn more deeply.

CASE STUDY 10.2 LEARNING TO PLAY A MUSICAL INSTRUMENT

If you are interested in or have learnt to play an instrument you will need to use visual (V), auditory (A) and kinaesthetic (K) learning in tandem. Holding the instrument (K), hearing the music played (A) and seeing how your body is positioned (V) are essential in this example. In this way it is clear to see that these learning styles can be present in a singular activity. The levels for each element will vary on what you are trying to accomplish. For example, if you are rehearsing a piece from memory, you might even close your eyes and listen to the notes produced in order to confirm your ability to create the correct melody. Conversely, as a beginner, you will probably focus more attention on where your hands and body are in relation to the instrument. This clarifies the varying levels of learning style linked to experience and proficiency in playing a musical instrument.

Work based

Kolb (1984) defined experiential (work) based learning, which is seen to combine visual, auditory and kinaesthetic forms. This is whereby a learner needs experience of an activity, reflection on the work, concluding elements from the work and knowledge learnt, and experimentation with new and alternative ways of working. Figure 10.1 outlines these stages in a cyclical model.

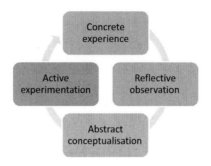

Figure 10.1 Kolb's (1984) *Cycle of work based learning*
Source: Kolb, 1984

Identifying learning as being a component of work based or experience based action requires reflective and reflexive practice. Experimentation in alternative ways of completing the activity and evaluating the outcomes of the activity enables you to process and accept new learning within current frameworks (Horn, 2009: p.64).

Honey and Mumford learning styles

Honey and Mumford (1992) classified four types of learning as follows:

1. Activist: generating and trying out new ideas.
2. Reflector: watching and gathering information before making decisions.
3. Theorist: logical and thorough steps taken to accomplish tasks (used in time management strategies noted in Chapter 8 of this part).
4. Pragmatist: experiencing something to evaluate its success.

Their classification of learning styles is based on Kolb's (1984) experiential learning style.

ACTIVITY 10.3 **IDENTIFYING YOUR USUAL PREFERENCE IN LEARNING STYLE**

Read each of the following statements and tick those that apply to you. Answer honestly (there are no right or wrong answers). It is advisable that you only briefly consider each statement and do not consider them in depth within lots of contexts. This will enable your answers to be spontaneous and an honest account of your opinions.

Active (Activist)

I usually initiate conversations first.
I enjoy participating and being involved in things.
I am outgoing and gregarious.
I am open minded and flexible.
I relish in trying out new things without full consideration.
I frequently have spontaneous ideas that are not perceived as fully thought out.
I like to try new things.
I talk quite quickly and think at the same time.

Visual

I enjoy observing and reading things.
I think before I talk.
I am known to be shy and quiet.
I often use lists to identify the stages and processes to complete tasks.
I cannot try something before I have fully researched it.
I am cautious and considered.
I am methodical in how I approach things.
I enjoy watching people.

Thinking

I would rather work alone than with others.
I always use facts to support actions.
I need to ask a lot of questions when trying to learn something new.
I have meticulous attention to detail when planning an event.
I read research and reports to ascertain issues and basic assumptions.
From observing others I mimic good practice and processes.

I am known for being formal and serious.
A strength of mine is that I am logical and rational.

Pragmatic

I try things out in order to get better at them.
I love working with other people.
I rely on my emotions to aid decision making.
I like tasks that are clear but flexible.
I am known for being expressive and verbal (sometimes informal).
People get to know me easily.
I seek information from others to understand a problem.
Emotions drive my motivation to complete tasks.

When you have done this, add up the ticks in each section and note them below:

Active =

Visual =

Thinking =

Pragmatic =

There are eight statements for each section. Consider where you feel strongest in the four areas and how this clarifies your usual learning style.

All learning styles noted in this chapter are needed in independent study (Part 3) and professional development (Part 4). Acknowledgement of the ones you use in different contexts is important in order to reflect and evaluate your own learning styles.

LEARNING FORMS AND STYLES TO AID ACADEMIC AND PROFESSIONAL DEVELOPMENT

In order to develop your employability and skills for work within THE businesses it is important you are able to align the form of learning and learning style necessary. Aligning these to important tasks or duties will enable you to clarify the time required to complete the task, identify what your motivation to complete the task is and what the outcomes from the learning are. Academic and professional tasks are outlined and linked to learning form and styles in Tables 10.1 to 10.4. Use these tables to understand and appraise how you usually complete this learning.

Table 10.1 Form of learning for academic tasks

Task	Behaviourist	Cognitive	Positivist	Social constructivist
New theory.	Being asked to read a paper on new theory.	Awareness of a lack of knowledge in an area.	Working with others to learn and discuss knowledge on new theory.	Talking and responding to others opinions on the theory.
Writing academically.	Sitting in the library to write assignment.	Awareness of improvements needed in writing style.	Asking teachers questions on the requirements for the assignment.	Proof reading others work to understand how yours differs (both positively and negatively).
Interviewing for a research project.	Verbal communication to ask questions.	Interpersonal skills to be developed to probe participants.	Completing a pilot on the interview and evaluating its success.	Watching others conduct interviews.

Table 10.2 Learning styles for academic tasks

Task	Visual	Auditory	Kinaesthetic	Work based
New theory.	Reading words, pictures and diagrams.	Talking to friends about knowledge developed.	Printing out a journal article and highlighting important sections.	Reflecting on past experience in learning theory and applying new techniques to complete actions.
Writing academically.	Reading words, pictures and diagrams.	Talking to a teacher on current progress of work.	Printing out the draft and making notes on it.	Using feedback from previous submissions to improve next assignment.
Interviewing for a research project.	Seeing the participant's body language and non-verbal cues.	Listening to participant responses.	Holding a tape recorder and interview question sheet.	Evaluating the success of a pilot study to improve interview technique.

Professional

Table 10.3 Form of learning for professional tasks

Task	Behaviourist	Cognitive	Positivist	Social constructivist
Building networks.	Attending networking events.	A need to increase business contacts for employability.	Using current network to gain access to new ones.	Discussing with a mentor how to build new networks; seeking best practice.
Writing CV.	Using the job description to write an individual CV.	Seeing others obtaining job interviews from CVs and wanting the same.	Reviewing example CVs from others.	Asking a colleague to offer a recommendation for your CV.
Understanding labour markets.	Finding government reports on labour markets and understanding them.	Using research skills to find, understand and evaluate sources of information.	Using a variety of sources of information to gain understanding.	Completing a labour market activity with your class.

Table 10.4 Learning styles for professional tasks

Task	Visual	Auditory	Kinaesthetic	Work based
Building networks.	Viewing others developing rapport at networking events.	Listening and speaking to others.	Obtaining a ticket to attend a networking event.	Reflecting on prior actions and improving these.
Writing CV.	Reading a job advert posted.	Asking for advice on CV development, or completing a 3 minute elevator pitch in support of CV writing.	Hand writing key aspects to include in your CV; printing and editing a draft copy.	Using past examples of CVs to develop for new roles.
Understanding labour markets.	Reading words, pictures and diagrams.	Watching videos and hearing discussion on labour markets.	Printing sources of information to highlight and organise.	Using past actions to aid finding articles in support.

**ACTIVITY 10.4 ACADEMIC AND PROFESSIONAL DEVELOPMENT
USING HONEY AND MUMFORD'S LEARNING STYLES**

Using the examples of learning style linked to academic and professional tasks, use the following table and identify how the different learning styles from Honey and Mumford would be evident.

Task	Activist	Reflector	Theorist	Pragmatist
New theory.				
Writing academically.				
Interviewing for a research project.				
Building networks.				
Writing CV.				
Understanding labour markets.				

SUMMARY

1. To understand different approaches to learning.

Four approaches to learning were identified as behaviourist, cognitivist, positivist and social constructivist. These outlined how determination, motivation, triggers and reinforcement are required from a learner and trainer. Appraisal of how these learning forms are present in this textbook will enable you to apply these to external learning completed in personal, academic and professional contexts.

2. To identify different learning styles.

Visual, auditory, kinaesthetic, work based and Honey and Mumford styles of learning were outlined in this chapter. One of these may appear dominant in specific tasks or duties. They are not static nor limited and they may also overlap.

3. To evaluate different learning forms and styles used in your academic and professional development.

This chapter aligned three academic and professional tasks to the different approaches to learning and learning styles discussed. This can be used to identify learning approaches and styles in practice but also to evaluate alternative learning methods to employ in your usual learning contexts.

Questions to support your learning and research

1. Why are students referred to as empty vessels?
2. Which learning styles are present when learning to play the guitar?
3. Can you learn on your own?
4. How do learning approaches affect your understanding on human psychology?
5. Do you find Kolb's cycle of experiential learning useful for reflecting on your usual way of learning?

References in support of your learning from this chapter

Campbell, A. and Norton, L. (2006). Teaching & learning in higher education: Chapter introduction. *Education*, pp. 1–8.

Drew, S. (1998). Students' perceptions of their learning outcomes. *Teaching in Higher Education*, 3(2), pp. 197–217.

Lave, J. (2010). The practice of learning. In *Understanding practice*. Chaiklin, S. and Lave, J. eds, (2nd ed.). Cambridge University Press (pp. 3–32).

Lave, J. and Wenger, E. (1991). *Situated Learning: Legitimate Peripheral Participation*. Pea, R. and Brown, J.S. eds, Cambridge University Press. [online]. Available from: http://books.google.com/books?id=CAVIOrW3vYAC&pgis=1.

Sternberg, R.J. (1997). The concept of intelligence and its role in lifelong learning and success. *American Psychologist*, 52, pp. 1030–1037.

Vygotsky, L.S. (1978). *Mind in society: The development of higher psychological processes*. Cambridge, MA: Harvard University Press.

Chapter 11
Effective communication

LEARNING OBJECTIVES

1. To recognise different forms of communication.
2. To appraise effective written and digital communication.

INTRODUCTION

In order for you to reflect on your employability and skills for work in tourism, hospitality and events (THE) businesses it is important for you to develop effective communication. Communication is required in every aspect of your personal and professional life to express yourself. The level and form of communication used will evidence your ability to communicate effectively. This chapter will outline forms of communication (verbal and non-verbal) as well as identify written and digital communication.

FORMS OF COMMUNICATION: VERBAL AND NON-VERBAL

Communication is accepted as a soft skill (Yorke, 2006; Jackson, 2010, 2012; Chan, 2011) used to express yourself. The situation and people with whom you are communicating with will alter your approach and the forms of communication you offer. In order to analyse your use of communication this chapter will outline verbal and non-verbal forms of communication and offer activities for you to consider how to alter these appropriately and professionally. Barriers to effective communication will also be discussed in order for you to understand how to overcome these and manage them appropriately.

Communication is linked to your ability to listen, read and understand information offered to you. As communication links to verbal language, the first area to consider is how your native and second language differs in communication situations. From an intercultural lens, Clyne (1994: p.3) noted that communication has three approaches:

1.   Contrastive approach – native language across cultures.
2.   Interlanguage approach – non-native speakers in a second language.
3.   Interactive inter-cultural approach – communication between two people of differing cultural and linguistic backgrounds using a lingua franca or one of the interlocutors languages.

(Clyne, 1994: p.3)

The contrastive approach to communication is whereby cultural differences in communication are evident in native language. How you convey politeness, manners, agreement within your own native language compared to others will be a potential barrier to effective communication.

> ## THINK POINT 11.1 AGREEMENT COMMUNICATED IN DIFFERENT LANGUAGES
> When you complete verbal communication face to face with someone, how do you know they are agreeing with your expressed opinions? Is this evident verbally or non-verbally? Have you encountered differences in this according to the language you and others speak?

Communicating agreement in a verbal language is clear in all native tongues (if you understand their language). However, when communicating a non-verbal agreement there are intercultural differences noted within the contrastive approach. Nodding your head up and down is a way of understanding agreement in America, most of Europe and India, for example. Conversely, countries like Lebanon, Syria, Turkey and Egypt nod their heads up and down to convey 'no.' In India they also offer a head bobble in agreement to communication.

Using verbal and non-verbal elements to communicate agreement has outlined how nodding can be used and perceived differently. Your own nationality and experiences in different languages will affect your interpretation of this.

The second approach noted by Clyne (1994), the interlanguage approach, is where a non-native speaker communicates in a second language. This form of verbal communication requires education and training to enable someone to speak a different language. A second language differs to your first as it is seen as not being your 'mother tongue.' There are exceptions to this in homes where children are brought up as bilingual and therefore may have two languages seen as their first language. Usually a second language is learnt after significant education on a new language when the person is older. It may be developed in studies or from working in a new country that has a different national language.

ACTIVITY 11.1 YOUR LANGUAGES

1. What would you consider to be your mother tongue?
2. Do you speak other languages?
3. How did you learn these?
4. How proficient do you feel in second and third languages?

Using your answers above, consider how second and third language is used when speaking to natives from that country.

1. Do you use gestures to aid your communication?
2. Do you ask for support when speaking in another language?
3. Do you clarify in verbal communication that you only speak a little?
4. How do you negotiate your level of ability with the other person?

Activity 11.1 on your language ability and use will enable you to reflect on the interlanguage approach to communication and how this affects your expression. If you do not speak more than one language, you can also apply this to situations where you encounter people from other regions. Regional communication in accent and language can also be seen as a second language due to the local traditions present.

The interactive intercultural approach to communication is the final area noted by Clyne and refers to how people communicate in a common language even if they do not share the same native and second language abilities. This is often perceived in THE contexts as the workers and tourists may be from differing cultural backgrounds and use English as a lingua franca. A lingua franca is the language chosen to communicate due to people perceiving this as a common language. English language is often the preferred lingua franca in THE contexts due to it being taught in most countries around the world and used extensively in international business and policy.

CASE STUDY 11.1 USING ENGLISH AS A LINGUA FRANCA: AMERICAN VERSUS BRITISH ENGLISH LANGUAGE

This case study will outline four differences between British and American English language. If you are a non-native English speaker you may be aware of the accent differences in native English speakers, but there are also other differences which may lead to confusion and conflict.

Vocabulary

In Table 3.1 in Chapter 3 of Part 1, we reviewed different British and American under-standing of certain words (chips being crisps or cooked potatoes). There are further differences noted in the specific words used to describe things:

British	American
Aubergine	Eggplant
Bill	Check
Boot	Trunk
Courgette	Zucchini
Driving licence	Driver's licence
Quilt	Comforter
Expiry date	Expiration date
Fire brigade	Fire department

Collective nouns

A collective noun is the way in which we communicate about a group of individuals. In American English, collective nouns are usually singular and in British English they can be either singular or collective. Examples of these are noted below:

British	American
My class is ready. My class are ready.	My class is ready.
Our government is great! Our government are great!	Our government is great!
The team are playing. The team is playing.	The team is playing.

A past action effecting the present

Here, American and British language differs in the words used to describe a past action effecting a present situation:

AmericanL:	Mike is not well. He ate too much!
British:	Mike is not well. He has eaten too much!
AmericanL:	I think I have lost my textbook. Did you see it anywhere?
BritishL:	I think I have lost my textbook. Have you seen it anywhere?

Ate/eaten and did/have are used differently in these examples. They convey the same information but are used specifically by people from the UK or USA.

Auxiliary verbs

Auxiliary verbs are used to express the time, voice and modality of a question. Examples of different auxiliary verbs used are noted as follows:

AmericanL:	Should we go now?
BritishL:	Shall we go now?
AmericanL:	I don't need to come to class today.
BritishL:	I needn't come to class today.
AmericanL:	Should we ask them to join us?
BritishL:	Shall we ask them to join us?

Case Study 11.1 on four differences in British and American language evidences how contradictions in verbal language are present. If you have learnt American English and speak to someone who has learnt British English you may be confused in the way they use this language. This is not due to a lack of ability in English but due to the national grammatical differences present.

By outlining Clyne's (1994) three approaches to verbal communication you need to consider your mother tongue and lingua franca used in order to complete communication. Your education, experience and level of ability in language will impact effective communication. Reflection on your language ability is therefore needed in order to identify why issues arise in verbal communication.

Native and non-native language ability is another fluid and difficult area to consider here. A native English person may not be able to understand another English person due to the regional differences present. As noted previously, this is pre-eminent in vocal accents (Scottish versus Welsh for example) but is also clear in regional vocabulary (see Table 11.1).

Table 11.1 outlines how a 285ml or 10 floz amount of beer has different names in a range of Australian regions. If you asked for a schooner in Perth they may not understand what you are asking for. In this way, being a native speaker of a language does not confirm your ability to successfully verbally communicate within the country.

Table 11.1 Names used for beer glasses in
Australian cities

Area	Name
Canberra	Middy
Darwin	Handle
Brisbane	Pot
Sydney	Middy
Adelaide	Schooner
Hobart	Ten
Melbourne	Pot
Perth	Middy

Source: The Aussies Beer Baron

Within verbal communication there are a range of additional elements to consider when using the same language (see Table 11.2).

The information offered in Table 11.2 enables knowledge of how terms, language, actions and meanings all vary the way in which verbal communication is offered and understood. A crucial component in addressing these is the amount to which you listen and apply meaning to them.

THINK POINT 11.2 REFLECTING ON ELEMENTS OF VERBAL COMMUNICATION

Using Table 11.2 on elements of verbal communication offered, consider the following:

1. How can these lead to misunderstanding in verbal communication?
2. How does your emotional state affect your understanding of verbal communication?
3. Does your ability to reflect and consider these differences change based on the situation and context you are listening in?

Although verbal communication is the primary area to convey and express yourself, it is present in our bodied selves. If we are communicating face to face, we will also be interpreting and communicating using non-verbal cues and actions (Table 11.3).

Table 11.2 Elements within verbal communication

Area	What does this sound like?	What does it suggest?
Linguistic relativity.	Communicating the same word in different languages.	Speech influences how we view things (world view). Germans use maternal aunts, we use just Aunt as the name.
Communicative relativity.	Language used when communicating with different people.	Informal language on Facebook. Formal language in a thesis.
Language inferences.	Meaning from words used can create an inferred belief, intention or understanding.	People can misunderstand language due to inferred meaning.
Speech act.	Situation in which communication occurs.	That two people want to communicate something to each other.
Speech event.	The phrase of communication offered to another person.	A person wants to request or state something to another person.
Low context culture.	The interpretation of the exact words spoken to mean all communication.	Communication relies on language solely.
Involvement.	A statement or question that identifies empathy or awareness of another person's involvement: *'I know just what you mean.'*	Awareness of other people having the same background or familiarity with a subject or action.
Independence.	A statement or question identifying an understanding of independence: *'It would be nice to do something, but I am aware you may be busy.'*	It does not take ownership from the other person. It communicates awareness of independence.
Prosodic patterns.	Intonation when speaking.	Intonation can suggest emotion, position and familiarity with the other person or situation.
Discourse system.	Words and language used based on an individual's background.	Each and every person will use different words and phrasing to communicate to another person.

Source: Piller, 2011; Scollon et al., 2012

All elements of non-verbal communication are present and understood by people in verbal communication. It is not simply your body language alone but a range of aspects based on your national culture and previous experiences.

Table 11.3 Elements in non-verbal communication

Area	What does this look like?	How it differs
Proxemics.	The distance between people communicating.	Brazilians speak standing closely to each other.
Chronemics.	The time between speech acts.	Pause = Thinking? No pauses = Urgency?
Kinesics.	Facial expressions and gestures.	Emotion, familiarity or instruction.
Adumbration.	Body language or breathing cues.	Deep breath = speech is about to happen.
High context culture.	Taking more meaning from the person's knowledge, situation and relationship between the people.	The context of the communication is more important than the words spoken.
Scripts.	The order in which situations are completed.	Some restaurants require customers to order, then pay, then collect, and then sit and consume. Others need customers to sit first, then order and then pay on exit.
Frames.	Explanation of a procedure.	One person has authority to another and describes the way something operates.
Schemata.	Complaining to someone.	A certain social understanding of a situation.

Source: Hall, 1959; Clyne, 1994; Scollon et al., 2012

ACTIVITY 11.2 EVALUATING NON-VERBAL COMMUNICATION

1. Find a video of a TV presenter interviewing someone.
2. Watch them communicating in the interview.
3. Use the eight areas of non-verbal communication listed in Table 11.3 and identify where each of these are seen, or where they may be influencing their verbal communication.

As noted earlier, communication is not only linked to your language development (native and non-native language) but also to your awareness of politeness, attitudes and manners. Different contexts will require you to communicate using different professional scripts and schemas. A personal and professional situation within which to address this is within a telephone conversation (see Table 11.4).

Table 11.4 Personal and professional telephone conversation

Personal	Professional
1. Answer when available. 2. Welcoming the caller by name and ascertaining the reason for the call. 3. Using colloquial and informal language. 4. Talking at length about personal or private issues. 5. Ending with a personal clarification of your feeling or satisfaction with the discussion.	1. Answer within three rings. 2. Noting your name on answering then asking how you can assist them. 3. Using professional terms and formal language. 4. Keeping the discussion to a minimum and ensuring you clarify how you will assist. 5. Ending professionally by thanking them for their time.

The example in Table 11.4 comparing personal and professional telephone call schema clarifies how differences in communication are not simply verbal or non-verbal but are context- and person-specific also. If you applied the usual methods of a personal telephone call to a professional one you might find the other person is confused and unsure why you are acting 'familiar' with them. However, personalisation is sometimes used as a competitive advantage in THE business as it enables customers to feel known and welcome. Conversely, if you used professional conversation in a personal telephone conversation, the other person may feel you have been rude and distant from them. Using either of these in the wrong contexts will lead to problems perceived by the other person.

CASE STUDY 11.2 CUSTOMER RELATIONSHIP ISSUES

Katy works in a five star hotel in Barcelona within the spa department of the hotel. She is Irish and has been working at the hotel as part of her placement year for her university studies. She serves a number of guests within her working week and usu-ally uses English as the lingua franca with guests (although she can speak some Spanish).

During a pedicure for one of her frequent customers, Katy's customer starts to inform her about their relationship issues. According to the customer, their marriage is breaking down due to infidelity. They discuss their observation of their partner being more secretive, that they are seen to be lying about their whereabouts and that they feel that something is 'not right.'

> Within this discussion Katy's customer asks Katy the following questions:
>
> - Do you think I'm being over sensitive?
> - How am I to find out if this is true?
> - Should I just trust them?
> - Do you know how this feels?
> - Maybe I should just have an affair also?
> - Maybe they think we are in a more open relationship than I thought?

Case Study 11.2 on customer relationship issues clarifies how professional conversations can easily turn personal within THE businesses. Serving guests in restaurants, bars and leisure activities will naturally lead customers to offer personal information. It is important for the employee to understand how to react to this and how to best respond. This is where communication is championed as a superior soft skill in THE and it is vital you consider appropriate responses in these situations. Appearing concerned (emotional labour) whilst maintaining professionalism with customers is essential in THE employment.

WRITTEN AND DIGITAL COMMUNICATION

Within your academic, personal and professional contexts you will have to use written communication effectively. Written communication in the form of emails is noted here (academic writing is considered in Part 3, Chapter 15) and social media written communication (Twitter, Facebook, WeChat and Instagram) are explored to enable you to develop and improve your current skills. Please note that written communication for employment (CVs) is considered in Part 4.

Emails are a form of digital letter sent using a computer and internet connection. In a personal context, you might use these when you want to communicate at times when the other person is unavailable. For example, you might write your parent an email when you know they are at work or abroad. This form of communication is useful at sending information and expression of opinions and feelings in the knowledge that the content is static. In business contexts, emails are a daily requirement for sharing information to a range of stakeholders. The following outlines the benefits and issues perceived in email written communication:

Benefits in email written communication include:

1. Written in any language.
2. Can be translated using computers to enable cross cultural communication without your own language ability needing development (not always advisable).

3. Can be sent and received any time of the day.
4. Connects you to people who are located abroad in a cheap and efficient way.
5. Communication is continuous and uninterrupted.
6. Extensive amount of information can be included (attachments and web links increase this further).

Issues in email written communication include:

1. They can be ignored by the other person.
2. Requires internet access, which may be expensive and lack infrastructure.
3. The other person needs a level of ability in reading in the language sent.
4. Non-verbal communication is missing, which can lead to a lack of understanding.
5. Increased time to read, re-read and consider the potential meaning behind the written words.
6. Writing in an incorrect manner or structure that portrays a lack of respect for the other person.

In acknowledgement of the benefits and issues present in email written communication, the following offers you a list of appropriate mechanisms to employ when writing to a friend or teacher/academic:

Friend:

1. Address them in a familiar tone (Hi Ben).
2. Use abbreviations, acronyms and colloquial language appropriate to them.
3. Ask a range of direct and rhetorical questions.
4. Inform them of your opinion.
5. Sign off in an appropriate manner.
6. Convey feeling using letter (a kiss seen as an 'x', for example).

Within the abbreviations and acronyms used to write emails to your friends it is important to outline acronyms appropriate to use. A list of well-known ones are offered below:

ROFL   Roll on the floor laughing
LOL   Laugh out loud
TBH   To be honest
BFN   Bye for now
FB   Facebook
CU   See you
DM   Direct message
BFF   Best friend forever

Misunderstanding these or using them incorrectly in a sentence can lead to issues in the communication. If this occurs you may not receive a response and could attribute this to a range of reasons.

Teacher/academic:

1. Address them in a professional tone (Dear …). An important element here is to use their formal title in the first email and then check how they sign off in future emails. If you write Dear Professor Smith in your first email, then note in their response they write Adam, then you are able to use their first name. If they repeat your use of Dear to start the email then continue to do so. If they use 'Hi …' then it is accepted to use this also. Start formally and reflect on their response to guide the start of emails to teachers/academics.
2. Clarify the purpose of the email. Do not state that you want or need something (a meeting, for example). Ask specific and direct questions: Are you available next Tuesday at 10am for a meeting?
3. Offer ways for them to respond: 'Or alternatively, if you are available on Wednesday next week that would work for me also.'
4. Clarify information you have already gathered: I am aware from Claire that you would like us to email to arrange a meeting?
5. Sign off professionally.

A key to successful written communication with teachers or other working professionals is to start as formal as possible and then mediate the areas of informality. If you see someone replying in an informal way then do so also if you feel comfortable. Do not maintain a formal tone if this is unnecessary as it will hinder effective relationship development. Examples of alternative ways to sign off a professional email are noted below for your consideration and use:

*   Best/Best regards/Best wishes.
*   Fond regards.
*   Kind regards.
*   Regards.
*   Sincerely.
*   Thank you.
*   Sincerely yours.
*   With appreciation.
*   With gratitude.
*   Yours sincerely.
*   All my best.
*   Warmest wishes.
*   Warmest regards.

Within all email written communication you have a number of choices to make. Considered thought on these is needed to ensure the writing conveys the correct intent and motivation. Around this, you also need to consider the email address you send from and the title of the email.

By discussing email use in personal and academic contexts guidance has been offered in the ways in which you can alter the communication appropriately. Use Part 3, Chapter 15 and Part 4 to consider academic and professional written communication in more depth.

Now moving to digital communication, social media is considered an integrated daily form of communication. Whether you use WeChat, WhatsApp, Facebook/FB Messenger, Twitter or Instagram, you will most likely use digital communication in your daily routines. Unlike written emails, you may find that this content uses far more informal language (see Figures 11.1 and 11.2).

Figures 11.1 and 11.2 clarify how abbreviation and acronyms can be used in text message written communication. The reason for this is that it reduces the number of characters used. The first example uses 13 characters and the second has 26. Some social media platforms limit the number of characters that can be used and so this is a common form of written communication, not because of informality but due to the lack of letters available. What is interesting in the example is how some people choose to use words like wuz instead of was

Figure 11.1 Text speak

Figure 11.2 Text speak translated

when this has the same number of letters. Here, it can inform regional differences in pronouncing a word. Similar to email written communication you need to consider where and how to use this form of language and whether it is appropriate for the platform and person you are communicating to. The second example is evidently clearer to understand, but social media restrictions (like Twitter for example) have led to more people communicating in the text speak style when writing.

THINK POINT 11.4 WRITING BY HAND

When was the last time you wrote something by hand?

When are you required to write by hand in your studies?

Do you use the same abbreviations and acronyms when you write by hand? Why?

Think Point 11.4 on writing by hand is offered to enable you to reflect on how this form is now less frequently used. If you are writing a sensitive or opinion-based account using digital communication and are unsure of how to write it, it is good practice to write it by hand first to see how you feel in communicating the written information. Would you hand write the same abbreviations and acronyms? If not, why not? Physical writing can often feel more personal and, therefore, this should be used in mind of your digital communication to enable reflection on what you want to communicate and how this may be perceived by others.

CASE STUDY 11.3 SOCIAL MEDIA COMMUNICATION ELEMENTS

Twitter is a social media platform used to communicate using written information. Twitter enables you to Tweet, Retweet, follow, search and hashtag in order to connect and communicate with others. To compose a Tweet you need to use the following process:

1.   Create a Twitter account.
2.   Sign in.
3.   Compose a Tweet using the compose button on the screen.
4.   Write your Tweet using less than 140 characters.
5.   Include photos if needed.
6.   Include a hashtag (#) so that others can find your communication in relevant areas of interest.
7.   Post it.

For more information see www.twitter.com.

Case Study 11.3 from Twitter clarifies how the words may be limited and include other communication elements like photos and hashtags. What is interesting here is that social media communication uses hashtags as a form of metadata tag to include your content in other streams of related content (subjectively decided by individual writers). However, the hashtag was originally used in information technology for coding and programming. It was not until 2007 that it was used to link communication content on social media platforms.

ACTIVITY 11.3 **THE INSTAGRAM CONTENT**

1. Create an account on Instagram.
2. Search for a THE business you have visited recently.
3. Review the posts from this business.
4. Consider the written and photo communication used.
5. Review the comments underneath each post.
6. How does this social media platform support their marketing and communications?
7. Is the communication formal or informal?
8. How does this compare to your friend's and family's use of Instagram?

Within social media written communication you must also consider the policies surrounding posting new content. Unlike verbal, non-verbal and hand written communication, social media is seen as public and therefore is limited in terms of what you are allowed to post. Privacy, violence and physical harm, harassment, intellectual property, adult material and distribution of personal information are all discussed in Table 11.5 to clarify appropriate behaviour in your online written communication.

Within email written communication, you may consider that only one other person will view this and therefore feel it is acceptable to share personal information or information relating to others. Caution is advised here as hackers are able to find email information and extract this to use and distribute without your consent. This is illegal on their behalf, but you can minimise and mitigate against it by adapting appropriate digital content behaviour.

From Table 11.5 there are some further issues to discuss. For example, if you want to post about your personal leisure holiday experience and have a picture of yourself in a swimsuit, is this considered adult material? If you want to share pictures of your new baby, is this considered a violation of your baby's privacy? There is a degree of subjectivity within consideration of posts on social media and this means that you also need reflexivity in considering what to post.

Table 11.5 Avoiding inappropriate digital content

Area	Appropriate content
Privacy	Posting information that refers to others (photos or by name) must have the consent of that other person. Even if you are in a social situation in which you think others will be happy with you sharing information, it is best practice to verbally ask them first.
Violence and physical harm	No content should portray or elude to the harm of others.
Harassment	No content on describing or identifying others as part of a group.
Intellectual property	If you learn of something from somewhere else, always check they are happy for you to share the information and site them as the source (see also Chapter 3).
Adult material	No content showing private body parts of yourself or other people.
Personal Information	If content informs any detail relating to someone's personal information (name, address, school etc.) this should not be posted.

ACTIVITY 11.4 REFLEXIVITY IN SOCIAL MEDIA POSTS

1. Identify one of your social media accounts to use for this activity.
2. Find a recent post you uploaded.
3. Read the post and answer the following questions:

   - How did you intend the post to be seen? Funny? Informative? Provocative?
   - If you printed and distributed this to your neighbours, what would they think?
   - If your parents saw this, what would they think?
   - If someone from another culture or religion read this would they be shocked or amused?
   - If your teacher saw this, what would they think?

4. Using your answers to these questions identify if you want to keep or remove this post.
5. How will you mediate future posts on social media in light of this activity?

Activity 11.4 on reflexivity in social media allows you to reflect on external opinions of your posts. If you are not considered in the content of your posts, you may distribute material that is not only unlawful but also offensive to others. Social media and email companies have the ability to remove these, but it is your individual responsibility to mediate appropriate content before clicking on send/post.

SUMMARY

1. To recognise different forms of communication.

Communication was outlined in both verbal and non-verbal forms. The language spoken and your language ability will affect your competence in communication. Knowledge of the three approaches to communication, verbal communication and non-verbal communication can be used to reflect on how you perceive information and are understood by others. Regional and individual differences in communication are always present and these are not only defined by the country in which you grew up in but also the experiences you have completed. Finally, personal and professional differences in communication were outlined in order for you to consider how these vary in THE contexts.

2. To appraise effective written and digital communication.

Digital written communication was discussed within the use of emails and social media posts. Etiquette in email writing was outlined to clarify how this is perceived by others and enables motivation for their response and reading of your letters. Abbreviations and acronyms were outlined to clarify usual forms of condensed digital communication used. Social media (like Facebook, Twitter and Instagram) were discussed alongside activities and case studies in order to increase your awareness of the public nature of these and the policies surrounding your public written communication.

Questions to support your learning and research

1. What is a lingua franca?
2. How do auxiliary verbs differ in American and British English?
3. What regional differences are known to affect verbal communication?
4. What is adumbration and how does this inform verbal communication?
5. How should you open an email written to a teacher?
6. What does ROFL stand for?
7. Why is privacy seen as violated on social media accounts consistently?
8. Which positions should you consider your written communication for social media from?
9. Can you be arrested for posting on social media?

Websites in support of your learning from this chapter

American and British Vocabulary www.englisch-hilfen.de/en/words/be-ae.htm

Bread vocabulary in Britain www.bbc.com/travel/story/20180717-why-the-uk-has-so-many-words-for-bread

Social Media Acronyms https://stylecaster.com/social-media-acronyms-abbreviations-what-they-mean/

Origins of the hashtag https://en.m.wikipedia.org/wiki/Hashtag

Part 3

Academic development strategies

Part 3 identifies academic development strategies and processes to support tourism, hospitality and events management students. Although the premise of this chapter could support a wide range of students I will offer specific examples for tourism, hospitality and events management students and link to the academic work they will be required to complete in industry. For example, group work is not only a usual assessment method for these students; it is a core component of their graduate work. Each of the sub-sections will therefore identify what students need to do in their studies and then link to graduate roles in the leisure sectors.

Chapter 12
Goals and targets

LEARNING OBJECTIVES

1. To understand research approaches and philosophies in order to ascertain the difference between knowledge and reality in setting and managing goals and targets.
2. To outline important areas to set goals and targets for academic development.
3. To evaluate and create strategies for meeting academic goals and targets.

INTRODUCTION

This chapter offers support for Part 2 of your skills journey (see Part 2, Chapter 6) but also requires awareness of your own learning style (see Part 2, Chapter 10). Academic development is naturally linked to goals and targets as you will be required to submit work and complete research to a deadline. A goal is seen here as the desired result from completion of work. A target is seen as an objective to aim towards the intended goal. The levels of performance are seen from the marks or grades established on your work. Grades are often an outcome of effective time management (Part 2, Chapter 9) but also from a determination and drive to reach set goals and targets. In order to understand the importance of goals and targets, this chapter will firstly align these to research philosophies. Understanding research philosophies will enable you to identify different positions from which to establish realistic goals and targets. The types of academic goals and targets are then outlined in order for you to evaluate your current and desired success in academic practice (including personal elements present in academic experience). Finally, strategies are outlined for you to meet the goals and targets you have set.

FRAMING YOUR GOALS AND TARGETS THROUGH RESEARCH APPROACHES AND PHILOSOPHIES

In order to create appropriate goals and targets you need awareness of what is required, what is feasible and the level to which you need to perform. Earlier chapters in the book support self-reflection for goals and targets in the following areas:

- Self-awareness: being reflective, reflexive and accountable for your own decisions and positions.
- Time management: using time effectively in task management.
- Learning approaches: how learning is usually completed.
- Learning styles: how you learn best in different contexts.

It is important to complete learning and activities from these chapters as they offer a foundation from which to appraise and develop goals and targets for your academic development.

Ontology: what is real?
Epistemology: what is knowable?
Axiology: what is good?

Research approaches are discussed here as they are a key component of developing researcher competence. Epistemology, ontology and axiology are firstly outlined to clarify the way in which you might perceive knowledge and truth. Being realistic in your goals and targets is essential and considering these approaches will also lead to enhanced awareness of how theory and knowledge are accepted and critiqued.

Epistemology

Epistemology is seen as '*how one aligns oneself*' in relation to research being completed (Cohen et al., 2009: p.7). Scott and Usher (1996) further clarify that epistemology enables a researcher to distinguish between knowledge and non-knowledge based on objective or subjective approaches to a study. Epistemology is, therefore, seen as the way in which you make assumptions about knowledge. For example, if you read a newspaper article, what assumptions do you make about the knowledge or information offered? Do you accept this as fact and truth or are you wary of the potential bias and unreliable sources supporting it? Within epistemology you need to consider the materials (books, verbal communication, pictures) and opinions made (by you) on the theory in order to evidence rigorous consideration of knowledge gained.

ACTIVITY 12.1 EPISTEMOLOGY FOR ACADEMIC ASSIGNMENTS

1. Find a recent piece of work submitted for your studies.
2. Review the reference list and classify the sources in the following ways:

    a. Websites.
    b. Journal articles.
    c. Books.

d. Newspapers.

e. Company policy or documentation.

3. From the content written, note the 'facts' taken from these sources and placed in your work. For example, if you stated that THE organisations require staff training, did you offer a reference and confirm this as a fact?

4. Did you offer any counter arguments to the 'facts' offered? If so, where were these from?

5. Can you offer other positions to these 'facts' based on your own experience and knowledge about reality?

Ontology

Your ontology is the way in which you make assumptions about reality. Activities to enable reflection on your own bias and subjectivity were offered in Part 2, Chapter 7 on self-awareness. Being aware of your ontology is important as it will enable you to critique your judgements made for a topic. For example, you may think that it is universally accepted that if you eat lots of ice-creams you will become obese. A more reflective thought on this would be that ice-cream eating within a healthy diet with regular exercise will not make you obese.

THINK POINT 12.1 ONTOLOGICALLY THINKING

What negative associations do you have when being asked to complete an academic assignment? What 'truths' have you accepted about your ability to manage goals and targets for academic work? Are these correct?

Axiology

Axiology is your ability to understand other people's perceptions and opinions on a subject. This is important for reflexivity (noted in self-awareness in Part 2, Chapter 7) but most importantly for gathering information in order to write your academic assignments. Managing contradictory information on a subject you feel competent within is a skill. Being able to manage and reflect on this will enable you to consider alternative ways of seeing and doing things.

Figure 12.1 clarifies that your epistemology, ontology and axiology are linked. Within each decision you make, you will use these three approaches to choose a course of action or

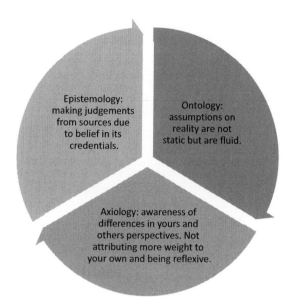

Figure 12.1 Epistemology, ontology and axiology

behaviour. What is important within acknowledging their existence is how you define and accept knowledge as truth. Do you accept all information as definite? Do you criticise others opinions? Do you make sound judgements on information? Our judgements and decisions are not separate from our emotions and contexts either. In this way your epistemology, ontology and axiology will vary dependent on other internal and external factors. To clarify the use and link between these research approaches and your goal and target setting, Table 12.1 has been created.

Table 12.1 How epistemology, ontology and axiology affect your approach to goals and targets

Epistemology	Ontology	Axiology
Using a range of sources to understand how to create goals and targets. Ensuring our subjectivity is justified from different 'facts' supported from different and appropriate sources.	Being able to perceive different ways to complete work and achieve targets. Identifying the reasons for differences perceived and where we sit and feel comfortable in our behaviour and actions for goals and targets.	Ignorance of other ways to work towards goals and targets due to a self-belief that your way is best and theirs does not work.

Although epistemology, ontology and axiology are research approaches they have been aligned to ways of managing or seeing goals and targets. This clarifies that your position or approach to goals and targets will also affect your ability to complete these in effective and efficient ways.

ACTIVITY 12.2 **YOUR APPROACH TO ACADEMIC WORK**

Use the following statements and allocate a number for each showing your strength of agreement (1 being strongly agree and 5 being strongly disagree).

1. I am aware of my learning style and that it differs to others'.
2. When completing tasks I consider a range of ways to complete it.
3. I need to gather information from a range of sources to understand something.
4. I do not care how others work as I am focussed on my own development.
5. My own opinions often override my ability to understand other people's points of view.
6. I often go to Wikipedia to understand something.
7. Once something makes sense to me I believe it is fact and true.
8. Classifying or grouping information and knowledge is the best way to learn.
9. I work best in a library around other students.

These statements were created in mind of the research approaches discussed. Statements aligned are noted as follows:

Epistemology: 3 (6, 7)
Ontology: 2 (8, 9)
Axiology: 1, (4, 5)

The statements in brackets are seen to be poor evidence of these. For example, if you note a number lower than 3 for statements 4–9 you can use this and interrogate your ability to reflect on alternative and wider positions to your usual behaviour.

Your epistemology, ontology and axiology are accepted as approaches to research that can represent your own approach to knowledge and reality. How you accept and investigate information as knowledge will determine your ability to be critical and aware of alternative perspectives (including your own). Saunders et al.'s (2009) research onion can be used to identify how these approaches fit the stages of researcher development (see Figure 12.2).

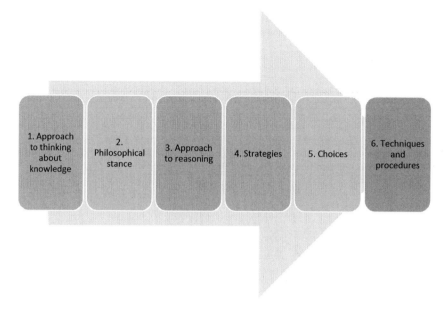

Figure 12.2 Research onion layers
Source: based on Saunders et al., 2009

The first stage in the research onion layers notes how your approach to thinking about knowledge (epistemology, ontology and axiology) will inform the following five stages in the onion. Inclusion of this is important in academic development as you need awareness of how knowledge is accepted as truth or compared and criticised from internal and external positions. In order to appraise these layers, the philosophical stance will now be discussed in support of your academic development. The latter layers of the onion are covered in Chapters 14 and 15 of this part to clarify how these differ in academic work.

PHILOSOPHICAL STANCES

Positivism

The Vienna Circle (see Maddy, 2007; Stadler, 2018) are seen as the founders to this philosophical position. The aim of this position is to offer information without human interpretation or bias. The use of the word 'posit' is important in this stance as it denotes how a researcher is positioned and offers knowledge from this. An epistemology using positivism would be where you use observable and measurable facts as a basis of knowledge. Government statistics on labour markets would be an example of how you develop knowledge using an epistemological approach with a positivist stance. An ontology using positivism would see one specific reality and process information as ordered elements within this one reality. The labour market statistics would be seen as the only measure from which to understand the economic standing for employment within a country. An axiology using positivism would be where a researcher has independence from the information and is objective and logical in offering the information. Removing any personal opinion or judgements on information is crucial in offering a positivistic stance with an axiology approach.

CASE STUDY 12.1 POSITIVISM IN ACADEMIC WORK

Amal is a second year student studying events and festival management. Within his course he needs to write an assignment on labour markets supporting festival growth in Sweden. He needs to offer economic statistics to justify how festivals are supported within areas of the country. The following outlines how positivism is seen in his creation of this assignment:

- Government statistics are seen as complete and representative of the country.
- He accepts the information portrayed for employment, GDP and industry as being the only way to measure economic support.
- As he does not know people living in Sweden he has no personal opinion or bias on the statistics presented and, therefore, has no judgement on how this is realised within communities.
- Without knowledge on Sweden's political and cultural history he is able to take the information and use it as detached from preceding events.
- As the assignment asks him to look at festival development in Sweden he feels that Sweden needs more festivals.

These examples outline how Amal has a positivism philosophy to the assignment task. Personal judgement and opinion on this task is absent and therefore leads to a universalist approach to writing knowledge for the assignment.

On obtaining his feedback from the submission, his teacher has noted that the work lacked critical awareness and critical reflection. This is due to him not commenting on the wider issues present in this research. Other areas the teacher wants him to consider in the future include:

- The history of Sweden.
- Current festivals in Sweden.
- Neighbouring countries and how they support festivals.
- The internal culture and usual creation of festivals.
- Personal opinions from the society on employment and GDP.
- How other THE businesses operate and perceive festivals.
- What the public understand to be a successful festival and the benefits they perceive from them.

This feedback for Amal's work clarifies that positivism has only allowed him to offer one position to the task. It is unbiased as he uses published information but lacks awareness of a range of positions.

Critical realism

Critical realism is seen in how we explain things. The experiences you have will lead to you constructing and shaping reality according to observable events. Fleetwood (2005) noted that ontology is crucial here as you need a structured judgement on reality. Layers, objectivity and causal relations are also important here in order for you to clarify and explain your position (Roberts et al., 2006). An epistemology using critical realism would accept that knowledge is based on events in time and that 'facts' are socially constructed. An ontology using critical realism would accept things happening as being real and attribute a cause to these things in how the world works. An axiology using critical realism would advocate for bias due to the knowledge that world views exist and are emergent and fluid. This philosophy not only accepts personal judgement and bias, it requires it in order to offer perspectives on how the world is seen.

THINK POINT 12.2 ARE YOU A CRITICAL REALIST IN CLASS?

When attending classes do you compare the information discussed on your own understanding and experiences? If not, why not? Do you offer counter points to knowledge discussed and outline different ways of viewing something with your experience as a source? If you do this, how does it aid others knowledge development?

Objectivism

Rand (2008) is seen as the originator of objectivism and her work (originally published in the 1950s) clarified how being selfish in your approach to tasks is beneficial and appropriate. Within this philosophy there are four pillars to objectivism:

1. Reality: accepting reality through self-awareness will enable people to work to appropriate goals and targets.
2. Reason: using logical thinking and avoiding making decisions based on your emotions.
3. Self-interest: a founding principle for objectivism is that you follow reason motivated by self-interest and self-esteem.

4.   Capitalism: as this philosophy requires selfish action based on individual realities it is also important that this be present within a capitalist society – one which allows for individual freedom from government control.

An epistemology using objectivism would accept all knowledge from your senses but reject religion of mysticism due to it being seen as illegitimate. If you see someone looking accomplished and proud, you may associate them as being effective and good at their job. This would in turn make you consider adopting similar traits in order for you to appear likewise. Critical realism can explain the ontology of objectivism as it requires you to be real and definite about what reality is and is not. An axiology of objectivism would require you to identify the values placed on the knowledge and link these to the four pillars.

Interpretivism

Researchers using an interpretivist paradigm emphasize human interaction with phenomena in their daily lives.

(Egbert and Sanden, 2014: p.34)

As noted by Egbert and Sanden (2013) interpretivism involves a researcher interacting and understanding humans in their daily lives. This means that the researcher is not simply separate from the foci of research but may be known or present in the research gathering process. Interpretivism involves thick description of the data and the research often analyses information from their *'compatriots'* (Geertz, 1973: p.9). One of the founding writers on interpretivism, Geertz (1973), identified that research participants need high levels of trust in the researcher in order to offer honest accounts of their daily lives. An epistemology using an interpretivism philosophy would create stories and new ways of seeing the world. For example, Firth's (2020) textbook uses staff narratives on customer service encounters in order to create new perspectives on theory relating to service contexts in THE. An ontology

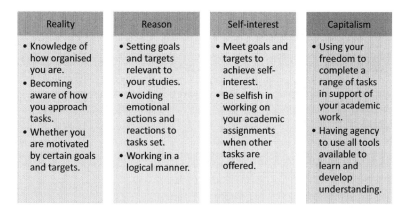

Figure 12.3 The four pillars of objectivism linked to goals and targets
Source: based on Rand, 2008; Ayn, 2019

using interpretivism would offer multiple values and meanings from a range of experiences. Your ability to communicate would be an example of this as you adapt and alter your communication style and behaviour based on a variety of experiences and positions. An axiology using interpretivism would include the researcher and, therefore, the associated values are inclusive of the person developing knowledge.

Postmodernism

Postmodernism is whereby information is interpreted but more attention is given to the language offered. Fluctuations, forms and types of language are seen as fluid and so this research philosophy tends to disregard objectivity. The world is seen via the langue offered in it, rather than how it is seen and accepted. Postmodernists (such as Derrida 1973, 1982; Foucault, 1972) deconstruct language and analyse the silences and pauses to understand and challenge current knowledge. An epistemology using post modernism would consider power and truth within language. For example, when discussing theory in class, your colleagues (class mates) will have preconceived knowledge on what is important in this discussion. A post modernist epistemology would be one that challenges any perceived dominant views. An ontology using post modernism would clarify that the classroom situation is socially constructed wherein some people are silent and some people dominate. This post modern ontology example, in a classroom, clarifies how social structures enable reality and dominant positions to form. Challenging this by examining the silences and quieting the dominating voices will allow the nature of this reality to be challenged. An axiology using post modernism would be whereby the researcher is present within the people and context being researched (similar to interpretivism). In the classroom example, the axiology is clear in who is silent and who contributes. The silent participants show power dynamics in the situation and the researcher should try to understand the silence and ascertain what this means in the creation of the situation and knowledge developed. If the silent people in class contributed, how would this change your understanding of the theory in discussion?

ACTIVITY 12.3 PRAGMATISM IN YOUR CLASSROOM

Using one of your classes where discussion in small or large groups occurs, complete the following:

1. Make a note of who contributes in verbal communication. Is it the same people each time?
2. Who remains silent? How do they look during the activity?
3. Make a note of the discussion and what was discussed and agreed on the theory.

4. After class, approach some of the people who you noted were silent and ask them their opinion on the discussion.
5. Do the 'silent' people have strong opinions on the information discussed? How would this have changed the discussion?

Pragmatism

This philosophy accepts that all action and behaviour is the outcome of concepts and knowledge. Dewey (1938) clarifies this in education contexts by noting that students need to interact and act in order to learn and change. An epistemology using pragmatism would see knowledge in specific working or practical situations. For example, if you learn about the operations in a restaurant kitchen and then apply this knowledge whilst completing work in a kitchen, the knowledge is tested via action and not memory recall. The ontology for pragmatism is multidimensional and reality is seen as external, complicated and action as a consequence of knowledge learnt. In the kitchen example, you would be able to try out and complete a range of duties in a working situation. Learning as you try, evaluating success and adapting new techniques are elements of this philosophy. An axiology using pragmatism requires reflexivity in considering the positions present. In the kitchen example, you have your own values in trying and changing your action, but this is within an environment where others and management have also applied their own values. Reflecting on these multiple positions is important to see where knowledge is taken and accepted through action.

THINK POINT 12.3 PRAGMATISM AND WORK-BASED LEARNING

From learning about the research philosophy pragmatism, and prior consideration in Part 2 on work-based learning, how are these two seen as linked? Does work based learning allow for full reflection on the ways in which information is seen and understood now that you have been reviewing other research approaches and philosophies?

TYPES OF ACADEMIC GOALS AND TARGETS

From the discussion of research approaches and research philosophies you will have considered differences in how reality is seen and researched. These are important for academic study and research and also a useful tool from which to understand your usual approach to goals and targets. Are you focussed on gaining a high mark or how your knowledge aids your actions outside of class? Do you use your learning to support part-time work or in your thinking critically for written assessment?

Before we move on to consider the types of academic goals and targets it is important to consider what you feel being 'successful' in academia is. When you first start at university or college it can feel like you are the only person that is unsure, and feels pressure and stress at the new situations presented for you. Even if you are excited and confident at starting your course (or returning after a summer break) all students will have a degree of apprehension. This apprehension will be due to your associations with academic life and what is required of you in the coming years.

ACTIVITY 12.4 YOUR APPROACH TO STUDIES: BEING SUCCESSFUL

Epistemology – which knowledge is seen as acceptable?

Ontology – what is seen as reality?

Axiology – how values affect your understanding of reality.

Using epistemology, ontology and axiology (discussed earlier in this chapter) answer the following questions:

E – What do you think university or college is for?
O – Which is more important for your studies: knowledge or skills?
A – Why have you chosen to study in that institution?
E – Do you accept information in class as truth and concrete or seek alternative per-spectives from classmates or textbooks?
O – Did you attend an open day for your course? Did this reflect the reality of study-ing on the programme? How different do you now perceive it?
A – How have your family informed your understanding of studying at a higher level? Has this affected your values and expectations?

Activity 12.4 enables you to consider your positions in coming to study THE and how epistemology, ontology and axiology are present in how you accept reality. The following also impacts the ways in which you perceive and feel pressure in academic contexts:

1. Family participation or financial support: if you have been informed of how university/college life will be by family members, then this will impact your understanding of what you are required to do and how you are to develop. If family have sponsored or funded

your academic studies, this will influence your perception of success as their requirements may be placed above your own.

2. Prior experience in education: in previous education you may have been required to
    complete exams at the end of the year and worked to achieve over 90% on all submis-
    sions. This will mean that you enter higher education with a similar expectation. If you
    attribute success as obtaining over 90% this will not sit comfortably if the marking or
    grading is shifted (to Grade Point Averages or degree classifications). This shift requires
    consideration so that you are reflective in what success in marks looks like in higher
    studies.

3. Friend's accounts of higher education: friends who have already completed higher
    education may have informed you of what is expected and needed. If they studied
    a different subject then they may mis inform you of the requirements for your
    course. For example, medical students often have lab time and work based learn-
    ing and therefore have high contact hours in a week of study. Comparatively, Eng-
    lish literature students may only need to attend four hours of class. The variance
    in expected (prior) versus perceived (actual) standards of education will naturally
    affect the pressure and demands felt in education.

4. Media and digital content depicting studies: how the media portrays being a university/
    college student will inform your understanding of how you should or should not
    behave. Whether this is studying for ten hours a day or partying every night, these per-
    ceptions will affect your self-confidence as a student.

5. Your motivation for studying: your own motivation (covered in Chapter 17 of this part)
    is crucial to understanding your success. if your motivation is based on a need to suc-
    ceed and gain high marks, this will affect the type of goals and targets you work to. If
    you are not motivated to study or learn, it will be futile to set academic goals and tar-
    gets unless you have non-academic rewards as outcomes.

6. Your perception of success in and from academia: if you are interested in doing the
    best you can then your goals will be linked to academic outcomes in marks. However,
    if you are competitive, you may associate success as doing better than your class-
    mates (regardless of the specific mark achieved). Your motivation to study could be to
    gain a managerial employment position and if this requires a specific level of academic
    achievment, this will also alter your perception of success.

The activity and discussion on your perceptions of success in your studies are a useful
starting point to reflecting on why you are completing the course and what you want to
achieve from it. Acknowledgement of what success in academia means to you will enable
you to outline the desired outcomes from your studies also. It is also accepted that there is
no 'perfect' student. Students who do their best, work to the best of their abilities, whilst
attending and communicating their learning needs are the basis of an excellent student.
How you engage and develop your knowledge and ability is entirely in your own agency.

Table 12.2 clarifies a few common outcomes from completing academic studies. This
list is incomplete and not all encompassing, but it allows clarification on the range of
outcomes from academic study. In THE, the professional outcomes are numerous. If

Table 12.2 Academic, personal and professional outcomes from academic study

Academic	Personal	Professional
Increased knowledge.	Increased personal relationships and networks.	Increased ability to apply for roles.
Ability to consider information from a range of positions.	Intercultural ability enhanced due to working with people of different nationalities and individual home towns.	Increased ability to complete tasks due to knowledge developed.
Ability to investigate and research to improve knowledge and operations of something.	Increased income (if family offer money in reward for work completed).	Academic approaches used will enable a reflexive and reflective approach to employment and management.

Figure 12.4 Understanding your perception of success: GROCERS

you are able to work or apply your knowledge and test this in working environments, within your course, you will reap significant professional rewards upon graduation. In order to appraise your own success, use the areas given in Figure 12.4, which create the mnemonic GROCERS. A grocer is a person who sells food and so was created with a hospitality field in mind!

Being **gentle** is whereby you need to accept the pressure and stress you put on yourself when considering success. Success is not static in everyone and therefore you will have varying success in a range of activities and courses.

Being **realistic** within the goals and targets created (covered in the later part of this chapter) will ensure you are able to complete the work in an appropriate and effective manner.

Being **objective** requires you to consider success without personal feeling or opinion. Reading feedback from tutors objectively will allow you to identify ways to improve without associating it with feelings of failure.

Being **clear** about what success you want to achieve by setting specific goals and targets will enable academic improvement.

Being **enthusiastic** about your success and working towards goals and targets will aid your motivation and ability to complete the work to set standards.

Being **reflexive** enables you to consider success from different positions. Whether this is success in completing tasks set, or achieving outcomes from successful work, you should reflect on how others establish the same success or attribute it differently.

Being **selfish** in owning and determining success to your own standards is important in showing self-efficacy and self-determination.

Being selfish has been considered within Rand's work on the philosophy of objectivism. This is important for establishing your own idea of success as this will be unique and individual to you:

- Follow reason, not whims or faith.
- Work hard to achieve a life of purpose and productiveness.
- Earn genuine self-esteem.
- Pursue your own happiness as your highest moral aim.
- Prosper by treating others as individuals, trading value for value.

(Ayn Rand Website, 2019)

This quotation clarifies how being selfish is seen as a component of self-development. Using selfishness in establishing your understanding of success for academic work will ensure you are satisfied with your work in your own terms. Being selfish does not mean you can ignore the requirements of your teachers, employers and relations. It can be the position from which you establish goals and targets to fit your own perception of success and meet your own individual goals in support of these people.

THINK POINT 12.4 USING GROCERS TO ESTABLISH YOUR VERSION OF SUCCESS

Consider each of the elements within GROCERS and identify if these are usually present in tasks you complete for your studies. How can these aid your understanding of your own perceived success? Are any missing or difficult to incorporate? How can you include these in the future?

From identifying what success might be for you and the outcomes perceived from completing academic work, we will now consider which short- and long-term goals you need to achieve this success. As noted in the introduction to this chapter, a goal is seen here as the desired result from completion of work. A target is seen as an objective to aim towards the intended goal. Table 12.3 identifies examples of short- and long-term goals and targets for academic development.

The goals and targets suggested in Tables 12.3 and 12.4 can be used in your own planning for academic success. However, if you already attend all timetabled sessions, a goal on attendance would not improve your ability further. Areas in which to create goals and targets in support of your academic development are listed as follows:

- Reading.
- Writing.
- Knowledge.
- Skills.
- Attendance.
- Engagement or Activity.
- Research.

Table 12.3 Academic goals: short- and long-term

Short term	Long term
Achieving a specific grade in a submitted assignment.	Achieving a degree result which is seen as a success.
Using a skill learnt in different situations.	Using a skill to evidence academic ability and employability for a role.
Acquiring knowledge.	An ability to express information on a topic or theory succinctly.

Table 12.4 Academic targets: short- and long-term

Short term	Long term
Attending all scheduled classes in a week.	Obtaining at least 90% attendance in a term.
Obtaining work experience in a local café or bar.	Ability to show experience to complete managerial duties in a café or bar (through skills appraisal).
Write 500 words on assignment in a day.	Finish assignment 5 days before submission to enable time to proof read and edit.

The seven areas listed can all be used to establish goals and targets for your academic development. Use the strategies suggested in the next chapter to create and manage these.

ACTIVITY 12.5 **SKILLS APPRAISAL FOR GOALS AND TARGETS**

Using the skills appraisal from Part 2, Chapter 6, identify skills which you have no evidence for and create goals and targets for these.

STRATEGIES FOR MEETING GOALS AND TARGETS

Now to consider the strategies to use in support of academic goals and targets: PDP and SMART will be discussed. PDP refers to professional development planning and SMART refers to specific, measurable, achievable, realistic and timely. PDP can be used for academic goals and SMART for your academic targets.

Professional development planning requires you to set goals and review and evaluate them at key time points. These are often used in employment in yearly appraisal meetings whereby your direct line manager considers the goals set and whether you achieved these.

CASE STUDY 12.2 **NYKYTA'S ACADEMIC PDP**

At the start of their second year of a tourism management degree, Nykyta sets himself the following goals for the year:

Reading
To spend at least 10 hours per week finding and reading academic publications.
Writing
To write at least 500 words per day (using five working days per week).
Knowledge
To have developed knowledge on topic areas covered in class and supplemented this with reading completed each week.
Skills
To evidence the use of skills in academic and professional contexts.
Attendance
To attend 90% of timetabled classes.
Engagement or Activity
To contribute towards the local sports team in at least four matches.
To set up and run a reading group with students in my seminar group.

Research

To use my research skills and develop further expertise researching environmentally sustainable tourism businesses.

Nykyta notes these goals and then sets dates for when he will evaluate his efforts in these areas. He plans to review these at the end of each term and then at the beginning of the next year.

Case Study 12.2 clarifies how PDP offers an example of how you can set goals and use these to evaluate your academic development. The key to effective PDPs is to reflect on your progress at set points. Nykyta plans to evaluate his progress at the end of each term, however, if you set a PDP it is important to review and reassess your goals if you are not meeting them within the time scales noted. For example, if Nykyta notes he cannot read for ten hours per week, this goal should be amended before evaluation at the end of term. Addressing areas where goals are not fully met during your studies is crucial for academic development. If you carry on and ignore issues in meeting these as the weeks go by, you will not achieve the goals set and this could be detrimental to your level of work and motivation to study.

THINK POINT 12.5 IGNORING ARISING ISSUES WITHIN ACADEMIC GOALS SET

Issues that may arise around the academic goals you create are varied. Part-time work, personal relationships, family duties, social clubs and sports participation are some examples of areas that can conflict with your ability to meet these goals. They may take your focus away from the work and use up time already set for academic tasks.

How do you usually manage these external demands? Do you give in at the mention of seeing friends, or do you manage your time effectively and stick to the planned action in support of your goal? Do you feel the goals were too labour intensive and need altering?

Think Point 12.5 is offered to enable reflection on how you will manage additional demands arising during completion of your goals. You may find you can complete the goals and have additional time remaining (in which case look to adjust your goals to complete more focussed work). The area of concern in managing a PDP is when you cannot complete your short-term goals in the set parameters. This requires you to manage your time (see Part 2, Chapter 9) and be reflexive of what you can achieve.

ACTIVITY 12.6 HOW DO YOU WORK?

Before writing own goals for a PDP, consider the following statements and think about how strongly you feel about them:

1. I will rush work to fit to a deadline rather than adjust the deadline to ensure work is to the correct standard.
2. I can prioritise my tasks and time to fit goals without too much stress or pressure felt.
3. I often set tasks and goals and then ignore them due to other demands around my studies.
4. I always finish my tasks before a deadline.
5. I am self-deprecating when it comes to academic work as I like to talk to class mates who have also missed personal goals in academic tasks set.
6. I do not like to talk about my academic success with class mates.
7. I praise others who complete academic work in a timely manner and seek advice from them.

Whilst considering these statements, think about other positions you tend to champion when completing academic work. What usual thoughts affect your actions for academic study? Are these supportive or detrimental? How can you alter these to fit and meet PDPs?

Within your PDP you will have set targets to meet. In addition to being flexible and reflexive you can use SMART to track your work. SMART was also used in Part 2, Chapter 6 within skills appraisal to clarify how you can develop each skill and evidence experience of your skills. Here, SMART is clarified for academic goals as:

S Specific – what task you will complete?
M Measureable – how much work will be completed?
A Achievable – does it fit in your ability and time frame?
R Realistic – how achievable the target is.
T Timely – where the work for the target fits within your current schedule.

For example, if you are a UK culinary arts student studying in your second year, your goal could be to achieve a 1st class degree. This goal is specific as it relates to competency gain, it is measurable as it has a level (1st class), it should be achievable as the person is already studying in their second year of a degree. Whether or not it is realistic and timely will depend on the student's individual ability and work ethos. Within this example the student would need knowledge of the degree and academic regulations within their course to set appropriate targets along the way. Some universities and colleges specify that your overall degree relates to second year and final year results. For example, your degree may use 75% or your final year and 25% of your second year results. If your final year marks are all 70% and your second year results are 45% with a weighted average of 75%/25% you would get an overall mark of 63.75% (2.1). However, some courses will say either weighted average OR best overall mark. In this case you can obtain a 1st with just your final year marks alone. So, be wary of stating this as a target without knowing your college/university regulations. This may not fit as a timely goal either. If there is a weighted average you may have already submitted assignments or completed parts that determine a future goal. Equally, the goal may be very near.

CASE STUDY 12.3 **MAKING A PDP SMART**

Referring back to the PDP goal example from Case Study 12.2, the following clarifies how Nykyta's research target can become SMART in support of a long-term academic goal:

Research
To use my research skills and develop further expertise researching environmentally sustainable tourism businesses.

Specific:
Acknowledgement of current research skills from prior experience and knowledge development is intimated here but not explicit. Reading, interviewing, surveying and critical analysis are all seen as crucial research skills. Completing work within this part will enable Nykyta to evaluate his researcher skill set.

Measurable:
The mention of 'environmentally sustainable tourism businesses' relates to a piece of work required within Nykyta's programme of study. The deadline and amount of work to complete for this can be used as a measuring tool. Using the marking criteria for the assignment is also a measurable area to use. For example, if the marking criteria states that he needs to gather primary research (see Chapter 16 of this part), this will be measurable in terms of type of method, number of participants and time taken to gather and analyse the data.

Achievable:
As a student in THE he will be both trained and expected to use research skills.

Realistic:
Reflecting on his current skill set and developing researcher competence will ensure this goal is realistic. It will not be realistic without supporting goals and attendance at timetabled sessions and extra curricular support in researcher skill development.

Timely:
This goal is timely as Nykyta is a THE student needing to complete research for a submission. The submission deadline will be appropriate within the range of topics being studied, but Nykyta will need to set personal deadlines to complete the research and edits on written work.

Using one of Nykyta's goals in Case Study 12.3, it is clear that these can be evaluated using SMART to ensure he is aware of the work he needs to complete in support of this. A goal does not need to be SMART in content, but the targets to complete in support of these do. A full and thorough appraisal of his skills, ability, schedule and work ethic (how he usually approaches academic work) is needed to meet these.

SUMMARY

1. To understand research approaches and philosophies in order to ascertain the difference between knowledge and reality in setting and managing goals and targets.

The research approaches of epistemology, ontology and axiology were defined in order to evidence how you approach knowledge and reality differs. Awareness of this approach is needed in order to clarify how you have accepted knowledge as fact and where you have critiqued this. The research philosophies of positivism, critical realism, interpretivism, objectivity, post-modernism and pragmatism were then defined to explore different approaches to processing and gathering knowledge. The approaches and philosophies were applied to actions and thoughts in academic development in order for you to understand and reflect on different ways of working and setting goals and targets.

2. To outline important areas to set goals and targets for academic development.

Through discussion of what success is and how this can be perceived, an outline of areas to establish goals and targets was offered. Using the mnemonic GROCERS you will be able to establish success in higher education by maintaining objectivity and ambition in your academic studies. Examples of goals and targets were noted for academic development and these can be created in seven areas of academic work.

3. To evaluate and create strategies for meeting academic goals and targets.

A professional development plan is noted as a useful tool to set goals in support of your academic development. Use this with class mates or other students you live with to clarify your goals for each term of study. Evaluating your progress in support of these is essential.

You need to be flexible and reflexive on how you are working towards them. SMART can be used to set targets in support of or in consideration of your longer-term goals. Creation and reflection on SMART targets will enable you to manage, organise and prioritise tasks in support of academic goals set.

Questions to support your learning and research

1. What is the research onion?
2. How is research philosophy evident in different research approaches?
3. Why is it ok to be selfish?
4. What is success in higher education?
5. What does GROCERS mean?
6. Is attendance suggested as a goal or target?
7. What does SMART stand for?
8. What is a PDP?

Chapter 13

Finding academic articles

LEARNING OBJECTIVES

----

1. To evaluate different forms of published material available in support of your studies.
2. To identify how to create themes and topics to discover linked or emergent knowledge.
3. To outline methods for searching for academic articles.
4. To apply search techniques in order to discover relevant articles for your studies.

INTRODUCTION

As a student on a tourism, hospitality or events management programme you will need to find academic articles. These are not simply given or available to you within the virtual learning areas of your units of study (topics). Further and wider reading is essential in academic study of THE as it enables you to develop and build on existing knowledge. Within research project work set in your studies, you will also be required to clarify the theoretical basis from which you probe and investigate current opinion from new participants. In this way, the published articles found are secondary existing material. This chapter will support your studies to enable you to appraise different forms of published literature available, clarify themes to use in your searches, and methods to narrow down your searches to find the most appropriate articles. From completing this chapter you will be able to create your own literature base from which to begin reading.

FORMS OF PUBLISHED ACADEMIC MATERIAL

As a student on a THE course, academic published material is at your fingertips. How you find this and whether it is appropriate for use in your assignments is what will be considered in this chapter. Not all literature is equal and the location and form of literature used will evidence your standard of academic work. Academic sources are noted as being either primary or secondary. These are critiqued in Chapter 16 of this part, but it is important to accept that academic articles published and available are seen as secondary sources. They are secondary as they have already been researched and published using existing literature and data analysis. Primary is whereby you offer your own conclusions from research completed yourself (this can be using either existing secondary data or gathering new primary data).

Primary – gathered by you, new comment and opinion on a topic. Requires surveys, interviews or other methods of data collection. Questions put to participants are based on secondary sources where your knowledge is developed from existing published academic material.

Secondary – existing published material. Either used for a literature review in support of an essay on a topic or used as a data source to draw new comparisons and connections (making it primary data).

CASE STUDY 13.1 SECONDARY MATERIAL USE IN AN ESSAY ON EMPLOYMENT RIGHTS FOR VOLUNTEERS AT A MUSIC FESTIVAL

Sophie has been instructed to write an essay on the employment rights for volunteers at a music festival. In order to understand employment rights for volunteers in music festivals she researches the following information:

- Laws, statutes and legislation on employment, including all forms of staff (employee, temporary and volunteer).
- Books and journal articles on volunteers at music festivals.

Sophie uses the above forms of existing literature to inform and develop her knowledge on what is known and concluded about volunteers in music festivals. Outlining this is seen as secondary material as she is mapping out information already published and available to her.

However, within the assignment she wants to draw from other sources of information on volunteer rights to compare and contrast this with. As such, she also researches the following:

- Volunteer employment rights in other countries.
- How volunteers are used and managed in other industries related to events management (like recreation, tourism and hospitality).

Using these additional areas she will compare this information with existing literature available involving events.

Case Study 13.1 shows two levels to researching existing literature for an essay assignment:

1. Basis of knowledge supporting the specific topic area.
2. Wider comparative literature to map and compare against the specific focus of your assignment.

If Sophie decides to create or offer new positions on volunteer employment rights at festivals using this literature she is creating primary material. If she compares and contrasts existing material showing her perspectives and knowledge on the existing literature, she is critically examining secondary material. Being aware of which of these is expected within an assignment is important as it will affect the type of material you search for.

THINK POINT 13.1 WHAT WILL YOU USE THE PUBLISHED MATERIAL FOR?

When you are asked to prepare for an academic assignment you will need to search for published literature in support of developing your knowledge. What is your immediate motivation for this? Is it to learn as much as possible about a topic? Or is it to offer new perspectives on existing literature? What does the marking criteria require of you? Is it just critical discussion or evaluation and new models?

When starting your search for academic published material you need to consider what you have access to. Whether this be a physical library or online e-books and journals, you need to acknowledge the form of content you are able to access. This reflection needs to be completed in tandem with reflection on your learning style. If you are a kinaesthetic learner, you may prefer to use physical material to highlight and hold physically. Use Part 2, Chapter 11 to appraise your learning style to consider if you want to find physical or virtual sources.

Academic sources can be found physically or virtually. As a student on a THE course you will probably have access to a library located on campus. However, this library is not the only place to source physical academic texts (see Figure 13.1).

Figure 13.1 clarifies how academic material is located in physical and virtual locations. The library is always the preferred and recommended location in which to source your academic articles. This is due to the subscriptions your institution will have and will therefore enable you access to a larger body of literature. News sources are noted as these often refer to academic research completed in support of a story on a societal issue. Using newspaper sources comes with a warning: the writer is not writing it to inform you of an unbiased position, but from a position of intent for a story or narrative. Newspaper articles are not blind reviewed, like academic textbooks and journal articles. Caution is needed when reading academic references noted in these as they may not be a true representation of the research conclusions.

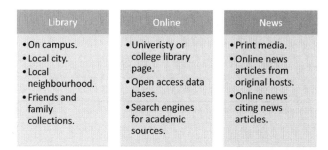

Library	Online	News
• On campus. • Local city. • Local neighbourhood. • Friends and family collections.	• Univeristy or college library page. • Open access data bases. • Search engines for academic sources.	• Print media. • Online news articles from original hosts. • Online news citing news articles.

Figure 13.1 Locations of academic published material

ACTIVITY 13.1 BUILD YOUR OWN LIBRARY

This is an activity where you can use your classmates, housemates and family.

1. How many books do you own related to the topic of your course?
2. Which textbooks do your classmates own?
3. Do your flatmates/housemates/family have books that can support your academic studies?

   a. Compile a list of the books you have access to from questions 1–3 above.
   b. Review your reading lists for your courses.
   c. Identify books missing from these and list them.
   d. Find them on second hand websites and note their prices.
   e. Agree to a budget with a group on your course.
   f. Allocate books to each other to purchase in support of your studies.
   g. Create an online library for your books (using www.lend-engine.com for example).
   h. Start borrowing and sharing books using the online library to track and use your network of books.

Textbooks in university of college libraries are accepted to be academic material. However, some may be opinion and positional, rather than research based. When you are reading textbooks and journal articles consider which of the following they are:

1. Written using research completed solely for the publication.
2. Written gathering information from a range of secondary sources (review of literature).
3. Discussion point to raise issues felt but currently lacking research support.
4. Reviews of other publications.

As a student on a THE course it is usual for you to focus on the first form of academic material: written work on research completed solely for the publication. This is not to say ignore all others as they are equally valid and useful forms of content, but a publication using research usually has a higher standard of academic validity. Before you look to create key themes to begin your searches, it is important to consider if the work you find is valid or trustworthy.

ACTIVITY 13.2 ESTABLISHING THE VALIDITY AND TRUSTWORTHINESS OF PUBLISHED LITERATURE

Is it valid?

The validity of an academic piece of literature can be established in the following ways:

1. What year was it published?
2. What year was the research completed in?
3. Where was the research completed?
4. What ethical considerations are noted in the research?
5. What limitations did the research have?
6. What funding was used to complete the research?
7. What objectives or research questions framed the research?
8. Does the topic of the research fit with the area in which I am interested in?
9. Do the authors use the same definition of the topic area as I do? If not, why and is this relevant?

Can I trust it?

The trustworthiness of an academic publication can be determined in the following ways:

1. Who is the author? Are they an academic at an established university or college? What qualifications and credentials do they have?
2. Who are the participants and are they related or linked to the author?
3. What motivations did the participants have for offering their data?
4. Were participants paid for participating?
5. Who is the original intended audience of the research and why did they want to know about this particular area?
6. Is the research approach and philosophy clear? How is this noted and accepted in the publication?

The questions raised in Activity 13.2 can be found in most academic publications. If you cannot find these details on the original source, the publishers should be able to clarify them for you. Any article which does not make these details explicit should be treated with caution and noted as potentially invalid or untrustworthy (see Chapter 15 on academic writing).

An initial glance at the authors affiliated institution, the year of publication and publishers will immediately inform you of the standard of work presented. For example, if the author is a business professional who wrote for the Adelaide Times in the 1970s it is unlikely the publication is relevant for your work on tourism sustainability practices in the 21st century in Pakistan, for example. This is not to say that it should be immediately excluded but that it should not be given as much weight as other academic publications evidencing valid and trustworthy content.

The final area to consider when looking for academic published material is whether it is reliable. This links to trustworthiness as it enables you to feel confident that knowledge from this research can safely inform your understanding of other similar issues. Here you need to consider what form of research methodology was completed and whether this enables a static or flexible understanding of an issue. For example, if you were to find published research that had surveyed every employee working in hospitality and it found that employees only liked to eat pizza for dinner, it would be a reliable assumption to state in your assignment (using a reference) that all hospitality employees like pizza for dinner. If the research is limited in methodology and participant size, you must treat the knowledge with care and not state this as definite truth (see Chapter 15 on writing this clearly).

THEMES AND KEY WORDS

Now that we have discussed where published academic material can be found and which sources can be seen as valid, trustworthy and reliable we can begin outlining strategies for formulating topics, themes and key words for your searches. In Part 1, Chapter 2, the following definition was offered on what tourism and tourists are:

Definition	Tourism is analysing what visitors do.
Characteristics	What tourists do and how they interact.
Themes in tourism	Travel to observe, learn, participate, relax, support and appreciate a local area.
Areas linked	Anthropology, economics, business management, history, sociology, leisure, recreation, geography, development studies, political science, international studies, architecture, urban studies, rural development, language and culture studies.
Active research	Since the 1990s research on tourism has been seen as a separate field of study.

The above definition can be used as a framework to begin clarifying key words and areas to start your search for published academic material. You can use the definition, characteristics, themes, areas and research dates to begin to list key words for your searches, however, this will lead to a large list of words which could be used. Case Study 13.2 from a tourism student will be used as an example to show how you can develop key words and narrow the focus of your work to enable clear themes and key words for searching with.

CASE STUDY 13.2 **KEY WORDS FOR AN ASSIGNMENT ON CONSUMER BEHAVIOUR**

Jonah has been instructed to write an assignment on consumer behaviour in Parisian tourists. He writes down the following key words for this topic area based on his completed studies so far:

Consumer
Behaviour
Paris
France
Europe
Tourism
Tourist

In addition, Jonah considers other key words that may be associated with the topic:

Consume
Holiday
Activity
Attitude
Leisure
Recreation
Customer
Service
Participation
Eating
Drinking

From completing a course on consumer behaviour, Jonah is particularly interested in younger tourist behaviour in and around historical sites. As such, he notes the following key words:

Youth
Young
Traveller
Gap year
Travel
Interest
Heritage
Historic

From considering one assignment and its associated key words, Jonah has 26 words from which to start searching for published material. Although this is too broad

> a position to start his searches from, it is an important step to begin your research as it allows you to outline the areas in which you naturally link and relate to an area of knowledge. Each assignment is unique to your knowledge and understanding of a topic and so listing words and key themes you associate with the topic will allow you to manage and focus your search criteria.

Case Study 13.2 clarifies how a student can easily end up with an abundance of key words from which to start searching for academic published material. This is an important first step, but needs situating within the process of writing academic work (see Figure 13.2).

Figure 13.2 clarifies the process within which key words are required for an academic assignment. Once you have clarified your keywords you can use these to search and find academic articles. Narrowing down your key words to clarify a focussed topic is an important step before you begin your searches. One way this can be completed is in the use of the forest metaphor. Using Jonah's case study, his forest would be the original topic area: Parisian tourists and consumer behaviour. Although there is a geographic location, area of the business and theoretical area noted here, it is still quite unfocussed (thus why it enabled 26 key words associated with it). To narrow this down further, Table 13.1 aligns Jonah's focussing to elements of a forest.

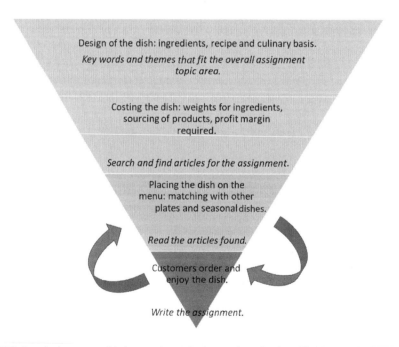

Figure 13.2 Developing a new dish for a restaurant: stages of academic writing

Table 13.1 Forest metaphor for focussing your topic area

Forest	Parisian tourists and consumer behaviour.
Tree	Young travellers in Paris and consumer behaviour.
Branch	Young travellers in Paris tourist experience affected by social media content viewed.
Leaf.	Could Instagram improve 18–21 year old tourist experiences of Museums in Paris? A critical analysis of current literature on youth travel linked to Instagram and consumer tourist behaviour.

Source: based on Buckler and Walliman, 2016

Using the forest metaphor, Table 13.1 clarifies how you can narrow down your focus for an assignment step by step. When using the forest metaphor and narrowing down your own topic area, ensure the following is explicit and focussed:

1. Geographic location (not the world or a continent – be specific).
2. Specific people, products or law.
3. Area of theory or knowledge.
4. Industry and business focus (even using one singular business on a road near where you are studying).

If the above four areas are explicit and clear then you will be able to create appropriate themes and key words in support of your search of the literature. The leaf noted in Table 13.2 is a clear and focussed topic for an assignment or research project as it specifies the age of customers, the location of the research, what action or behaviour is being investigated and what motivators affecting behaviour are to be researched.

After narrowing down your topic or title, use the branch content to clarify the themes. Still using the same example, the themes to address would be tourist experience, social media, traveller and young. These themes should be noted before you start searching as they are important links to be aware of in your searches. Use the leaf to outline the key words also (see Table 13.2).

Table 13.2 Themes and key words from the forest

Themes – branch	Key words – leaf
Social media Tourist experience Young Traveller	Instagram 18–21 year old Museum Paris Experience Tourist

By using the forest metaphor and narrowing down your topic title, you can reduce the number of themes and key words to use in the search. Continuing with this example from the case study, we have narrowed 26 key words down to four themes and six key words. These are clearer, more focussed and will enable efficient searches for academic literature.

METHODS FOR SEARCHING

Methods for searching are available in your campus library, your community library, online areas and printed news media (those which accurately reflect academic research). Within these locations there are a range of methods to use to complete the searches. Strategies for searching are noted in the next section, but here we will consider the methods and locations of the searches. From the previous section you should have created a clear title, themes and key words related to the literature search you want to complete. These are required for tasks in this section as they will inform the method and approach taken.

To begin, students often prefer to use the internet to search for publications and sources, however, this can often lead to the use of non-academic and biased content in your submission and knowledge development. To avoid this and aim for a higher standard of academic work, complete Activity 13.3.

ACTIVITY 13.3 MAKING A LIBRARIAN YOUR FRIEND

You will need access to the campus or local city library in order to complete this activity. It will require you to also use confidence, assertiveness and a natural curiosity for you to gain the most from it. These are all core employability skills for THE and you can also use this as an example for your skills appraisal completed in Part 2.

1. Go to your campus or local city library.
2. Find a member of staff (librarian) who is there to help and support visitors.
3. Inform the librarian of the work you are planning to complete (essay or assignment).
4. Clarify the title of the work and perhaps the key words.
5. Ask them for the following information:

    - What forms of material are offered in the library? (Books/journals etc.)
    - Which areas in the library can you find literature in support of your title and key words?
    - How can you search for sources located in the library and how do you then find them?
    - What workshops or classes does the library offer on sourcing and reading literature?
    - Are all sources in the library considered 'academic' and if not, why not and how can you learn to distinguish these?

6. Make a note of the librarians name and the information gained from the above questions.

On gaining access to your library and getting to know a librarian you have overcome a key barrier to literature searching. Friends on your course and tutors are not experts in finding literature – librarians are! Once you have met and talked to one of your librarians you can also ask for their email address or attend any classes and workshops they offer in support of your studies. This will not only improve your knowledge on methods for searching but will also widen your network of academics.

From completing Activity 13.3 you will have noted a range of sources and areas in the library to find literature. Make a note of these for future reference. The next step is to then use your course reading list. Refer to this and outline key texts on the reading list that you think will aid your assignment. The third method for sourcing literature is then using the internet.

Journals are publications that contain a number of small journal articles. The articles are usually around 5000 words long, are written by academic researchers and offer outcomes from work, which conclude new knowledge or alternative positions on current knowledge. These are used by academics to ensure their research is published and available to a wide range of readers. Journal articles are important as they may offer more up to date, contemporary research on a topic.

Figure 13.3 clarifies how a journal article is created. The blind reviewers are usually academic colleagues who have a similar interest or knowledge in the themes addressed in the submitted piece. Journals filled with articles are published 3–4 times a year and they remain within that publication without further editions, unlike

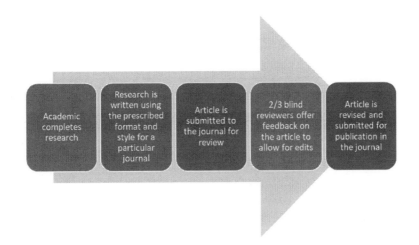

Figure 13.3 The process of journal article publishing

textbooks, which may have a number of revisions and future editions. Use Activity 13.4 to find journals that are relevant to your topic, themes and key words.

ACTIVITY 13.4 FINDING THE RIGHT JOURNAL

You will require a computer and internet access for this task.

1. Open your web browser on a search engine.
2. Search for Google Citation Metrics.
3. Open the page (which should look like the following):

≡ Top publications   🔍

Categories ▾   English ▾

Publication	h5-index	h5-median
1. Nature	362	542
2. The New England Journal of Medicine	358	602
3. Science	345	497
4. The Lancet	278	417
5. Chemical Society reviews	256	366
6. Cell	244	366
7. Nature Communications	240	318
8. Chemical Reviews	239	373
9. Journal of the American Chemical Society	236	309
10. Advanced Materials	235	336

4. Using the search button (a magnifying glass in the top right of the page) type in the themes for your assignment, one by one.

5. If you put in tourism as a key theme, a new list will appear ranking the top 20 publications. All of these are different journals.

6. Look at the H5 index and H5 median figures (see clarification on these after the activity).

7. List the journals you would like to search within (aim for 4/5) using the following table:

Journal Name	H5 Index	H5 Median	Years publishing	Theme linked
Tourism management	85*	135*	Vol 3 from 1982	Tourism

* accurate at the time of publication but likely to change.

The H5 index and H5 median score aligned to each journal will inform you of the citation level of articles published in the last five years. The higher the H5 index and H5 median, the better the journal is.

For those interested in how these are calculated and what they mean, the H5 index outlines how many citations (references) have been noted for the same number of published articles. For example, if the H5 index is 244, then 244 articles published in the last five years have received at least 244 citations. This shows that the journal has a high number of articles published in the last five years and that these articles are also highly cited (referenced), suggesting that other academics rate the publications highly. The H5 median figure represents the middle number of citations from articles in the journals publications over the last five years. For example, if a journal had published seven articles in the last five years and had the following citations from each (in descending order of citation): 25, 22, 19, 18, 10, 8, 5, the H5 median would be 18. Eighteen is the middle number when you order the citations on articles in descending form.

Journal citations and metrics are important for you to recognise that not all journals offer high quality research publications. By using the Google Citation Metrics to find journals, you will now have a list of these to search within. Although journals are an increasingly open source (freely available) there are still a number which require subscription. Therefore, before you finish your lists of journals to use, ask your librarian friend if you have access to these through your institution.

It is acknowledged that the H5 index and H5 median are one of a number of metrics you can use to establish the quality and citation ranking of a journal. Other areas you can note to clarify the journals success include cite score, impact factor, SCImago journal rank, Source Normalized Impact per Paper (SNIP) and five year impact factor (to name a few). The google metric scores of the H5 index and H5 median are offered in this textbook as they are clear figures to check for citation value on first glance. They are also visible when searching using Google Metric Citations across all journals published. If you were to search using a specific publishing house, like Elsevier for example, they would only show you journal titles that they publish.

The final area to ascertain literature for your academic work is then your community library (created from the activity earlier in this chapter). Review this and identify which textbooks you want to use for the piece of work.

From completing the tasks in this chapter you will now have a list of sources from which to search for content in support of your assignment. These are located in the following areas:

1. Library.
2. Reading list from course.
3. Online journals.
4. Community library.

SEARCH TECHNIQUES AND CHOOSING THE LITERATURE

Now that you have identified a theme, topic and key words, and have a list of sources to find information in support of your assignment, you can complete the searches to narrow down the linked content and pick the specific literature to use. Search techniques are clarified here for physical and online sources. When searching for information you need to use a cursory review of the material. Searching does not mean reading. If you start reading the content in detail, you may find you spend time reading the wrong sources (poor use of time). The techniques offered here are to support your shortlisting of sources for an academic assignment.

Searching in physical sources

Physical sources are textbooks, printed journals, news publications and anything which is on your current list that is tangible and physically printed. For textbooks, complete the following action:

1. Using your list of key words, look at the index pages of the textbooks on your list.
2. Identify the page numbers aligned to the key words.
3. Skim over these pages and make a decision as to whether the content is relevant to the focus of your assignment.
4. Compile your decisions using a table as exemplified by Table 13.3.

Table 13.3 Chapters of textbooks to use for your assignment

Author	Title	Year of publication	Keyword found	Page number	How important?
Heart, P.	Social Media in Tourism Management	2020	Instagram	114–117	Very – some notes on Instagram use by customers.

Using the processes and Table 13.3 will enable you to make effective notes on your decisions from searches completed in textbooks. It is important at this stage that you do not simply read everything, but use your time to reflect and consider the importance and relevance of every source.

THINK POINT 13.2 HOW MUCH DO YOU EXPECT TO KNOW?

In completing actions for search techniques in this chapter you will be starting to gauge the importance and relevance of the literature available to you. Do you expect to know everything about a topic? Do you expect to have read everything published on the topic? Can you access all content published in this area? Do you read in all languages which content may have been published?

Think Point 13.2 offers you time to reflect on your capability in knowing and reading all information published on your key words and themes. You are not expected to know everything about the topic area. You are expected to have completed a sufficient amount of reading to write an informed assignment. This is important when you are searching and narrowing down the literature to use. Your rejection or acceptance of the literature is also subjective and will differ to others. This again is accepted and appropriate.

Next, to printed journal articles and news media. With the ones you have listed, look at the key words, themes or topic areas listed. Do they match the focus of your topic? Are they written using academic work? How relevant are they to your area of enquiry? Academic journal articles often refer to these themes in their titles or key word chapters. For example, a journal article you find could have the following title and key words:

Title: How does TripAdvisor impact tourist behaviour in Dublin? An ethnography of the bars of Temple Bar.
Key words: Social Media, Consumer Behaviour, Hospitality, Tourism

Table 13.4 Physical journals and news media to read

Form	Author and title	Year of publication	Keyword/ theme found	How important?
Newspaper – New York Times	Phil Tragen, Instagram influencers supporting tourism economy in Bali	2019	Instagram and Tourist	Moderate – matches key words but may be biased in account.

By considering the title and key words of a journal article you can see how the branch themes (from the earlier case study example) might be listed as key words. When confirming you want to read these physical sources, use Table 13.4 to list your choices.

Again, in this example, your notes on how important the literature is will enable you to rank the literature found and align the appropriate time for reading and amount of power given to this in your assignment when writing up.

When you have compiled your tables for physical sources you are able to move on to the online sources. It is accepted that textbooks may be available online as well as in physical form and the same procedure should be followed to find content relating to the assignment topic.

Searching in online sources

Searching within online sources is a skill. It is not simply one search using one set of key word and themes and this section will outline techniques to use to aid your searching competence. Online searches will be outlined in the use of Boolean logic and then in minimising your search results using key criteria. As this requires online access, you will need to use a computer and internet access to complete these techniques.

Boolean logic originates from computer coding. It is a way of writing words and phrases in order to inform the computer or search engine that you require specific words and not others. We will use the same key words from Jonah's case study earlier in this part to evidence this:

- Instagram.
- 18–21 year old.
- Museum.
- Paris.
- Experience.
- Tourist.

As you were directed to use the themes to identify the textbooks and journals to search within, here it should be acknowledged that you need to use the key words to search within the larger publications.

CASE STUDY 13.3 USING BOOLEAN LOGIC TO SEARCH USING YOUR KEY WORDS

Phoebe is studying the same course as Jonah and has decided to use the same topic, themes and key words as him. They decide to complete their online searches in the library one afternoon together but use different search techniques. Using one of their listed journal articles, the *Journal of Destination Marketing and Management* (www.journals.elsevier.com/journal-of-destination-marketing-and-management) each use the following words and obtain the following results:

Jonah		Phoebe	
Search words	**Articles**	**Boolean search**	**Articles**
Instagram	14	Tourist and Paris	35
Museum	100	Tourist and Instagram	14
18–21	106	Tourist and Instagram and museum	3
Paris	36		
Experience	345		
Tourist	357		

By using the key words alone, Jonah has found 958 articles in one journal that could help him with the assignment. By using Boolean logic, Phoebe has narrowed down the search results to three articles which all refer to tourist and Instagram and museum. She did one further search using tourist and Instagram and museum and Paris, but this yielded no results.

Case Study 13.3, which compares Phoebe and Jonah's techniques for searching within an online journal, clarifies how Boolean logic will enable focussed results more quickly. Within three searches, Phoebe is able to note three articles that are likely to be relevant to her assignment.

Only one element of Boolean logic was used in the case study on Phoebe and Jonah's searching – another two words used in this form of logic are Or and Not. An example of how these can be used for this assignment is noted in Table 13.5.

Table 13.5 Boolean logic for Phoebe and Jonah's searches

And	Or	Not
Tourist and Paris	Paris or France	Paris not Europe
Tourist and Instagram	Museum or "Art exhibit"	Experience not product
Tourist and Instagram and museum	Tourist or visitor	Young not old

And, Or and Not can be used in your online searches to clarify the specific area you are interested in. Another technique noted in Table 13.5 is the use of double quotation marks. If you put " around two or more words, the search will only yield results where these words fall next to each other. If you type in art exhibit, the computer would show you results of every article with either or both words written anywhere within the document. By using "art exhibit" you are clarifying that you want results that refer to this as a key term and that the words remain next to each other.

Once you have searched within the online journals and ascertained a focussed smaller number of results, you can then narrow down in the following ways:

1. Date of publication – not older than five years.
2. Location of research – completed in Paris.
3. Form of research – empirical using primary data from tourists.
4. Form of publication – research paper.

You can usually narrow in these ways using the filters within each journal website. If this is not possible, it is possible to ascertain this by a quick scan of the abstract (discussed in the next chapter).

When you have found the articles and online sources to read, save each one as a PDF with a clear title and organise into appropriate folders. For example, it is best practice to save the article using the reference *Firth, 2019,* and follow this with a note on its content *skills in hospitality.* If you have themes within which you have searched for the key words, use the themes for folder names and save the relevant articles within these.

From completing searches of physical and online sources of academic literature you will have created lists of content, parts and folders of journal articles to read through. This is your literature base.

THINK POINT 13.3 HOW MANY SOURCES SHOULD I FIND?

One question often raised by students searching for academic literature to read and use in their assignment is 'How many sources should I find?' There is not an easy answer to this, but it is dependent on the time you have and the length of writing needed on the literature. If you are writing an assignment based on secondary literature and need to write 1000 words I would aim for around 15 sources in your initial search using your key terms. After this, the search using your key words may result in around 25 sources. These should be a mixture of textbooks, journal articles, physical and online sources of academic literature. The final number used in your submission will depend on the content and argument offered.

When completing your searches and saving academic sources you should also consider that the reference lists and references cited within the literature may also be useful sources to find. This is why the think point on how many sources to find is an important, but difficult question to answer. Using five sources for an assignment of 1000 words will be insufficient. However, if you start with five and use the reference lists for these five, you may end up with around 20 sources. The importance in searching is that you gain specific and focussed results on the relevant topic area you are interested in.

In summary of the discussion and activities in this chapter, a process for finding academic articles is clarified as shown in Figure 13.4.

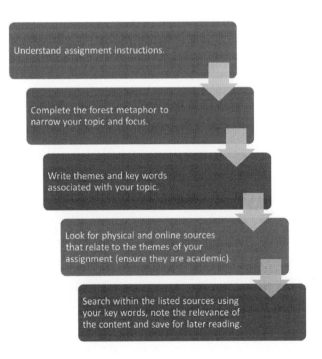

Figure 13.4 A process for finding academic articles

SUMMARY

1. To evaluate different forms of published material available in support of your studies.

Not all forms of literature are equal. Primary and secondary literature was defined to clarify how these differ in both literature reviews and desk-based primary research using secondary data. This opening section clarified the usual components of academic articles and how you can appraise the standard and value of articles to use. The author, motivation for the research, participants, funding body and location of the research all need consideration in order to identify the correct form of material to read and use for academic assignments. The validity, trustworthiness and reliability of published literature was outlined to clarify that personal judgement is needed when choosing or shortlisting publications to read.

2. To identify how to create themes and topics to discover linked or emergent knowledge.

Using your assignment instructions, this section enabled you to clarify a focussed topic, themes and key words from which to search for academic articles. The stages of identifying these will ensure that your assignments have a focussed and clear frame from which to look for academic literature.

3. To outline methods for searching for academic articles.

The library, reading lists, online journals and community library were all noted as methods to search for academic articles. Understanding how your campus or local librarian can support your searching is a vital first step in academic development. Clarification of what journal articles are, how they are created and how they are ranked was also offered here. Journal articles are essential for your academic studies as they enable knowledge of new theory as well as counter perspectives to existing knowledge. Activities here enable you to identify which journals you will use for your searches.

4. To apply search techniques in order to discover relevant articles for your studies.

Index analysis, Boolean logic, year of publication, author and form of content were all noted as important techniques to complete searches for academic literature. Using these techniques will ensure your search results within the listed sources are relevant and appropriate for the planned assignment. It is important to allocate a specific amount of time for your searches so that this is completed effectively but is not seen as an endless task. Second searches may be required after reading the sources to support knowledge of specific and related areas. You may also use the reference lists from your first search to support and understand the content of these sources.

Questions to support your learning and research

1. How do primary and secondary research differ?
2. Can published literature be used alone in writing primary data analysis?
3. What constitutes your community library?
4. What is the H5 median of a journal?
5. Which elements of a publication make it trustworthy?
6. Which is more focussed, a tree or a leaf?
7. Are key words used to search for textbooks and journals or parts and journal articles?
8. What three words can be used to assist searing using Boolean logic?
9. Can you work in pairs when creating your topic, themes and key words?
10. If you are instructed to write a 2000 word essay, how many sources should you aim to find using your key words?

Websites in support of your learning from this chapter

Google Scholar https://scholar.google.co.uk/

Google scholar citations – lists of journals (https//scholar.google.com/citations)

Cornell University review of Google Metrics http://guides.library.cornell.edu/c.php?
g=32272&p=608789

Chapter 14

Reading academic texts

INTRODUCTION

Reading is not understanding. Reading is a component part of knowledge development but requires activity and reflection in order to become explicit or tacit knowledge (see Chapter 1) that can be used at a later time. This means that if you write at the same time as reading, you will not have full knowledge of the area being read. Reading is one part of a process to knowledge development and is crucial to your studies in tourism, hospitality and events (THE) management. Your tutors and lecturers will require you to complete the recommended reading, but also look to read around a topic area. Use Chapter 13 of this part to enable you to find wider sources of literature to use in academic assignments and follow the guidance here to improve your reading skills.

MOTIVATIONS FOR READING IN PERSONAL, ACADEMIC AND PROFESSIONAL CONTEXTS

You read information without conscious intention most of the time. Words, pictures and information surrounds our daily routines and we naturally read and reflect on these in passing moments. However, for academic studies in THE you need to complete focussed, in-depth and reflective reading in order to increase your knowledge on key topic areas to be assessed. Employers will also need evidence of your reading ability, not just in content but for accuracy of understanding also. This opening section will offer you time to explore and consider your current position and motivations on reading. Once these are clear and addressed, we will discuss types of reading and strategies to improve and develop your reading skills.

ACTIVITY 14.1 **WHAT DO YOU READ?**

Consider your usual routines within one week and outline the following:

1. Places of travel.
2. Places of study.
3. Places of rest.
4. Places of eating and drinking.

Within each of the above four locations, note the form of reading you complete in these. Are the words on physical and tangible things or virtual on technology products?

Is the reading to assist your ability to complete actions or develop knowledge and information?

What percentage of your reading is completed using technology?

Do you ever test your reading by thinking about what you read later in the day?

Do you seek out reading as a hobby or social activity with friends?

Questions in Activity 14.1 are designed to focus your attention on the variety of reading completed in a usual week and also to understand the motivations behind your usual reading. It is expected that the majority of your reading is to enable action and discussion within social contexts. Reading for academic and professional purposes has different motivations and may fall outside of your usual routines and activities. As such, it is important to consider how you motivate yourself to complete this reading in an effective and efficient manner.

Reading for academic purposes will be motivated from your desire to complete an assignment or develop knowledge for an upcoming test or submission. Sources which are usual in this form include:

- Journal articles.
- Textbooks.
- Reports.
- Government publications.
- Peer-reviewed open-access content.

Each of these have a different format and layout to consider. For example, a journal article will use the abstract to clarify the contents and a textbook would usually use the back cover for a summary of the contents. Knowledge of the location of information within each source is essential to maintain your motivation and feel successful in completing the reading.

Knowledge of the structure and chapters to academic publications is important for your searching of sources as well as your initial reading of them. If you read an abstract or summary of a publication and feel it is a harder level of writing, you may need to portion more time to the task of reading and understanding it.

Within professional reading, you may find that the level of writing and information is lower than academic publications. Magazines, websites, blogs and industry association publications are included within these. Professional publications are usually open access and written for a wider audience than academic articles and are therefore written in a more accessible or clear tone.

Table 14.1 Structure of academic sources to aid reading

	Textbook	**Journal article**	**Report (gov or industry)**
Summary	Back cover	Abstract	Abstract or summary
How usually sectioned?	Contents page Introduction/preface Chapters: each having introduction, main body, summary and reference lists Glossary Index	Title Abstract Introduction Literature Methodology Findings Conclusions References	Title page Contents page Introduction Key sections Conclusions References Appendices
Conclusions	At the end of each chapter or section. Or a chapter at the end to conclude overall.	Final section.	Final section before reference list.
References	At the end of each chapter, section or whole text. Usually listed in alphabetical order as well as indexed locale.	After the conclusion.	After the conclusion.

CASE STUDY 14.1 DIFFERENT FORMS OF READING FOR CHEF BURNOUT

Three examples of writing are offered below. One is from a magazine, one from an academic journal article and the third from a government report. They are all written on burnout (the first two linked to chefs). Use these examples to consider the tone, language and information offered. How easily can you read each one? How does the style aid your understanding of the content?

Price (2019)

Through the Burnt Chef project, Hall hopes to improve working conditions within the trade, raise awareness of mental health issues, and raise money for Mind mental health charity.

Starting with his freelance photography business, Nose 2 Tail Photography, last year he started taking black and white portrait photographs of chefs wishing to support the project to raise awareness and spark conversations regarding mental health.

Hall, who works at a Bournemouth-based foodservice firm, said: 'I've been working closely with the chefs for around eight years and have seen first-hand the struggles of mental health issues within the trade with both clients and friends.

'Long antisocial hours, tough environmental conditions and pressures to perform are just some of the issues that hospitality professionals are fighting against on a daily basis. Years of these conditions provide a hotbed of mental health issues such as anxiety, stress, alcohol abuse, drug abuse and depression. Not to mention the impact of these conditions attributing to the breakdown of relationships with husbands, wives, spouses and families.'

Hall and chef Pete Tofis of Toff Chef Event Catering aim to raise money through boxing matches and marathons as well as exhibitions of the photographs, and the campaign is asking business owners to pledge to allow chefs three consecutive days off at least twice a month.

Hall added: 'The industry and business owners need to start taking more responsibility for the ongoing health and state of mind of their workforce to ensure high levels of retention and continued strong employment continues.'

Lee and Shin (2005: p.100)

Job burnout consists of three sub-constructs: emotional exhaustion, depersonalization and diminished personal accomplishment (Maslach, 2000). Emotional exhaustion (EE) refers to a lack of energy and a feeling that one's emotional resources are used up due to excessive psychological demands. Depersonalization (DP) is characterized by the treatment of others as objects rather than people through cynical and uncaring attitudes and behaviors. Diminished personal accomplishment

(DPA) denotes a tendency to evaluate oneself negatively due to the failure to pro-duce results. Each sub dimension of job burnout captures unique aspects of job burnout (Maslach, 1993). EE is about the stress component, whereas DP is about interpersonal relations and DPA is a self-evaluation dimension.

Public Health England, 2016: p.4

Burnout is defined by the International Statistical Classification of Diseases and Related Health Problems as a 'state of vital exhaustion' (Z73.0) under the category of 'problems related to life-management difficulty' (Z73.0). Burnout is a prolonged response to long-term emotional and interpersonal stressors on the job. The key dimensions of this response are overwhelming exhaustion, feelings of cynicism and detachment from the job, a sense of ineffectiveness and a lack of accomplishment.

Burnout is related to workload and time pressure, role conflict and role ambiguity, lack of social support, lack of feedback, lack of autonomy and lack of participation in decision-making. Burnout has been associated with absenteeism, intention to leave the job and staff turnover. Among those who remain in the job, burnout leads to lower productivity and effectiveness at work, decreased job satisfaction and a reduced commitment to the job or organisation. Burnout is associated with adverse health outcomes associated with stress, such as depression, musculoskel-etal pain, type 2 diabetes, cardiovascular disease and premature mortality.

Reading was not explicitly outlined within the skills appraisal in Part 1. This is due to reading being a pre-requisite to a whole range of skills. Reading informs your knowledge and, as such, it enables you to think and act differently. It is, therefore, a more important skill than others noted in the skills appraisal as it is the entrance and access for you to be able to consider alternative positions and information. What you do as a result of the reading will then clarify the degree to which you processed and understood the information (or agreed with the content!).

THINK POINT 14.1 **DID YOU REALLY READ THAT?**

Have you ever skim read something only to think seconds later that none of the infor-mation went into your head? This is due to your being distracted and unable to focus on the information being 'digested.' How do you stop yourself doing this? How do you feel when you realise you are not reading properly? What is affecting this ability?

Think Point 14.1 enables you to consider how reading can take place without you even understanding or interpreting the words. This feels odd when you realise it has happened. It is often due to a lack of motivation and focus when completing the task. You can subconsciously read information around you on a daily or minutely basis, but when reading something of length you can also forget to consciously process the words. This is detrimental when completing reading for academic and professional purposes as you need to interpret and consider the information in order to impact your understanding and behaviour.

INDUCTIVE AND DEDUCTIVE REASONING FOR READING

From consideration of the motivations to read, structure in published literature and ways in which we process and consider written information, this section will now apply two forms of reasoning to your reading: inductive and deductive. Inductive and deductive reasoning are clarified in the approaches to research (Saunders et al., 2009) and are necessary when considering your philosophy and approach to research information.

It is accepted that you will use both inductive and deductive reasoning when completing a research project within your studies. Both are present and required as you are expected to understand current information and apply this to external positions and historical experience.

Starting with inductive reasoning, this is whereby you observe something, make generalisations and then create a map or overview of your learning. For example, you may read five articles on sexualised labour practices in tourism and hospitality businesses. Within these five you will observe definitions, research and conclusions on a topic area. The observations you make on these will naturally lead you to consider generalisations on the subject as a summary of your learning. Inductive reasoning is therefore usual in writing literature reviews of reports on existing secondary literature as you observe, generalise and summarise them.

Deductive reasoning is where you begin with a theory, predict how this influences something and then test it within an experiment or research group. This is used when gathering primary data for analysis as you need to base your enquiry on existing knowledge in order to test it in alternative positions or groups.

Inductive and deductive reasoning are clarified in Figure 14.1 to show how theory and published literature is used in both but result in different outputs. Inductive reasoning enables you to apply knowledge to create new paradigms of thought, whereas deductive reasoning is used to test current knowledge in new experiments or research projects. Both forms of reasoning are present in reading. You will apply your understanding of the content read to your existing knowledge (inductive and based on existing patterns). In parallel you may also note how your knowledge fluctuates due to applying new principles (deductive based on new rules and information).

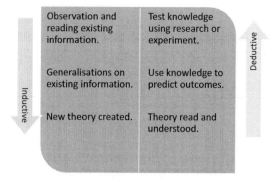

Figure 14.1 Inductive and deductive reasoning

SURFACE AND DEEP READING

Your ability to skim over words or to read without conscious thought has been noted already. This relates to your skill in surface and deep reading. Both are necessary to read effectively but you need to apply these in the appropriate contexts to ensure you do not waste time deep reading material that is unsuitable or irrelevant to the task at hand. In appraisal of your surface and deep reading ability, this section offers three activities and a case study activity to enable you to reflect on your reading ability.

ACTIVITY 14.2 **SPEED OF READING**

Read the following excerpt out loud and record the time it takes you to complete the reading:

Descartes's (1989 translation of 1649 text) quotation below outlines the first position on humour: the Superiority Theory.

> Derision or scorn is a sort of joy mingled with hatred, which proceeds from our perceiving some small evil in a person whom we consider to be deserving of it; we have hatred for this evil, we have joy in seeing it in him who is deserving of it; and when that comes upon us unexpectedly, the surprise of wonder is the cause of our bursting into laughter …

(pp.178–179)

This quotation outlines how people use humour to show superiority (or to mock others or ourselves). Mocking humour described above also involves hatred or dissatisfaction with the observed behaviour or action. Stating that something is inadequate can be amusing if the other person or self is able to reflect and understand the point is not an insult, but it can easily lead to interpretations of insult.

'Observing the imperfections of other men.'

(Hobbes, 1651, Part 1, Chapter 6)

The above quotation from Hobbes simplifies Descartes's definition by noting that this humour is through awareness of the inadequacies of others. In order to create this form of humour you need awareness of a status quo from which any deviancy can be noted and mocked. For example, if a worker arrives to work with a creased shirt and their colleagues states 'did your iron run off today?' (stated with a laugh) the colleague is mocking the employee by pointing out that their uniform is below standard. This example also uses sarcasm as an iron cannot run. By stating something which is impossible, about an action (ironing), which the colleague could have done, they are also mocking their knowledge and ability to use irons.

The second definition of humour relates to the need to relieve stress or tension. This is seen to originate from Lord Shaftsbury in the 1700s when he wrote a paper on how humour and wit enables the release and venting of tension. Freud (1905) developed this earlier definition and concluded that humour is needed to release nervous energy to support psychological well-being. In this way, humour is used as a medicine to relieve psychological stress or anxiety. For example, if a worker states 'I think I need to go on another training course to learn about time management, but I think I'd be late to that also!' This example uses both superiority and relief theory in that it allows the worker to relieve their stress at being late to work through making a joke, whilst also acknowledging their lack of time management (superiority). May (1953c cited in Kuiper et al., 1993: p.82) suggested that humour has the function of:

> preserving the sense of self … It is the healthy way of feeling a 'distance' between one's self and the problem, a way of standing off and looking at one's problem with perspective.

This confirms Freud's writings on humour used for psychological well-being as it allows a person to self-reflect and acknowledge problems in a light hearted stance. Finally, in Plesters (2009) article on relief humour, swearing is acknowledged as a key linguistic tact used here. They even warn readers of the profanities contained in the article in case readers are offended by the strong language used. If a customer or worker was to use swearing in this form it may again be perceived as insulting, rude or provocative.

Source: Firth, 2020: pp.127–128

From completing Activity 14.2 on the speed of your usual reading you will now be aware of how many words per minute you can read. It is usual for you to be able to read around 225–250 words per minute (in your first language or mother tongue). If you cannot read to this speed, the best way to improve is to read more and practice. Speed reading is a skill learnt through repetition and mastery. Conversely, you may find you can read many more than 250 words per minute. If this is the case, how much of the content do you remember and actively understand?

CASE STUDY 14.2 READING ENGLISH REGARDLESS OF NORMAL CONVENTIONS

The following two paragraphs are examples of English writing where two changes have been made to the words. These are followed by the original text.

Example 1

Iae ikelae otai isitvae ethae useumae onae ymae unchbreakslae. Erethae areae otslae of areasae otae itsae, eadrae andae hinktae boutae the istoryhae and ignificancesae of iencescae and umanitieshae inae ourae orldwae.

Example 2:

I lkee to viist the mesuum on my lchunbareks. Tehre are ltos of aeras to sit, raed and tnihk aobut the hrotisy and scignanecife of sniecce and heitinaumas in our wlord.

Original Example:

I like to visit the museum on my lunchbreaks. There are lots of areas to sit, read and think about the history and significance of science and humanities in our world.

The two examples of English writing offered in Case Study 14.2 use alternative ways of writing. The first example uses something called pig-latin. Here, each opening consonant sound is moved to the end of the word and ae or ai is added. For example, Miriam becomes iriammae. If you read the first example it may be difficult to understand. Try speaking them out loud instead. Upon speaking the words you may find it is easier to understand the content. To read this example you not only have to consider the way the words are phrased and sound but also work on moving the consonants back to the beginning of the word to clarify its meaning. Speaking them out loud is more efficient in understanding the content. The second example shows words where the first and last letter remain, but the inside letters are scrambled. How many of these words can you understand without needing to move the internal letters back to their original place? Are you amazed at your ability to understand the words even though they are spelt incorrectly? If you can read the second example clearly, this showcases your ability to speed read.

ACTIVITY 14.3 RECALL INFORMATION 1

Read the following paragraph and answer questions on its content:

The word 'leisure' is apparently harmless, almost neutral in its intent and certainly in its effect. Indeed, in the papers presented in both parts of this special issue, consumption is often assumed to be a space of enactment, fulfilment, and identity construction. For this reason, research into leisure can often feel rather descriptive in nature. But the point here is that in a world of prosumption leisure spaces are simply not neutral. If I may return briefly to the world of fitness, Frew and McGullivary (2005) suggest that the gym is a factory of fear; it provides a space in which consumers believe in the sovereignty that consumption can provide, whilst avoiding any conception of the mechanisms that underpin it. Leisure convinces us that it can provide us with the arenas we need to escape the monotony and the constraints of everyday life. Prosumption gives the consumer control, but that control comes at a cost. The challenge for leisure research lies in understanding what that cost might be. Back in 1991, Susan Willis argued that the consumption of fitness, on the part of women specifically, is liberating insofar as it involves the propagation of the image of women as independent, self-assured and powerful individuals. But in this context, dress is as constraining as it is enabling. For Willis, the workout is a highly evolved commodity form which obliges women to define themselves through the adornment of their bodies. This tension permeates prosumption and as such is worthy of particular attention by leisure researchers. Prosumption offers leisure research a means of re-framing the leisure experience as pro-active, yet ideological in nature. By doing so, it may be the case that the leisure research of the future can aspire to a promised land which is less about the insecurities of a group of scholars unsure of their own place in the world and more about standing up to and challenging the increasingly difficult pressures that a consumer society puts in front of it.

(Miles, 2016: p.273)

Questions:

1. Which section of a journal article do you think this writing is taken from?
2. What is the intention of the author in this excerpt?
3. Is the writing clear and easy to understand? Why?
4. Do you need to re-read the content to answer these questions? Why?

ACTIVITY 14.4 RECALL INFORMATION 2

Read the following paragraph and answer questions on its content:

'The third season of Stranger Things *promises to transport audiences to the summer of 1985 when it premieres on July 4. But for fans who just can't wait – or those who want to see first-hand what the setting of the coming season could be like – there's a solution. And it doesn't require time travel or a visit to Indiana.*

In anticipation of the new season, Los Angeles' Santa Monica Pier is hosting a Stranger Things season 3-themed fair that promises to deliver an imagined glimpse into Hawkins, Indiana in the summer of 1985. The two-day fair kicks off Saturday, June 29 and runs until Sunday, June 30 – giving Stranger Things' biggest fans four days to recuperate before the new season drops on Netflix.

Like any good fair, the Stranger Things 3 Fun Fair will be packed with carnival games, a slime-filled dunk tank, and a Demogorgon-filled Curiosity House. At the center of the event, guests can watch '80s cover bands, magicians, and the Hawkins High School Cheerleaders, while those who visit Hawkins Bike Shop will have the chance to win a Max-inspired BMX bike.

The Stranger Things-driven fair doesn't stop there. Expect to find the Santa Monica's iconic Pacific Wheel transformed into the Hawkins Wheel, while the Playland Arcade will become Hawkins' Palace Arcade.

For a full '80s fair experience, come hungry. There will be eating contests and an old-school Scoops Ahoy ice cream truck that's slated to be featured in season 3. The fair runs from 11 a.m. to 9 p.m. both days and will be located at the Pier Deck parking lot at Pacific Park on the Santa Monica Pier. Admission is free.'

(Carrick, 2019)

Questions:

1. What type of publication do you think this writing is taken from?
2. What is the intention of the author in this excerpt?
3. Is the writing clear and easy to understand? Why?
4. Do you need to re-read the content to answer these questions? Why?

Activities 14.3 and 14.4 on recalling information offer different forms of writing to work with. The first example is from a journal article and the second from a news article. The second is easier to recall and remember as it follows a story arc, which you will be more used to recalling. This is not due to less complex words but due to the use of short paragraphs and descriptive information, common phrasing, short sentences and simplistic language. The second uses more complex language.

STRATEGIES FOR EFFECTIVE READING

Reading requires you to consciously and actively understand words and meaning within sentences. The information should build upon prior learning and enable you to reflect and consider alternative perspectives. This final section will clarify strategies to help develop better reading techniques for personal, academic and professional development.

To begin, consider the following three elements for reading, noted as the 3 Rs (shown in Figure 14.2).

Figure 14.2 The 3 Rs of reading

Use Figure 14.2 to aid your development of this skill. Firstly, repetition is whereby you repeat the reading to check for meaning and understanding. On your first read of something, you may have understood some but not all of the content. Re-reading therefore allows you the time to consider and question information previously assumed. Reflection is where you make notes, highlight and comment upon the reading completed. This reflection will clarify your understanding but also enable you to stand back from the information and consider how the words could be interpreted or written differently. The final area is to review. Here, you should review your own knowledge and question this. Is your reading based on the reading or based on knowledge from your life experiences? How does your experience interfere with your understanding of written information?

ACTIVITY 14.5 **USING THE 3RS IN PRACTICE**

Read the following excerpt:

Philosopher Thomas Nagel suggests that some of the most crucial problems in human knowledge revolve around the following question: 'How to combine the perspective of a particular person inside the world with an objective view of that same world, the person and his viewpoint included. 'With a minimum of polemic, Nagel's comment summarizes one of the central problems in postmodern discourse. Contemporary postmodernism challenges the notion of a self-contained and transcendent self able to stand apart from experience and observe the 'world' from some privileged and 'uncontaminated' viewpoint. Any knowledge we have of our world, most postmodernists maintain, is 'insider knowledge.' When self-knowledge is the issue, the problem is compounded. We are ineluctably insiders in developing self-awareness.

(Kondrat, 1999: p.456)

1. After the first reading, write down what you understand from this.
2. Read it again and highlight key words and make comments on the content.
3. Now consider what you understand from the content.
4. Next, align the comments and highlighted key words to your own prior understanding and experiences: do you agree or disagree with the content?

Using the short excerpt of reading in Activity 14.5, you will observe how the three Rs can aid your ability to read and understand published information. The extract from Kondrat (1999) is neither simple, nor clear writing. By using the three Rs you should be able to dissect the content, consider its meaning and relate it to your own prior knowledge and experiences.

In addition to the 3Rs for effective reading, there are six supporting techniques and areas to consider to aid your reading skill development:

1. *Ensure the material is valid and appropriate for the task at hand.*

The first and most important element to consider when completing reading is whether or not it is valid and appropriate for the area of knowledge you want to develop. Use Chapter 13 of this part to ensure you gather and save published literature that is valid and appropriate for your knowledge development.

2.   *Plan your time to fit the reading and ensure you won't be disturbed.*

Reading requires devoted time and effort to complete it efficiently. If you are to read and understand words effectively, you need to ensure you have minimal distraction and enough time to read the work set. This means you need knowledge on your usual, or average, reading words per minute, the length of the reading to be completed, and how you intend to repeat the reading and make notes in support. Time management is also linked to this and you must consider which articles can be read within the time allowed for reading.

THINK POINT 14.2 NOISY OR QUIET? WHICH READER ARE YOU?

When beginning allocated time to read, do you look to sit in a quiet and secluded space or in the middle of a café with noise and music? What is it about that atmosphere which supports your reading? Why do you feel most comfortable reading there? Are there different locations you use for different forms of reading?

3.   *Make notes when reading.*

Using highlighters, scribbling notes in the margins, drawing mind maps and writing out themes and sub-themes are all examples of how you can make notes when reading. Table 14.2 can also be used to summarise some of these.

Table 14.2 Reading notes and reflections

Author	
Title	
Key words	
Why have I picked this to read?	
What is the intention of the authors?	
Is the content relevant to my studies?	
Is the piece convincing? Why?	
Which aspects can I use in my writing?	
What gaps are there in the logic expressed?	
Does the writing fit my prior knowledge and experience?	

Table 14.2 is based upon the Cornell note template (see Burns and Sinfield, 2012: p.169) and Wallace and Wray (2011) questions for critical reading. Use of this table, or one similar, will enable you to reflect upon the content and your motivation for using information gained from it. This will support the justification of reading and writing about the literature found.

4. *Memory check.*

After your first and second (and third, even) read of an article, you should put it to one side and write out what you remember from reading the piece. This will clarify your emergent knowledge from the reading but also signal the aspects which you have found most important. This is not a test of memory, but a check on which aspects your consciousness and subconsciousness have retained. This is a useful activity completed in pairs also. Read and complete a memory check with a partner who has read the same literature piece as you and check to see their understanding compared to yours. If there are differences, these can be discussed to aid emergent knowledge from the reading.

5. *Record and listen.*

Reading in silence is not the preferred method of reading by everyone. Similarly to your varied learning styles, reading can also be completed in different ways. This technique is whereby you record yourself reading the information out loud and then listen to it later as an audio file. This is beneficial in a number of ways. Firstly, reading information out loud makes you read each word in turn and inhibits speed reading. By speaking the words, you are also making sense of them within the sentences and paragraphs. As an audio file, the reading can be repeatedly considered in a wider variety of situations. The gym, bus and grocery store are three locations within which you would not usually sit and read an academic textbook but would be a space to enable you to think about the content.

6. *Think deeper.*

On review of the reading completed you should also consider how it affects your position and emotions. Are you comfortable with the content? Does it relate to personal experience? Has it affected the way you think or consider something? Are you anxious or more concerned about the topics it discusses? Consider deeper questions: what does the author expect me to take away? How could others understand or see this? Which research and philosophy approach is taken here?

SUMMARY

1. To appraise different motivations for reading in personal, academic and professional contexts.

This chapter offers you activities and case studies to reflect on your usual habits and methods of reading. When directed to complete an academic submission you need to find journal articles, textbooks, reports, government publications and peer-reviewed open-access content. These are important for your developing knowledge. Different forms of writing were offered to allow you to consider how motivated you are when faced with alternative styles of published literature. It is important to acknowledge your feelings towards more difficult reading and allow additional time to complete this.

2. To evaluate whether you need to use inductive or deductive reasoning in your reading.

Inductive reasoning was defined as theory generated from observations and generalisations from existing secondary data. Deductive reasoning is where you test knowledge learnt using research methods or experiments. You are required to use both of these within your reading for academic development. Reading, understanding and applying this to emergent knowledge and skills will enable you to create research questions. Likewise, using your knowledge to test and apply theories in different contexts will be of importance to research projects you complete.

3. To understand what surface and deep reading is.

Surface reading was explored through working out how quickly you can skim read. This is an important skill in the initial stages of finding appropriate literature. Deep reading and re-reading is then necessary for you to consider, understand and apply knowledge learnt from literature against previous knowledge and other sources of theory and critique on the topic area.

4. To outline strategies to aid effective reading.

The 3 Rs of reading and six techniques for effective reading were offered to enable you to follow clear processes in your reading tasks.

Questions to support your learning and research

1. What is an abstract and what does it contain?
2. What is deductive reasoning?
3. What do the 3 Rs stand for?
4. How many words can you read in a minute?
5. How can you tabulate information from an article or chapter read?

Chapter 15

Academic writing

LEARNING OBJECTIVES

1. To understand the basic conventions required within academic writing.
2. To identify where judgement, power and balance are present in academic writing.
3. To outline strategies for academic writing.

INTRODUCTION

Academic writing is unique in its content, form and structure. You may have written essays and reports at school or college previously which has been descriptive and fact based, but this chapter aims to develop your writing using the knowledge gained from academic sources and academic research. Using the previous chapters in this part you should have found and read academic literature to develop your knowledge for an assignment. This part will appraise your ability to write about these sources and weave your authorial voice into the submission. Although this chapter focusses on academic styles `of writing, it can be used for professional and formal writing in part.

CONVENTIONS WITHIN ACADEMIC WRITING

Figure 15.1, repeated from Chapter 13 of this part, outlines the stages required before you start writing. Identifying a focussed topic, themes, key words and reading academic sources are all required before you begin writing. These are important steps as they ensure your writing is informed and relevant to current research published by academics. To assist with your writing skills, this section will outline paragraphs, grammar, referencing, spelling, sentence construction and rhetorical questions. These are all important skills for employability and you will already

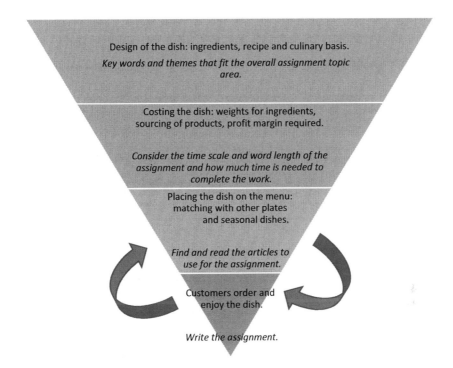

Design of the dish: ingredients, recipe and culinary basis.
Key words and themes that fit the overall assignment topic area.

Costing the dish: weights for ingredients, sourcing of products, profit margin required.

Consider the time scale and word length of the assignment and how much time is needed to complete the work.

Placing the dish on the menu: matching with other plates and seasonal dishes.

Find and read the articles to use for the assignment.

Customers order and enjoy the dish.

Write the assignment.

Figure 15.1 Developing a new dish for a restaurant

have some competence within all of these. This review is offered in order for you to appraise and consider your usual practice in writing.

Before reviewing the key components in your writing, it is important for you to have created an assignment plan to work within. This plan should contain the following:

1. Topic/title.
2. Word length.
3. Chapters with word counts and aligned academic sources to discuss.
4. Positions and arguments to discuss.
5. Chapters linking to marking criteria for the submission.

These five areas can be used for any form of written submission. An essay, report, blog, discussion board or social media post will all require these in planning. Assignment planning is clarified as a strategy for academic writing at the end of this chapter but is summarised here to clarify this is a precursor needed before you begin writing.

Paragraphs

Within your assignment you need to ensure the work meets the criteria of the marker and evidences your ability in critical writing. Meeting the marking criteria means you need to convey clear information under chapters or areas of writing. If in report format you can use titles to signpost the content to follow, however, if you are writing an essay or blog post, you will need to use paragraphs to signal this. Chapters and paragraphs are also needed in order to plan and inform the reader of your argument within a topic. To enable effective paragraph writing use the following strategies:

Opening paragraphs start with a clear sentence on what the submission intends to do. This is followed by listing in separate sentences the areas to consider. The final sentence will then confirm how the submission will conclude or close.

Main body paragraphs will clarify the area for definition or discussion in the first sentence. This is then followed with sentences using references to clarify the author's knowledge and position. A concluding and linking sentence then completes the paragraph to move on with. Use the following as a guide:

Sentence	Content.
S1	Open and introduce the area for discussion.
S2	Overall knowledge of an area.
S3	Position 1 offered with a reference.
S4	Position 2 offered with a reference.
S5	Your understanding of positions 1 and 2 and how these relate to each other.
S6	Positions not found in the literature but which may be important in consideration of the topic.
S7	Conclude and link to the next paragraph.

Concluding paragraphs will note that there is a summary and conclusion being drawn in its opening sentence. Sentences following this will conclude the previous discussion from main body paragraphs. Notes for further research or recommendations.

The format and font within your paragraphs may be explicit in the assignment instructions. If you are unsure, use the following as a guide:

Font	Times New Roman
Size	12
Line spacing	1.5

To enable a clear view of your paragraphs it is advised that you separate with a line break.

The above space between this and the previous sentence shows a line break.

Grammar and Style

Every language conforms to a set of grammatical rules. In academic writing the following outlines ten essential rules when writing in a formal and appropriate tone (using English as the lingua franca). In some of these rules, the sentences and words use examples to enable you to perceive how these can be managed effectively or ineffectively.

Rule 1 – Do not contract

Contracted words are don't, can't, shouldn't and shan't (for example). These are easy ways to verbally communicate information but are to be avoided in written academic assignments. The correct ways to write some of these are noted as follows:

Contraction	Correct words
They're	They are
We're	We are
Don't	Do not
Can't	Cannot
Shan't	Shall not
Couldn't	Could not
Wouldn't	Would not
They'll	They will
Aren't	Are not
We'll	We will

Rule 2 – Never interject emotion

Interjections are exclamation phrases used like Ouch! Wow! Or Watch out! These are not usual in academic writing as they are emotive and express spoken language. It is advised that exclamation marks never be used in academic writing as they infer meaning and judgement!

Rule 3 – Use apostrophes correctly

Apostrophes can be used to signal missing letters or the ownership of something. Miriam's socks clarifies that the socks belong to Miriam. However, students' socks shows that there is a group of people (plural) who own the socks. Use the following as a guide for apostrophe use:

Sahar and Mohammed Said have two dogs. Woof is 5 and Pickle is 3. The Saids' house is on the first floor. The dogs' bedrooms are next to the front door and their owners' bedroom is past the living room. Woof's bed is clean and tidy and Pickle's bed is full of fur and toys. The Saids' schedules are busy today. Sahar's netball team have a match in the morning. Mohammed's car needs repair at 1pm, and Woof and Pickles' dog walkers cannot collect them until 2pm.

This example shows plural and singular possession using apostrophes correctly.

Rule 4 – Commas and colons have a rightful place

Commas are needed in a sentence where you want to signal a pause in the flow of information. Different ways in which commas can be used are evidenced in the examples below:

a. Munich, Germany.
b. So, to begin this discussion (for, and, nor, yet, or, but also relevant here).
c. *'At the end of a direct quotation,'* used in a sentence.
d. Monday 2nd September, 2019.
e. When this was published, there seems to have been fewer publications available.
f. Tourism, hospitality and events.

The examples above all offer different ways in which commas can be used in sentence construction. The colon and semi-colon are also useful tools that can be used when structuring sentences.

Colon	Used to signal the start of a list or to separate content in a title.
Examples	This part contains three elements: conventions for academic writing, using authorial judgement and voice, and strategies for academic writing.
	Artificial Intelligence in catering: a critical analysis of the use of robotics in fast food manufacturing in Beijing.
Semi-colon	Aids in the separation of a list which already uses a comma or is used to separate clauses.
Examples	Dr Steven Courtney, Education; Dr Shirley Jenner, HR; and Professor John Swarbrooke, Tourism.
	I have read this part in one day; it really helped me reflect on my academic development.

Rule 5 – Write numbers up to ten in full

If you are writing for an academic submission it is usual to write out numbers as words up to ten. This is a stylistic rule but is usual and applied widely. For numbers one to nine ensure you write the number as a word.

Rule 6 – Use references appropriately

Students entering higher education will often feel most comfortable copying and pasting words from sources they have read. This needs to be avoided. Higher level academic writing uses paraphrasing and short snippets of direct quotations in order to clarify knowledge learnt. Paraphrasing is when you re-write information learnt in your own words. A reference is still needed as you cannot state you learnt the information from research completed (unless you are an academic and have completed research on this!).

Consider the following direct quotation:

> Academic writing follows a similar pattern of planning and decision making.
>
> (Cottrell, 2008: p.171)

Two points to consider in the use of direct quotations:

1. Never presume the reader interprets the quotation in the same way as you.
2. Never use direct quotations for simple and clear information.

The direct quotation from Cottrell is simple and easy to read and understand. As such, there is no reason to use it as a direct quotation. The area of interest is the notion of academic writing being like a *'pattern.'* If I was using knowledge when writing an academic assignment I would state:

> Academic assignments are seen as linked to planning and decision making as they both require *'patterns'* and processes in order to complete them to a high standard.
>
> (Cottrell, 2010: p.171)

This second example using a direct quotation from the same source and sentence is of a higher academic standard as the writer has informed the reader their own understanding and link between the quotation, their knowledge and how this informs their thinking.

If you find a direct quotation that cannot be paraphrased, it is best to put it in as a direct quotation, but always unpack the meaning and relevance of it in your work. Refer to point one above on why you must note your understanding of the quotation.

Paraphrasing and using short direct quotations will also guard against plagiarism. Plagiarism is when an academic assignment is seen to be made from other people's work. In academic writing the focus is on showing your knowledge and understanding of secondary material. This is not the same as repeating information from these publications. In paraphrasing you should not simply re-organise the words from the original source, but consider exactly what is meant by the literature and interpret it within the requirements of your assignment task.

ACTIVITY 15.1 **PARAPHRASING SECONDARY LITERATURE**

Read the following extract from an essay on Global Citizenship Education:

Definitions of Global Citizenship Education (GCE) has evidenced a variety of components. Exploration of UK and EU government support is now required to highlight its importance for today's educational leaders. As previously mentioned, the UK and EU have implemented various offices and policies in order to regulate and maintain Citizenship education and agendas (Crick, 1998; GHK, 2007). The Department for International Development (DfID) and Development Education Association (DEA) are examples of such government offices. These are funded to formulate strategies on promoting the work of NGOs via educating concerning development and global issues. In developing initiatives around GCE, these political bodies have also documented specific outcomes for schools and higher education (McKenzie et al., 2000; DEA, 2000; Oxfam, 2006; and the DfES, 2005).

Starting with the DEA and Bourn's (2006) publication to the Education and Skills committee for Citizenship education highlighted how imperative the global dimension is within Citizenship education. This appeal was based on the premise that current Citizenship curricula retained its focus on the local and regional aspects, with little linkage or relevance to global impacts. The argument developed in this documentation was based around similar authors reviewed in Chapter 2.1, but also mirrors Said's (2008) and Kant's (1794) work, in that Bourn wanted to engage in developing students' cultural and local opinions to embrace new and different opinions. In embracing new and different opinions, students would need a transparent recognition of their own opinions and identity in order to identify other ones and embrace new ones. Further, Bourn's (2006) paper noted that ethnic allegiances and local foci could be a problem, and GCE should not just be about nationalistic attitude, but enhancing and creating new relationships across global industries. Spring's (2009) text equally posits this in that UK education is no longer about creating human capital, but social capital via multicultural education. Therefore, global education should focus on both local and global practices, expand student opinions and also create a labour market that is socially equipped, not just economically active.

Evidently, there has been an increasing interest in encouraging Citizenship education agendas into global Citizenship or multicultural Citizenship. But the question posed now is how is it available in UK education, and at which levels?

Questions:
1. What direct quotations are used in this abstract?
2. How is the information written as learnt knowledge from secondary sources?
3. How does the content lead to clarification of a research question?
4. Are there affirmative statements suggesting a lack of flex in the knowledge?
5. Can you paraphrase the content included into a 250 word summary?

In terms of how references are formatted, this will depend on the style of reference your institution requires you to follow (Harvard, APA etc.). In academic assignments it is usual for direct quotations to be written in *italics* and if this is longer than one line, to indent by one inch at both sides. They should also be offered in double or single inverted commas as a consistent style throughout your assignment. Brackets are usually required in noting the reference at the end of a sentence (Author, year). And the year is usually in brackets if the name is within the sentence. Author (year) as an example.

Rule 7 – Spell it out clearly

Spelling, similar to grammar, is important in conveying the correct meaning and intent in your academic writing. This is tricky when two words are spoken in the same way but spelt differently. For example, they're and there are spoken in the same way but written and mean entirely different things. When writing in English you also need to consider which type of spelling to adopt: British or American? A classic example of American spelling is the use of z instead of s: personalized, stylized and categorized is written using the American English spelling, whereas British English would use personalised, stylised and categorised.

When editing your work the easiest way to check your spelling is to firstly use the spelling software in the word processing document. However, this will not pick up on words spelt correctly but written incorrectly. Fair, fare and fayre are another example of words spoken in the same way but spelt differently. If you were to say to someone 'Being fair to someone having fare hair at a fayre' they would probably look entirely lost and not know what you meant. Reading these three words in written form makes it easier to understand the meaning intended.

Rule 8 – Use different fonts and formats correctly

Fonts, *formats, and* **style** *is* important **in written** work as it **enables you to *read the words*** *clearly.* Standard writing should not use any bold, underline or italics. These fonts should be used to signal titles or emphasis of words written. Similarly, if you have used a specific font style and size, continue with this throughout the writing. Fonts and formats are important as they ensure the reader can understand the letters and words clearly. Used incorrectly, they can signal confusion and lack of organisation.

Rule 9 – Sentences allude to control of knowledge

Sentences written in English have a clear beginning and an end. Begin with a capital letter and end with a punctuation mark such as a full stop. Long sentences that use commas, semi-colons and continued narrative lead the reader to become lost and unsure of the content and direction of the work as they try to follow the stream of thought and understand the intention behind the words. Short sentences are clear. Using a mixture of short and one line sentences is useful in academic writing, but long sentences should be avoided. Short sentences are useful for punctuating information. They are clear. They clarify specifics and they allow the writer to show management of knowledge clearly. Reading sentences that are clear and controlled enables the marker of your work to understand your ability and knowledge. Reading sentences that are unclear and disorganised will lead to lower marks and a lack of clarity on your knowledge and thought processes.

Rule 10 – Is that rhetorical?

Rhetorical questions are questions that cannot be answered by the reader. When writing an academic assignment students may feel that these are necessary, but are they? If you are writing an academic assignment it is usual for you to clarify the following elements:

1. Your level of knowledge on a topic area.
2. Comparisons between publications on a topic area.
3. Your position in relation to the knowledge learnt.

None of the above requires you to persuade or convince the reader of something. As a caveat, if you are asked to write a persuasive written piece, ignore this advice!

Rhetorical questions in an academic assignment may make the reader think one of two things. Firstly that you are unsure and are asking the reader for their opinion (impossible as the reader cannot write back to you in an essay). Or, secondly, that you want to raise a question based on contradictory information learnt from theory. Both of these show a lack of command and knowledge on the topic set. If this is seen the marker may reduce the overall mark due to a lack of ability in offering knowledge and positions on academic literature.

CASE STUDY 15.1 ACADEMIC WRITING CONVENTIONS IN PRACTICE

The following is an example of academic writing submitted by a first year student in university that uses paragraph formation and the ten rules accurately:

Current research on the impact of the European Working Time Directive (EWTD) mainly shows medical staff working hours through their shift work patterns (Fitzpatrick et al, 1997; Böheim and Taylor, 2004; Douglas, 2005). The new 2006 EWTD notes that training doctors are to have reduced weekly working hours phased from 2007 until 2009 to ensure they do not work over the 48 hour limit each week (Department for Employment and Learning, 2006). Labour processes within the hospitality industry, similarly to medical work, vary according to demanding customer interaction, and therefore shifts constantly alter according to the customer requirements (Sosteric, 1996). The EWTD was primarily created to ensure better health and safety within the work place, in consideration of the link between excessive hours and ill health (Lucas, 1983). Employees working in shifts have higher rates of coronary heart disease, gastro-intestinal problems and higher blood pressure, (Reeves et al., 2004). Therefore, the EWTD legislation should ensure reduced health risks in the workplace through reduced working hours.

Working hours have also been seen to have a significant impact on job satisfaction, motivation and retention of employees (Clark, 1996, 2001; Cully et al., 1998). Long working weeks have been an ongoing concern in the NHS, resulting in recruitment and retention problems (Kapur et al., 1999; Machin, 1999). Turn-over of staff within restaurants currently lies in excess of 120% per year (Tracy and Hinkin, 2006) and Enz's (2001) study found that 57% of hospitality managers found retention a key problem. European hospitality managers also found implementing EU regulations, such as the EWTD, a fundamental problem through higher training costs linked to low retention of staff (Enz, 2001). It is clear that prolonged working hours result in similar management problems for both the NHS and the hospitality industry. However, the revised EWTD has been adapted for doctors, but not for hospitality managers.

WRITING USING JUDGEMENT, POWER AND BALANCE

When you write academic assignments it is important to acknowledge that they are not for you to repeat or regurgitate information from other people. Assignments are usually set to enable you to showcase your knowledge and ability in critical thinking and writing. Your knowledge is unique to you and so your writing style will reflect this. When planning academic assignments you need to consider the authors and your positions to the existing body of literature. Do you agree with the literature you have read? Can you see issues or gaps in the literature available? Does it accurately reflect reality in society and business? These questions will enable you to consider your position and authorial voice when writing for academic purposes. To clarify how to use your authorial voice and write effectively for academic assignments, this section discusses judgement, power and balance.

Your judgement of secondary published material has been outlined in Chapter 13 of this part. As you searched and selected literature for your assignments you were already making decisions on whether the literature was appropriate to inform your existing knowledge base. Accepting this as an appropriate action in your academic writing is the first step to using and owning your own judgement. It is important here to accept that you will not be able to read everything published on an area of study. Do your best to find and read appropriate sources linked to the reading list and academic searches completed.

Another consideration when using your own judgement in reading and critiquing academic work is that the published literature you find may not be correct and you may disagree with it. Refer to Chapter 12 of this part whereby the different research approaches and philosophies are clarified to aid your consideration of how you approach knowledge. On learning about different research philosophies you will see how authors of academic research are not detached nor impartial all of the time. The position and place in which the researcher completes research and writes about their findings will affect their conclusions. Surrounding this are their personality, nationality, life and work experiences. Therefore, no written research can be accepted as definitive fact as it is attached to a researcher and participants. This position is asserted from a humanities and not a scientific basis. Scientific experiments that are recorded within laboratory and controlled situations would be seen as accurate and evidencing factual information.

CASE STUDY 15.2 CHALLENGING ACADEMIC PUBLICATION WITH YOUR OWN JUDGEMENT

When reading academic literature do you take every piece of information written as correct and accurate? Have you read academic research that seems to be incorrect from your own experience? How comfortable are you at writing this challenge or discussing this with classmates?

In using your judgement you are accepting that you are liking or disliking literature in a subjective way. This can feel awkward if you have learnt that academic research is correct and cannot be critiqued or judged. In higher education, however, you are marked on your ability to show judgement and patterns and issues within the published literature. Appropriate personal judgements made on existing literature can be clarified in three areas:

1. Trustworthy: can you believe the content can be applied to similar situations? Do you believe the publication accurately represents the research completed?
2. Reliable: could you depend on the conclusions written based on findings and analysis presented?
3. Valid: does the content refer to realistic issues in an area of concern?

Areas 1–3 have been discussed in Chapter 13 of this part. When writing about these, use the strategies noted later in this chapter.

Power given to academic literature will be evident in your use and rejection of sources. When writing your assignments you might have read over 50 articles but only choose to reference 20. This is accepted and appropriate but clarifies that you are not using all of your knowledge to write a submission. In this way, you are giving more power to certain published literature. This area for consideration links to your judgement on the reliability of the findings and conclusions within a publication. It may also be that you have singular research publications on different but linked issues. It is important in your writing that you use a number of sources in order to justify and clarify your knowledge and argument.

ACTIVITY 15.2 JUSTIFICATION OF NOT USING SOURCES

Once you have your assignment plan and list of references and sources to use in your academic writing, note your answers to the following questions:

1. Which articles did you shortlist but not read?
2. Which articles have you read but will not include in the assignment?
3. Which parts of the source are you planning to use?
4. Why do you think you have made these choices?
5. Are these choices informing a clear argument and structure to the submission?

Discuss your answers to these in a small study group and consider the following:

1. How have others chosen to select the sources of academic literature to use in their assignment?
2. What rationale do others have for omitting sources?
3. Have some people included all sources? Why have they done this?
4. Has anyone chosen less than five sources to use? Why is this?
5. Has anyone chosen over 30 sources to use? Why is this?

Activity 15.2 is designed to ensure you are accountable and reflective on the decisions you make for your academic writing. It is appropriate not to include all sources of academic literature you have read relating to a topic, but it is equally inappropriate to only have five sources.

The balance (or weighting) you give a publication is evident in the number of times you reference (or cite) it within your work. This can also suggest poor planning and a lack of wider reading. For example, students who read an article and write about it immediately may use the reference for a whole paragraph, rather than weave it into a discussion using a range of sources. If you heavily rely upon one or two sources it will also make your writing biased. When writing it is important that you consider how you want to answer or approach the task and which articles and research you feel is most appropriate. Areas to consider if you want to use a specific definition or source more than others include:

1. Is this due to your research approach and philosophy?
2. Does the assignment ask you to consider this researcher and theory specifically?

3.   Is it easier to read and digest than other sources?
4.   How has it affected your reading of other sources?
5.   Are you focussing on this more than others due to a lack of time and ability to find alternative sources?

If you use a source three or four times within a small assignment I would suggest you consider your answers to the above in order to reflect on your motivations behind this consistent use.

STRATEGIES FOR ACADEMIC WRITING

This section will outline a process to assist your planning and writing of academic submissions. In addition to this section, please also consider your research approach, research philosophy, time management, skills appraisal and self-awareness (all covered previously in this textbook). Completing learning in these areas will aid your ability to plan and reflect on your ability to write clearly and succinctly. This section will clarify how to plan your assignment, key phrases to use in your writing and how to show judgement, power and balance in your submission.

To plan your academic submission, please follow the ten steps discussed below to aid a clear plan for your writing:

Step 1: Understand the task

Your assignment may be rigid and specific, or open and fluid. You must start with the assignment instructions to understand the amount of work and time needed on the submission. Examples of these are noted in Case Study 15.3.

CASE STUDY 15.3 TWO ENDS OF THE ASSIGNMENT INSTRUCTION SPECTRUM

Assignment 1:

You are instructed to write a 2000 word essay answering the following question:

'Is artificial intelligence affecting service encounters in tourist destinations?'

Assignment 2:

You are instructed to write a 2000 word essay on artificial intelligence in tourist destinations. Specifically consider:

1. Areas where AI is used.
2. People who have to manage or interact with AI.
3. Organisational strategy which would support and develop AI.
4. Interpersonal skills required in AI.
5. Staffing concerns in replacing their work with AI.

On reading the assignment instructions make a note of the key questions you feel you need to answer in the submission. Do you need to define and clarify, or to analyse and investigate? The type of action to be shown in your writing is important. If you need to define and discuss, then you can offer a range of definitions from similar sources. Investigation and analysis is where you need to show a deeper level of knowledge from a wider array of sources. Before moving on to your reading for the submission, check with your class mates and tutors that you have understood the task instructions correctly. Ask for examples of previous submissions to aid your understanding of the criteria and writing style, and also if there is a set list of reading to complete in support of the submission.

Step 2: Complete the set reading

From your understanding of the assignment instructions it is then important to start your reading using the recommended set reading lists and articles offered in class. The assignment will likely be based upon work completed in class and the reading list linked to the topic. This is an important starting point for your reading as the unit will be based upon testing your learning outcomes in skills and knowledge linked to content already delivered.

Step 3: Complete further reading

Use Chapters 13 and 14 of this part to aid your search for additional sources and reading to supplement recommended reading lists. Spending time finding and reading these is essential for your writing as it informs new knowledge and supports existing beliefs and theories gained from your current studies. The notes you make during this reading can be used to support the next step of planning your arguments.

Step 4: Outline your planned arguments

This step is the most important in terms of how you will achieve high marks from your submission. Please note that by arguments, I am not stating you need to be angry and persuade the reader of your position, but instead clarify a position and train of thought you want to take the reader on. Each academic assignment you complete is based upon showing your own individual knowledge of an area. This knowledge is individual to your own reading and life experiences. Showing an ability to clarify this position and stance on a subject is a high academic skill.

ACTIVITY 15.3 **PLANNING THE LINE OF THOUGHT TO TAKE YOUR READER ON**

Before you start writing your submission, use the following questions and actions to clarify your line of thought and argument.

Clarifying your knowledge and outlining potential lines of argument:

1. How much do you know about the topic? Is it enough to start writing?
2. What elements of the literature do you agree with? Which do you disagree with?
3. What are the usual considerations made in the area?
4. What gaps are there in the literature you have used?
5. Are there areas linked to the literature and industry practice that could be seen as contemporary and interesting to discuss?
6. What story do you want to tell?

Planning your argument and line of thought:

1. Clarify what position you want the reader to understand. Is this an existing position from literature or a new one you have seen in gaps in current literature?

Note the end position you want your reader to get to and work backwards:

1. What is your concluding statement (written without references)?
2. What definitions are needed to clarify the focus?
3. What do current researchers conclude around this?
4. What industry practice supports or refutes the literature?
5. Which lens are you using to critique the information (refer to research approach and philosophy)?

Step 5: Outline key chapters and paragraphs

Once you are clear on the assignment instructions and your own position and line of argument, it should be relatively easy to plan your chapters and paragraphs. If you are writing a report with specific headings and chapters, you can write these in at this point. For an essay without titles, use the following as a guide:

P1 – Introduction. Set out the aim of the writing and the contents to be offered.
P2 – Introduction to key topic. Definitions and areas to be discussed.
P3 – Argument 1. What is my position and understanding of this?
P4 – Argument 2. What is my position and understanding of this?
P5 – Conclusion on content offered and answer to the task set.

The above paragraph plan examples could be used for an essay of 1000 words in length. It is important to plan the chapters and paragraph contents before you begin writing as you may wander to different points of positions when writing from memory.

Step 6: Note the sources to be used in each paragraph

Within each paragraph or chapter, write out the references planned. An example is offered in Case Study 15.4.

CASE STUDY 15.4 SOURCES WITHIN REPORT PLANNING

Ben's report plan is noted below:

Title: A critical analysis of the event authenticity of the Munich Christmas Markets
Chapter 2.1 Research on authenticity in Event Tourism Contexts
Baker and Crompton (2000)
Casteran and Roeder (2012)
Goulding (2000)
McIntosh (2004)
Robinson and Clifford (2012)
Chapter 2.2 Definitions on Event Authenticity
MacLeod (2006)
Novello and Fernandez (2016)
Waitt (2000)
Wang (1999)
Kolar and Zabkar (2010)
Chhabra et al (2003)
Jacobs (1995)
Chapter 2.3 Research on Event Authenticity in Christmas Market
Brida et al (2012)
Brida and Tokarchuk (2015)
Brida et al (2013)

Reference List:

Baker, J. and Crompton, D. (2000). Quality, satisfaction and behavioral intentions. *Annals of Tourism Research*, 27(3), pp. 354–375.
Brida, J. G., Disegna, M. and Osti, L. (2012). Segment visitors of cultural events by motivation: A sequential non-liner clustering analysis of Italian Christmas Market visitors, *Expert Systems with Applications*, 39, p. 11, 349–11, 356.
Brida, J. G. and Tokarchuk, O. (2015). Keeping mental budgets: visitors' spending at Christmas market. *Tourism Economics*, 21(1), pp. 67–82.
Brida, J., Disegna, M. and Osti, L. (2013). Visitors' expenditure behaviour at cultural events: The case of Christmas markets. *Tourism Economics*, 19(5), pp. 1173–1196.

Castéran, H. and Roederer, C. (2012). Does authenticity really affect behavior? The case of the Strasbourg Christmas. *Tourism Management*, 36(1), pp. 153–163.

Chhabra, D., Healy, R. and Sills, E. (2003). Staged authenticity. *Annals of Tourism Research*, 30(3), pp. 702–719.

Goulding, C. (2000). The commodification of the past, postmodern pastiche, and the search for authentic experiences at contemporary heritage attractions. *European Journal of Marketing*, 34 (7), pp. 835–853.

Jacobs, J. M. (1995). That dangerous fantasy of authenticity: A review of the J. C. Slaughter Falls Community Arts Project, Brisbane. *Ecumene*, 2(2), pp. 211–214.

Kolar, T. and Zabkar, V. (2010). A consumer-based model of authenticity: An oxymoron or the foundation of cultural heritage marketing? *Tourism Management*, 31(5), pp. 652–664.

MacLeod, N.E. (2006). The placeless festival: Identity and place in the post-modern festival. *Festivals, Tourism and Social Change: Remaking Worlds*, 8, pp. 222–237.

McIntosh, J. (2004). Tourists' appreciation of Maori culture in New Zealand. *Tourism Management*, 25(1), pp. 1–15.

Novello, S. and Fernandez, P. (2016). The influence of event authenticity and quality attributes on behavioral intentions. *Journal of Hospitality and Tourism Research*, 40(6), pp. 685–714.

Robinson, R. N. S. and Clifford, C. (2012). Authenticity and festival foodservice experience. *Annals of Tourism Research*, 39(2), pp. 571–600.

Waitt, G. (2000). Consuming heritage-perceived historical authenticity. *Annals of Tourism Research*, 27(4), pp. 835–862.

Wang, N. (1999). Rethinking authenticity in the tourist experience. *Annals of Tourism Research*, 26, 349–370.

Step 7: Ensure chapters and paragraphs meet marking criteria

From completing steps 1–6 you should now understand the task, have planned your paragraphs/chapters and listed the references to use within the submission. It is vital you now take a moment to reconsider the marking criteria before you begin writing. During your reading and consideration of the literature it is possible that you ended up down an incorrect path of thought. So, before you begin writing the submission, go back to your tutor/professor or online learning area and check for what the marking criteria contains. What percentage is critical analysis or further reading? What percentage are references and writing style listed as?

Use the marking criteria percentages and areas to identify if your planned submission will meet these. Check with a class mate or tutor/professor and ask if there are any areas that look as though they could be improved or altered before you begin writing.

Step 8: Write the assignment

With your planned paragraphs, reading and sources ready it should be easy to start your writing now. Allow yourself a couple of days free of other work to complete this without distraction. During your writing, ensure you complete the following:

1. Stick to your plan and word limits.
2. Note the references and compile your reference list as you go.
3. Note down any questions or further reading required.

The three areas above are important when you complete your writing as you need to keep track of your progress. In your referencing for the assignment you can utilise a reference or source programme/software (see Activity 15.4).

ACTIVITY 15.4 USING MENDELEY FOR CITING YOUR SOURCES

This activity offers information on how to use Mendeley, a source/citation management software for academic writing. Go to www.mendeley.com for more information.

*'**Mendeley Desktop**: Mendeley Desktop is the downloaded part of the software installed onto your computer. Download Mendeley Desktop (www.mendeley.com/ download-mendeley-desktop/) if you haven't already.*

Mendeley Web: *This is the Mendeley website where you can access the web version of your library, edit your profile and search for papers, groups or people. You can also access Mendeley's social features.*

Sync: *The process of synchronizing your Mendeley data across devices.*

Web Importer: *The browser extension that lets you quickly add references to your library from anywhere on the web.*

Citation Plugin: *A plugin you can install that allows you to create and format your citations and bibliography according to your chosen style.'*

Task for the activity:

1. Visit Mendeley.com.
2. Create a profile.
3. Download the desktop software.
4. Import your articles and reading to use in your academic work.
5. Check the plug in works in Word or Pages (or the processing software you prefer to work with).
6. When inputting references into your sentences, use the plug in software to allocate and build the list for the document.
7. Insert a bibliography (call this a reference list if sources are used in the submission) and ensure this uses the correct style (Harvard, for example) for your studies.
8. Check the reference list and sources used in the submission to ensure they are correct.

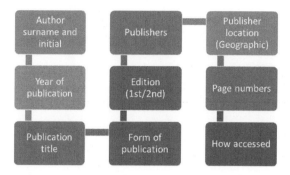

Figure 15.2 Information needed in a reference

Even though you may have read enough and planned all sources correctly, you may still find you need further knowledge to effectively write the assignment. Make sure any questions on the content are raised using a comment or separate file to use in future searches and edits.

Nota bene: In this step we have noted that your sources and references be listed within a reference list. A bibliography is a list of sources, which includes those read whilst researching and writing an academic assignment, but not necessarily used in the final assignment, and those references actually used within the assignment.

Step 9: Add and improve words to clarify your position

One of the most difficult areas in academic writing is your ability to clarify your position and then convey this correctly to your reader. Table 15.1 offers some key phrases to pick and use when clarifying or establishing your position.

Step 10: Edit and proof read

The final step in your academic writing is to edit and proof read the work before you submit it. Firstly, go back over the queries raised when writing the submission and establish if the queries have evident gaps in the knowledge or train of thought offered. If there are still gaps, find or use literature that supports the answer to the question and weave this into your paragraphs. You should then complete three edits of your work to tighten and improve before submission:

1. Meaning and intent.
2. Spelling and grammar.
3. Assessment instruction and marking criteria.

The first sweep of edits is best completed by another person. You could read a paragraph three times and not see an obvious omission in meaning or direction (due to the fact that you have written it!). Ask a course mate, family member or friend to

Table 15.1 Words and phrases which convey your position

Aim of the sentence/section	Words to assist your writing
Passive assertion from knowledge learnt from reading.	It can be seen that It is suggested that Empirical evidence has demonstrated It has been reported that It is argued that
To introduce similar or further ideas linked.	Moreover Furthermore Also Additionally Similarly
Introduce a theory or topic.	Author (year) suggests/articulates the view/ posits/argues/offers/adopts the position that/ take the view that
To show agreement with something.	This theory … … has good descriptive power … is well supported … is appropriate and clear … has excellent face validity
To show disagreement with something.	This theory … … neglects to consider … underestimates … ignores … assumes without evidence
To clarify your logic and train of thought.	It follows from this Therefore, It is clear that This position suggests that These ides could be used to support
To offer caution in consideration of a position.	However, Nevertheless, Despite this, Caution must be used To introduce a caveat
Signposts to help the reader understand where you are in your argument/discussion.	To clarify In summary This means that For example Essentially then Firstly/to follow/to discuss More simply

read the work for consistency, meaning and intent. Are they clear on what you wanted to discuss or analyse? Is your position in relation to the assignment and literature clear? Ask them to highlight or raise questions on areas that are unclear to them. Then the second sweep is in spelling and grammar. This can be completed using the work processing software you may have written the piece of work within, however, as some computer checks will only confirm the spelling and not the correct word used in a sentence, it is advisable you ask a colleague to check this for you also. Finally, you need to align the work written in accordance with the assessment instructions and marking criteria. You have used these twice within the ten steps on academic writing, but here you must review one final time before you submit to ensure the work is clear and completes the task set.

SUMMARY

1.   To understand the basic conventions required within academic writing.

Before you begin writing, it is important you have an assignment plan in place and academic sources read to support your writing. Once your reading is complete and you have an assignment plan, use the opening section of this chapter to reconfirm your usual habits and practices when writing academic assignments. Paragraph formation and ten rules were offered to aid your reflection on basic writing conventions. These may differ in style according to the requirements of the marking criteria.

2.   To identify where judgement, power and balance are present in academic writing.

Your own judgement of articles, the power you attribute to published literature and balance for each source you cite are considerations to make when writing academic assignments. Your judgement is important in consideration of your authorial voice and sources to discuss. The sources you pick to include in your work shows the power you have to control and manage information, and the balance in writing is seen in the number of times you use the same or similar references. If you consider your judgement, power and balance in your writing you will be able to reflect on how to alter and improve your writing style using academic sources.

3.   To outline strategies for academic writing.

Ten steps were outlined in completing your academic writing. This was offered from the position of completing an assignment within your studies. Drafting, editing and checking your work throughout the writing process is important for developing and improving your writing skills.

Questions to support your learning and research

1. How are colons and semi-colons used differently?
2. Which words should be italicised in an academic assignment?
3. When is it ok to use a direct quotation longer than one line?
4. What do rhetorical questions suggest in a standard critical writing assignment?
5. How are apostrophes used differently?
6. What is the obvious area of difference when using British versus American spelling?
7. When you use the same reference repeatedly in a paragraph what does the reader think about your knowledge?

Chapter 16

Secondary and primary sources

LEARNING OBJECTIVES

1. To understand types or categories of sources.
2. To align primary and secondary sources to different research methods.
3. To analyse how primary and secondary sources are used in academic and professional contexts.

INTRODUCTION

This chapter will offer you an overview of what primary and secondary sources are. These forms of sources are vital for your academic development as you will be required to find secondary sources and create primary sources in your assignments. Your ability to distinguish between these will also aid your researcher competence and critical thinking skills. Identification of the types or categories of sources will be offered to begin with to establish what these are. This is followed by aligning them to research methods in order to appraise their use in different approaches to research. Finally, evidence of how these sources are used in academic and professional contexts will outline how you can use these in developing your researcher competence.

TYPES AND CATEGORIES OF SOURCES

Primary and secondary data was defined in Chapter 13 of this part. Here, it is important to consider types or categories of sources in order to understand the variety of ways in which they can inform your academic and professional development.

Brotherton (2011) noted that there are three categories of information that can be used in the development of knowledge: primary, secondary and tertiary. Primary data is new

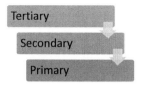

Figure 16.1 Stages of using types of data in your academic work

information gained with the specific purpose of answering a research question or objective. Secondary is information collected by other people and published to consider or learn new knowledge. Tertiary is then paraphrased or summarised secondary data to form a new type of publication (like encyclopaedias or indexes). Cameron (2010) confirms this assertion in three types of data (primary, secondary and tertiary) and notes that tertiary sources are often used to begin development of your knowledge within a topic.

Figure 16.1 clarifies how you should use the types or categories of data in your academic research. Beginning with indexes, glossaries or encyclopaedias you can understand generic definitions of key topics. Next, look to the secondary data published in academic, peer-reviewed sources (textbooks and journal articles) to understand research and positions concluded on these within practical and theoretical positions. Depending on the type of work to complete, you may then be required to complete primary data collection. Primary data collection involves you gathering new information. This could be either via approaching research participants and asking for their perspectives on the topic, or by completing new desk-based analysis on secondary data (usually quantitative reports or previously analysed qualitative data).

USING PRIMARY AND SECONDARY SOURCES IN DIFFERENT RESEARCH METHODS

In Chapter 12 of this part you will have learnt about the various approaches and philosophies used in academic research. Within this discussion, the levels and layers of research were clarified from Saunders et al.'s (2009) research onion. When completing research you have choices to make in consideration of the data and method to use in answering your specific area of investigation. This section will discuss the fourth through sixth layers of this onion and outline the forms of primary and secondary data that may be present.

Starting with the fourth layer, choices, you have to consider whether you are going to research using one, multiple or mixed methods. Examples of research methods which could be used in singular form are noted below:

- Literature review.
- Survey.
- Interview.
- Focus group.

If you choose to use one of the above methods, you will still require both primary and secondary data to support your research. The level of importance of each of these sources, however, will vary. For example, if you use the conclusions from a literature review of secondary data the conclusions may be based on new positions not tested with primary analysis. In this way you may want to utilise publications of secondary source critique to test with primary data and analysis to draw comparisons to previously suggested positions. Comparatively, if you use the conclusions from research that gathered and analysed primary data your research will be testing an existing theory in alternative contexts. It is usual in mono method for you to place importance on the emergence of primary data analysis. However, the secondary data should inform creation of the data collection tools for primary data and so should be included at each stage.

Multiple and mixed methods data is dependent on the order and timing of the methods employed to gather the data. Mono method will allow you to collect data in one go, but mixed and multiple will be completed over time.

Figure 16.2 offers a visual example of how mono, mixed and multiple research can operate. A mono method would see a simple line of research from secondary to primary, to results and conclusions. Mixed methods would employ more than one method and use these to explore different areas or consider the same topic from different perspectives. Multiple methods are seen in longitudinal research whereby the researcher may use a number of years to explore, reconsider and evaluate information and data in a range of contexts and with a range of participants. Another example of this is clarified in Table 16.1.

Table 16.1 clarifies how mixed and multiple methods may be used in the same piece of research. On the one hand, the stimulated recalls are based on the submitted data from each participant, but they are questioned using a suite of questions developed from previous recalls. In this way the questions to participants are based upon both primary and secondary data. The first set of questions being based on secondary data, and this then altering in mind of primary data gathered within the process of completing the research. This example showcases how mixed and multiple methods can enhance the results of research as it is tested and verified within the project. This detail is not to say this way is superior or best but that secondary and primary research is not simply available and found – it can also be emergent within a research project.

A common form of mixed method employed by THE students is to interview one group of participants and survey another. For example, you might survey a group of customers (due to the availability of a number of participants) and interview staff and/or management. In this way you will be able to offer comment and analysis from two groups of participants who may be present within the area of analysis. This is seen as a form of triangulation as the secondary data is tested and verified from multiple positions (Denzin, 1978).

Data triangulation is seen as the time, space and people within the data and these are offered from different perspectives;

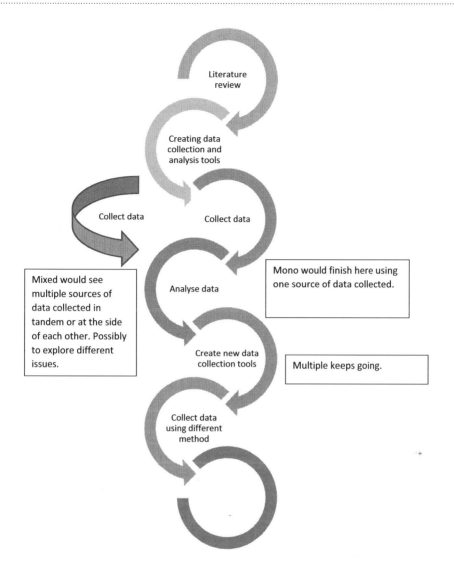

Figure 16.2 Mono, mixed and multiple methods of data gathering

Table 16.1 Using multiple and mixed methods

Date	Data gathering and analysis being completed
Wk1	Critical incidents recorded by P1 on mobile phone.
Wk2	Receive and listen to P1 incidents. Make a note of questions to raise.
Wk3	Stimulated recall with P1 and P2 gathering incidents.
Wk4	Interview with P1 and listening to P2 incidents. Using P1 data to create questions to P2.
Wk5	Stimulated recall with P2 and P4 gathering incidents. Using questions from previous stimulated recall to check for accuracy and similarity in P2.

Note: P = participant

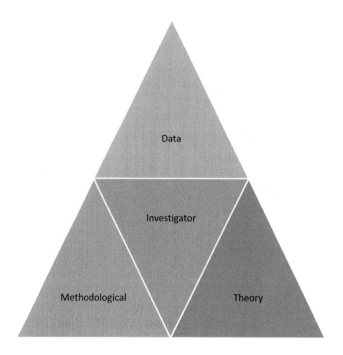

Figure 16.3 Forms of data triangulation
Source: based upon Denzin, 1978

Investigator triangulation is when there are multiple versus single researchers observing and analysing the data.

Theory triangulation is whereby multiple perspectives on a theory are considered within the analysis of data gathered.

Methodological triangulation is whereby multiple analyses are completed within the data or between methods.

THINK POINT 16.1 WHICH FORM OF TRIANGULATION?

David uses survey data to investigate customer opinions on the service standards offered at his hotel. After completing analysis himself, he passes on the raw data to his area manager to analyse and comment on also. What form of triangulation, noted by Denzin, 1978, is being used here?

Within the fourth layer, choices, it is clear that primary and secondary data are both required. These will either be static within mono method, or emergent and tested within mixed and multiple methods. Triangulation may also be present and dependent on the people completing the research and perspectives required.

The next layer from the research onion is the time horizon. This indicates the time and amount of information required and gathered. If you are conducting a review of an activity, for example, you may decide to survey participants at the beginning, middle and end. This would be sectional over a period of time and be considered longitudinal data. The time of the activity and points in between the gathering of data does not need to be of a minimum or maximum length. The importance is that you can track or observe the data from similar people, or tasks, at key points. The sectionality of the data is when the data is gathered within the usual stage of a process. For example, to gain customer satisfaction data, you would need to survey them at the end of their experience rather than at the beginning. Examples of longitudinal and sectional data gathering of primary data is clarified for THE as follows in Table 16.2.

Table 16.2 Sectional and longitudinal data in THE

Sectional	Longitudinal
Interviewing management after one year of work experience within a company.	Gathering skills appraisals before, during and after a training event.
Surveying customers after receiving an experience.	Surveying customers before and after they have completed a leisure experience.
Focus group with new staff before induction into the company.	Interviewing staff three times within a year at work to establish patterns of motivation.

The sectional and longitudinal elements to data gathering are all linked to primary data. The time horizon is important within these as they situate and contextualise the data according to the time and people completing the research. Time horizon can also be considered for secondary data in the following ways:

1. Age of literature used.
2. Perspectives that are considered in the literature.
3. Whether authors consider this from different stages of a process or one singular point.

These points enable you to consider whether secondary literature is also sectional or longitudinal. One such longitudinal dataset seen as secondary are economic reports or labour market statistics. These publish information in cycles and are seen to explore the same information at different times.

The sixth and final layer of the research onion relates to the specific technique or method employed for the data analysis. These are outlined below with examples of the primary data usual in its completion:

- Case study: location of the case study should be specific. A city, business or group of people are examples of an appropriate focus. These participants evidence the case study as they all belong to a narrow context.
- Survey: participants are gathered from a sample of a larger population. For example, if you survey 100 students out of a total cohort of 200 you would have a 50% sample of the total population. The response rate from this 100 asked to complete the data is then important in noting the relevance of the analysis to the total population of 200.
- Grounded theory: a question is posed before a review of the secondary and primary data. This question forms the basis of a theory and as you gather and analyse more data the theory is tested and altered according to the results gained.
- Ethnography: the study of people, cultures and histories. You would usually gather diary accounts or observations on situations in order to understand issues and activities occurring in the area.
- Action research: this should consider a new activity or seek to solve an identified problem. If there is a new training course you can complete action research to evaluate the success of the training. Conversely, a problem identified by an employer can be researched through evaluating actions taken to solve it.
- Experiment: a scientific method within which something is analysed under control conditions. Analysis of the results of the experiment would need a controlled group and a group that has had significant change.
- Archival research: primary research is created based upon analysis and comparison of secondary data. New analysis is completed on archived data in order to understand links or reasons for societal issues.

SOURCES USED IN ACADEMIC AND PROFESSIONAL CONTEXTS

Finally, to appraise the use and need for secondary and primary sources, this section will outline case studies in which both sources of data are required in academic and professional contexts. The cases discussed include creation of a menu, group presentations and writing a business plan. These four examples are discussed using the processes for completion and alignment of primary and secondary data gathering and analysis linked at key points.

Menu creation

Menu creation is seen as needing all three types of data in order to create a dish and serve this to customers. Data gathering is not linear and static as you will need to reflect and repeat the gathering of some data (particularly feedback on perceptions on the dish).

Table 16.3 Menu creation

Stage in the process	Form of data gathering or analysis
Write menu components.	Use existing knowledge of menu creation from tertiary sources.
Source ingredients.	
Practice making the dish.	Use secondary data on guidance for cooking.
Try the dish.	Primary data in understanding a perspective on the dish.
Alter the dish to ensure it meets the required standards.	Check secondary data on legislation for food standards and hygiene.
Ask others to try and evaluate the dish.	Primary data with other perspectives.
Cost the dish.	Secondary data gathering on prices and quality of ingredients from different suppliers.
Place on menu.	
Customers order.	
Obtain feedback from customers and alter the dish accordingly.	Primary data gathering to obtain customer perspectives.

Table 16.4 Group presentation

Stage in the process	Form of data gathering or analysis
Read assessment instructions.	
Meet as a group and identify who will complete which aspects of the work.	
Gather information to support your work.	Secondary data collection.
Analyse other group members' information and apply this to the assignment.	Secondary data analysis.
Create the presentation using all knowledge gained.	Primary data created.
Practice the presentation.	
Rehearse and make changes to improve.	Primary data analysed (opinions on the presentation).
Check the presentation meets the marking criteria for the submission.	

Group presentation

Within a group presentation you will need to gather primary and secondary data and analyse these. Applying analysis on both will ensure the data forms a cohesive presentation on existing information available and your groups' position on this literature.

Writing a business plan

Creating a business plan will require you to gather a range of primary data from different sources. Secondary data will be required when aligning the business idea to theories or positions on the idea. For example, if you create a staffing company you should look to human resource and talent management theory in order to outline potential issues, barriers and triumphs feasible within the business.

Table 16.5 Writing a business plan

Stage in the process	Form of data gathering or analysis
Identify a business idea.	
Find existing companies offering this service or product.	Primary data collection.
Investigate theories and positions on this business idea.	Secondary data collection and analysis.
Identify gaps in the current market related to your business idea.	Primary data analysis.
Identify customer markets or segments who would use your business.	Primary data collection.
Create business objectives.	
Find suppliers for your business.	Primary data collection.
Outline costs of sales and prices within your business.	
Identify the legal frameworks you need to work within.	Primary data collection.
Create a business plan based on your knowledge.	Primary data analysis and conclusions.
Trial aspects of your business with customers who will use your business.	Primary data collection and analysis.
Ask industry networks opinions on your business plan.	Primary data collection and analysis.
Alter the business plan from feedback gained.	
Create the business and go to launch.	

SUMMARY

1. To understand types or categories of sources.

Three types or categories of data were outlined here. Primary data is new data gathered or analysed. Secondary is existing published literature. Tertiary data is located within encyclopaedias, indexes or glossaries. All three forms of data are essential for your academic studies. It is usual for you to use secondary data in essays and critical reviews of a topic. Dissertations and research projects will require you to gain and analyse primary data. Tertiary data can be used to supplement your knowledge but are not often demanded as part of academic submissions for THE.

2. To align primary and secondary sources to different research methods.

This chapter offered information to support your awareness of the use of primary and secondary sources in completing a research project. Singular research methods, multiple and mixed methods were outlined as needing different levels of data types. Triangulation was defined as a way of analysing a topic from a range of perspectives in order to verify conclusions and assertions from your and others research. Sectional and longitudinal data clarified how your primary data has a position and therefore relevance within the context in which you analyse the data. Finally, different methods of research were outlined to clarify examples of primary and secondary data to use within each.

3. To analyse how primary and secondary sources are used in academic and professional contexts.

Menu creation, group presentation and business plan writing were offered as three tasks that require primary and secondary data gathering and analysis. Outlining the stages within each of these enables links to be made to different forms of data gathering and analysis. All require primary and secondary data and the skills learnt from your academic studies can be applied in problem solving in industry contexts.

Questions to support your learning and research

1. What is tertiary data?
2. Do you have to gain participant data to analyse and offer primary data?
3. Where should secondary data be gathered from?
4. What is the difference between mixed and multiple methods?
5. What is triangulation?
6. How do sectional and longitudinal data differ?
7. What data types are required in a case study?
8. What data types are needed for action research?
9. How can archival research be conducted?

Further reading to support of your learning from this chapter

Bell, J. (2009). *Doing Your Research Project: A Guide for First-time Researchers in Education, Health and Social Science*. UK: Open University Press.

Creswell, J. (2009). *Research Design: Qualitative, Quantitative and Mixed Methods Approaches*, 3rd ed. UK: Sage Publications.

Field, A. and Hole, G. (2003). *How to Design and Report Experiments*. UK: Sage Publications.

Johnson, J. (1990). *Selecting Ethnographic Informants*. London, England: Sage Publications.

LeCompte, M. and Goetz, J. (1993). *Ethnography and Qualitative Design in Educational Research*, 2nd ed. Academic Press Inc. [online]. Available from: www.loc.gov/catdir/description/els032/92028787.html.

Lecompte, M.D. (1982). Problems of reliability and validity in ethnographic research. *Review of Educational Research*, 52(1), pp. 31–60.

Moustaka, C. (1994). *Phenomenological Research Methods*. Thousand Oaks, USA: Sage Publications.

Pallant, J. (2011). *SPSS Survival Manual: A Step by Step Guide to Data Analysis Using the SPSS Program*, 4th ed. Crows Nest, Australia: Allen and Unwin.

Silverman, D. (2006). *Qualitative Research: Theory, Method and Practice*, 2nd ed. London: Sage Publications.

Strauss, A. and Corbin, J. (1994). Grounded theory methodology. In *Handbook of Qualitative Research*, pp. 273–285.

Chapter 17
Motivating yourself

INTRODUCTION

Motivation has already been noted and linked to your ability to develop initiative (Part 2, Chapter 6), have self-awareness and reflexivity on your actions and behaviour (Part 2, Chapter 7) and acknowledgement of your motivations for reading for academic success (Part 3, Chapter 12). You may also develop knowledge of motivation theory within the study of human resource management on your course. This chapter will offer an overview of key motivation theory and enable you to critique and explore your usual motivation when completing tasks for academic and professional development.

NURTURING AND DEVELOPING YOUR MOTIVATION

'Being motivated' is often seen as a personality trait or skilling level. This is due to your natural tendency to want to do something and if you are interested, driven or inspired to act and learn more. However, as a student of THE you also need to critique your motivation and nurture this in order to maintain standards of work and learning for your course. Motivation is often easier when in full-time work as you will have set shift patterns and daily tasks to complete. As a student you will have time around your classes, which will need to be used effectively to complete your reading, research and applied understanding of THE working contexts.

Within human resource management publications and studies you will be required to consider how you can motivate others. This is a usual position to consider in THE studies as you need to ensure your staff and suppliers offer high levels of service to satisfy your customers. The THE literature on staff motivation often neglects the personal and academic development entwined within motivating staff in that you also need to nurture and develop your own motivation.

If you are motivated you are also often happy, content, driven, satisfied and clear on the task at hand. These linked positions mean that completing tasks that you are motivated to do will be done to a good or high standard. De-motivation as the opposite will lead to you feeling dissatisfied, unhappy and potentially anxious about the work to complete. Lacking motivation can also lead you to ignore key tasks and postpone work until the last minute, again resulting in lower standards of work completed.

As motivation links to a basic need to complete tasks it is often considered using Maslows (1943) hierarchy of needs (offered and discussed in Part 2, Chapter 6). Completion and support for the levels in this hierarchy is said to lead to self-actualisation in that you are fully capable and competent to complete tasks and work set. When completing academic and professional work you might lack some of these elements, which then leads to demotivation. The levels of this hierarchy are offered below and are linked to academic motivation to complete work set.

Physiological needs

In order to feel capable and willing to complete a task you need to support your basic physiological needs. These include being rested, hydrated and having eaten appropriately. If you have not slept well you will find it harder to find your motivation to complete the most basic of tasks. Travel leading to jet lag will also affect this and may make you feel less able to complete tasks. An important position to take here is to recognise that you need to support your physiological needs and that if you are unfit to complete work, don't! Sitting at a desk or in the library forcing yourself to complete work when you are hungry and only had three hours sleep will only lead to poor quality work and a sense that you are incapable of doing the work. Furthermore, you will have a natural tendency to work better with specific physiological needs met. Do you work best in the morning? Do you need to snack on food whilst working to satiate your appetite?

**THINK POINT 17.1 WHAT PHYSIOLOGICAL NEEDS
DO YOU HAVE?**

Consider the last time you completed a large piece of writing for academic studies. What were your usual times of working? What practices did you employ to support this work? How do you feel about these usual practices and did they help or hinder your motivation?

Safety needs

Similar to your physiological needs, your safety needs are surrounding support required to make you feel comfortable to complete tasks. If, for example, you are worried about money and are unsure if you will be able to pay your rent or purchase food for the week, this will greatly affect your motivation as you will feel unsafe and unsecure. Being able to work and live in a safe and secure environment is crucial to motivation as it allows you to feel content and capable. In situations where you are feeling unsecure or unsafe consider the degree to which you have control over them. Are you able to earn more money? Are you able to work in a more safe location? If you feel unwell are there actions you can take to make yourself feel better? Your reflection and ability to use agency is important here to develop better safety frames for you to complete tasks set.

Love and belonging

Procrastination is commonplace when completing academic studies. Finding academic articles, understanding content, figuring out the theoretical positions and terminology can all lead to you whinging about the work at hand. This is important as you need to accept difficult tasks and overcome them to feel competent and capable to repeat the tasks in the future. A key element to procrastination is having friends and family whom you can confide in and communicate with. This could be face to face, verbal or virtual. The relationships you have to complete this communication is, therefore, important. Having a friend on your course to discuss, ask questions and validate your feelings about academic work is vital to maintain your motivation. In addition, your personal relationships outside of work and study will equally support your motivation as you may be working towards living with someone and marriage. In this way the love and belonging you receive and offer to friends, family and romantic partners is crucial to your ability to discuss your feelings and feel supported to complete work.

Esteem

As discussed in Part 2 Chapter 6, your self-awareness and self-esteem are linked and require development. Having confidence in your ability to complete academic and professional tasks will enable you to be motivated to complete the work. Without self-esteem you will not feel capable to do the work. Esteem is evident if you manage and take care of your physiological, safety and love and belonging needs first. Once you are comfortable with these first three levels you will have evidenced self-respect and have nurtured your self-esteem. Negative thoughts will inhibit your self-esteem and become a barrier to successful academic development.

THINK POINT 17.2 NEGATIVE THOUGHTS IMPACTING SELF-ESTEEM

When starting a task you will naturally consider your ability and competence to complete the work. This is due to you needing to consider how you will approach the task, the time set aside to do the work and the level which you expect the final product to achieve. Within this you naturally have positive and negative thoughts. Negative thoughts will impede your motivation to complete the work to a high standard. So what are your negative thoughts? How do you beat yourself up mentally when completing academic work? How can you challenge these? Would your class mates and friends agree with them? If you can accept them as biased and subjective are you able to put them to one side and acknowledge that they are hindering your motivation?

Self-actualisation

Being self-actualised is where you are capable and competent to do the best you can. At this level you will be as motivated as possible and willing to take on the tasks at hand. All previous levels of Maslow's (1943) hierarchy need to be complete to a basic level in order for you to feel self-actualised. For example, to read a book chapter and two journal articles you need to:

- Be rested and have eaten and drank.
- Sit in a location that is safe and quiet to allow you to read.
- Have connection to people to ask and discuss the reading.
- Feel capable of completing the work.

Nurturing motivation to complete this task is simply to check you have each of these elements before you begin. Problems in your motivation will arise when you disregard one or more of them as you will lose concentration and feel unable to complete the work.

Maslow's (1943) hierarchy of needs is a useful framework to consider your basic needs for motivation to complete academic tasks. Within these basic levels you will be unable to complete the work for a sustained and high level. However, motivation is also linked to outcomes, reward and achievement. It is unusual for someone to complete a task without an external or internal feeling of satisfaction. This is where the expectancy model of motivation (Vroom, 1964; Lawler and Porter, 1967) needs consideration. The expectancy model of motivation is whereby you consider the potential outcomes resulting from the exerted effort and the degree to which you need to work. For example, if you are reading a newspaper article you immediately know you do not need high levels of concentration and you will obtain a biased account of a news or research topic. Conversely, if you read a journal article from a relevant and high ranking journal you will have to exert more focus and expect to work hard to understand the content and resulting conclusions. Both of these academic tasks require knowledge of a reason to complete the task and expected outcome to support the level of exertion.

You may have been asked to complete an assignment for your studies and be doing so to enable a high mark and high degree award. However, if you expect a high mark to be above 90% and you received 72%, your perceptions on the actual outcome may not match the expectation. Therefore, there is some movement and reflection needed when using this model of motivation as your expectations and perceptions may not be accurate. Further, if you do not understand the criteria or feedback offered on the work you have completed it is easy to become disenfranchised and disengage with the outcomes from the work. This will result in lower motivation to repeat the task in the future.

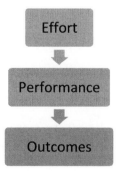

Figure 17.1 Expectancy model of motivation
Source: based on Vroom, 1964; Lawler and Porter, 1967

In order to understand the expectancy model of motivation and use this to nurture your own motivation in tasks, we will consider the extrinsic and intrinsic outcomes. These are categorised outcomes resulting from effort and performance and you have control of how these can support your motivation.

Extrinsic outcomes

Extrinsic outcomes are the results and rewards seen as a physical and external product of your performance in a task. For example, in employment you will receive monetary payment for completing time at work. In academic studies you will be working towards a desired degree level, which in turn will lead to paid employment. Extrinsic outcomes are seen as

- Payment.
- Marks.
- Presents or physical rewards on achieving an outcome.

Payment and marks will be an outcome set and prescribed by a job description and marking criteria. These are explicit and clear prior to completing the task. Your ability to interpret the marking criteria and instructions for an assignment is important to ensure you do not exert effort in incorrect ways. Examples of this are offered in the following chapter. Presents or physical rewards are things you can create and control yourself. For example, you may set yourself the task of reading for two hours before class. If you achieve this goal you could reward yourself with a bar of chocolate or a trip to the local charity shop to look at clothes. Family members may also offer you extrinsic outcomes from meeting your targets. Money, employment or a holiday are examples of extrinsic rewards you may be offered if you meet certain targets. All of these can assist your motivation so long as you are interested in the outcome offered.

THINK POINT 17.3 PERCEIVED DIFFERENCE OF MOTIVATION IN YOUR PEERS

Have you ever been shocked by a classmates lack of motivation to complete the work set? Are you amazed by people who do work last minute? Are you curious as to why some people start their work the day the assignment is set? These positions are due to your own perceptions of extrinsic motivations. They are individual to you and yet your perceptions of them make you question how you and they differ so dramatically. The reasons behind this is due to their differing motivations to exert effort. Neither is right or wrong and both work to a set of expectations from completing the work. The difficulty is that as a human, and someone who reflects and empathises, you automatically ask how and why you work differently and if that method results in different outcomes. If you work consistently hard on a piece of work and see a class mate start the assignment the night before and you both achieve the same outcome in marks you can feel cheated and annoyed at seemingly exerting more effort than them. This is not the case, however. Yours and others abilities in exerting and competing work differs in a number of ways. Think about your position and reflections on your work ethic and others around you. Ask them why they work in that way and what motivated them to continue efforts in a set method.

Intrinsic outcomes

Intrinsic outcomes are based on your self-esteem and sense of achievement gained from completing the work. If you have never written 5000 words, and you achieve this, regardless of the standard you will feel a sense of achievement in having completed the task set. Self-esteem and an appreciation of the task completed is an internal and individual position. Celebrating these successes is important to nurture your self-worth and appraise your abilities. Doing so will lead to development and improvement in your work. Examples of intrinsic outcomes from academic and professional tasks are noted below for consideration:

- Completing a task for the first time.
- Achieving your highest mark for a submission.
- Receiving customer or management feedback on doing a job to a good or higher than expected standard.
- Finishing work within the time set.
- Perception of improved ability in completing a task.
- Acknowledgement of your ability to set and achieve higher standards.

These examples will vary in occurrence due to your personality and natural disposition to appraise and reflect on your abilities. Some people may always challenge themselves to do better and achieve higher. In these instances it is important to utilise friends and family to ground you and reflect on the strides and improvements you have made. Conversely, others may over attribute their outcomes and feel they have done better than they needed to and, therefore, this reduces their motivation. Understanding and managing these self-esteem elements to motivation is important to maintain a balance in your sense of achievement.

Discussion on motivational theory here has clarified how your ability to appraise and manage the effort and perceived outcomes from tasks will help develop and nurture your motivation. Acknowledgement of motivation and how you can control this will lead to your ability to manage expectations and outcomes from the effort put in.

MOTIVATIONAL THEORIES APPLIED IN ACADEMIC AND PROFESSIONAL CONTEXTS

In addition to the theories explored to appraise and nurture your motivation, this section will now apply a range of motivational theories to academic and professional contexts as evidence of how these are manifest and result in perceived outcomes. Outcomes exemplified span both extrinsic and intrinsic forms to clarify how a mixture of these are present in tasks you complete.

Incentivise your work

Incentives are rewards you identify as being an outcome of work completed. You establish these before starting a task to motivate yourself to complete it to a set standard or level. The type of incentive you allocate to a task will depend on the task itself and availability of extrinsic outcomes possible. Within professional development it is accepted that completing academic work will lead to increased knowledge and ability to undertake critical examination and thought. This is a desired outcome required by your tutors and, however, this may not be a personal incentive you actively consider. It is a required outcome from completing academic studies, but not one often sought specifically by students.

THINK POINT 17.4 CRITICAL THINKING AS AN INCENTIVISED SKILL

A core skill to develop within your THE studies is to become a critical thinker. Through active reading and examination of published literature and research you will naturally develop a critical lens when considering knowledge, theory and opinion. This is an intrinsic outcome from completing work and can enable you to adapt and offer flexible alternatives to the usual ways of doing and thinking about something. Consider for a moment why this is a skill and how it will aid your self-esteem. If you only consider one position and have one version of the truth how will this impede your development? How can you establish and acknowledge developed critical thinking? What outcome will be an incentive as a result of this?

Incentives can be seen as a form of hygiene or motivational factor in motivational theory (Herzberg, 1959). Hygiene factors include extrinsic outcomes like improved pay and marks. Motivational factors are intrinsic and relate to personal growth, achievement and advancement. Herzberg's (1959) two factor theory can be applied in review of incentives as an additional dualism similar to extrinsic and intrinsics. Herzberg's theory was written to support job satisfaction and retention of employees, but can be applied to academic contexts as it outlines how satisfaction and dissatisfaction in a task can result in motivation and drive.

Rewarding loyalty

Hospitality cafés and coffee shops are common places for loyalty schemes. When purchasing your hot beverage you may be offered a loyalty card that is stamped each time you purchase a drink. Upon purchasing a set number of these you are rewarded by being given a free product. This form of loyalty is commonplace in THE business, but it can also be utilised to support your own motivation. For example, if you set yourself the task of reading for two hours per day, you could reward yourself upon completing this. Intrinsically, you could allow yourself an alternative exercise or activity from completing repeated effective work. For example, at the end of a day of writing, you could reward your loyalty to sitting at a desk by going for a run or a walk.

CASE STUDY 17.1 SEEING LOYALTY REWARDED THROUGH THEORY X AND THEORY Y

Rewarding loyalty can be applied to McGregor's (1957) theory of X and Y of employees, which was published in support of human relations theory. McGregor saw employees as being either theory X or theory Y and that they were innately liking or disliking work required. If you acknowledge that a person either likes (X) or dislikes (Y) the task at hand, you can offer support to motivate and manage their completion of the task better.

McGregor's (1957) theory was created in support of managing employees, but can be used to support academic development in addressing your position to a task at hand.

If you accept that you do not want to do something, you need to scaffold support around the task and reward loyalty in repetition of good behaviour.

If you are happy to complete a task, then the loyalty rewarded should be based upon going above and beyond the usual tasks associated.

Theory X and theory Y can be used as a frame to support loyalty in repeated effective task completion but it requires individual appraisal of your own feelings towards the task. If you consistently reward good practice you will not push yourself and develop further. Equally, if you accept you do not want to complete a task and ignore it, you will not achieve the highest standard as an outcome.

Badges and certificates of completion

Within employment your work will be rewarded by pay and promotion. This may result in further responsibility or income but will outline your ability to complete tasks to a set level. In academic practice your marks, grades and degree classifications will denote your completion of work to a set standard. Around these there are other badges and certificates you can complete in support of the end goal. Attending a workshop on referencing, being trained on health and safety law or going to a networking event are all examples of attending extra professional and extracurricular activities. These will often result in you being awarded or certified in a new skill or activity.

ACTIVITY 17.1 FINDING ADDITIONAL COURSES AND TRAINING TO SUPPORT YOUR GOALS

Regardless of the level of study you are currently in, there will be additional courses and training events that can support your academic development. These can be used as incentives to motivate and increase your employability and skills.

1. Find out which extracurricular courses are offered at your education institution.
2. Identify which of these courses will support your academic development based on your current knowledge and skill level.
3. Book to attend.
4. Identify the learning objectives for the course and the outcomes from completing the training.
5. Attend the course.
6. Appraise the knowledge and skills developed from the course and identify a future course to attend to develop your skills further.
7. Discuss the training completed with class mates and tutors in terms of how they see it as beneficial to your studies and ability.
8. Add the course to your CV as extracurricular training.

Team and group work

Any activity completed with a team or group of people will require motivation and effort in different ways to individual work. Chapter 18 of this part considers group work in detail. Here, team and group work is noted as it is a component part to employment duties in THE but also a usual motivator to completing academic studies. Revising in pairs or groups, attending a reading group, sharing lecture notes and discussing literature in class activities

Table 17.1 Theory of achievement for motivating yourself

Area	Evident in usual motivations for work
Affiliation	You want to work in a group. You need intimacy and trust with others to be motivated. You have a need to be liked and will go a long way to seek affirmation from others. You prefer to work collaboratively rather than in completion with others. You avoid risks and work that is uncertain in effort and outcome.
Power	You prefer to win arguments rather than discuss positions. You seek status and recognition. You enjoy influencing and leading others. You achieve satisfaction in winning.
Achievement	You want to work alone. You have a desire to obtain feedback within stages of completing a task. You use goals and targets to organise work set. If you do not achieve the goal set it inhibits your future motivation.
Avoidance	You allow anxiety to inhibit motivation. You feel fear leads to avoiding tasks. You are concerned about failure and so avoid work. You do not like power relations present and so avoid tasks to avoid conflict.

Source: based upon McCelland, 1988

are all usual actions in academic study. These will support your motivation in a different way as you are being relied upon to enhance the work and knowledge of others.

An aspect of McCelland's (1988) theory of human motivation (see Table 17.1) links to team and group work as being *affiliated* with others may be important for you to achieve tasks set. Being motivated through affiliation means you naturally want to work with others to complete tasks set and achieve group goals. Working in collaboration with others to achieve group satisfaction and group development is core in this aspect of motivational theory. If you are set a task that is individualistic and you conform to this form of motivation, you will need to establish additional support frames to enable affiliation in the work set. This theory of motivation refers to four aspects: affiliation, power, achievement and avoidance, as outlined in Table 17.1.

Plan and evaluate

In the opening chapter of this part we discussed how goals and targets can be created and managed to support your academic development. Using a similar construct, use plans to organise your tasks and evaluate the outcomes at key points to support appraisal of your academic and professional development. Annual appraisals completed in work can aid your professional development plans and set a time limit on when these need to be achieved by. These are often called professional development reviews (PDRs) and can be used to plan and evaluate development within a set career trajectory. Equally, you can set plans and evaluate work completed for a single academic assignment.

Social activities after a task or event

As humans, we require social interaction and experience in order to reflect upon ourselves, feel valued by others and contribute to society. A useful motivator in support of our basic human needs is to offer a social event or activity after completing or achieving a task. A usual social activity in THE studies is to attend a celebration event after completing a year or submitting a large research project (like a dissertation, for example). These social events are not rewards for achieving a high standard but for completing a task within the required timeframe. Celebrating with others is also used as a motivational tool in THE industry. If you work in a restaurant, for example, you may be offered a meal together with staff and management at the end of a shift. Resort reps in tourist destinations may offer social activities where they and their customers participate together in the activity in order to signal the end of an experience.

The review of techniques to support your motivation has enabled application of further motivational theories. Nurture your motivation by applying different practical exercises and personal reflection to support your academic work. Motivation is not seen as individual and fixed but fluid and reliant on external people who will support you in completing the work or task at hand.

SUMMARY

1. To understand how motivation is nurtured and developed.

Motivation is enabled by control and management of your basic needs. Eat well, rest and keep hydrated to maintain your levels of human function. Work in a safe location that supports your concentration. Utilise your friends and family to discuss the work and task at hand. Be aware of your expectations on the outcomes from completing the task to ensure these are placed correctly and appropriately. Outline the extrinsic and intrinsic outcomes from completing a task to enable you to reflect on the additional outcomes from the work completed. Evaluate and appraise your continued development to enable you to actively promote your motivation through a sense of achievement and self-esteem.

2. To apply motivational theory in techniques for improved motivation in academic and professional tasks.

Six techniques were outlined and linked to motivational theory. These enable reflection on a range of tasks and approaches to work, which can enhance your motivation. Using a variety of these for each task will ensure you promote and advance your academic development. Motivational theory was critiqued as being from a desire to manage the performance of employees, but this chapter used key motivation theory in analysis of how you would approach usual academic and professional tasks.

Questions to support your learning and research

1. What is theory X?
2. What can friends and family do to support your academic achievement?
3. What does the power element of McClelland's human motivation refer to?
4. How does perceived effort link to perceived outcomes?
5. What are intrinsic and extrinsic motivations?
6. What are hygiene and motivation factors?
7. How does sex affect motivation? (Read McClelland's text for this!)

Further reading

Harding, S. et al. (2018). Maslow's hierarchy of needs. In *MBA Management Models*.

Herzberg, F., Mausner, B. and Snyderman, B.B. (2009). *The Motivation to Work*, 12th ed. Wiley.

Lawler, E.E. and Porter, L.W. (1967). *Antecedent Attitudes of Effective Managerial Performance*. Organizational Behavior and Human Performance.

Lundberg, C., Gudmundson, A. and Andersson, T.D. (2009). Herzberg's Two-Factor Theory of work motivation tested empirically on seasonal workers in hospitality and tourism. *Tourism Management*, 30(6), pp. 890–899. [online]. Available from: http://linkinghub.elsevier.com/retrieve/pii/S0261517708001969 [Accessed August 29, 2013].

Maslow, A. (1973). *On Dominance, Self-Esteem, and Self-Actualisation*. T. Books, ed.

Mcclelland, D. (2016). McClelland's theory of needs.

Taormina, R.J. and Gao, J.H. (2013). Maslow and the motivation hierarchy: Measuring satisfaction of the needs. *American Journal of Psychology*.

Chapter 18

Group work and alternative assessments

LEARNING OBJECTIVES

----

1. To appraise the importance of group work in your studies and how this links to team working in industry.
2. To understand different forms of academic group work required for tourism, hospitality and events management students.

INTRODUCTION

Part 1 of this textbook outlined the skills needed by employers in tourism, hospitality and events (THE) management applicants. Within these skills, group and team working was noted as an important skill to evidence. This is due to the businesses related to THE, requiring teams of people to create and produce leisure experiences. This chapter will offer an overview of group work to clarify what this is within your studies, how to be a good team member and how this feeds into a range of assessments to complete on your course. Working within a group is reliant on your ability to cooperate, collaborate and consider others positions and abilities. As such it also involves your self-awareness and ability to lead.

GROUP WORK IN STUDIES LEADING TO TEAM WORKING IN INDUSTRY

This chapter will begin by defining group and team work to clarify its position in academic study and employment. From this, Belbin's team roles will be discussed to enable you to appraise your usual position within a group. Finally, an overview of the achievements and barriers in successful groups.

Group and team work is where you are a component part of a larger group of people working towards the same goal. In academic studies this may be due to a group assessment where you need to plan, present or form a piece of work. In industry you may be part of a supply chain in creating an experience and rely on others to support and deliver this with your input within the chain of operations. Universities and colleges often use group work as an assessment to enable you to collaborate and develop skills in team working.

Groups and teams are collections of more than two people. Within this there needs to be a shared goal or shared sense of identity in order for the group to succeed in the task. Tuckman's (1965) work on the stages of group formation is often applied to group and team work to analyse the success within each stage and strategise effective outcomes from the people working together. The later article from Tuckman and Jensen (1977) offered four stages of group formation in order to clarify the necessary hurdles which present themselves, as shown in Figure 18.1.

Figure 18.1 Stages of group formation
Source: based upon Tuckman and Jensen, 1977: p.421

The four stages of group formation were seen to be necessary components to effective performance by the group. Each stage is not a simple action completed by the group but an emergent state felt within the group. In order to expand upon these, the following uses eight stages to align to your position with a group task set.

Stage 1: Getting to know the individuals and group as a new collective (forming)

In the initial stages of a group coming together you need to adjust to your role within the group. You may have already developed a friendship or relationship with some of the others and this needs readjustment to fit with the roles ascribed for the task. Feelings on the group make-up will be present and you need to acclimatise to cooperating with the others, learning about how they approach tasks and if this differs to your usual approach. This is an important stage as it allows you to get to know other group members and establish your position within it.

Stage 2: Release of your emotions/catharsis (storming)

When getting to know others in your group you will perceive differences and clashes in the ways you approach and identify the goal set. These conflicts are important in the opening stages and they need addressing in order to complete the cathartic release of your feelings to these positions.

THINK POINT 18.1 EXPRESSING YOUR FEELINGS WITHIN THE GROUP

When starting within a group do you naturally express your opinion? Or do you sit back and let others dominate the discussion? Are you clear on your motivations and expected outcomes? Are you cooperative in noting the tasks you can support and lead in? How does it feel if you do not express these opinions? How do you think it will affect the group if you are not open and clear on your expectations from the start?

Stage 3: Focus (norming)

Once your group are comfortable with each other and clear on their intentions and direction, you can begin to focus on active collaboration and cooperation to address the task at hand. This focussing is not simply as a group, but can be within the individual tasks allocated to group members. An issue for groups can arise if participants perceive others are not as focussed within the task.

Stage 4: And ... action! (norming)

Once the individual and collective work starts to merge and support the overall task there is an increase in action and behaviour. The ground work set up and agreed should support this. If the group has set clear deadlines and tasks there will be a natural point within the work where all members come together to support and build towards the final outcome of the task. This is often a busy (and frantic, even) position in group work.

Stage 5: Limbo (norming)

A natural progression after the action and merging of the group's work is for there to be a state of limbo. This does not mean that all members go and rest for two days but that there is a sense of relief and anxiety around the work. There will be a natural lull in activity once the bulk of the work is completed. This break and settling is important in group activity as it allows for all members to get to the same point of satisfaction before continuing with the tasks set.

Stage 6: Purposive (performing)

Using the example of a group report to be submitted, this stage is after all sections have been combined into one document and the members begin to check and verify the order, flow and contents of the submission. There is a clear purpose and task to complete and all members work to improve the submission.

Stage 7: Evaluative (exiting)

This stage can be within preparation to submit the work or after receiving feedback from your tutors. Before submission you need to complete final edits, proof reading and spelling checks on the work.

ACTIVITY 18.1 GROUP EVALUATIONS BEFORE SUBMITTING GROUP WORK

In order to complete your evaluation and final edits, follow these steps to ensure the work submitted is of a high standard and flows clearly. Split the group members into four and assign the following tasks. It is important to complete each step in order.

1. Marking criteria.
Review the marking criteria and consider the assignment instructions to check all elements are clear. To what level do you feel you have met these criteria? Which areas could you improve upon?

2. Flow and style.
Are the sections within the submission appropriate and clear? Are introductions and conclusions drawn at the right points? Is the style of writing consistent or are there differences due to the group members varied abilities? Could one person edit for style to maintain this? Are there any paragraphs ending without a clear point? What argument is offered? Are there enough secondary sources to support points made?

3. Grammar and spelling.
Read the submission out loud. Does it make sense? Where are the places you become stuck and unable to continue reading? Complete a spell check. Ensure all words are spelled correctly and also that they are the correct word for the context in which they are used (there/their etc.). Ask a friend or family member who is not on the course to read it for grammar and check it makes sense.

4. Accuracy and position.
Which forms of sources and citations have you used? Are these reliable and valid? If you have paraphrased sources, are these accurate? If you use direct quotations are

these unpacked and explained from your understanding of these? Is it clear all group members understand these in the same way? What positions are asserted in the work? Do these contradict each other due to members differing positions? How is this clarified in the submission?

Upon receiving the marks and feedback from your submitted group work it is advisable that you discuss this feedback as a group. If you consider the marks and feedback individually you may not fully understand areas where the group could have improved. As it is a group submission, the feedback is upon the group work and not individual elements you each completed. Discussion together will also enable you to be more objective in your evaluation of the task completed. If you are not able to complete this in a classroom exercise or environment, complete it in a social or study location and consider the following:

1.   Where did we meet the marking criteria?
2.   How could we improve the submission if repeated?
3.   What aspects of our work together worked well?
4.   What aspects did not work to plan and how could we address these in the future?
5.   What did the individuals in the group enjoy about working as a group?
6.   Does the group want to continue and form a reading or critical friend group to support other submissions?

Stage 8: Disentangle and disengage (exiting)

A final stage to consider is how you exit from the group. After evaluating the success and feedback on the work completed you will naturally go back to working as an individual within your studies. This can result in negative or positive emotions arising. If you enjoyed working with the group, as others supported and nurtured your development, you may feel sad and isolated. If this occurs, ensure you actively communicate this to the members of the group and ascertain future work you can complete together. If you are delighted at not being linked to the other members, consider why this is and how you may have missed opportunities to utilise other member's expertise and ability. Students are often relieved to exit from group work when they perceived an imbalance in effort from other members. If this was the case, how did you challenge and lead them to improve the work?

The eight stages of group formation offered above are based on the work from Tuckman and Jansen (1977). The four components of group formation have been developed to eight stages in order for you to apply this to discreet group work completed in academic studies.

Within the group, you may fit a specific type of team role. Belbin's (2004, 2013) publications on team roles are often applied in THE and business contexts as they enable you to identify and reflect on how you naturally work within a team. Identification of your usual team role, and approach to group work, will clarify your natural aptitude for this work but also outline barriers to the success of the group as a whole. For example, if you identify that all group members work as a plant (see this role noted below), you may find the group communicates poorly. Complete Activity 18.2 to identify your team role.

ACTIVITY 18.2 WHICH TEAM ROLE ARE YOU?

1. Go to the following website on your computer: https://www.belbin.com.
2. Download the Belbin questionnaire.
3. Complete the questionnaire.
4. Identify your individual report results.

From Activity 18.2 you will now be aware of the team role you mostly fit within. Each of the nine roles are outlined below (based on Belbin, 2013).

Resource investigator

This group member is enthusiastic and outgoing. They develop and explore opportunities. They can tend to be overly positive in their outlook and may overlook issues arising or lose interest once the group gets to the storming stage.

Teamworker

This member will enable the group to merge and cooperate better. They are seen to be diplomatic and attentive to members' positions and opinions. They need to be challenged to offer conclusions or decisions and may avoid confrontation in order to keep peace within the group.

Co-ordinator

This member will enable the group to create clear objectives and delegate tasks appropriately. They are confident and able to allocate tasks to the most suitable members of the group. They may be seen to be manipulative and offload work to others. Ensure they have enough work to complete in order to disperse tasks fairly.

Plant

Creative, good at solving problems and generates new ideas within the group. They may become too focussed within a task to communicate effectively though. This can lead to them being absent from group work and perceived as distant and seeking their own outcome for the task set.

Monitor evaluator

This member offers a logical and impartial eye on the groups work. They are considered in their position to the work set and can be seen to accurately judge options available. They may not be able to inspire others as they are seen as rigid in their approach.

Specialist

This group member will offer specialised knowledge to support the group. They may be seen to be individualistic. In discussion they may focus on minutia of details instead of being able to see the overall task at hand. They may want to inform the group of information they know on a particular aspect of the work without considering the relevance of this within the whole submission.

Shaper

The shaper will ensure the group sticks within the parameters of the task. They will challenge deviations from the work set and encourage other members to overcome issues as they arise. They may be easily provoked into conflict and may offer flippant or offensive remarks in response to being challenged. If they see a clear path to complete the task they could become angry or bad tempered if you suggest alternative ways to complete the work.

Implementer

Working to a specific strategy and being efficient in their work is a trait of the implementer. They are practical in being able to turn knowledge into action. They may be reticent to make suggested changes or alterations to an agreed plan.

Completer finisher

This member is essential to the final stages of the work. They will effectively edit and evaluate the work to ensure high standards are met. Caution is needed if this person begins to over evaluate the work as they may become anxious about whether the work is of the correct standard. Over evaluation and editing can lead a deterioration of the quality of the work.

Within the team roles outlined above, you may find that you are a mixture of two or more of the roles. This is due to your position when completing the team role questionnaire and the variety of ways you will complete tasks within the group.

These team roles can enable you to create an effective team by grouping members who appear to reflect each of the nine types. However, as the survey is self-reporting and

Table 18.1 Success and barriers in effective groups

Success	Barriers
Clear and consistent communication.	Lack of communication.
Plan created and agreed by all with specific dates to check on progress.	Unclear plan of action.
Conflict and issues are aired within the group to address and discuss professionally.	Too much procrastination.
Group works with the individual strengths of members to ensure their contribution works with their current ability.	Imbalance in academic ability.
Where tasks are perceived as simplistic or easy, the group actively works to challenge and develop better and more efficient working.	Simplistic task perceived.
Renegotiation will be required throughout the group work. Being open and flexible to this will ensure members are not dissatisfied of the group's efforts.	Missing deadlines agreed.
Within every group there will be a mix of personalities. Treat the group as a professional body and act as though you are working with them in an industry context. Be open with your feelings and clarify how you feel about situations as they arise.	Personality clashes or conflicts.

self-reflective, this may not necessarily mean the members act in this way within your group. As such, any group formed will need to consider how to succeed and overcome barriers that may arise.

The final barrier noted in Table 18.1 relates to personalities of the individuals within the group. It is rare that all group members get on throughout the task. It is advisable in situations where you are not happy with how someone is working to adopt 'I' statements. For example, instead of saying 'You aren't doing enough work!' try 'I am feeling worried about our progress as we have not completed this section yet.' Using 'I' statements is a clear form of communication whereby you can take ownership of how you feel and your concerns whilst avoiding blaming others. It may be the case that one person has not completed the work to the right deadline or standard, but blaming others will only lead to conflict and group breakdown. After you have clarified your positions, others will either agree or disagree in consideration of their own feelings and a resolution can be discussed and agreed.

FORMS OF ACADEMIC ASSESSMENT FOR GROUP WORK

Group work in academic studies for THE is considered usual and traditional due to the needs for team working skills for graduate employment. However, the types of assessment requiring group work will vary according to the topic being studied. The following assignments may require group work within your studies:

- Report.
- Research project.
- Discussion board.
- Blog.
- Live operation (event, restaurant, for example).

Each of the above assessment forms can require group work explicitly or implicitly. Clarification on how these may operationalise are offered in Table 18.2.

Table 18.2 clarifies how even if these assignments are set as individual pieces of work, there may be a natural implicit element of group work underlining it. I have not completed the implicit elements of group work in a live operation as it is usually always explicit.

In addition to these assessment forms, which may explicitly require group work, your other assignments will lead to group work in support of your writing and research. An essay, for example will require you to communicate with others, source and find literature and complete edits and proof reading. This can be seen as an emerging and built group of colleagues who you refer to at specific stages of your assessment.

Table 18.2 Assessment linked to explicit and implicit forms of group work

	Explicit group work	Implicit group work
Report	Instruction is to write the submission with others as collaborators.	You may need to work with others to find information to support the submission. Work experience in groups may also lead to your position or argument within the submission.
Research project	You require research participants to analyse primary data.	You are reading and using research from other people in order to inform your inquiry.
Discussion board	You need to set up and create a discussion board with others.	You may look to other examples of discussion boards and collaborate with them to understand the process of these.
Blog	You are asked to write a blog with others on a specific topic area.	You may comment on others blogs or require comments on your own posts.
Live operation	Dependent on the operation, you will have to work with stakeholders to realise the operation.	

ACTIVITY 18.3 CREATE YOUR CRITICAL FRIENDSHIP GROUP

In order to support your assignments, this activity is designed to enable you to create a group of critical friends. Consider the following people and identify who you could ask or find to complete the role:

The librarian

This person can work in a library or be someone who you know can successfully navigate libraries. They will aid your development and ability to source and find articles for your work.

The industry mentor

This person will work in a role in the THE industry that links to the work and topic you are investigating. They are needed for discussion on your thoughts from academic knowledge gained and reflection on its application to working practices.

The criticiser/s

This could be one or a group of people who you discuss and explore positions and perspectives on a topic. They should offer you alternative positions to a topic in order to allow you reflexivity and objectivity on your knowledge.

The expert

Find someone who is academically successful in their work and approach to studies. Use their guidance to aid your strategies in completing work.

The developer

This person will have a natural talent at supporting and inspiring you to consider and complete work to a higher standard. They will have a natural aptitude for training and teaching you.

The socialiser

A person who will offer you access to networks and groups of other people. The networks may be industry or academic in nature but should support your ability to discuss and communicate positions in social or informal contexts.

> ### The proof reader
>
> This person is needed to check and proof read your writing. They should check your work for clarity in meaning, spelling, grammar and referencing. If using a course friend, also ensure they have a good level of ability in checking academic work.

Activity 18.3 on creating your critical friendship group may appear to be a list of individual stakeholders who can support your academic development. As they all feed into your developing skills and knowledge they can be seen as a group, even if they do not meet together. Inform each of these members of the goal you are working towards and their supporting role required. Being clear in this direction and support will enable you to create an individual supportive group of people who will nurture and develop your abilities.

SUMMARY

1. To appraise the importance of group work in your studies and how this links to team working in industry.

Group work was noted as important in both academic and THE contexts. The stages of group formation were outlined and discussed in relation to a group task set in your studies. Understanding these stages and identifying which one the group is at will ensure the group works effectively to evaluate and develop a successful submission. Understanding of Belbin's team roles was then offered to clarify your usual approach and part within a group.

2. To understand different forms of academic group work required for tourism, hospitality and events management students.

This chapter outlined explicit and implicit group work present in academic assessments. As a student in THE it is likely you will be explicitly required to complete an assignment as a group, as this links to employer needs for team working. However, even within individual work, you will draw upon groups of others to support and develop your knowledge. Your ability to reflect and apply knowledge in different contexts is important to evidence critical awareness, and so utilising groups will enable you to critically analyse topics appropriately. The activity on creating a critical friendship group can be completed to establish a group of people who will support your academic assignments and improve your submissions.

Questions to support your learning and research

1. What are the four stages of group development?
2. What is the 7th stage offered in group formation?
3. How can you continue within the group after the submission?

4. What are team roles?
5. Which team role are you?
6. Does an effective team have to have all nine team roles?
7. How can you overcome barriers to effective group work?
8. Is group work implicit in every academic assignment?
9. How are others required to support your individual essay writing?

Further reading

Cumming, J. (2010). Student-initiated group management strategies for more effective and enjoyable group work experiences. *The Journal of Hospitality Leisure Sport and Tourism*, 9(2), pp. 31–45. [online]. Available from: www.heacademy.ac.uk/assets/hlst/documents/johlste/vol9no2/03AP284Cum ming31to45.pdf [Accessed September 28, 2013].

Knight, P.J. (2006). The Tuckman team development model's ability to explain small short duration technical team development as evidenced by DAU teams. The University of Alabama in Huntsville. [online]. Available from: http://search.proquest.com/docview/304987539?accountid=13460.

Napier, W. and Hasler-Waters, L. (2003). Building team collaboration in the virtual classroom. *Educational Perspectives*, 35(2), pp. 13–20. [online]. Available from: www.ncbi.nlm.nih.gov/entrez/query.fcgi? cmd=Retrieve&db=PubMed&dopt=Citation&list_uids=3665916.

Watkins, M. (2013). Making virtual teams work: Ten basic principles. Harvard Business Review Blog. [online]. Available from: http://blogs.hbr.org/2013/06/making-virtual-teams-work-ten/.

Zammit, K. and Whitelaw, P.A. (2005). Is there room at the inn for Belbin? An investigation of team structure in senior hospitality management teams. In *EuroCHRIE*.

Part 4

Professional development

Part 4 defines and examines four types of work experience for tourism, hospitality and events management students. The benefits and challenges associated with these experiences will also be explained to allow students to choose their work placements carefully. Career mapping will be used as a guide to explore how a range of experiences can aid students targeting a specific career path within these industries. Finally, consideration of leadership, influence, manipulation and management is explored to enable reflective and reflexive thinking for leadership roles in tourism, hospitality and events management.

Chapter 19

Leadership styles

Evidencing reflective and reflexive thinking, learning and doing

LEARNING OBJECTIVES

----

1. To define reflective and reflexive thinking and learning.
2. To reflect on what leadership, management, manipulation and influence are.
3. To establish a reflexive position on leadership, management, manipulation and influence in tourism, hospitality and events management contexts.

INTRODUCTION

Being reflective and reflexive is important for both academic and professional development. These have been offered to begin this part on professional development as they are important skills for completing your career mapping (Chapter 23 of this part). This chapter will define reflective and reflexive thinking in order to outline how these are life-long skills supporting your employability for tourism, hospitality and events (THE). From these definitions, reflection will be offered on four topics supporting your studies and skills for THE: leadership, management, manipulations and influence. These four terms are often attributed to being a successful senior manager in THE and so we will reflect on these and consider how they are manifest in working contexts. Within the reflection on these terms you will consider your natural approach to these and whether you can develop skills to support these further. Following this, reflexive positions will be outlined on leadership, manipulations, management and influence. This will offer you a critical lens on these and enable you to consider what type of manager or leader you aspire to be in the different working contexts you will occupy.

LEARNING AND THINKING REFLECTIVELY AND REFLEXIVELY

Being reflective and reflexive will enable you to place yourself in different positions. Multi-positioning links these terms to the academic skills in being a critical thinker and writer (see Chapters 14 and 15 in Part 3). Within Part 2 Chapter 7 on Self-awareness, an overview on reflective and reflexive self-awareness was also offered to enable you to consider how you position yourself for personal development. The whole skills journey outlined in Chapter 6 of Part 2 also requires you to embed reflection on where you are and where you want to be in the future. As such, reflective and reflexive thinking is not just an element of professional development but an entire outlook to utilise in your personal, academic and professional development. It will enable you to consider positions for coaching (Chapter 21 of this part) and lead to a clear career map for your continued career professional development (CPD). Use these other chapters to support your ability to complete reflective and reflexive thinking and learning for personal and academic development.

To begin, reflective thinking is where you consciously consider something. For example, you may put the kettle on, get distracted with something else and then return to find the water hot. This forgetfulness will proceed with a reflective thought like '*I was meant to make a cup of tea, how did I forget that? Best start again and make one now!*' This is reflective thinking, as you are considering something consciously which should have happened and attributing a future action to it.

THINK POINT 19.1 REFLECTING ON YOUR CAREER

Up until this point, what employment experience have you completed? Which roles have you been paid for? What levels of responsibility have you occupied? Have you completed work as a volunteer with the purpose of accessing experiences or developing skills and knowledge in a difficult field to enter?

Reflective learning is then where you consider what has been learnt and what you need to learn more of in order to feel competent in the topic. The skills appraisal in Part 2 of this handbook requires you to do this with your current skills base. Once you have reflected on gaps in your skills and knowledge, you then need to identify a plan to develop and evidence these skills to feel fully competent in them.

ACTIVITY 19.1 HOW TO DEVELOP COMPETENCE IN A SKILL

To complete this task you need to have completed the skills journey and appraisal from Part 2, Chapter 6 beforehand.

1. Identify one of the skills missing on your skills appraisal.
2. Outline examples of current learning completed on this skill from education, industry and personal contexts.
3. How will this skill be needed in employment?

4. What level of competence do you want on this skill?
5. What plans do you have in gaining employment experience to support the development and use of this skill?
6. Are there personal and academic situations in which you could learn about this skill?
7. What plan can you identify in order to develop and use this skill?

Activity 19.1 on developing competence in a skill enables you to action reflective learning. You will consider your current skills base, outline a gap and identify ways to learn and develop competence in one skill. The activity enables you to reflect consciously on your skills development. Other ways to complete this are listed below:

1. Identify employment areas where the skill will be needed and note a level of importance in developing it.
2. Brain storm the skill and link it to skill and knowledge actions and evidence.
3. Diarise incidents when you use the skill and note your ability demonstrated.
4. List future incidents where your use of the skill will enable you to effectively complete a task.
5. Talk to industry contacts and ask them where this skill is used, ask if another skill is used in its place.
6. Search for journal articles (see Part 3, Chapter 13) that investigate this skill in THE working contexts and learn about their conclusions on this from industry research.

The list of different ways to approach reflective learning on your skills is noted in mind of your varied learning styles (see Part 2, Chapter 11).

Reflexivity is when you consider something with a critical eye. Reflexive thinking is thinking about your thinking and reflexive learning is learning from your learning. Reflexivity is therefore important in CPD as you need to consider how you thought and learnt something in order to improve for future incidents. Garcia-Rosell (2014) noted that tourism and hospitality management education completes this in the use of problem-based learning. This is seen as a critical pedagogy in that it forces a person to be critical of a position or issue and seek to solve it through work-based learning.

THINK POINT 19.2 WHEN DO YOU THINK ABOUT THINKING?

Within your daily routines and schedules, do you notice yourself repeating the same thought or reconsidering an earlier thought? How much time do you rest upon this? Do you unpack how the original thought and repeated thought are part of something else in your subconscious?

Think Point 19.2 on thinking about thinking (thinking thinking!) gives you a chance to reflect on your usual thought processes. Reflexive thinking is not simply something actioned from conscious decision but, often, a spontaneous occurrence. As such, reflexive thinking is not something you need to create or begin, it is something to nurture from your current habits.

CASE STUDY 19.1 ZHANG'S PROBLEM SOLVING IN CUSTOMER SERVICE

Zhang is a second year events management student studying in Melbourne, Australia. Outside of his studies he works part time in a café. During a busy shift at work he interacts with a customer – a woman who has come with her baby. The woman asks for Zhang to heat up some milk to give to her baby and that it needs to be a set temperature in order for it to be safe for her baby. Zhang has never completed this action before and he is concerned about the following aspects:

- What equipment to use to heat up the milk (microwave, coffee machine milk heater or oven).
- Whether this is a service requiring a charge.
- If he should agree to the action in mind of his managers opinion.
- If it goes wrong the implications of hurting a baby and the resulting legal action or bad review, which could be made public.

Zhang informs the customer he will check with his colleagues and management on how he can complete the task requested. He finds out the possible ways to complete this and informs the mother. He asks her which she prefers and she confirms that heating it up using a pot of boiling water and sitting the container in this is the method she would prefer. Zhang completes this and offers the milk to the customer and checks if it is at the correct temperature for the baby.

Case Study 19.1 on Zhang's problem solving uses a customer demand that is unusual for café products and services. However, from my own experience working in cafés and being a mother, this is an expected demand from this form of customer. Zhang shows reflective thinking in his acknowledgement of the tasks and positions to complete the service but is then also reflexive in his ability to utilise other positions (manager and customer) in completing the task. Therefore, when solving THE business problems, you will naturally reflect on the potential outcomes but will also need to reflexively think about alternative ways of completing the task.

Areas in which you can evidence and improve your reflexive thinking and learning are outlined below:

1. Classroom discussion on theory learnt (different positions and conclusions).
2. Work-based problem solving (customer and management).
3. Self-awareness activity for personal development.

All three of the above will be presented to you within your studies and employment experiences. In order to develop and improve your reflexive thinking and learning you need to take time to review and analyse the ways in which you approached and completed the task. In later full-time or fixed employment this will be a component part of your professional development reviews (PDR) or appraisals (see Chapter 21 of this part on coaching and mentoring).

This opening section has outlined the importance of reflective and reflexive thinking and learning for your studies and employment in THE management. Completing these consciously and analytically will enable you to complete PDRs on your skills and knowledge for employment.

REFLECTING UPON LEADERSHIP, MANAGEMENT, MANIPULATION AND INFLUENCE

This section will reflect upon leadership, management, manipulation and influence, as these are core THE topics required in completing senior roles in industry. In order to reflect upon common definitions and knowledge on these terms, this section will outline their common interpretations separate from specific industry or working contexts. This will then be followed by reflexively outlining literature on these from THE sources in order to consider them from multiple positions.

Leadership

Leadership is sometimes linked or used instead of management. You might occupy the position of General Manager but be perceived as an inspirational leader. Therefore, managing is part of a role and action and leading is the ability to show and action management work. However, you can also be an effective leader within a group of people as you can be seen to encourage and inspire others (see Chapter 18 on group work in Part 3).

Being an effective leader links to your ability to use soft skills. Goleman (1998) identified that a core component to being an effective successful leader is your emotional intelligence. Excellent leaders will be seen to use self-awareness, self-regulation, self-motivation, empathy and social skills in their management roles. These have all been considered within this handbook in order to enable development of your leadership capability for THE employment. Leadership is considered in a range of leadership styles. For learning on this topic, seven styles of leadership are offered: trait, behavioural, contingency, transformational, democratic, authoritarian and charismatic.

TRAIT STYLE OF LEADERSHIP

This leadership style is seen in a person's natural ability to complete the skills for a good leader. People are seen as born with natural capabilities to be effective and successful leaders. Carlyle (1849) originated discussion on this style and created the theory of the 'great man.'

THINK POINT 19.3 WHO ARE YOUR HEROES?

Who are the people who inspire you? Who would you consider to be your heroes? What traits do these people have? Have they struggled to gain knowledge and skills for their positions? Have they natural ability in performing or completing their work?

Think Point 19.3 clarifies how your heroes will either be naturally talented or have had to work and gain knowledge and skills to become successful. Arts-based heroes (like singers, musicians or actors) are often seen to have natural talents in their roles. These are depicted as heroes as they appear to use a natural talent in their ability. This is accepted without full knowledge of their training and difficulty in preparing for their performances.

BEHAVIOURAL (OR PARTICIPATIVE) LEADERSHIP

This leadership style focusses on how the leader behaves towards people whom they lead. Using the example of your heroes, how do they react to their followers? If they are on Twitter or Instagram, how do they respond to comments or direct messages? This leadership requires a dualism in that you consider how the leader reacts and participates with people they interact with.

CONTINGENCY LEADERSHIP

Contingency leadership acknowledges that people will require different forms of leadership in different situations. The person can also identify which situation their natural leadership thrives within. Being aware of how leadership is effective or ineffective in different contexts is important to evidence reflexivity in your professional development. If you continue to lead people in the same manner in every situation you may find your colleagues or staff are demotivated.

TRANSFORMATIONAL LEADERSHIP

This leadership style is seen when people are transformed, motivated and elevated to do their best in the situation. Members of the group working with a transformational leader will feel valued, respected and autonomous in order to complete the work to their best standard.

DEMOCRATIC LEADERSHIP

Democratic leadership originated from a group of researchers completing the Harwood Studies in the 1940s. A democratic leader was perceived when subordinates were offered equal power and ability in completing a task, regardless of the hierarchical structures present (Bavelas and Lewin, 1942). Gastil (1994) later confirmed that democratic leadership is when a manager distributes tasks and responsibility across members of a group in order to ensure group work is effective and efficient.

THINK POINT 19.4 DEMOCRATIC LEADERSHIP IN GROUP WORK

Within group work completed in your studies, was there a clear division of responsibility to completing the task? Were there some members who held and carried the rest of the group? How could you have divided and delegated the responsibility and tasks more fairly to evidence democratic leadership?

AUTHORITARIAN LEADERSHIP

An authoritarian leader is someone in a role of management where their position is not questioned due to the power and formality of their position. This is often seen in military conditions whereby the manager relays orders, commands respect and demands action without question. It is usual for subordinates of managers to offer their respect and motivation without question, however, once the manager has demanded or required unfair actions in work, the respect will be lost and the employees will not work to the same standard. Respect, fear and obedience are evident in individuals working for people using authoritarian leadership styles.

CHARISMATIC LEADERSHIP

Bryman (1992, 1993) clarifies this form of leader as someone who can use their natural personality to charm and energise people. Charismatic leaders use their skills in interpersonal communication, confidence, self-awareness, emotional intelligence and flair in appearance to guide and motivate others. They are seen as people who others want to follow due to the appeal in their personality and positive outlook.

ACTIVITY 19.2 REFLECT ON YOUR NATURAL LEADERSHIP STYLE

From reading the discussion on the seven styles of leadership, consider each of the following scenarios and which leadership style you would usually offer or expect from others:

1. Teacher in a lecture room.
2. Organising meals for your flat or house for the following week.
3. You tube channel presenter.
4. Business owner.
5. Nurse in a hospital.
6. Researching information on a topic related to your studies.
7. Talking to your parents about a personal issue.
8. Talking to your friends about a personal relationship.
9. Working with class mates on reading for an assignment.
10. Part-time work as a food server.

Management

There are countless books and articles of research published on managers and management theory. This section will outline three positions on management in order to clarify how this is defined and situated. As noted within leadership, a manager may be seen as a form of leader, but a manager is only acknowledged as a manager through an official job title or senior position of responsibility. You cannot be seen as a manager without a hierarchy structure present.

Firstly, Fayol's (1916) five elements of management outline the classic theory on management:

1. Forecast and plan for future outcomes.
2. Organise resources.
3. Command and complete action to support the plans.
4. Coordinate activities needed in support of targets.
5. Control and monitor the activity maintaining standards of work.

These elements to management offer an overview of the processes and actions managers need to complete in order to effectively manage. They relate to an authoritarian form of leadership as they instruct, command and control aspects of work.

Mintzberg's (1989) research and publications on managers are seen as seminal. He classified management into three roles, each containing task roles within:

1. Interpersonal: figurehead, leader, liaison.
2. Informational: monitor, disseminator, spokesman.
3. Decisional: entrepreneur, disturbance handler, resource allocator and negotiator.

These forms of management enable a manager to reflect upon their ability to manage within a senior position. A person is given formal authority and status and they should complete each of the three roles in turn to become a good manager.

On review and acknowledgement of management within business, Horn (2009) offered his own list of ten management activities, paraphrased below:

1. Evaluating.
2. Planning.
3. Analysing.
4. Organising.
5. Financial practice.
6. Motivating others.
7. Monitoring work and resources.
8. Negotiating.
9. Providing support.
10. Completing paperwork.

Horn's experience within business management is clear as he has the addition of financial management, omitted in Fayol and Mitzberg's models.

ACTIVITY 19.3 ASK A MANAGER

Identify someone who is a manager who you can communicate and complete discussion with easily. This could be within your family and friendship or professional networks.

1. Ask them for the usual tasks they complete each week.
2. Align their tasks to the three models of management in this chapter.
3. Where are there gaps in their work?
4. How does their position within the company affect their ability to complete all aspects of management discussed?
5. Does the industry in which they work in affect your ability to apply their tasks to the management models?
6. Ask them for their opinion on the management models. Do they agree? What would they add?

Manipulation

Feeling that you have been manipulated to think or do something is seen as a wicked (or bad) thing. Awareness of manipulation will either be conscious or subconscious. If you become consciously aware of having been manipulated you need to consider what the intentions and outcomes of your changed thinking or behaviour were. For example, if someone suggests you should purchase three rather than two chocolate bars (due to there being a discount on multi-buying), you cannot say this was manipulation to eat all three chocolate bars but as a result of good intentions and an inability to stop eating the chocolate available! Subconscious manipulation is where you will have altered thoughts and behaviour but not be aware of these changes.

THINK POINT 19.5 **THINK THINGS THROUGH**

Do you act or speak without thinking? Do you consider what you think and how you act based on others guidance or direction? If you complete an action from attending to commands or suggestions from others, how do you feel? If you follow someone, why is this a better or nicer way to be manipulated?

Quite often it is only after you have completed a thought or action that you become aware of prior manipulation. This can also be evident when someone directly asks or reacts to something you have done. When this happens reflect and consider if your position is clear and according to your own intentions. Your acceptance of manipulation will be, in part, due to the perceived intentions from the manipulation, the level of the change and your acceptance of this, and the moral framework in which this change is perceived. If you perceive all manipulation as acceptable you will not gain confidence and self-awareness of appropriate and inappropriate thought and action. These are vital in your professional development as you need to be aware of how your thoughts impact your actions and how your actions lead to beliefs and understanding on how things work effectively.

Influence

March (1955) is noted to have introduced theory on influence. He noted three elements present within influence: origin, intention and time. The source of the influence clarifies the origin of the influence, for example, wanting to try a new brand of deodorant due to an advert on TV. The intention behind the influence is whether there were good or bad motivations for the influence. For example, your friend might tell you that an item of clothing looks good on you in order to support your confidence. If the item looks awful, their intention is misleading as if you buy the item you may not achieve the look or appearance you want. Equally, influence can lead to humorous incidents. A person might have the intention of making light of a situation or making you look funny. This could be immediately perceived as a negative outcome, but on consideration of their intentions could be seen as a humorous event with friendly intentions. Therefore, the intentions of the influence is an important consideration from your influenced thoughts and actions and these can easily be misunderstood or misinterpreted. The simplest way to clarify intentions from someone influencing you is to ask them for their motivation for the influence to understand their position. Time is the final element in influence and outlines whether the influence is actioned immediately, as an outcome of an action, or is a long-term influence on thoughts and beliefs.

CASE STUDY 19.2 WHISTLING TO MY CATS

When I was young, my parents used to use a specific whistle with our cats when it was time to feed them. In turn, they used this whistle when we were in public if we had become separated in shopping centres or grocery shops. Now as an adult with my own house and two cats, I still use this whistle to signal to my cats that food will be available. This form of conditioning (similar to the Milgrim experiments) means that I can influence my cat's behaviour and thoughts relating to a sound. Other cats will hear a whistle and not associate it with food. If I whistle any tune, my cats will immediately perceive food to be available. As I whistle a lot at home, my intention in whistling is not always to get the cats into the kitchen, nor to feed them. If I whistle a different tune and the cats come running, I feel guilty about influencing their behaviour due to a noise which is not dissimilar to the whistle for them to receive food. However, if it is bonfire night or New Year and I know there will be fireworks in our neighbourhood I will whistle them with the intention of getting them safely in the house so that they can find a cupboard or box to hide in when the fireworks start.

Cast Study 19.2, from my own practice in influencing my cats' behaviour, evidences how the origin of the influence is from my desire to manipulate my cats' behaviour. They are conditioned to respond to my whistling due to the repeated reward for their actions. Over time, any whistling I complete has led to a repetition of their behaviour, making me feel guilty for their speed of arrival into the kitchen and thus I then feed them at a point I was not intending to give them treats! The length of time in repeating this influence has led my cats to consistently come home as well as make me more aware of when I whistle and how I whistle.

CASE STUDY 19.3 TRAITS OF GOOD LEADERSHIP IN TOURISM AND HOSPITALITY

1. Adaptability

Adaptable leaders are not afraid to get their hands dirty. Individuals who can adjust to change possess great people skills and poise under pressure.

Flexible hospitality and tourism professionals are ready to tackle any task at hand, including responding to a weary traveler's demands or completing a team checklist.

2. Team-oriented

Being a team player is an essential trait to develop as an individual in the hospitality and tourism industry. Team players work constructively with everyone in the business, from employees and coworkers to managers, customers, and guests. They create weekly schedules to staff the hotel or event, and they resolve conflicts between employees should they arise.

A team leader is a positive force all the time – when profits are high and when cash flow is tight. Knowing what strengths are essential to company performance helps team players make valuable use of time and resources. In fact, CEO of Zipline Logistics, Walter Lynch, told Business News Daily *that leaders 'need to be genuinely interested in growing the skills of others, not just in delegating tasks or managing processes.'*

Likewise, when team members need reassurance, guidance or additional support, an exemplary team player is there to offer assistance, trust, and clear communication.

3. Entrepreneurial

Not every person with an entrepreneurial mindset is a business owner. Entrepreneurs come in all shapes, sizes and ranges of abilities. They have different strengths and weaknesses, but there are a few common ways most entrepreneurs think and act in order to become successful leaders.

First, entrepreneurs seek out new opportunities. Whether they are working toward a managerial position or they're starting a new career from scratch, entrepreneurs have a clear vision of the future they want.

Most importantly, entrepreneurs take ownership of outcomes. Good, bad and everything in between – entrepreneurs step up to the plate when it comes to scheduling preventative maintenance on a property or resolving a shortage of housekeeping supplies.

4. Passionate

Finally, to keep growing and improving, leaders in hospitality and tourism management must be passionate about what they do each day. Passion takes the form of energy, excitement, kindness and other characteristics that will make a difference for you and your guests or clients.

It's important to remember it takes practice and commitment to become an effective leader. 'Becoming a leader is a marathon and not a sprint. It takes time and effort to develop effective leadership skills,' Lynch says.

Source: https://ohiobusinesscollege.edu/4-leadership-traits-for-hospitality-and-tourism-careers/

CASE STUDY 19.4 HOW TO BE AN EFFECTIVE LEADER IN HOSPITALITY AND TOURISM

Lead by example

In hospitality and tourism, leadership entails complete participation. Where in other businesses it is accepted and even expected that leaders will work from behind a computer, the fast-paced nature of day-to-day hospitality operations will keep you involved in many ways. Put simply, our leaders are working leaders. If you're the type who feeds off the energy around you, there's no better industry in which to immerse yourself.

Experiences spread quickly

Online channels have made it easier than ever for guests to instantly share their experiences with the masses. What that means for leaders in hospitality and tourism is that they need to be able to resolve issues quickly and effectively, while maintaining complete composure. On the flip side, the wildfire works to your advantage when you're able to create positive experiences. In both instances, the information age instills endless motivation to uphold high standards of service.

Promotions take perseverance

Hospitality and tourism is very much a 'climb the ladder' industry. There are plenty of opportunities to advance, but it often takes many steps to rise to the top. I specifically use the word perseverance over patience here, because I don't want to imply that promotions just happen. You have to work with a purpose, position yourself and your team for success, and seize every opportunity you are given.

Collaboration is key

Effective hospitality leaders have a knack for making everyone around them feel comfortable and included. You can build organic support for your leadership simply by learning how to interface with everyone in your organization – from the leaders above you, to the ones alongside you, and of course, the countless staff members who keep the day-to-day running smoothly. The more pleasant and seamless interactions with you are, the more your team will realize that you are there to support their efforts rather than simply direct them.

Quiet time is essential

The ability to take a step back before you take a step forward will save you from making careless errors. One of the most important pieces of advice I can give you is to designate a time every day – even just 10 minutes – to gather your thoughts, process your priorities, and develop thoughtful solutions. You might also find that this practice sparks new ideas that would otherwise go unrealized.

Source: https://mastershtm.sdsu.edu/2017/02/17/expect-leader-hospitality-tourism/

CASE STUDY 19.5 LEADERSHIP RESEARCH IN EVENTS MANAGEMENT

The theoretical contribution made by this study is that Human Resource Development should focus on the six key leadership practices of engaging communication, strategic perspectives, critical analysis and judgement, resource management, emotional resilience, and interpersonal sensitivity in order to successfully deliver their events and lead their event teams. Additionally, this study indicates that event managers believe that it is not the technical skills (such as financial planning and event design) that ensure successful event delivery but rather that it is the soft skills and the human resource that drive successful events. The study concludes then that, in terms of HRD, business event managers need to combine the acquirement of the technical skills needed to undertake the role and to incorporate these 6 key leadership practices into their every day in order be successful events leaders.

The study has also highlighted the tension at the heart of leadership within events – event projects are intangible and temporary in nature, with only one opportunity to get it right and this results in attempts by event managers to control all aspects of the event delivery. However, in order to be successful leaders, they also need to work in teams, motivate and empower others, and develop team members. How event managers resolve this tension, and whether this makes them successful leaders, should be a focus for future events-related HRD research.

This study has shown that those working within the industry have already acknowledged that the 'person' or personality is central to the role of event management. This notion has yet to be fully explored by academic research; future research should therefore attempt to focus on the management and development of the human resource who are seen as key by the industry, and yet largely ignored by those of us studying the industry.

Source: Abson, 2017: p.418

ACTIVITY 19.4 **REFLEXIVE THINKING ON LEADERSHIP IN THE**

1. Read the three case studies (Case Study 19.3, 19.4 and 19.5) that give examples of leadership advice for THE.
2. Compare their components to the forms of leadership style discussed earlier.
3. What are the differences and similarities across the three case studies?
4. How do their component parts match with general leadership styles?
5. Are there any significant differences in THE leadership which outline a different approach to leadership style?
6. Can you find other academic articles to support specific leadership styles in THE?

CASE STUDY 19.6 **MANAGEMENT DUTIES IN CARLSON WAGONLIT**

Global sales director

Global sales directors target and win profitable large multi-national and global clients who want to consolidate their corporate travel management in two or more regions. They aim to gain new global clients in a specific region or globally and need to:

- *Focus on winning new, profitable business for CWT.*
- *Think globally and collaborate across different cultures.*
- *Work in a customer-centered way to develop strategy and deliver results.*

Your responsibilities

1. *Initiate and manage the sales relationship with the key client contacts.*
2. *Represent CWT at key industry trade shows and functions.*
3. *Manage the entire global or multinational proposal response and process.*
4. *Manage to the maximum possible profitability for the new client of new business won.*

5. *Have sound knowledge of our value proposition, including global products, tools and service offerings.*

Desired skills

1. *Strong negotiation and problem solving skills.*
2. *Drive for growth.*
3. *Drive for financial decisions.*
4. *Excellent interpersonal and communication skills.*
5. *Project management skills.*
6. *MS suite proficiency.*
7. *Fluency in English.*

Abilities and traits

1. *Results-driven personality with energy, commitment and a strong drive to succeed.*
2. *Adaptability and resilience.*
3. *Cumulative learning.*
4. *Collaboration.*
5. *Interpersonally savvy.*
6. *Executive presence.*
7. *Influence and inspire.*
8. *Strategic thinking.*
9. *Courage.*
10. *Ability to interact in a multicultural, global and matrix environment.*

Source: https://careers.carlsonwagonlit.com/content/careers/global/en/find-your-job/sales-program-management.html

CASE STUDY 19.7 MANAGEMENT PRINCIPLES IN MARRIOTT

1. Keep physically and mentally fit, and spiritually strong.
2. Guard your habits – bad ones will destroy you.
3. Pray about every difficult problem.
4. Study and follow professional management principles. Apply them logically and practically to your organisation.
5. People are no. 1 – their development, loyalty, interest, team spirit. Develop managers in every area. This is your prime responsibility.
6. Decisions: men grow making decisions and assuming responsibility for them.
   a. Make crystal clear what decision each manager is responsible for and what

decisions you reserve for yourself. b. Have all the facts and counsel as necessary – then decide and stick to it.

7. Criticism: don't criticise people but make a fair appraisal of their qualifications with their supervisor only (or someone assigned to do this). Remember; anything you say about some may (and usually does) get back to them. There are few secrets.

8. See the good in people and try to develop those qualities.

9. Inefficiency: if it cannot be overcome and an employee is obviously incapable of the job, find a job he can do or terminate now. Don't wait.

10. Manage your time. a. Short conversations to the point. b. Make every minute on the job count. c. Work fewer hours – some of us waste half our time.

11. Delegate and hold accountable for results.

12. Details: a. Let your staff take care of them. b. Save your energy for planning, thinking, working with department heads, promoting new ideas. c. Don't do anything someone else can do for you.

13. Ideas and competition: a. Ideas keep the business alive. b. Know your competitors are doing and planning. c. Encourage all management to think about better ways and give suggestions on anything that will improve business. d. Spend time and money on research and development.

14. Don't try to do an employee's job for him – counsel and suggest.

15. Think objectively and keep a sense of humor: make the business fun for you and others.

Source: www.marriott.com/Multimedia/PDF/Marriott_Management_Philosophy.pdf

CASE STUDY 19.8 SELF-EMPLOYED EVENT MANAGER

Freelance Events Manager – Totnes Christmas Festival Nights 2019

We're looking for a talented freelance events manager and logistical co-ordinator to help run three community festival nights throughout December 2019.

In this key role you will manage the development and delivery of these major events for Totnes, which are expected to attract up to 7,000 visitors each night. You will also play a crucial part in the development and implementation of policies and best practice to ensure long term sustainability and that events are delivered to the highest level, including the post-event analysis.

Blending creative and collaborative thinking with a solid grasp of logistics, this is an opportunity to make a real difference to the community. The role includes:

* *All pre-event booking and administration.*

- *The event and market management.*
- *Working with community partners to enrich and diversify the events.*
- *Deliver multiple events with creativity, flair and imagination.*
- *Lead an onsite management team for all three events.*
- *Manage budgets and work with the Town Clerk to monitor income/expenditure of public funds.*

What we're looking for:

- *Solid experience in events and project management, drafting event management plans and implementation of site infrastructure.*
- *Experience engaging and co-ordinating independent blue light service provision.*
- *The ability to engage with stakeholders and the community across all levels.*
- *Excellent customer service and organisational skills.*
- *A flexible approach to working hours.*
- *Strong experience working within budgets and time limits.*
- *Experience of writing and implementing comprehensive risk assessments.*

The successful applicant will:

- *Commit to a minimum of 10 hours a week working from the Town Council offices.*
- *Be available on the day of the events to coordinate and manage.*
- *Will be available to start work as soon as possible and be willing to work flexibly to meet the needs of the project.*

Source: www.indeed.co.uk/cmp/Totnes-Town-Council/jobs/Self-Employed-Event-Manager-811af4ad078d27e4?sjdu

ACTIVITY 19.5 REFLEXIVITY ON MANAGEMENT MODELS AND DUTIES FOR THE

1. Read the three case studies on management role requirements and principles from THE contexts.
2. Compare their components to the models of management discussed earlier.
3. What are the differences and similarities across the three case studies?
4. How do their component parts match with general management actions?
5. Are there any significant differences in THE management which outline a different approach to management?
6. Can you find other academic articles to support specific management models or principles in THE?

CASE STUDY 19.9 MANIPULATION BY HOTEL MANAGERS

This study has investigated aspects of manipulation from the viewpoint of managers. Results confirm the significance of online reviews and ratings for business success, and indicate that concerns over online reputation have become a major force for product improvement and focus on hospitality and service management. However, reviews and ratings have also been revealed as a source of frustration and suspicion, and they have introduced competitive structures as a result of direct comparison and struggles for top ratings and listings. Importantly, results also show that opportunities for customers to rate and review, and growing awareness of the importance of consumer-generated content for business success, have initiated changes in consumer culture due to the encouragement of judgement. In these emerging consumer judgement cultures, evaluating a business becomes a consumer responsibility.

With regard to manipulation, results indicate that many businesses find themselves at a crossroads, aware of the growing importance of online reputation, wary of the power of guests to judge service quality and to decide over the fate of businesses, as well as longer term concerns about the credibility of reviews. This research has thus argued that businesses are increasingly caught up in a Prisoner's dilemma, where engaging in manipulation is the most rational choice. Even though many manipulation strategies were identified, virtually all of which are in breach of ethics codes as published by TripAdvisor, there is only limited evidence of systemic manipulation in this study of hotels in southern Sweden. Yet, in the future, pressures on businesses to engage in dishonest practices may increase, as there is already evidence of winners and losers, and a growing share of income lost to reservation platforms.

Source: Gössling et al., 2018: p.499

ACTIVITY 19.6 MANIPULATING RATINGS AND CUSTOMER FEEDBACK

Read the excerpt from Gössling et al. (2018) (given in Case Study 19.9):

1. What form of manipulation is noted here?
2. Who is manipulating whom?
3. What reason and motivation is there for this form of manipulation?
4. What ethical considerations are needed in this manipulation? Is it ok?
5. How have you manipulated others based upon your own subjective experience of a tourist experience?
6. How do you read reviews reflexively?
7. Do all customers have a reflexive lens when considering customer reviews?

CASE STUDY 19.10 USING SOCIAL MEDIA INFLUENCERS FOR BUSINESS GROWTH

'Fyre was basically like Instagram coming to life.'

Or at least, that was the idea, says DJ/producer Jillionaire in the new Netflix documentary Fyre: The Greatest Party that Never Happened.

The organisers spent eye-watering sums on an extravagant launch campaign with 10 of the world's top supermodels sharing gorgeous promotional pictures and videos of themselves partying in luxurious style on a sun-drenched island in the Bahamas.

Kendall Jenner was reportedly paid $250,000 (£193,000) for one single Instagram post announcing the launch of ticket sales and offering her followers a discount code.

Despite the 'luxury' tickets costing thousands of dollars, the event sold out – many snapped up by social media influencers keen to document their exclusive experience, many in exchange for free accommodation.

The festival was supposed to run annually for five years.

However, just like Instagram, away from the filters and the supermodels, the reality turned out to be somewhat different.

The 'private jet' in which the guests were supposed to arrive, turned out to be an old rebranded aeroplane. The luxury accommodation consisted of rain-drenched tents, and the gourmet cuisine was a cheese sandwich.

The event never took place.

The organiser, Billy McFarland, is now in prison for fraud.

Bella Hadid, one of the models who took part in the promotions, later apologised to her followers and said she had 'trusted' the event would be 'amazing and memorable.'

Kendall Jenner deleted her post.

Two new documentaries about the luxury event that never was – one by Netflix, the other by US streamer Hulu – have thrown a spotlight on the influencers and celebrities who promoted it.

You'd be forgiven for thinking this all sounds like extremely bad news for the influencer industry. But you'd be underestimating their Teflon-like resilience in the face of adversity.

Rohan Midha, managing director of the PMYB influencer agency, says that while Fyre itself was a disaster, the marketing choices behind it were not.

'It just shows how powerful influencers can be,' he told the BBC.

On the subject of Fyre, he agrees that while the sheer size of the influencer campaign was 'unusual,' the results were not.

'Influencers can reproduce the largest return on investment,' he says. 'That's across the board.'

Source: www.bbc.co.uk/news/46945662

ACTIVITY 19.7 HOW ARE YOU INFLUENCED?

Read the BBC article on the Fyre festival (given in Case Study 19.10). Watch the documentary on Netflix if you have access to this also.

1. What are social media influencers?
2. Where do they post content and what do they usually post?
3. How are these seen as influencing others?
4. Are you influenced by social media influencers? If so, which people and why?
5. How could you influence others through social media?
6. What questions should you ask yourself upon seeing social media posts on products or events?
7. What is the usual resulting action of being influenced by social media posts?
8. What are the resulting beliefs or thoughts on a product as a result of social media posts?

SUMMARY

1. To define reflective and reflexive thinking and learning.

Reflective thinking was defined as your ability to consciously consider something. This is required in your work to develop skills and knowledge for THE employment as you need to actively outline areas of growth and create plans to complete actions in evidence of your employment expertise. Reflective learning is the second part of development in that it clarifies the plan of action to learn and develop knowledge and skills. Using reflective thinking and learning will enable you to approach professional development with clear actions aligned to your goals in employability. Reflexivity is then the ability to understand various positions on something. Thinking about your thinking and learning from your learning were outlined here to enable you to critically appraise your usual thinking and learning habits. This multi-positional aspect is important in your studies as it links to your ability to write and think critically on published literature. It is equally important in professional development as you need to appraise and consider your thinking and learning styles in order to address bad habits or solve problems which will occur in working contexts.

2.   To reflect on what leadership, management, manipulation and influence are.

Leadership was defined as a form of behaviour motivating others to complete action. This can be evident in any person in any role. Management is seen in people completing management roles and their duties and tasks are clarified in a range of models. Manipulation is a form of making someone think or do something without their conscious consent. You will feel manipulated after acknowledgement of a change in your usual thoughts or actions. Influence was defined in three areas: origin, intention and time. These are components of influence and alter the ways in which someone acts or behaves. All management are accepted to use different leadership styles in the influencing of others and manipulations of work to be completed.

3.   To establish a reflexive position on leadership, management, manipulation and influence in THE management contexts.

This chapter offered case studies from THE contexts in which leadership, management, manipulation and influence are evident. Activity on these enables your reflexivity on definitions and common assertions on these.

Questions to support your learning and research

1.   What is reflective learning?
2.   What is reflexive thinking?
3.   What are the seven leadership styles discussed?
4.   How is whistling to your cats at dinner time a form of influence?
5.   How do the different leadership styles in THE compare to the seven styles discussed?
6.   What management principles and practices are outlined from THE?
7.   How are social media influencers used by THE management?
8.   How can you manipulate Trip Advisor reviews and is this ethical?
9.   What further research can you complete on manipulation and influence in leadership and management to support THE business operations?

Further reading in support of your learning from this chapter

Blake, R. and Mouton, J. (1964). *The Managerial Grid: the Key to Leadership Excellence*. Houston: Gulf Publishing Company.

Bourdieu, P. (1977). Outline of a Sociological Theory of Art Perception.

Burns, J. M. (1978). Burns Transformational Leadership Theory. Burns Transformational Leadership Theory.

Desmond, J. and Wilson, F. (2018) Democracy and worker representation in the management of change: Lessons from Kurt Lewin and the Harwood studies. *Human Relations*, doi:10.1177/0018726718812168.

Firth, M. (2020). *Service Encounters in Tourism, Events and Hospitality*, 1st ed. Channel View Publications.

Kuehn, R. (2003). *Transforming Leadership, A New Pursuit of Happiness (book)*. Human Development.

Kunhert, K.W. and Lewis, P. (1987). *Transactional and Transformational Leadership : A Constructive/Developmental Analysis*. Academic of Management Review.

Lyons, A. P., Bourdieu, P. and Nice, R. (2006). *Outline of a Theory of Practice*. ASA Review of Books.

Moua, M. (2010). *Culturally Intelligent Leadership: Leading through Intercultural Interactions*. J. Phillips and S. Gully, eds. Business Expert Press.

Chapter 20
Networking

LEARNING OBJECTIVES

1. To understand what networking is and its importance within academic and professional development.
2. To examine skills needed for effective networking.
3. To examine methods and processes involved in individual networking: face to face and online.

INTRODUCTION

When you arrive at college or university your social and academic networks expand vastly. The people you live with, your class mates and your student union groups all represent new networks of people with whom to develop and maintain relationships with. Part 2, Chapter 8 outlined ways to create and maintain effective relationships for personal development, but here we consider how networking is an essential tool for developing academic and professional relationships. In this chapter, discussion will be offered on what networking is, the skills you need to network effectively and face-to-face and online networking. As tourism, hospitality and events (THE) employment often requires temporary, fixed term or self-employment, networking is not simply an add on to your professional development, but a superior skill needed to maintain your industry contacts, knowledge and future employment.

NETWORKING FOR ACADEMIC AND PROFESSIONAL DEVELOPMENT

Networking is an action and activity in which you develop contacts, maintain relationships and understand different positions. It is supported by a common belief in that '*it's not what you know, but who you know.*' This mantra goes against the academic position in that learning and knowledge is a priority to enable critical thinking, but critical networking can be used as a strategic add on to your studies and support your professional development in graduate life.

Within your academic studies you will have created networks simply by being enrolled within a course. The degree cohort, classes, accommodation groups, societies and academic study groups are all forms of networks which you can engage with. These are essential networks for your academic studies as they can offer you support in discussing and aiding your academic development.

THINK POINT 20.1 YOUR ACADEMIC NETWORKS

Within your current course, what access do you have to different networks? How engaged are you within these? How easy would it be for you to communicate with members from these if you needed support or guidance?

Think Point 20.1 is offered to make you consider the level to which you are currently able to utilise your academic networks. Being a member of these does not mean you will be able to utilise and engage with them easily. Your ability to use and engage is based upon your relationships with other members within the networks. For example, if you signed up to join a society within your university or college and you receive updates and social media information but do not attend or meet with these members, this network is redundant. It can inform you of the society's efforts and work, but is not an active resource for you to use and build your knowledge from. Engagement in your academic networks is therefore essential for you to be able to demonstrate and contribute your knowledge and learning needs. The rise in technology use in education has also led to distance learning courses and lectures being recorded so that students can catch up online without physical attendance. These aspects can inhibit your face-to-face networking and you will need to complete online networking and group discussion in order to support your development. A further perceived barrier to networking in academic studies is when you choose to live with family instead of other university students.

ACTIVITY 20.1 ACADEMIC NETWORKING WHEN YOU ARE NOT PHYSICALLY PRESENT

Consider times when you are unable to develop face-to-face networks linked to your academic studies and complete the following:

1. Who do you not have access to?
2. How can you gain access to these people?
3. What do you want to gain from access and relationships with these people?
4. Does technology support your networking?
5. How can you use technology to aid your connection and communication with these networks?
6. How active are you in using the engagement points available?
7. How can you improve your engagement to enable network development?
8. Create a plan for developing and improving your engagement with the groups you want to access and build relationships with.

Plan for building networks:

1. Communicate and clarify your needs and intentions.
2. Ask for a meeting to discuss your needs.
3. Offer information about yourself and your current situation.
4. Build a relationship through meeting and discussing issues relating to your common interests and beliefs.

Activity 20.1 will enable you to consider and reflect upon your access to and ability to engage with academic networks. Using technology is discussed later in this part and is essential for building networks as a distance learner or student living at home. Once you have made contact it is important to meet physically or virtually to develop a relationship on common interests or beliefs. A common issue in this relationship development for academic studies is that you look for people who can be your friends foremost.

THINK POINT 20.2 DO MEMBERS OF YOUR ACADEMIC NETWORKS HAVE TO BE YOUR FRIENDS?

Your historical experience of education will have naturally led you to develop long-term friendships with class mates. These are important personal relationships for you to enjoy social and personal activities with. When completing academic studies you may also find you develop friendships, which are important for your self-esteem and self-worth when moving to and living in different cities.

As you will naturally place high importance on these relationships as being for your social connections and networks, how does this affect your ability to develop and access people who can support your academic development? Are there people who's academic ability inspires or impresses you? Why have you not developed connections with these people? How could you do this professionally?

Think Point 20.2 relates to your natural objective in making friends during your studies. Friendships are important when living away from home or living in a different city or country as they enable you to use personal networks to support your emotional and social support systems. When considering networks for academic development, you need to accept how these connections are important professional relationships as well.

Figure 20.1 clarifies how academic, personal and professional relationships are all required when completing studies for THE. Your academic networks will aid your learning and critical skill development, the personal networks are needed for social and emotional support and the professional networks will enhance your knowledge of industry working practices. All three of these forms of networks are important and need development when completing your studies. The following list outlines the types of people and groups you can approach in support of developing these.

Figure 20.1 Academic, personal and professional networks

Academic network members and groups

- Programme director.
- Teachers and tutors.
- Library staff.
- Reading group members.
- Research group members.
- Post-graduate students.
- Academic association members.
- Invited academic speakers or presenters.

CASE STUDY 20.1 ACADEMIC RESEARCH ASSOCIATION

The Travel and Tourism Research Association offers the following benefits for members:

Multi-Sector Membership

ALL MEMBERS

TTRA offers access to a unique membership combination of academics, practitioners and consultants/agencies. A full listing of its membership is available to members online.

Chapter Membership

MEMBERS RESIDING WHERE A CHAPTER EXISTS

As part of your membership fee, all members of TTRA automatically belong to their local chapter, providing localized communications and networking opportunities. If not geographically aligned with a Chapter, or if you have a specific regional interest, members are able to nominate a Chapter to join.

Local Focus

MEMBERS RESIDING WHERE A CHAPTER EXISTS

TTRA's chapter structure provides members with an additional venue for networking and communication with a local focus and many great opportunities for involvement.

Industry Education

ALL MEMBERS

Through conferences, papers, proceedings, reports, presentations, white papers, webinars, live streaming, YouTube sessions and professional development experiences, TTRA members stay up-to-date on the latest travel industry research and methodologies, hot topics, industry matters, trends and more.

Member Communities & LISTSERVs

ALL MEMBERS

TTRA offers members platforms for discussion and collaboration that provides them with access to timely information on current issues in the field.

Range of International and Local Conferences

ALL MEMBERS

TTRA hosts two conferences a year – the Annual International Conference in June (held around the world) and the Marketing Outlook Forum (held in the U.S.) in October. In addition, the seven TTRA Chapters hold localized conferences each calendar year. That's a total of nine conferences each year, each with a unique topic and perspective on travel and tourism research and marketing.

Career and RFP Boards

PARTNER, ORGANIZATIONAL, LIFETIME (FREE)

PREMIER, STANDARD, GLOBAL SOUTH STANDARD, NON-MEMBER ($)

TTRA members can advertise their careers and RFPs with us to find the 'just right' talent for their organization. OR they can search our open opportunities to find a new career or project.

TTRA Webinars

ALL MEMBERS

Webinars allow our members to stay up-to-date on the information that interests them the most and gives TTRA members the opportunities to share their expertise with the world.

Source: https://ttra.com/membership/why-join-us/

Personal network members and groups

- Students on your course.
- Students in your classes.
- Halls/student living members.
- Colleagues who you work with (paid or voluntary outside of your studies).
- Friends from school who are also in the same city or institution.
- Student society members.

CASE STUDY 20.2 **PROFESSIONAL AND ACADEMIC RESEARCH ASSOCIATION**

The American Hotel and Lodging Association offers students the following benefits through student membership:

To qualify for student membership you must currently be enrolled in a hospitality pro-gram at an accredited college or university.

For just $45 per year, your annual membership includes:

News and Information

To keep you in the know of all the trends, challenges and legal matters affecting the hospitality industry, you'll receive:

- *access to our Research, your one-stop shop for research, fast answers, and a wealth of industry data*
- *free subscription to* Lodging *magazine*
- *free reports via the Members Only section on our Website, covering security, government affairs, sustainability, and more*

Education

Advance your skills and give yourself an edge on the competition, by taking advantage of:

- *up to a 40% discount on all products and services from the American Hotel and Lodging Educational Institute (EI), the premier provider of hospitality training and certifications worldwide*
- *access to the American Hotel and Lodging Educational Foundation, alerting you to new academic scholarships and research grants*

Career

Begin setting the foundation for your future hospitality career through:

- *networking opportunities through AHLA meetings and conferences, where general managers and property owners meet to discuss their future plans*

Placement in the AHLA Annual Resume Database, hosted on the Hcareers Website and made available to key executives in the industry.

Access to AHLA's Career Center, powered by Hcareers.com, where you can search the largest online database of hospitality job openings, from line-level to management positions.

Source: https://www.ahla.com/student

Professional network members and groups

- Careers office at your university or college.
- Guest speakers from industry who attend classes.

- Student society members.
- Colleagues who you work with (paid or voluntary outside of your studies).
- Research participants.
- Presenters at academic events and conferences.
- Members of THE associations and bodies of knowledge.

CASE STUDY 20.3 INDUSTRY ASSOCIATION NETWORKS

The meetings and events Australia association offers members the following benefits which can support professional development through an external network:

What MEA can do for you

Management and Development of Staff

Professional Development sessions are held around the country covering a variety of topics and featuring speakers from wide ranging backgrounds willing to share their knowledge and expertise for the benefit of members.

MEAs education and training arm, the Australian Events Academy, conducts accredited and non accredited qualification courses as well as seminars and workshops on specific topics. All seminars, workshops and courses are developed specifically for the meetings and events industry and delivered by experienced trainers with the aid of industry professionals.

The MEA website includes a Jobs listing page (JobsMEA) for the listing of industry related job vacancies. Members can post vacancies free of charge to be viewed by potential candidates specifically looking for work within the meetings and events industry.

MEA Future Leaders events and workshops are designed specifically for the future leaders of the industry to provide a platform for networking and to hear from experienced industry professionals and motivational and specialist speakers. Including mentoring programs and scholarships, the Future Leaders initiative provides the basis of a succession plan for the industry.

MEA coordinates mentoring programs to bring together employees of members wishing to develop their careers with experienced industry practitioners who can provide guidance and often a different perspective to the challenges facing those building a career within the industry.

The USI Young Professional Scholarship program is open to employees of members under 30 years of age, with state and territory winners having the opportunity of an expenses paid attendance at the MEA Annual Conference thus gaining exposure, knowledge and experience they would otherwise not have the opportunity to acquire.

Resources

The MEA website includes a Member Resources area containing a variety of research documents and resources available for members to view or download. From time to time MEA undertakes industry research as well as participating in research of industry significance, with the resulting reports available to members through the MEA website.

Source: https://secure.meetingsevents.com.au/membershipbenefits/member-benefits

---

The lists offered on the networks and members who can support your academic and professional development can enable you to reflect and consider new people and groups to join to support your studies in THE. The three case study examples of associations are offered to support your knowledge of research and industry associations. There are hundreds of these associations supporting THE and they are an important network to join during your studies. Through joining an association you will gain access to professionals and research publications that underpin and drive industry standards. These will ensure you are aware of current industry issues and emerging trends. This knowledge is vital for your employment as it will evidence your ability to keep up to date with research and practice and show that you are a determined and well-informed student.

From discussion of what networking is, how it links to the relationships developed within your studies, and how you can develop academic, personal and professional relationships on your course in THE, it is important to now consider which networks you want to build and develop and for what purposes (see Activity 20.2).

ACTIVITY 20.2 DEVELOPING YOUR PLAN FOR NETWORKING

Which networks?

- Review components of the academic, personal and professional networks.
- In which of these do you already have contacts and relationships developed?
- Where are the gaps?

Purpose of the network:

- Which skills do I currently lack (use the skills appraisal in Part 2)?
- What roles of employment am I interested in?
- What topic of research or industry practice do I want to know more about?
- Which networks will aid my ability to learn more about these?

The questions in Activity 20.2 will aid your reflections on your existing networks and which networks you want to develop. This reflection will be based on your awareness and understanding of your need for employment or academic knowledge development. The industry and research associations (outlined in case studies earlier) will support a wide range of knowledge and industry support for your professional development, but you may also have individual needs in understanding how to gain employment for a specific role. The following sections on face-to-face and online networking will aid your individual networking for these tasks.

SKILLS FOR NETWORKING

Before considering techniques and processes for individual networking it is important to assess your skills to support your ability to network. When developing networks you will use a range of soft skills. Soft skills were outlined in Part 1, Chapter 1 of this text as core employment skills required by THE employers. These were further explored within Part 2 on personal development whereby communication, empathy and relationship skills were explored. In terms of the skills required for networking, communication, presenting, assertiveness and confidence are all linked. Some of these relate to personality traits, but all can be developed and utilised to create successful networks.

Communication

When finding, joining and engaging in networking, it is essential to communicate. This is due to the phases of professional networking requiring interaction and discussion:

Phase 1: contact the network or person within a network.
Phase 2: establish a reason for the connection and ask to meet or join in with the networks events and activities.
Phase 3: meet or complete the activity.
Phase 4: reflect on the learning and ability developed and reassess its importance for your employment.
Phase 5: outline new reasons for being within the network/leave the network when it is no longer required.

The five phases of professional networking offered above clarifies how interaction and communication is embedded throughout. The form of communication required (verbal, non-verbal or written) will depend upon the location of the member of the network and the function of the network. If you join a network and passively watch or read information you will not be completing networking action nor activity.

When communicating in a new network you should consider the tone, language and content of the communication. If you are joining a professional network, do they need to know what your favourite TV show is? If you are communicating to an academic, should you use colloquial phrases or curse?

Table 20.1 Communication for academic, personal and professional networks

	Academic	**Personal**	**Professional**
Tone	Formal Clear and polite	Informal Unclear at times Can be impolite in the use of humour	Formal Clear and polite
Language	Academic Standard or high version of the language	Familiar Colloquial	Professional
Content	Ensures opinion is based upon academic knowledge learnt Questions positions and does not assert fact as confirmed	Based on supporting you and others as individuals Around hobbies, likes and dislikes	Uses common phrases for the context Sticks to hierarchy and power relations present

Table 20.1, which looks at communication differences for academic, personal and professional networks enable you to consider the changes you will need to make when completing these actions. This table is not rigid. Humour is often used in professional and academic situations in order to relieve anxiety or pressure within a situation or make light of serious issues.

Presenting yourself

When engaging in your networks you will need to present yourself in an appropriate way. This will be in physical appearance (if online, via a profile photo) and people will see how you look and attribute judgements to this. This is seen as a skill as you have choice and flexibility in creating how you are presented. In professional contexts you may be informed of the specific dress code, but in academic and personal networks it is usual for you to choose this independent from instruction. To support your ability to present yourself appropriately consider the following steps in dressing for success:

1. Consider options available in your wardrobe.
2. Identify the usual level of formal or professional attire for the activity.
3. If you have these in your wardrobe then put them together as an outfit and try them on. If you do not have them, identify key pieces which would help create an outfit for the activity. Purchase the additional item/s.
4. Try on the outfit.
5. Ask others what they think of the outfit: what does it suggest? Is it formal? Is it casual? What does it say about your personality?
6. Make alterations and additions to the outfit including shoes, accessories, hair style, make-up and bags.
7. Attend the networking event or activity.

These rules can be addressed a week before attending a networking activity or event to ensure you are organised and prepared for the event. In addition to these steps you need to consider local and regional commonalities in appearance.

THINK POINT 20.3 LOCAL AND NATIONAL CUSTOM IN DRESS

Consider the place/s you will be seen and presented. Are these local, national or international? What are the cultural norms in dress associated? Are you wanting to match, fit in or stand out from these?

Is it appropriate to wear a short shirt? Are trainers too casual? Do people wear clothes showing their skin or do they cover up? What degree of fitting is usual and is it acceptable to show underwear or the contour of your body?

The questions surrounding your attire and appearance are often overlooked or presumed. By addressing these in Think Point 20.3 you will ensure your appearance is not only appropriate but considered.

Once you have attended an activity with network members once, you will have a clearer idea on the group norms on presentation. Look at what other members wear and how they present themselves and adjust your presentation accordingly in follow-up activities. In following the guidance in this section you may also find that your dress is more formal for the first occasion with the network. If this is the case, you need to be confident and clear that it is better to attend looking more formal than informal as you are treating the occasion as serious and important for your academic, personal or professional development.

Assertiveness

Being assertive is sometimes linked to being arrogant. They are not the same thing. Assertiveness is your ability to clearly communicate your requirements. Arrogance is ignoring others positions and asserting yourself with little to no awareness of others abilities linked to the discussion. Some people may feel you are being arrogant if you assert your position with little to no self-awareness of other network member's position. In this way, showing and using assertiveness is a skill for effective networking.

Confidence

Being confident in yourself and the work you do is an important development, which will emerge through completing your studies in THE. At the beginning of your course you may be lacking in confidence due to the perceived low level of knowledge in the subject area. It may be daunting to meet your teachers and class mates and learn about the new rules and social norms within academic studies. Similarly, on entering employment you may be nervous about working with new colleagues, unsure of who your manager is and the type of manager they may be. As networking requires you to enter new situations and develop relationships with members in the network you have to use confidence in putting yourself forward in new environments. If the network requires you to complete multiple new activities you will also need to maintain your energy to be and seem confident.

Figure 20.2 should be used as a process and actions to support your self-reflection. Identify who you want to be perceived as when meeting others. State positive aspects about yourself to affirm your ability. For example, if you are nervous about meeting a new person, say 'I am looking forward to this experience and I am not the only person who is nervous,' four times to yourself when going into the situation. Affirmation is a neat psychology trick that persuades your subconscious you are able to complete something. This builds inner confidence. Being critical of your inner voices means addressing the negative thoughts that may arise. Instead of accepting these and feeling worse, challenge them and think about them logically. Would others agree? Why has the thought come up? Why is it irrelevant? Finally, create a diary and note situations where you are praised. These can be simply comments on your dress or hair style but may also be on your ability to act professionally or support others. By documenting these you will force yourself to reflect and acknowledge these to a more subconscious level. All of these processes are aimed at telling your subconscious that you are capable of completing the task at hand.

Through discussion of communication, presentation and assertiveness you will be able to plan and implement these skills for effective networking. Conversely, through completing the act of networking you will also be witness to the skills from other people. Being aware of these and reflecting on them will allow for further development of your own skills. One of your goals for networking may also to be ascertain and understand the skills needed to complete specific employment roles. In this way you will be using your own skills to identify new ones to develop. It is a skilling circle!

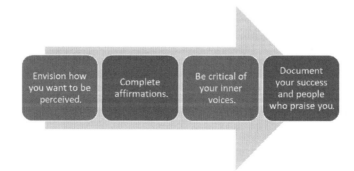

Figure 20.2 Flowing into increased confidence

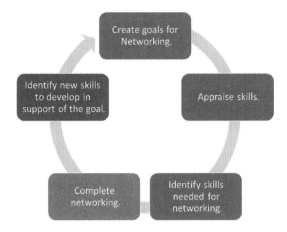

Figure 20.3 Skilling circle in networking

METHODS AND PROCESSES FOR INDIVIDUAL NETWORKING

This final section will examine the methods and processes for your individual networking in face-to-face and online environments. In order for these to be successful, identify goals for the networking (use Part 3, Chapter 12 for support). Education institution events, networking events and social media will be outlined as forums for networking in support of your professional development.

Education institution events

Events at university enable you to access new networks, learn new knowledge and contribute towards the institutions success. These events are varied but usual ones available in most institutions include:

- Career workshops (professional).
- Academic writing training sessions (academic).
- Well-being classes (personal).
- Social events (academic, personal and professional).
- Student union events (personal and professional).

These events are a form of network as they allow you to become a member of a new group of people whom are all actively participating in something.

Career workshops may be offered in support of specific career routes or industry. These usually include industry representation and offer you new contacts to discuss your employability and career trajectory with. Attend these to learn more about the industry and career routes from your programme of study.

Academic writing sessions will provide you with members of an academic network. You can learn from these in terms of academic practice and improvement, but alongside this you need to utilise the group members to collaborate and support your academic development. Once you have met other students, establish relationships with these and ask to utilise their skills in discussing literature, proof reading or checking your work for grammar and spelling.

Well-being classes support your personal development as they will offer you strategies and methods to combat stress, anxiety and pressure. These are all component parts of your personal, academic and professional life. Being aware and actively managing your well-being will ensure you are able to tack and complete tasks to a high standard without compromising your metal health. The members of these classes will have a similar perspective on well-being and can be approached to discuss and build personal relationships in support of your academic and professional development. They may be interested in different career routes, but their knowledge on coping mechanisms and completing academic studies within a busy student schedule will be useful as a comparator to your usual habits.

Social events are often the focus and priority of new students. Meeting new people within social environments and building personal relationships are vital to feeling safe and comfortable in education. These enable you to gain new social networks as well as meet tutors and teachers in a less formal setting. If you attend university or college run social events, ensure you behave appropriately and are not offensive. Education institution ran social events are where you are both integrated and representing the institution in which you study. As such, you need to present yourself professionally and ensure you are respectful of the environment you are socialising within.

Student union events run by your university or college will enable you to develop your skills in activities, hobbies, beliefs and interests important to you. These networks will offer a range of events and activities for you to participate within. Again, it is unlikely that your course mates will be present in these and it will offer an additional network for your personal and professional development

Actions to complete when attending events with new networks:

1. Write a list of questions before you go.
2. Research the presenters or content to be discussed.
3. Take pens and paper to the session.
4. Make notes during the session on questions and knowledge gained, and further actions to complete.
5. Ascertain the contact details of members of the event.
6. Follow up with members of the event or presenters to support your development.

These actions are applicable to the majority of academic and professional events when engaging with new networks. They are not, however, advisable when attending a club night or going to the movies with course friends!

Networking events

Networking events are specific events intended to create opportunities for you to meet new people. These are usually personal or professional in nature. For example, you may decide to attend a speed dating night. This is a form of networking event as you are required to sit and talk to a number of people within a period of time in order to establish if you want to develop a relationship with them. Business, industry and sector networking events are commonplace in most major cities.

CASE STUDY 20.4 BUSINESS NETWORKING

The Young Tourism Network (YTN) is a not-for-profit organisation that was established in 2005 with the aim to provide students and new entrants the opportunity to learn and grow through professional development workshops and networking opportunities, gaining valuable knowledge and building strong relationships across the broader industry. Anyone can join YTN! There is no age restriction and our network is relevant to those in the tourism, travel, hospitality, events and accommodation sectors.

Events:

Career Confidence

Whether you're about to enter the tourism, hospitality or events industry, or have been involved for a number of years, selling yourself to employers is always a daunting task – something we all need to learn how to do better. Learn from HR experts how to make your resume stand out and how to use LinkedIn to your advantage.

Building Big Ideas: Discover your inner Entrepreneur

Ever been curious about how to start your own business? Do you have a great idea but don't know how to get it off the ground? Come and learn from people who started their own tourism ventures about how they turned an idea into a great business.

Source: https://youngtourismnetwork.com.au/about/

The Young Tourism Network in Australia is an example of an established network supporting tourism students and staff who are interested in professional development. They offer a range of events to enable people to meet industry professionals and share knowledge and best practice from the tourism industry and studies.

ACTIVITY 20.3 FIND A LOCAL NETWORKING EVENT

To complete this activity you will need an internet connection.

1. Go to Eventbrite, Meet-ups, or a local THE network page.
2. Find an event that offers you an opportunity to network with people in the field of employment you are currently interested in.
3. Look at the criteria for attending and ensure you are able to register or purchase a ticket.
4. Review the learning outcomes or intended aims of the event to ensure it is suited to support your current goals.
5. Prepare for the event using the action list noted earlier in this chapter.
6. Dress professionally and appropriately.
7. Attend the event.

Social media

Social media is a tool used for networking by most students. However, this is usually used for personal networking in linking to friends or family members. This section will outline how to use LinkedIn, Twitter and Instagram to aid your online networking for professional development.

LinkedIn

LinkedIn.com is a professional online network whereby you create a profile and link to other business professionals. Your profile will contain major academic and professional accomplishments and you can use these to promote your availability for work, as well as examine how others have progressed in employment roles to achieve their current job.

ACTIVITY 20.4 9 STEPS TO CREATE A LINKEDIN PROFILE

Step 1: Upload a professional photo.
Step 2: Add your industry and location.
Step 3: Customize your LinkedIn URL.
Step 4: Write a summary.
Step 5: Describe your experience.
Step 6: Add 5 skills or more.
Step 7: List your education.

Step 8: Connect with 50+ contacts.

Step 9: Turn ON 'Let recruiters know you're open.'

Source: www.linkedin.com/pulse/linkedin-beginner-all-star-8-easy-steps-clifford-wessel/

LinkedIn is particularly useful for people who completed fixed-term work or are self-employed. It allows you to search for job postings and find people in key positions to contact and request paid work. An example of how to complete this is noted below:

1. Find the person who you want to contact and ask for employment.
2. Locate their business phone number using a search engine.
3. Call them and inform them you have found them via LinkedIn and want to meet to discuss opportunities to support their work in the future. OR

If you cannot find a phone number to speak directly, write them a personal message within LinkedIn and offer your number for them to call directly.

4. Follow up a week later to check on the progress of your request.
5. Meet and discuss employment opportunities. OR

Ask for other contacts they have who may be interested in supporting your employment.

The above list of actions will ensure you are showing assertiveness and contacting professionals via appropriate methods. It is usually best to call and speak to them directly as you immediately begin to develop a relationship. If you get no response after two weeks, move on to consider other contacts you are linked with. Within LinkedIn you are able to find a high number of business professionals. As such, do not contact these people one by one but in bulk according to the task or goal you want to achieve.

Table 20.2 is offered blank to allow you to complete the rows of detail when using LinkedIn. If you are systematic and clear in how you organise and approach contacts on this social media website, you will quickly and effectively source employment opportunities.

Another useful tool within LinkedIn is the function to gain recommendations. These are similar to references and enable you to showcase recommendations on your work from other people. Once linked to other people, use this function to request people to write recommendations on your work. This is then visible to employers looking for new employees and can be clarified as a link for employers to review within your job application. N.B. If you use this on a job application, ensure the profile is up to date and filled with information to showcase your ability. A blank or partly completed profile will make you look less capable.

Table 20.2 LinkedIn contact chasing

Contact name	Business	Phone number	LinkedIn profile URL	Role or title	When contacted?	Follow up on?

LinkedIn has been discussed in terms of a tool for your professional development. However, a number of THE companies will also need you to use LinkedIn as part of your work supporting their goals and targets. Employees are often asked to use LinkedIn to search for customers, suppliers and markers to support their company. As such, even if you do not feel LinkedIn has members who you could contact to develop your understanding of roles and skills for professional development, it is essential you observe and try out its key functions as a skill for employment.

Twitter

Twitter is an online social media platform where people communicate using short written pieces, photos, gifs and links. You will create a profile using two photos and be able to describe yourself in under 160 characters.

ACTIVITY 20.5 SETTING UP A TWITTER ACCOUNT

1. Go to http://twitter.com and find the sign up box, or go directly to https://twitter.com/signup.
2. You will be guided through our sign up experience and prompted to enter information such as your name and email address.
3. If you choose to sign up with an email address, we will require you to verify your email address by sending you an email with instructions.
4. If you choose to sign up with a phone number, we will require you to verify by sending you an SMS text message with a code. You may also request a voice call to verify your phone number. Enter the verification code in the box provided. Learn more about having a phone number associated with your account.

5. Once you sign up for an account, you can select a username (usernames are unique identifiers on Twitter). We'll tell you if the username you want is available.
6. Learn how to customize settings for your new account.

Source: https://help.twitter.com/en/using-twitter/create-twitter-account
Other sites in support https://help.twitter.com/en/managing-your-account/phone-number-faqs https://help.twitter.com/en/managing-your-account/new-account-settings

CASE STUDY 20.5 ADVICE ON WRITING YOUR TWITTER PROFILE

Write about your interests – especially on Twitter. *Why are you on Twitter in the first place? Try to answer this question in your bio. You don't have to do it directly, but if your bio says you are a social media expert and all you do is share cat photos and videos on Twitter, your followers will probably start to fall off.*

Get your priorities straight. *You are a complex person and your business is too. It might take some serious thinking, but you need to prioritize just what it is you want to get across to your followers that defines you. Being a happy husband, a proud daddy and a golf addict might be large parts of who you are, but if you are using Twitter to promote your online graphics designing business, these might not have a place in such a short bio.*

Keep keywords in mind. *Twitter is a search tool, too, so you'd do yourself a favor if you included keywords in your bio. Think about things that people would search for to find you, and try to include those keywords in your Twitter bio. Your followers will be more likely to stick if they were searching and found you based on relevant keywords.*

Twitter Bio Don'ts

Along with the three tips above, you should be careful to avoid some of these common pitfalls of Twitter bio creation:

1. *Don't waste space on a quote or something that has nothing to do with you or your business. You might live and die by someone else's words, but your followers want to know about you, not the people you admire.*
2. *Don't use a bio you've written elsewhere without editing it. 160-characters is pretty short, and you don't want any text cut off. That's a big turn-off for followers.*

> 3. *Don't leave this space empty! After reading these tips, you've got lots of theory under your belt. Go put it into practice and start getting more targeted followers!*
>
> *Source*: www.adweek.com/digital/3-tips-for-writing-a-killer-twitter-bio-to-get-targeted-followers/

The advice offered from Lauran Dugan in Case Study 20.5 is one of many pieces written on how to improve and support your profile bio writing. When you have set up your Twitter profile (using an appropriate photo and profile description) you can then start following others and tweeting information to the internet. Please note that unless you change the settings, your tweets will be public and accessible to anyone with another Twitter profile.

To use Twitter for professional development start by searching for hashtags (#) related to your area of interest. For example you could search for #culinaryarts. This search would then bring up all comments using this and would enable you to view tweets and people who are discussing this. You can then request to follow people whom you find interesting. Tweets discussing topics you are interested in can then be commented upon and offer your opinion or perspective. This is how you will receive feedback, followers and support within the social network.

Unlike LinkedIn, you can use Twitter as an emergent network for you to discuss, comment and interact with others to enable your knowledge development. Its purpose is not simply for business professionals and is used for personal and social connection and comment.

Instagram

Instagram is a social network different to LinkedIn and Twitter as it requires you to post photos rather than written content. This is an essential professional development network for THE as it will offer you access to photos on THE businesses and operations from both the business and its customers.

ACTIVITY 20.6 **CREATING AN INSTAGRAM ACCOUNT**

1. Go to instagram.com.
2. Enter your email address, create a username and password or click Log in with Facebook to sign up with your Facebook account.
3. If you register with an email, click Sign up. If you register with Facebook, you'll be prompted to log into your Facebook account if you're currently logged out.

If you sign up with email, make sure you enter your email address correctly and choose an email address that only you can access. If you log out and forget your password, you'll need to be able to access your email to get back into your Instagram account.

Source: https://help.instagram.com/155,940,534,568,753

Once you are using Instagram you can search for businesses you are interested in working in, culinary dishes, tourist experiences and event photos. These will support your understanding of industry practice but also offer you access to comments and links made by others. As a student on THE your ability to appraise and reflect on business operations is important and will be seen as a core skill by future employers.

Furthermore, some companies only operate using Instagram and decline the traditional website home for their marketing and business operations.

Global Source Kitchen is an example of a hospitality business that only operates on Instagram and Facebook. This is due to their need to connect with customers and suppliers in social channels. They are found more easily within these websites and networks and it enables them to save on the cost of creating a bespoke website.

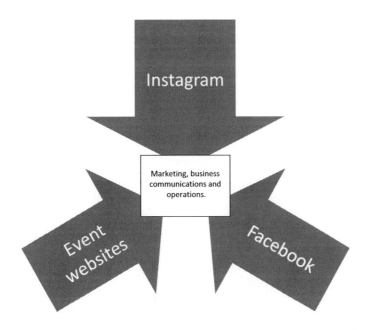

Figure 20.4 Global Source Kitchen's social media accounts

Advice in support of your online academic and professional networking:

- Use a high quality and professional photograph of yourself.
- Use appropriate language and terminology.
- Search for people who are aligned to your professional development goals and topics of interest for employment.
- Connect with as many people as possible to link yourself to other professionals.
- Engage and comment on others' posts to request and offer your opinion.

SUMMARY

1. To understand what networking is and its importance within academic and professional development.

Networking was defined as an action or activity in which you develop links with other people in order to improve your knowledge or access to information. Your ability to develop relationships and build networks is a vital employability skill as it will enable you to consider industry practice and research from wider positions. Within your studies you can create academic, personal and professional networks which will support your self-esteem and supplement your awareness of industry practices for THE. These three forms of networks are important for your transition into graduate life and the skills used in developing them will be valued highly by prospective employers.

2. To examine skills needed for effective networking.

The soft skills of communication, assertiveness and confidence were discussed briefly in this chapter. Other parts and chapters offer more depth on these particular employment attributes. Here, we applied them to your ability to complete networking efficiently. Consideration of the form, tone and language used in the communication will ensure you are understood clearly and your requirements are transparent. Your physical appearance online and face to face will be judged and interpreted by network members. Ensuring you dress appropriately for each network activity will result in being accepted and involved within the network. Mistakes made in presentation may result in you being rejected from the group, not being taken seriously or being overlooked for further activity that could support your development. Being assertive is core to networking. As it relies on action, you need to assert your intentions and requirements clearly to ensure you get the most from the network. Finally, it was outlined how there is a skilling circle in networking as you may often find a purpose of the network is to clarify the skills needed for academic and professional development.

3. To examine methods and processes involved in individual networking: face to face and online.

LinkedIn, Twitter and Instagram have all been discussed as methods to aid your professional development. The processes to create, contact, upload and offer comment on others' posts has been offered in support of your networking using these websites. They should not be used alone, nor remote from attending events and meeting people. Use them as a tool for improving your knowledge of key topics in your studies and learning about key experts in the fields you aspire to work within.

Questions to support your learning and research

1. What tone should you use within personal networks?
2. How should you plan to present yourself in networking activities?
3. How can a research association aid your networking?
4. What does the skilling circle contain?
5. How can affirmations aid your confidence?
6. How can Twitter be used for professional development?
7. What contents does the table for LinkedIn contain?

Websites in support of your learning from this chapter

My LinkedIn, Twitter and Instagram Accounts:
www.instagram.com/mirifirth/
https://twitter.com/DrMiriamFirth
www.linkedin.com/in/mirifirth/

Chapter 21
Coaching and mentoring

INTRODUCTION

Coaching and mentoring are seen as part of performance management. Your own professional performance is based on your ability to reflect and build upon current skills and knowledge in industry contexts. You may either be satisfied with the level to which you can perform in an industry role, or be asked or driven to improve in areas of performance. This chapter will outline what performance management is, how coaching and mentoring are defined and how to utilise these in your own career planning and development. Use the activities in this chapter at different levels of your career to enable you to pro-actively support and manage your professional development planning.

PERFORMANCE MANAGEMENT

Performance management is a process in which you outline goals and targets for improved performance, and evaluate the progress made in meeting these goals at set times. A number of tasks can be completed in support of performance management. Induction and appraisal are discussed here to clarify how you can utilise these aspects for your professional development within THE industry.

Induction

When you enter employment it is usual for you to be offered an induction to the company. This may be a training event or a week of activities in support of clarifying the company's goals or culture. THE companies often use these to establish good working teams as new recruits enter the working environment. Induction can both clarify the organisational strategy and indirectly assert the organisational culture of a business. Knowledge of their organisational strategy is important for you to complete your role in support of overarching operation targets as well as to understand how the company focusses and attributes its success.

CASE STUDY 21.1 STRATEGY IN A THE BUSINESS

The following is an excerpt from TUI's (TUI, 2019) strategy. It clarifies the existing environment in which it operates, the extent of the group's operations and its future direction:

Holiday Experiences

TUI operates 380 hotels and 16 cruise ships globally through ownership, JVs, management contracts, leases or franchise, and maintains a strong position in the growing tours and activities market with our 150k excursion and activity offerings. Our differentiated hotel and club brand portfolio, our uniquely positioned German and UK cruise brands, and our global tours, activities and services destination business is well diversified to mitigate content cluster risks.

Our strong and in the future fully digitalised risk management tools within distribution and purchasing, allow us to optimise occupancy and yield. 23 m customers come through our Markets and Airlines, including joint ventures in Canada and Russia, complemented by 4 m customers sold either directly by Holiday Experiences, or via third parties. An optimised and in the future fully dynamic allocation of around 100 m bed nights and approx. €5 bn third party hotel beds purchasing volume globally, will further contribute to our yield maximisation. As part of our divisional strategy, we continue to invest into the growth and diversification of our hotel and cruise portfolio, leading to a more seasonally robust business mix delivering superior margins. Looking ahead, building a new Southeast Asia hotel cluster is a strategic priority. In addition we have a strong pipeline of new ship deliveries in the coming years.

The global and pre-dominantly offline, fast growing tours and activities market, worth over €150 bn is highly fragmented with over 300 k providers and therefore offers a strong growth and consolidation opportunity for TUI Group.

Markets and Airlines

TUI operates a customer centric and diversified distribution and fulfillment business across Europe. We combine leveraging our strong market and customer knowledge, driving customer satisfaction and retention, with service and fulfillment. Packaging and purchasing is increasingly driven through our digital platforms and our own airlines, supported by third party flights, facilitate the link between customer demand and our own, as well as third party committed and non-committed hotel and cruise offerings.

Enhancing efficiency by harmonising these regional market organisations, which include our airlines as well, is a key strategic priority.

In addition, we intend to diversify our existing market footprint further. Through our fully digital LTE platform, we are pursuing a low risk entry strategy, simultaneously improving our position to yield our Holiday Experiences' risk capacity through additional new source market demand.

On review of the above detail taken from TUI's strategy, consider how employees working within its businesses are required to perform to meet the strategy. Is the level of performance or customer service standard explicit or implicit?

In addition to being made aware of the strategy the company works within, THE business inductions often relay information on their organisational culture through key business mantra.

ACTIVITY 21.1 MAKE YOUR OWN PERFORMANCE MANAGEMENT MANTRA

On completing an induction course at the Hilton Metropole, London, blogger Ayeshan 2014 noted the following content explained to all new starters:

In the first part of my induction; I took note about the values of Hilton Hotel.

H – Hospitality, this is the most important thing which Hilton specialize in.

I – Integrity, staff must be honest, honorable towards customers.

L – Leadership, staff should have some kind of leadership of themselves as well as others.

T – Teamwork, teamwork is very important at any Hilton Hotels; when staff work together things will run smoothly.

O – Ownership, staff should take ownership in their actions and decisions.

N – Now, in Hilton it is all about what happens now; not tomorrow or in the
future.

Source: http://ayeshan2014.blogspot.com/2014/11/induction-for-work-experience-hilton.html

1. Using the same method, write out the letters to your first and second name on
separate lines.
2. Next to each letter, consider a word that reflects yourself and your approach to
professional development in THE.
3. Write a sentence after each word to clarify your own professional development
and ways in which you approach working tasks.

Mission statements, objectives, mantra and business buzz words are all used in induction
to support the overall strategy. This ensures all staff are able to represent the brand clearly
and feel motivated to work to a high standard in insupport of achieving these targets. In
addition to learning about these aspects, you will often have health and safety and legal
training within the induction.

The information relayed within induction will clarify the business ambitions and goals. These
will enable you to consider how the organisation is structured and perceive where
promotion, development and training will fit in support of your employment with them.
Within the induction find out the following:

1. Where is your position in relation to the overall business hierarchy?
2. What on-the-job training is available to you?
3. What personal development activities are supported by the business?
4. What is the usual timescale for performance management and promotion in your particular career track?

Obtaining answers to these questions within the induction will aid your understanding of
your position and ability to develop within the company.

If you work within a small- to medium-sized enterprise (SME) you may find that there is
no provision for induction. Equally if you are a fixed-term worker who contracts their
work to a variety of businesses, you are not expected to understand the overall strategy
as you are seen as a stakeholder within a supply chain of staff. Self-employed workers
are also not expected to induct themselves! As a high proportion of THE businesses rely
on staff who are transient, fixed term, or employed for particular activities, it is
appropriate to complete your own induction checklist in order to satisfy your
performance management.

ACTIVITY 21.2 AN INDUCTION CHECKLIST FOR FIXED-TERM OR SELF-EMPLOYED WORKERS

Go through the following and outline the areas you are competent in or those for which you need further advice or support:

1. Health and safety legislation surrounding your duties and role in the business.
2. Employment law supporting your role.
3. Strategy you are working towards.
4. Mission statement and objectives for the company.
5. Standards of customer service.
6. Financial targets to achieve.
7. Training required to develop your ability in the role.
8. Resources needed within the development of your role and business.
9. Policies and procedures you work within (external and internal).

Using this checklist, compile your own operational manual for the work and role you complete.

Appraisals

In employment, you may be offered an appraisal meeting with your manager or direct line supervisor. If working in a full-time position, it is usual for these meetings to be completed once per year. If you are on a probation period to start your employment, you may be offered an appraisal before this time finishes in order to establish if you will be made a permanent employee. Appraisals are therefore used by company management to track and monitor an employee's performance, but can also be used by the employee to establish clear career goals and targets for professional development.

CASE STUDY 21.2 CARIBBEAN HOTEL AND TOURISM ASSOCIATION APPRAISAL FORM

The following has been adapted from the Caribbean Hotel and Tourism Associations Appraisal form.

Numbers noted against each criteria relate to the following:

5. Outstanding
Level of performance in completing all tasks consistently exceeds the standard established, especially in key areas of quality, quantity and timeliness of output. Shows team spirit, initiative, contributes ideas and assists in activities outside of key areas of responsibility.

4. Exceed expectations

Often exceeds performance standard for the completion of tasks. Requires minimum supervision, is reliable, professional and capable of rising to the occasion in handling the demands of work.

3. Meets expectations

Meets performance standard and fulfills duties and responsibilities of the position in a satisfactory and timely manner. Performance is competent with some supervision generally required.

2. Needs improvement

Does not always meet performance standard in all major areas of responsibility. Demonstrates ability to complete some assignments but needs supervision. Need for appropriate training and personal development.

1. Unacceptable

Level of performance in completing tasks is consistently below performance standard in spite of supervision, coaching and training.

To access the full version please visit www.caribbeanhotelandtourism.com.

The exemplar grading criteria above utilises a usual system of organisation. Areas of work are outlined to clarify levels within each. These are then given a number according to the perception of performance on the employee. Goals are then clarified separate to this and can include on-the-job training, industry accreditation, or customer satisfaction feedback targets. If you are a temporary or self-employed worker you can still complete these appraisals. Instead of calling them appraisals they are a form of customer feedback as you are offering your work for payment and your employer is treated as a customer. The feedback they offer within the same areas of working standards will enable you to appraise and understand how your competences and competencies are perceived.

An important aspect of the appraisal is that it is a discussion between the manager and employee. It is not designed to be instructive whereby the manager informs the employee of the level they are working within. Individual ability, personal life, perceived expectations and the scope of targets should all be discussed. It is the opportunity for you to appraise your ability but also signify your intended career goals.

THINK POINT 21.1 DO YOU ALWAYS NEED TO SET CAREER GOALS?

In review of the appraisal process within performance management it has been established that you need to be evaluated on your standards of work and career goals. Is it always necessary to create career goals? Are you someone who is content in maintaining a good level of work and remaining in the same position? How can you clarify this to management within your appraisals?

Think Point 21.1 is to clarify that it is not necessary for you to set high standard targets and goals within the appraisal. You may feel content in achieving high customer satisfaction and a good work–life balance, meaning you are not driven to achieve higher targets and goals. In this instance, the appraisal is mainly for management to confirm their employees are aware of the standards of work required and document these have been discussed.

In terms of the goals you can set within your appraisal these can be personal, career and professional goals.

Table 21.1 clarifies how the goals set on your appraisal are not simply related to the performance of the business you work within, but can include career, professional and personal aims. Use Part 3, Chapter 12 to develop your ability to create and manage goals and targets effectively.

COACHING AND MENTORING

Coaching and mentoring are support mechanisms to aid your professional development. Within performance management, you will be required to work to set standards and receive

Table 21.1 Goals for appraisal meetings

Personal	Career	Professional
• To have more time for activities with family and friends. • To support family by getting an increase in wages. • To be recognised as outstanding in order to support and develop personal self-esteem.	• To achieve a promotion within a fixed time period. • To complete industry accreditation on a specific area. • To be recognised by others in your position as a leading example.	• To be identified by customers as offering high service standards. • To support colleagues' development. • To enable a company to meet its targets and strategy.

feedback upon the level and ability demonstrated. Coaching can be utilised to develop your ability and reflexivity in work. Mentoring is whereby you seek inspiration and support from a more senior colleague within the same career track. This section will outline positions on coaching and mentoring to define and explore known positions. The final section will then outline how to use these in your own career planning and development.

Coaching is whereby an employee seeks to improve their skills and knowledge with the goal of improving work performance (Horn, 2009). There is relatively little currently researched and written upon coaching and mentoring with THE working contexts. Within existing literature, coaching referred to in relation to sports tourism (Blackman, 2008, for example) and mentoring is mostly aligned to students being given industry mentors (Nash, 2009, for example). Nevertheless, this chapter is offered on coaching and mentoring as there is a surge in using these in the development of leaders across economic supporting industries (Hawkins and Smith, 2013). Coaching is a form of counselling offered on an individual basis, which aims to specifically develop a skill, competence or aptitude for career development:

> helping the individual to gain self-awareness, but is not goal focussed and action is required so that the individual can move forward.
>
> (Harrison, 2009: p.168)

This quotation outlines that progression and development has been halted and that coaching is used to remedy a person's ability to progress. The action completed by the employee is as a result of supportive coaching, which can be offered either internally or externally to the company they work within. As it is not welded to the career tracks, organisational strategy or direct line managers within your employment, this is an essential professional development tool to support your life-long learning.

CASE STUDY 21.3 CALIFORNIAN HOSPITALITY COACH

Donna Bond is a coach in California, USA, who offers coaching to hospitality professionals. Donna clarifies her coaching will assist employees in the following way:

My coaching practice offers hospitality coaching benefits for individuals and teams who:

- *Seek work–life balance, integrating the whole person and all aspects of life.*
- *Need help identifying and addressing blocks which may be causing stagnation.*
- *Desire to overcome specific issues and benefit from an experienced and objective perspective.*

> *The results look like this:*
>
> * *Supporting oneself in using your gifts and talents for success.*
> * *Increased confidence, optimism and self-awareness.*
> * *Uncovering blocks that have kept you from greater success and personal fulfilment.*
> * *Releasing limiting beliefs and reframing them to support your life.*
> * *Improved self-awareness and communication skills.*
> * *Increased engagement with what matters.*
> * *Clarification on priorities.*
> * *Manifesting a clear pathway to step forward as your true self.*
>
> *My approach assists by:*
>
> * *Exploring possibilities in a safe and loving environment.*
> * *Gathering information and offering feedback and perspective in a non-judgmental environment.*
> * *Helping my clients Vision their future and how their career fits into that Vision.*
> * *Determining the strategy and gaining commitment for taking action.*
> * *Instilling personal accountability for outcomes.*
>
> *Source*: https://donnabond.com/

In review of the case example offered in Case Study 21.3, it is clear that coaching not only develops professional practice but supports career and life-long learning.

Coaching can also assist whole businesses. Tourism Growth (https://tourismgrowth.co.uk/) is an example of a company that can coach tourism companies in the UK to develop and enhance their current policies and processes. This approach is mainly directed at supporting the overall strategy and revenue of a company. Personal coaching is navigated more towards self-improvement.

Within the increase in coaching, noted by a number of human resource professionals and researchers, there are a number of questions arising from this form of support:

1. How does individual coaching link to the organisational goals of the business?
2. How is it measured in relation to the strategy of a business?
3. What standards are applied in coaching?
4. What are the ethical considerations in personal coaching if it is paid for by a company but results in the employee leaving the business or changing career?
5. Who should lead in coaching? The individual or manager of an employee?

As coaching links to individual self-improvement it also supports mindfulness and well-being. These are two important aspects within professional development as they enable a person to be reflective of their ability and state of mind as well as maintain a healthy structure and routine in their life (see Chapter 19 of this part for more information on these).

THINK POINT 21.2 COMPLETING MINDFULNESS AND WELL-BEING TRAINING WITHIN YOUR STUDIES

Well-being and mindfulness are two contemporary topics supporting your ability to lead a successful and happy life. Have you been offered courses on these from your institution of study? Have your friends been on a course on these? Are you able to make time to attend these in support of your professional development?

Now moving onto mentoring, this is seen as a one-to one activity whereby a colleague supports a junior employee to develop professionally. Mentoring is usually established when you join a company as you may require advice and support from another colleague. The intention of mentoring is to enable you to fit within the organisational culture and at the same time support individual duties and roles (Harrison, 2009). There are two common models of mentoring used within business management, the 5Cs and the GROW model. These are discussed as examples of how mentoring should facilitate professional development.

The 5Cs of mentoring

Challenges are the issues or goals required for the mentoring session. The mentee is required to outline the current position and identify the results they want to achieve.

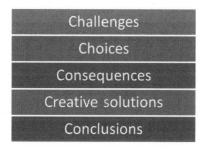

Figure 21.1 The 5Cs of mentoring
Source: based upon Keele, 2019 and Cambridge, 2019

Choices enable the mentee to outline the possible options and routes to complete or solve the issue noted. Discussion should enable a range of choices to be outlined as well as note of prior actions completed.

Consequences are the advantages and disadvantages of completing the choices listed in order to appraise and evaluate each one in turn.

Creative solutions is when you begin to consider the issue from external positions. This position often includes using a blank piece of paper to consider if the issue has to exist or whether there are background or foregrounding factors present.

Conclusions are then outlined from discussion of the previous four Cs. A plan of action is created based upon the options which were most achievable and realistic.

GROW: A MENTORING MODEL

Goals require you to create an aim, objective and specify a topic. This is used to focus the mentoring and allow for a framework of reference to discuss.

Reality involves self-reflection on the current situation and discussion of assumptions made relating to the issue.

Options clarify the range of approaches available to solve or address the goal.

Will is the commitment to complete actions within agreed deadlines in support of the goal.

Goal

Current Reality

Options (or Obstacles)

Will (or Way Forward)

Figure 21.2 GROW: a model for mentoring
Source: based on Bishop, 2015

CASE STUDY 21.4 MENTORING THROUGH THE INSTITUTE OF HOSPITALITY

Mentor Me is mentoring with a difference; it focuses on career growth and development for both experienced and new hospitality managers.

Our student members and Associates (AIH) are matched with experienced Members (MIH) and Fellows (FIH) to undertake some guided learning on topical industry issues alongside monthly meetings.

If you can commit to a one-to-one meeting each month for a six month period and you are keen to undertake professional development as well as supporting a colleague then Mentor Me could be for you! Meetings do not always need to be in person, you can choose to meet via Skype, Face Time etc. if more convenient.

To take part in **Mentor Me** you need to be a current member. It's one of our most valued member benefits. Find out how to join the Institute of Hospitality.

Register your interest:

mentorme@instituteofhospitality.org

"I have been paired with an Institute of Hospitality Fellow through the Mentor Me scheme. My mentor has helped me to create a set of professional goals and given advice on a variety of work-related topics, which have been very beneficial to my development." Louise Balderson AIH, Graduate Manager, Hilton

Source: www.instituteofhospitality.org/professional-development/mentoring/

In addition to individual mentoring, team mentoring can aid team working within an organisation. If mentoring is used for a team or group of employees it needs to address the following aspects:

1. A business case for mentoring of a team. This should link to the strategy and organisational goals to meet or exceed.
2. Piloting of the mentoring with other groups in order to establish it is fit for purpose and adds value for the company.
3. Workloads adjusted for individuals within the team to allow for time spent on completing actions to support issues or goals.
4. An agreement with all individuals and mentors that the process is reciprocal and requires team working in order for it to be a success.
5. Mentors trained and qualified to complete the work to a consistent standard.

If the following is addressed in team mentoring, it can be used effectively for meeting organisational targets.

UTILISING COACHES AND MENTORS FOR YOUR CAREER PLANNING AND DEVELOPMENT

Activities 21.3 and 21.4 are designed to allow you and a partner to complete coaching and mentoring whilst completing your academic studies.

ACTIVITY 21.3 COACHING FOR YOUR SKILLS

This activity is designed for you to approach professional development using a coaching framework:

1. Complete your skills appraisal using activities and information in Part 2, Chapter 6.
2. Identify a skill you have not gained experience for from this appraisal.
3. Using this skill complete the following four As:

Awareness

What do you know about the skill?
What does the skill require you to know or do?
How relevant is this skill to your professional development?
How motivated are you to develop this skill?
Do you know others who have this skill already?

Analysis

How can you develop an ability in this skill?
Do you need a working or study context in which to develop and complete this skill?
Do you know of any managers or business owners who would employ you as a volunteer to develop and practice this skill?
Do you need to develop knowledge in order to apply this to the skill?
Are there forms and types of this skill to be practiced?
Are there barriers or limits known in using this skill?

Action

What time scale do you want to work to?
What level of experience and standard of skill do you want to achieve?
Will you need to work with others to evidence the skill?

Achievement

How will you know you have achieved the skill?
Who will confirm your level of ability?
How will you add this to your curriculum vitae?

ACTIVITY 21.4 MENTORING FOR YOUR PROFESSIONAL DEVELOPMENT

1. Identify a role or position in industry you would like to complete in the future.
2. Find someone on LinkedIn or within your business networks offline who already completed this role.
3. Ask them or review their work experience completed prior to gaining this role.
4. Search for current job opportunities available for this role.
5. List the essential criteria needed to apply for the post.
6. List the desirable criteria needed for this post.
7. Align your own skills, knowledge and experience to these criteria and identify gaps currently missing.
8. Contact your industry mentor (step 1 above) and ask for their advice on how you could gain this experience in support of you completing a role similar to theirs in the future.

SUMMARY

1. To identify what performance management is.

Performance management was defined as a way in which managers track and evaluate employee's working standards. They are often explained within induction training and evaluated within appraisals. Students in THE can create their own mantras for professional development and outline their own induction checklist for completing work in these industries. Students aiming for self-employment and fixed-term work can also apply these individually to obtain employer perceptions on their standards of work.

2. To understand tenets of coaching and mentoring.

Coaching and mentoring are relatively new additions to human resource management and life-long learning support for employees. Coaching can be completed internally or externally to the company you work for and aims to support your development in a skill or competence. Mentoring can assist your transition into a company and also aid problem solving within professional development. Both of these originate from counselling and psychology professions whereby individuals seek counsel on how to manage their usual approach to tasks and dealing with issues.

3. To appraise the use of coaches and mentors at different levels of your career in support of professional development.

The two activities offered in this final section enable you to complete work on professional development using the coaching and mentoring models discussed. Self-awareness, motivation and aspiration to improve your professional skills are needed for completion of these. When working as a fixed-term or self-employed worker, use these activities in regular intervals to aid your professional development.

Questions to support your learning and research

1. What is performance management?
2. How is organisational culture communicated in an induction?
3. Why might you need an appraisal after a probation period?
4. What would your personal goals be within an appraisal of your academic or professional work?
5. What does GROW stand for?
6. How is coaching supportive of your skilling development?
7. What are the 5Cs of mentoring?

Further reading in support of your learning from this chapter

Drake, D. and Stelter, R. (2014). Narrative Coaching. In *Mastery in Coaching: A Complete Psychological Toolkit for Advanced Coaching*.

Eby, L.T. et al. (2008). Does mentoring matter? A multidisciplinary meta-analysis comparing mentored and non-mentored individuals. *Journal of Vocational Behavior*.

Ghosh, R. and Reio, T.G. (2013). Career benefits associated with mentoring for mentors: A meta-analysis. *Journal of Vocational Behavior*.

Jacob, Y. and Jacob, Y. (2019). Existential coaching. In *An Introduction to Existential Coaching*.

Neenan, M. (2018). Cognitive Behavioural Coaching.

Neenan, M. and Palmer, S. (2001). Cognitive Behavioural Coaching.

Newfield Community, the and Olalla, J. (2010). Ontological Coaching. In *The Routledge Companion to International Business Coaching*.

Waljee, J.F., Chopra, V. and Saint, S. (2018). Mentoring millennials. *JAMA – Journal of the American Medical Association*.

Chapter 22

Forms of employment experience

LEARNING OBJECTIVES

1. To offer tools to write an effective curriculum vitae.
2. To clarify traditional forms of employment experience to support your graduate career in tourism, hospitality and events management.
3. To outline non-traditional locations for THE employment experience to consider.

INTRODUCTION

This final chapter outlines tools and techniques to write an effective curriculum vitae (CV) to apply for employment positions. From this, forms of employment experience will be outlined. These forms of employment experience are clarified as a range of different forms from which you can develop and build your skilling experiences. It is unlikely that you will graduate and work in one role or position until retirement. As such, consideration of the non-traditional locations of THE employment is then clarified in order to appraise how you can develop experience and evidence skill use in a wider array of businesses and sectors.

EFFECTIVE CV WRITING

Writing CVs is an art form. A CV is a document explaining your current qualification and work experience, which showcases your ability to complete working tasks. There are a variety of ways in which CVs can be presented (blogs, word documents, LinkedIn profile and videos, for example). This chapter will outline a traditional form of CV usual for applying for positions within THE businesses and industry. It is usual for you to write a cover letter in support of your application. This may be within an email or separate word document and should outline your reason for applying for the post.

A cover letter should be unique to the role you are applying for and should clarify the following:

1.   What you are applying for.
2.   Why you are interested in the business/company/organisation.
3.   How you feel you meet the person specification.
4.   How you want to support their strategy and objectives within employment.
5.   When you are available for interview and how to contact you to discuss the application further.

CV structure:

- Name.
- Address.
- Email and phone number.
- Qualification list.
- Training completed (including industry accreditation and certification).
- Relevant work experience.
- Additional work experience.
- Roles with responsibility.
- Languages spoken.
- Driving licence held.
- Hobbies and interests related to the post.
- References (usually available on request or via your LinkedIn page).

Within the work experience section of your CV use the CAR technique (see Figure 22.1) to outline how this evidences your skills and abilities.

The CAR technique involves three sentences in a bullet point under each work experience listed in your CV. For example, if you have worked part time within

C – Case
A – Action
R - Result

Figure 22.1 CAR technique for CVs

a restaurant and wanted to clarify this evidences your interpersonal skills, the following would be an appropriate bullet point:

- I have excellent interpersonal skills. I used verbal communication, empathy, understanding and awareness to serve and meet guests' needs. As such, I have received 90% customer satisfaction.

The case sentence states your ability. The action is what you did to use this and the result is the outcome from using this skill or knowledge.

ACTIVITY 22.1 USING THE CAR TECHNIQUE WITH YOUR SKILLS

1. Look at the essential and desirable criteria on a job advert.
2. Identify where you have experience of these within your work experience and link them to skills.
3. Write bullet points using the CAR technique for each of these under your work experience.
4. If there are multiple examples of using the skill, pick the one with the most impressive result.

CASE STUDY 22.1 STUDENT'S CV USING THE CAR TECHNIQUE

Theresa Higinbottom

Crawford House, Booth Street East, Manchester, M13 9QS tel: 0161 123 4567, mob: 0123 456 7891 email: xxx.xxxxx@live.com, LinkedIn: www.linkedin.com/xxxxx

Education

2018–2021 The University of Manchester BA (Hons) Management, Leadership and Leisure. Expected result 2:1

First year result: 58% Second year result: 65%

- Achieved a first class grade for a comparative case study of two local businesses on sustainability and ethical business practices.
- Utilised both primary and secondary research sources, conducting 100 questionnaires and five focus groups to produce a paper.

- Undertook a group project on behalf of Manchester Student Homes looking at improving waste management in student residential areas as part of a Career Management Skills module.

2000–2016 Silverdale Secondary School, Sheffield

A level: English (A), Economics (B), French (B)

AS level: Psychology (B)

GCSEs: 9 (5A, 3B, 1C) including Maths and English

Relevant work experience

June–September Hofbrauhaus, Munich, German 2019

Internship in Sales Management

- Set up four appointments with buyers through cold calling. Successfully persuaded a buyer who initially did not want to book a meeting to immediately place an order over the telephone, which has helped to improve my confidence in both my German language abilities and my negotiation skills.
- Promoted Hofbrau's presence at a national trade fair. Identified potential new clients and marketed the fair through Facebook, LinkedIn and by delivering a five minute presentation at a small business breakfast meeting. Three of the businesses went on to place orders.
- Assisted Sales Reps in two meetings with key clients, providing data and answering questions about the trade fair. Developed excellent knowledge of advanced sales techniques and the principles of good account management.
- Researched and investigated three 'pre-sale' competitor products. Produced a ten-page report and wrote and delivered a presentation of my findings to the Sales Director and Marketing Team, taking questions from the group.

Additional Skills

IT Proficient in the use of Microsoft Office, including Excel to create spreadsheets and analyse complex data sets.

Driving: Full clean driving licence.

Languages: Fluent German (second language). Basic conversational level Spanish (GCSE plus visits).

Interests and Activities: Societies Member of the Debating Society and enjoy participating in competitions and events. I recently organised an evening of guest speakers from industry to speak on persuasive public speaking.

References available on request

Source: based on CV examples from students at the University of Manchester

Further guidance in CV writing:

1.   Create a different cover letter and CV for every application.
2.   Keep your CV shorter than two sides of A4.
3.   List your qualifications and work experience in descending order starting with the most recent one completed.
4.   Remove unnecessary qualifications (if you need to prove you have a degree, there is no need to include all lower levels of education and their topic names).
5.   Be clear and explicit in why you want to work for them.
6.   Outline how you will be of benefit to the company using your own skills and qualifications.
7.   Offer references on request.

Using the above guidance and techniques, you will be able to create a tailored and specific CV addressing the requirements of a job advertised. However, you do not need to wait to see a job posted to apply to work within a company. If you find a company you would like to gain employment experience from, use the following steps to apply for a position:

1.   Find the details of the manager or HR manager.
2.   Call them and identify your expression of interest in working for them.
3.   Clarify the form of employment experience you are seeking.
4.   Clarify what skills you want to offer in the role.
5.   Identify the skills you want to develop within the experience.
6.   Ask how you can send in your CV and how to proceed.
7.   If they do not have availability for you to work with them, ask for advice on similar businesses/organisations who may support you.

FORMS OF EMPLOYMENT EXPERIENCE

This section will discuss nine forms of employment experience. These can all be completed in support of your career mapping (see Chapter 23 of this part).

1.   Freelance work.

Freelance work is often fixed term and temporary. You can offer your specialist skills and knowledge to complete tasks in support of the overall business. This may involve working for an event or business for a fixed amount of time. You will work and be paid by a number of employers.

2.   Gap years.

A gap year is often completed before higher education. Students choose to take a gap year after their school qualifications at the age of 18 in order to travel, work or complete new experiences. However, gap years can be taken at any point during your life. In employment these are called sabbaticals and within your university or college studies, are called an interruption year. These are locations of employment experience as people often complete working roles to support their financial needs within the year. These are abundant with skilling development as you will be completing a range of tasks and activities which can be linked to your skills appraisal (see Part 2, Chapter 6).

3.   Placements.

A placement is usually a year of work experience completed within a business. Students are often able to choose university and college courses which specifically include a placement year. This year out of your studies is aimed at offering you the opportunity to apply your knowledge and skills in a working context. If completed within academic studies it is usual for students to aim for a role at a supervisory level in order to experience a role with responsibility and leadership requirements.

4.   Internships.

An internship is a set period of time when you work within a business/organisation. It is aimed at giving you an insight into a specific role or department of a business in order to assist your career development. Internships are offered by companies to support their business strategy but also to meet and get to know potential employees of the future.

5.   Part-time jobs.

A part-time job is where you are paid for a set number of hours per week. Full time hours are usually +35hrs and so part-time work would tend to be around 15 hours per week in two shifts.

6.   Working abroad.

Working abroad from your native country is often completed within a gap year. However, it may also be a requirement of other positions available. For example, freelancers may travel abroad to complete work on different events, internships might not be available in your home country and so you may travel abroad to complete these.

7.   Volunteering.

Volunteering is whereby you offer your time and effort without any payment. This role is usual for people wanting to gain experience in an area that is difficult to get into. It is also usual for students to volunteer during holiday periods from their courses to attend festivals and events they are interested in.

8.   Work shadowing.

Work shadowing is where you work within a company but follow a person completing a specific role. This is an observational employment experience whereby you usually shadow someone with senior leadership responsibilities. Similar to volunteering, this position is usually unpaid. It can enable you to consider the skills and knowledge used in senior positions as part of your career mapping.

9.   Other: workshops, training and competitions.

Workshops, training and competitions are examples of employment experience linked to specific skills or knowledge. Workshops enable you to complete actions based upon your

Table 22.1 Examples of THE roles within the nine employment experiences

Type of experience	THE role examples
Freelance	Event photographer. Coach driver in a resort. Social media influencer.
Gap year	Resort worker. Volunteer. Guide.
Placement	Front of house supervisor at a hotel. Marketing assistant manager within a tourist board. Assistant site manager for events.
Internships	Marketing internship within a national hospitality business. Financial management internship in a travel agents. Artist liaison internship at a festival.
Volunteering	Event stewards. Restaurant host.
Work shadowing	Directors of companies. Managers of large multi-national corporations (MNCs).
Workshops, training and competitions	Association workshops (academic or professional). Training within accreditation (WSET, for example). Worldwide Hospitality Awards.

learning and can evidence your ability to apply and develop skills for employment. Training sessions are often in tandem with work and often require you to develop your skills and knowledge to apply to working contexts. Competitions enable you to apply for certification or awards in an area of expertise or ability. Again, these usually rely upon work experience to appraise the level of expertise and ability.

NON-TRADITIONAL LOCATIONS FOR THE EMPLOYMENT EXPERIENCE

The usual locations of employment experience for THE were outlined in the previous section, however, it is not necessary for you to source employment in THE specific businesses/organisations from completing studies in THE. Leisure, recreation, sport, creative arts and business sectors are all locations of employment whereby your skills and knowledge from THE can be applied. Core areas of management and linked industries are outlined here as two areas for non-traditional THE employment experience.

Aligned with your management and leadership studies for THE are a range of management areas you can look for employment:

- Human resource management.
- Financial management.
- Operations management.
- Marketing management.

These are just some of the core management areas you will have completed studies within during your course.

ACTIVITY 22.2 SEARCH FOR CORE MANAGEMENT POSITIONS

1. Use your LinkedIn account (discussed in Chapter 20 of this part).
2. Identify a core management area to investigate.
3. Search for the title of this role on LinkedIn.
4. Review the profiles of people completing these roles.
5. Which companies do they work for?
6. What skills and experience do they use in the role?
7. Find the business/organisation online and see if there is an organisational hierarchy of staff and management. If this is unavailable, connect with the person on LinkedIn and ask for these details in support of your professional development.
8. Ask the contact if they know of other THE graduates who have worked in their role or similar.

Table 22.2 THE linked industries for employment experience

Arts	Business	Charity	Public
Museums Clothing design Architecture Design company Décor/furnishing company	Banking Product manufacturing Information technology Retail Research and development	Cause awareness Fundraising Research and development	Sporting events Government management Education

By completing Activity 22.2 you will be able to appraise your ability to work in a range of businesses/organisations. Using your networks you can ask other working professionals for their advice on how your course and skills are applicable to their core management position. Another method for finding non-traditional employment experiences with your skills and knowledge is to consider linked industries and sectors. Table 22.2 can be used as a guide to support.

Table 22.2 is not an exhaustive list but is offered to enable you to consider other, non-traditional THE industries within which you will find the usual THE roles.

SUMMARY

1. To offer tools to write an effective curriculum vitae.

Covering letters, structure for a CV, the CAR technique and guidance on CV writing was offered here. Using these you will be able to write individual applications for jobs advertised. It was highlighted that you do not need to wait for a job to be advertised in order to apply for an employment experience. Job adverts are published after internal analysis and financial planning, but any company will benefit from employing staff who have the skills and drive to support their organisational goals.

2. To clarify traditional forms of employment experience to support your graduate career in tourism, hospitality and events management.

Nine forms of employment were discussed and linked to traditional THE roles. These employment experiences should support your developing abilities and knowledge. The variety in employment experiences means that you can fit these around your studies, or even around full-time employment. They are discussed to offer you consideration of alternative methods to gain and develop your skills for employment in THE.

3.   To outline non-traditional locations for THE employment experience to consider.

The final section gives a reflective discussion on non-traditional locations for THE employment. This is important for your career mapping as you may find THE positions in other industries, or core management positions within non-traditional THE businesses. In this way, you are advised to consider linked roles and industries to complete employment experience within, as these will enable further application and development of your THE competencies.

Questions to support your learning and research

1.   How long should your CV be?
2.   What is a cover letter?
3.   What does CAR stand for?
4.   Do you need to find a job advertisement to apply for employment experience?
5.   What are the nine forms of employment experience?
6.   What is a gap year termed when you are in employment?
7.   How can work shadowing aid your career mapping?
8.   What are the core management topics usual within a THE course?
9.   Which industries were outlined as non-traditional to THE but places where you can seek employment experience?

Websites in support of your learning from this chapter

WSET – www.wsetglobal.com/

Chapter 23

Career mapping

After completion of this handbook, follow each of the outlined steps below to complete your own career map.

Outline the role you want to obtain upon graduation.

↓

Find job adverts for this role in the location or business you want to work within.

↓

List the essential and desirable criteria for the role.

↓

Within these lists note your current experience and ability.

↓	↓
Identify topics of knowledge you need to develop in support.	Identify skills, knowledge and experience needed to complete the role, which are currently missing in your CV.
↓	↓
Use these topics to focus your academic assignments and research projects on.	Identify forms of employment experience that will offer you the opportunity to develop and use these skills.
↓	↓
Complete research in these areas to develop your research competence and understanding of working context positions to these.	Obtain employment experiences using your networks.

↓

Update your CV with new skills and knowledge gained.

↓

Once you have all of the requisite evidence in skills and knowledge for the role, apply for a job advertised.

Figure 23.1 Career map

References

Abson, E. (2017). How event managers lead: Applying competency school theory to event management. *Event Management*, 21(4), pp. 403–419.

Aggett, M. and Busby, G. (2011). Opting out of internship: Perceptions of hospitality, tourism and events management undergraduates at a British University. *The Journal of Hospitality Leisure Sport and Tourism*, 10(1), pp. 106–113. [online]. Available from: www.heacademy.ac.uk/assets/hlst/documents/johlste/vol10no1/10PP310AggettBusby106to113.pdf [Accessed October 11, 2013].

Alexander, M., Lynch, P. and Murray, R. (2009). Reassessing the core of hospitality management education: The continuing importance of training restaurants. *The Journal of Hospitality Leisure Sport and Tourism*, 8(1), pp. 55–84. [online]. Available from: http://www.heacademy.ac.uk/assets/hlst/documents/johlste/vol8no1/AP0203Format55to69.pdf [Accessed March 30, 2014].

Arasaratnam, L.A. and Doerfel, M.L. (2005). Intercultural communication competence: Identifying key components from multicultural perspectives. *International Journal of Intercultural Relations*, 29(2), pp. 137–163. [online]. Available from: http://linkinghub.elsevier.com/retrieve/pii/S014717670500074X.

Arcodia, C. and Barker, T. (2002). The employability prospects of graduates in event management: Using data from job advertisements. In *CAUTHE Conference 2003, Coffs harbour, New South Wales, Australia*. p. 16.

Arnstein, S.R. (1969). A Ladder of citizen participation. *Journal of the American Planning Association*, pp. 216–224.

Atkins, M.J. (1999). *Oven-ready and Self-basting: Taking stock of employability skills. Teaching in Higher Education,* 4(2), pp. 267–280.

Bailly, F. and Lene, A. (2013). The personification of the service labour process and the rise of soft skills: A French case study. *Employee Relations*, 35(1), pp. 79–97.

Bakar, A. and Hanafi, I. (2007). Assessing employability skills of technical-vocational students in Malaysia. *Journal of Social Sciences*, 3(4), pp. 202–207.

Bandler, R. and Grinder, J. (1979). *Frogs into Princes: Neuro Linguistic Programming*. USA: Real People Press.

Bandura, A. (1989). Human agency in social cognitive theory. *American Psychologist*, 44(9), pp. 1175–1184. [online]. Available from: www.ncbi.nlm.nih.gov/pubmed/2782727.

Bandura, A. (1993). Perceived self-efficacy in cognitive development and functioning perceived self-efficacy in cognitive development and functioning. *Educational Psychologist*, 28(2), pp. 117–148.

Barclays. (2012). UK hospitality and leisure sector outlook third quarter 2012. p. 7. [online]. Available from: www.business.barclays.co.uk/BBB/A/Content/Files/Hospitality_and_Leisure_Outlook_Q4.pdf.

Bateman, J. (2014). *Developing an Employability Skills Portal*. Advance Higher Education report. Available from: https://s3.eu-west-2.amazonaws.com/assets.creode.advancehe-document-manager/documents/hea/private/hea_university_of_bolton_1568037345.pdf.

Baum, T. (1991). Competencies for hotel management: Industry expectations of education. *International Journal of Contemporary Hospitality Management*, 2(4), pp. 13–26.

Baum, T. (1996). Unskilled work and the hospitality industry: Myth or reality? *International Journal of Hospitality Management*, 15(3), pp. 207–209. [online]. Available from: http://scholar.google.com/scholar?hl=en&btnG=Search&q=intitle:Unskilled+work+and+the+hospitality+industry:+myth+or+reality+?#0.

Baum, T. (2002). The social construction of skills: A hospitality sector perspective. *European Journal of Vocational Education and Training*, 54(3), pp. 74–88.

Baum, T. (2006a). *Human Resource Management for Tourism, Hospitality and Leisure Industries: An International Perspective*. 1st ed. London, England: Thomson.

Baum, T. (2006b). Reflections on the nature of skills in the experience economy: Challenging traditional skills models in hospitality. *Journal of Hospitality and Tourism Management*, 13(2), pp. 124–135. 10.1375/jhtm.13.2.124.

Baum, T. (2007). Human resources in tourism: Still waiting for change. *Tourism Management*, 28(6), pp. 1383–1399. 10.1016/j.tourman.2007.04.005 [Accessed October 6, 2011].

Baum, T. and Nickson, D. (1998). Teaching human resource management in hospitality and tourism: A critique. *International Journal of Contemporary Hospitality Management*, 10(2), pp. 75–79. [online]. Available from: www.emeraldinsight.com/10.1108/09596119810207228.

Bavelas, A. and Lewin, K. (1942). Training in democratic leadership. *Journal of Abnormal and Social Psychology*, 37(1), 115–119.

Belbin, M. (2011). Management Teams: Why They Succeed or Fail (3rd ed.), *Human Resource Management International Digest*, 19(3). https://doi.org/10.1108/hrmid.2011.04419cae.002

Belbin, M. (2013). *Team Role Summary Descriptions*. [online]. Available from: www.belbin.com/content/page/49/BELBIN(uk)-2011-TeamRoleSummaryDescriptions.pdf.

Bennett, M. (1986). A developmental approach to training for intercultural sensitivity. *International Journal of Intercultural Relations*, 10(2), pp. 179–196.

Birdwhistell, R.L. (1955). Background to kinesics. *A Review of General Semantics*, 13(10–18), pp. 10–18.

Bishop, J. (2015). An investigation into the extent and limitations of the GROW model for coaching and mentoring online: Towards 'prosthetic learning'. In *International Conference for e-Learning, e-Business and e-Government*.

Blackman, A. (2008). Perspectives on leadership coaching for regional tourism managers and entrepreneurs. In Moscardo, G. (ed), *Building Community Capacity for Tourism Development*. UK: CABI, pp. 142–154.

Bridgstock, R. (2009). The graduate attributes we've overlooked: Enhancing graduate employability through career management skills employability through career management skills. *Higher Education Research & Development*, 28(1), pp. 31–44.

Brotherton, B. (2011). *Researching Hospitality and Tourism*. 2nd ed. SAGE Publications.

Brown, P., Hesketh, A. and Williams, S. (2003). Employability in a knowledge-driven economy [1]. *Journal of Education and Work*, 16(2), pp. 107–126.

Bryman, A. (1992). *Charisma and Leadership in Organizations*. London: Sage Publications.

Bryman, A. (1993). Charismatic leadership in business organizations: Some neglected issues. *The Leadership Quarterly*, 4(3–4), 289–304.

Buckler, S. and Walliman (2016). *Your Dissertation in Education*. UK: Sage Publications.

Burns, P.M. (1997). Hard-skills, soft-skills: Undervaluing hospitality's 'service with a smile'. *Hospitality*, 3, pp. 239–248.

Burns, T. and Sinfield, S. (2012). *Essential Study Skills*. 3rd ed. SAGE Publications.

Busby, G. (2005). Work experience and industrial links. In Airey, D. and Tribem, J. (eds), *An International Handbook of Tourism Education*. Oxford: Elsevier, pp. 93–107.

Butler, R. (2015). The evolution of tourism and tourism research. *Tourism Recreation Research*, 40(1), pp. 16–27.

Byram, M. (1997). *Teaching and Assessing Intercultural Communicative Competence*. Multilingual Matters. [online]. Available from: http://books.google.com/books?id=0vfq8JJWhTsC.

Cameron, S. (2010). *The Business Student's Handbook Skills for Study and Employment*. 5th ed. Prentice Hall.

Carlyle, T. (1849). On heros, hero-worship, and the heroic in history. In *Lecture V. The Hero as Man of Letters*. London: James Fraser.

Carrick, E. (2019). California's Santa Monica Pier is Getting a 'Stranger Things' Makeover. *Travel and Leisure*, p. 1. [online]. Available from: https://www.travelandleisure.com/culture-design/tv-movies/santa-monica-pier-stranger-things-themed-fun-fair.

Christou, E.S. (1999). Hospitality management education in Greece: An exploratory study. *Tourism Management*, 20, pp. 683–691. CIPD. (2012). Performance Appraisal. [online]. Available from: http://www.cipd.co.uk/hr-resources/factsheets/performance-appraisal.aspx.

Challis, N., Robinson, M. and Thomlinson, M. (2009). "Employability" skills in mathematical courses. *MSOR Connections*, 9(3), pp. 38–41.

Chan, J. (2011). Enhancing the employability of and level of soft skills within tourism and hospitality graduates in Malaysia: The issues and challenges. *Journal of Tourism*, 12(1), pp. 1–16.

Chang, S. and Gibson, H. (2010). Comparing the active and on-active leisure-tourism connection: Leisure involvement, leisure habit, tourism motivation, and tourism behavior. In *Travel and Tourism Research Association: Advancing Tourism Research Globally*. p. 12.

Chon, K. and Maier, T. (2009). *Welcome to Hospitality: An Introduction*. 3rd ed. New York: Cengage Learning.

Christou, E.S. (1999). Hospitality management education in Greece: An exploratory study. *Tourism Management*, 20, pp. 683–691.

CIPD. (2012). Performance appraisal. [online]. Available from: http://www.cipd.co.uk/hr-resources/factsheets/performance-appraisal.aspx.

Clarke, L. and Winch, C. (2007). *Vocational Education - International Approaches, Developments and Systems*. Abingdon, UK: Routledge.

Clyne, M. (1994). *Inter-Cultural Communication at Work*. Cambridge, UK: Cambridge University Press.

Cohen, L., Manion, L. and Morrison, K. (2009). *Research Methods in Education*. 6th ed. Oxon, England: Routledge.

Coleman, S. and Crang, M. (2002). *Tourism: Between Place and Performance*. Oxford: Berghahn Books.

Cottrell, S. (2008). *The Study Skills Handbook*. 3rd ed. London: Palgrave Macmillan.

Cottrell, S. (2010). *Skills for Success: Personal Development and Employability*. 2nd ed. London, UK Palgrave Macmillan.

Crawford, D. and Godbey, G. (1987). Reconceptualizing barriers to family leisure. *Leisure Sciences*, 9(2), pp. 119–127.

Daniels, K. and MacDonald, L. (2005). *Equality, Diversity and Discrimination: A Student Text*. London: CIPD.

Deardorff, D. (2006). Identification and assessment of intercultural competence as a student outcome of internationalization. *Journal of Studies in International Education*, 10(3), pp. 241–266. [online]. Available from: http://jsi.sagepub.com/cgi/doi/10.1177/1028315306287002.

Deardorff, D.K. (2009). *The SAGE Handbook of Intercultural Competence*. Sage Publications.

Denzin, N. (1978). *The Research Act: A Theoretical Introduction to Sociological Methods*. Transaction Publishers.

Derrida, J. (1973). *Speech and Phenomena, and Other Essays on Husserl's Theory of Signs, Philosophy*. USA: Northwestern University Press.

Derrida, J. (1982). *Margins of Philosophy, Philosophy*. USA: University of Chicago Press.

Dewey, J. (1938). *Experience and Education*. New York: The Macmillan company.

Dhiman, M.C. (2012). Employers' perceptions about tourism management employability skills. *An International Journal of Tourism and Hospitality Research*, 23(3), pp. 359–372.

Druckman, J.N. (2001). The implications of framing effects for citizen competence. *Political Behavior*, 23(3), pp. 225–256.

Dunne, J. and Ryan, S. (2014). Enhance employability skills in work placements with the use of blogs as a reflective peer-peer learning tool: Lessons learned. In *STEM Annual Conference 2014*.

Duval, T.S. and Silvia, P.J. (2002). Self-awareness, probability of improvement, and the self-serving bias. *Journal of Personality and Social Psychology*, 82(1), 49–61.

Edensor, T. (2001). Performing tourism, staging tourism. (Re)producing tourist space and practice. *Tourist Studies*, 1(1), pp. 59–81.

Egbert, J. and Sanden, S. (2014). *Foundations of Education Research: Understanding Theoretical Components*. New York: Routledge.

Enterprise and Industry, E. (2012). Small and medium-sized enterprises (SMEs) what is an SME? [online]. Available from: http://ec.europa.eu/enterprise/policies/sme/facts-figures-analysis/sme-definition/index_en.htm.

Ewert, G.D. (1991). Habermas and education: A comprehensive overview of the influence of Habermas in educational literature. *Review of Educational Research*, 61, pp. 345–378.

Fadel, C. and Trilling, B. (2012). Twenty first century competencies. In *Encyclopedia of the Sciences of Learning*. New York: Springer, pp. 3353–3356.

Fantini, A. (2001). Exploring intercultural competence: A construct proposal. In *National Council of Less Commonly Taught Languages*. Arlington, USA.

Fayol, H. (1916). Administration industrielle et générale. In *Bulletin de la Societe de lIndustrie Minderale*. Vol X. 5th series.

Feinman, J. (1976). The development of the employment at will rule. *The American Journal of Legal History*, 20(2), pp. 118–135.

Firth, M. (2020). *Service Encounters in Tourism, Events and Hospitality*. 1st ed. Channel View Publications.

Fleetwood, S. (2005). Ontology in organization and management studies: A critical realist perspective. *Organization*, 12(2), pp. 197–222.

Foucault, M. (1972). *The Archaeology of Knowledge*. London: Tavistock.

Franklin, B. (1729). A modest enquiry into the nature and necessity of a paper-currency. [online]. Available from: http://etext.lib.virginia.edu/users/brock/webdoc6.html.

Garavan, T.N. (1997). Interpersonal skills training for quality service interactions. *Industrial & Commercial Training*, 29(2), pp. 70–77. [online]. Available from: http://search.ebscohost.com/login.aspx?direct=true&db=bth&AN=17693514&site=ehost-live.

Garcia-Rosell, J. (2014). Promoting critical reflexivity in tourism and hospitality education through problem-based learning. In Dredge, D., Airey, D. and Gross, M. (eds), *The Routledge Handbook of Tourism and Hospitality Education*. Abingdon, UK: Routledge, pp. 279–291.

Gartner, W. (1989). 'Who is an entrepreneur?' Is the wrong question. *Entrepreneurship Theory and Practice*, pp. 47–67. [online]. Available from: business2.fiu.edu/1660397/www/Session2Readings/Gartner_1988_All.pdf.

Gastil, J. (1994). A definition and illustration of democratic leadership. *Human Relations*, 47(8), 953–975.

Geertz, C. (1973). *The Interpretation of Cultures: Selected Essays*. New York: Basic Books.

Getz, D. and Page, S. (2016a). *Event Studies: Theory, Research and Policy for Planned Events (Events Management)*. 3rd ed. Abingdon, UK: Routledge.

Getz, D. and Page, S.J. (2016b). Progress and prospects for event tourism research. *Tourism Management*, 52, pp. 593–631. 10.1016/j.tourman.2015.03.007.

Goleman, D. (1998). *What Makes a Leader? The Best of Harvard Business Review*, 93–102.

Gössling, S., Hall, C.M. and Andersson, A.C. (2018). The manager's dilemma: A conceptualization of online review manipulation strategies. *Current Issues in Tourism*, 21(5), pp. 484–503.

Government, U. (2012). Your contract and working hours. [online]. Available from: www.gov.uk/browse/working/contract-working-hours.

Griffin, P., McGraw, B. and Care, E. (2012). *Assessment and Teaching of 21st Century Skills*. London: Springer.

Habermas, J. (1971). *Towards a Rational Society*. London: Heinemann.

Haldrup, M. and Larson, J. (2009). *Tourism, Performance and the Everyday: Consuming the Orient*. London: Routledge.

Hall, B.E.T. (2000). The silent language in overseas Business. *Language*, 78(6), pp. 131–137. [online]. Available from: http://scholar.google.com/scholar?hl=en&btnG=Search&q=intitle:The+SILENT+LANGUAGE+in+Overseas+business#0.

Hall, E. (1959). *The Silent Language*. New York: Doubleday, ed.

Hall, E.T. (1966). *The Hidden Dimension*. Anchor Books Doubleday, ed. Doubleday. [online]. Available from: www.bookforfree.org/pdf-download/The-Hidden-Dimension-BY-Edward-T.-Hall-ID3764.pdf.

Harrison, R. (2009). *Learning and Development*. 5th ed. London: CIPD.

Hassanien, A. et al. (2010). *Hospitality Business Development*. England: Butterworth Heinemann.

Hawkins, P. and Smith, N. (2013). *Coaching, Mentoring and Organizational Consultancy: Supervision, Skills and Development*. 2nd ed. London: McGraw-Hill.

Henderson, K. and Bialeschki, M. (2005). Leisure and active lifestyles: Research reflections. *Leisure Sciences*, 27(5), pp. 355–365.

Henry, I. (1990). *Management and Planning in the Leisure Industries*. 1st ed. London: Macmillan Press.

Henry, I. (1993). *The Politics of Leisure Policy*. London: Macmillan Press.

Hertenstein, M.J. et al. (2006). Touch communicates distinct emotions. *Emotion Washington DC*, 6(3), pp. 528–533. [online]. Available from: www.ncbi.nlm.nih.gov/pubmed/16938094.

Herzberg, F. (1959). Herzberg's motivation-hygiene theory (two factor theory). *Netmba.Com*.

Hibberd, S. and Grove, M. (2009). Developing graduate and employability skills within a mathematical sciences programme. *MSOR Connections*, 9(2), pp. 33–39.

Hinchliffe, G. (2013). Workplace identity, transition and the role of learning. In Gibbs, P. (ed), *Learning, Work and Practice: New Understandings*. London: Springer, pp. 51–66.

Hochschild, A. (2012). *The Managed Heart: Commercialization of Human Feeling with a New Afterword*. 3rd ed. London: University of California Press.

Hodge, C. et al. (2015). Family leisure. *Journal of Leisure Research*, 47(5), pp. 557–600.

Hofstede, G. (2006). Dimensionalizing cultures: The Hofstede model in context. Lonner, W.J. et al., (eds). *Online Readings in Psychology and Culture*, 2(1), p. 8.

Holecek, D. (1993). Trends in world-wide tourism. In Van Lier, H. and Taylor, P. (eds), *New Challenges in Recreation and Tourism Planning*. London: Elsevier, pp. 17–33.

Holliday, A. (1999). Small cultures. *Applied Linguistics*, 20(2), pp. 237–264.

Honey, P. and Mumford, A. (1992). *The Manual of Learning Styles*. Maidenhead, UK: Peter Honey.

Horn, R. (2009). *The Business Skills Handbook*. London: CIPD.

IBD. (1996). *Investors Business Daily Guide to the Markets*. Canada: J. W. and S. Inc, ed.

INCA. (2004). Inter-cultural awareness. *Assessors Manual*. [online]. Available from: www.incaproject.org/en_downloads/21_INCA_Assessor_Manual_eng_final.pdf.

International City Management Association. (1965). Basic concepts of organisation. Bulletin 3, Effective Supervisory Practices, ICMA, Washington, DC.

International, M. (2012). Assistant manager catering sales for marriott international. *Job Advert on Marriott*. [online]. Available from: https://marriott.taleo.net/careersection/2/jobdetail.ftl.

Jackson, D. (2010). An international profile of industry-relevant competencies and skill gaps in modern graduates. *The International Journal of Management Education*, 8(3), pp. 29–58. [online]. Available from: www.heacademy.ac.uk/assets/bmaf/documents/publications/IJME/Vol8no3/3IJME288.pdf [Accessed April 1, 2013].

Jackson, D. (2012). Testing a model of undergraduate competence in employability skills and its implications for stakeholders. *Journal of Education and Work*, (April 2013), pp. 1–23. [online]. Available from: www.tandfonline.com/doi/abs/10.1080/13639080.2012.718750 [Accessed March 5, 2013].

Jackson, E. (2000). Will Research on leisure constraints still be relevant in the twenty-first century? *Journal of Leisure Research*, 32(1), pp. 62–68.

James, P. (1995). Models of vocational development revisited: Reflecting on concerns. *Vocational Aspects of Education*, 47, p. 298.

Jin, X. and Wang, Y. (2016). Chinese outbound tourism research: A review. *Journal of Travel Research*, 55 (4), pp. 440–453.

Jones, K. and Wills, J. (2005). *The Invention of the Park; from the Garden of Eden to Disney's Magic Kingdom*. Cambridge, UK: Polity Press.

Kay, C. and Russette, J. (2000). Hospitality-management competencies: Identifying managers' essential skills. *Cornell Hotel and Restaurant Administration Quarterly*, 41(2), pp. 52–63. [online]. Available from: http://cqx.sagepub.com/cgi/doi/10.1177/001088040004100217 [Accessed March 7, 2013].

Kelley, H.H. (1973). The processes of causal attribution. *American Psychologist*, pp. 107–108. Accessed at http://www.communicationcache.com/uploads/1/0/8/8/10887248/the_processes_of_causal_attribution.pdf.

Kelley, H.H. and Angeles, L. (1973). The processes of causal attribution 1. *American Psychologist*, 28(2), pp. 107–128.

Kelly, J. (1983). Social benefits of outdoor recreation: An introduction. In Lieber, S. and Fesenmaier, D. (eds), *Recreation Planning and Management*. State College, Pennsylvania: Venture Publications, pp. 3–14.

Kim, Y.Y. (2008). Intercultural personhood: Globalization and a way of being. *International Journal of Intercultural Relations*, 32(4), pp. 359–368. [online]. Available from: http://linkinghub.elsevier.com/retrieve/pii/S0147176708000278.

King, P.M. and Baxter Magolda, M.B. (2005). A developmental model of intercultural maturity. Samovar, L.A. and Porter, R.E. eds. *Journal of College Student Development*, 46(6), pp. 571–592. [online]. Available from: http://muse.jhu.edu/journals/journal_of_college_student_development/v046/46.6king.html.

Knowles, M.A. (1980). The modern practice of adult education. From pedagogy to andragogy. *Training & Development Journal*. Cambridge Adult Education. New Jersey, USA: Prentice Hall.

Kolb, D. (1984) [2014]. *Experiential Learning: Experience as the Source of Learning and Development*, 2nd edition (p. 377). New Jersey, NJ: Pearson Education.

Kondrat, M. (1999). Who is the "self" in self-aware: Professional self-awareness from a critical theory perspective. *Social Service Review*, 73(4), pp. 451–477. [online]. Available from: https://www.journals.uchicago.edu/doi/10.1086/514441.

Lamers, M. and Van der Duim, V. (2016). Connecting practices: Conservation tourism partnerships in Kenya. In G. Spaargaren, D. Weenink, and M. Lamers (Eds.), *Practice theory and research. Exploring the dynamics of social life* (pp. 179–201). London: Routledge.

Lamers, M., Van Der Duim, R. and Spaargaren, G. (2017). Annals of tourism research the relevance of practice theories for tourism research. *Annals of Tourism Research*, 62, pp. 54–63. 10.1016/j.annals.2016.12.002.

Lashley, C. and Morrison, A. (2007). *In Search of Hospitality; Theoretical Perspectives and Debates*. 2nd ed. Abingdon, UK: Routledge.

Latour, B. (2005). *Reassembling the Social: An Introduction to Actor-Network Theory*. Oxford: Oxford University Press.

Lawler, E.E. and Porter, L.W. (1967). Antecedent attitudes of effective managerial performance. *Organizational Behavior and Human Performance*, 2(2), pp. 122–142.

Lee, K. and Shin, K. (2005). Job burnout, engagement and turnover intention of dietitians and chefs at a contract foodservice management company. *Journal of Community Nutrition*, 7(2), pp.100–106.

Lee-Ross, D. and Lashley, C. (2009). *Entrepreneurship and Small Business Management in the Hospitality Industry*. Butterworth Heinemann. [online]. Available from: http://books.google.com/books?id=pSYwYrp-70kC&pgis=1.

Leitch, S. (2006). *Prosperity for All in the Global Economy - World Class Skills*. [online]. Available from: www.official-documents.gov.uk/document/other/0118404792/0118404792.pdf.

Lieber, S. and Fesenmaier, D. (1983). *Recreation Planning and Management*. State College, PA: Venture Publications.

Light, D. (2017). Progress in dark tourism and thanatourism research: An uneasy relationship with heritage tourism. *Tourism Management*, 61, pp. 275–301. 10.1016/j.tourman.2017.01.011.

Louviere, J. and Timmermans, H. (1990). Stated preference and choice models applied to recreation research: A review. *Leisure Sciences*, 12(1), pp. 9–32.

Lucas, R. (1983). The role and regulations in recreation management. *Western Midlands*, 9(2), pp. 6–10.

Lucas, R. (2004). *Employment Relations in the Hospitality and Tourism Industries*. London: Routledge.

MacLeod, N. (2006). The placeless festival: Identity and place in the post-modern festival. In Picard, D. and Robinson, M., *Festivals, Tourism and Social Change: Remaking Worlds*. UK: Channel View Publications, pp. 222–237.

Maddy, P. (2007). *Second Philosophy: The Naturalistic Method*. Oxford, UK: Oxford University Press.

March, J.G. (1955). An introduction to the theory and measurement of influence. *American Political Science Review*, 49(2), pp. 431–451.

Maslach, C. (1993). Burnout: A multidimensional perspective. In Schaufeli, W.B., Masalch, C. and Marek, T. (eds), *Professional Burnout: Recent Developments in Theory and Research*. Washington, DC: Taylor & Francis, pp. 19–32.

Maslach, C. (2000). A multidimensional theory of burnout. In Cooper C.L. (ed), *Theories of Organizational Stress*. Oxford: Oxford University Press, pp. 68–85.

Maslow, A. (1973). *On Dominance, Self-Esteem, and Self-Actualisation*: Germinal Papers of A. H. Maslow (Ed: Richard Lowry). Monterey, CA: Brooks/Cole Publishers.

Maslow, A.H. (1943). Theory of human motivation. *Psycological Review*, (50), pp. 370–396.

McClelland, D. (1988). *Human Motivation*. Cambridge, UK: Cambridge University Press.

McGregor, D. (1957). The human side of enterprise. *Management Review*, 24, pp. 41–49.

McLaughlin, M. (1995). *Skills Profile: What Are Employers Looking For? Employability Skills Profile: What Are Employers Looking For?* [online]. Available from: https://files.eric.ed.gov/fulltext/ED399484.pdf.

McShane, S. and Travaglione, T. (2003). *Organisational Behaviour on the Pacific Rim*. Australia: McGraw-Hill.

Miles, S. (2016). What clothes should leisure research wear? *Annals of Leisure Research*, 19(3), pp. 270–274.

Mintzberg, H. (1989). *Mintzberg on Management: Inside Our Strange World of Organizations*. London: Simon and Schutser.

Moodie, G. (2002). Identifying vocational education and training. *Journal of Vocational Education & Training*, 54(2), pp. 249–266.

Morrison, A., Rimmington, M. and Williams, C. (2012). *Entrepeneurship in the Hospitality, Tourism and Leisure Industries*. 8th ed. London: Butterworth-Heinmann.

Moua, M. (2010). *Culturally Intelligent Leadership: Leading through Intercultural Interactions*. Phillips, J. and Gully, S. (eds). New York: Business Expert Press.

Mowatt, R. (2018). The case of the 12-year-old boy: Or, the silence of and relevance to leisure research. *Leisure Sciences*, 40(1–2), pp. 54–70. https://doi.org/10.1080/01490400.2017.1296389.

Munar, A.M. and Montaño, J.J. (2009). Generic competences and tourism graduates. *Journal of Hospitality, Leisure, Sport and Tourism Education*, 8(1), pp. 70–84.

Nash, C. (2009). Development of a mentoring system within coaching practice. *The Journal of Hospitality Leisure Sport and Tourism*, 2(2), pp. 39–47.

Needham, M. and Szuster, B. (2011). Situational in fluences on normative evaluations of coastal tourism and recreation management strategies in Hawai'i. *Tourism Management*, 32(4), pp. 732–740. 10.1016/j.tourman.2010.06.005.

Nickson, D. (2007). *Human Resource Management for the Hospitality and Tourism Industries*. Oxford, UK: Butterworth Heinemann.

O'Shannessy, V., Minett, D. and Hyde, G. (2002). *The Road to Tourism*. 1st ed. Frenchs Forest, New South Wales: P. E. Australia, ed.

OECD. (2019a). *OECD industry list worldwide*. [online]. Available from: www.oecd.org/sti/ind/40729523.pdf.

OECD. (2019b). Tourism. [online]. Available from: www.oecd.org/cfe/tourism/ [Accessed April 13, 2019].

Office, I.L. (2012). *Global Employment Trends 2012 Preventing a Deeper Jobs Crisis*. International Labour Office. [online]. Available from: www.ilo.org/wcmsp5/groups/public/—dgreports/—dcomm/—publ/documents/publication/wcms_171571.pdf.

Okumus, B., Ali, M. and Ma, F. (2018). Food and gastronomy research in tourism and hospitality: A bibliometric analysis. *International Journal of Hospitality Management*, 73(October 2017), pp. 64–74. 10.1016/j.ijhm.2018.01.020.

Omerzel, D. (2016). A Systematic review of research on innovation in hospitality and tourism. *International Journal of Contemporary Hospitality Management*, 28(3), pp. 516–558.

Page, S. and Ateljevic, J. (2009). *Tourism and Entrepreneurship: International Perspecitves*. Oxford, UK: Butterworth-Heinmann.

Patton, W. and Mcmahon, M. (2002). Theoretical and practical perspectives for the future of educational and vocational guidance in Australia. *INternational Journal for Educational and Vocational Guidance in Australia*, 2, pp. 39–49.

Pavlov, I. P. (1927). *Conditional Reflexes: An Investigation of the Physiological Activity of the Cerebral Cortex*. London: Wexford University Press.

People 1st. (2011). *State of the nation report 2011*. Uxbridge.

People 1st. (2013). *State of the nation report 2013*. [online]. Available from: www.people1st.co.uk/web files/Research/StateOfTheNation/2013/SOTN_2013_final.pdf.

Piaget, J. (1950). *The Moral Judgment of the Child* (M. Gabain, trans.). Glencoe, IL: Free Press.

Piaget, J. (1964). Part I: Cognitive development in children: Piaget. Development and learning. *Journal of Research in Science Teaching*, 2(3), pp. 176–186.

Pigram, J. (1985). *Outdoor Recreation and Resource Management*. 2nd ed. New York: St Martins Press.

Piller, I. (2011). *Intercultural Communication: A Critical Introduction*. Edinburgh: Edinburgh University Press.

Platek, S.M., Critton, S.R. and Myers, T.E. (2003). Contagious yawning: The role of self-awareness and mental state attribution. *Brain Research and Cognitive Brain Research*, 17, pp. 223–227.

Polanyi, M. (1966). *The Tacit Dimension*. New York: Anchor Day.

Price, K. (2019) Burnt Chef project to tackle mental health in the sector. *The Caterer*. 24th June 2019. [online]. Available from: www.thecaterer.com/news/restaurant/burnt-chef-project-to-tackle-mental-health-in-the-sector [Accessed July 10, 2019].

Prospects. (2009). What skills do employers want? [online]. Available from: www.prospects.ac.uk/faqs_s kills.htm [Accessed March 1, 2013].

Public Health England. (2016). Interventions to prevent burnout in high risk individuals: Evidence review about Public Health England. [online]. Available from: https://assets.publishing.service.gov.uk/govern ment/uploads/system/uploads/attachment_data/file/506777/25022016_Burnout_Rapid_Re view_2015709.pdf

QAA. (2008). *Subject Benchmark Statements: Hospitality, Leisure, Sport and Tourism*. [online]. Available from: www.qaa.ac.uk/academicinfrastructure/benchmark/statements/HLST08.asp.

Rand, A. (2008). *Atlas Shrugged. Original E*. New York: Paw Prints.

Rand, A. (2019). Advancing your potential. [online]. Available from: www.aynrand.org/ideas/overview [Accessed June 6, 2019].

Roberts, J.M. (2014). Critical realism, dialectics, and qualitative research methods. *Journal for the Theory of Social Behaviour*, 44(1), pp. 1–23.

Rogers, S. and Burn-Murdoch, J. (2012). US jobless data: How has unemployment changed under Obama? *Guardian Article*. [online]. Available from: www.guardian.co.uk/news/datablog/2011/oct/07/us-jobless-unemployment-data#data.

Rojek, C. (1989). Leisure and recreation theory. In Jackson, E.L. and Burton, T.L. (eds), *Understanding Leisure and Recreation: Mapping the Past*, Charting the Future. State College, PA: Venture Publishing, pp. 69–88.

Rojek, C. (1993). *Ways of Escape: Modern Transformation in Tourism and Travel*. Buckingham, UK: Palgrave Macmillan.

Rotter, J.B. (1954). General principles for a social learning framework of personality study. In Rotter, J.B (ed), *Social Learning and Clinical Psychology*. Englewood Cliffs, NJ: Prentice-Hall, pp. 82–104.

Rousseau, D.M. (1989). Psychological and implied contracts in organizations. *Employee Responsibilities and Rights Journal*, 2(2), pp. 121–139. [online]. Available from: http://www.springerlink.com/index/10.1007/BF01384942

Russell, E. (2014). Working with alumni and STEM professionals to enhance the employability skills of undergraduate mathematicians. In *STEM Annual Conference 2014*. p. 1.

Saunders, M., Lewis, P. and Thornhill, A., (2009). *Research Methods for Business Students*, 5th edition. London: Pearson Education.

Schatzki, T. (2016a). Keeping track of large phenomena. *Geographische Zeitschrift*, 104(1), pp. 4–24.

Schatzki, T. (2016b). Practice theory as flat ontology. In Spaargaren, G., Weenink, D. and Lamers, M. (eds), *Practice Theory and Research. Exploring the Dynamics of Social Life*. London: Routledge, pp. 28–42.

Scollon, R., Scollon, S. and Jones, R. (2012). *Intercultural Communication: A Discourse Approach*. 3rd ed. Oxon, England: John Wiley & Sons Ltd.

Scott, D. and Usher, R. (1996). *Understanding Educational Research*. New York: Routledge.

Seymour, D. (2000). Emotional labour: A comparison between fast food and traditional service work. *International Journal of Hospitality Management*, 19(2), pp. 159–171.

Shavelson, R. and Bolus, R. (1981). Self-concept: The interplay of theory and methods. *Journal of Educational Psychology*, 74(1), pp. 3–17.

Shoval, N. and Ahas, R. (2016). The use of tracking technologies in tourism research: The first decade. *Tourism Geographies*, 18(5), pp. 587–606. 10.1080/14616688.2016.1214977.

Shove, E., Pantzar, M. and Watson, M. (2012). *The Dynamics of Social Practice: Everyday Life and How It Changes*. London: Sage.

Silvia, P.J. and Duval, T.S. (2001). Objective self-awareness theory: Recent progress and enduring problems. *Personality and Social Psychology Review*, 5, pp. 230–241.

Sjollema, S. and Yuen, F. (2017). Evocative words and ethical crafting: Poetic representation in leisure research. *Leisure Sciences*, 39(2), pp. 109–125. 10.1080/01490400.2016.1151845.

Smale, B. and Fowlie, J. (2009). *How to Succeed at University: An Essential Guide to Academic Skills and Personal Development*. 1st ed. London: SAGE Publications.

Smith, J. and Warburton, F. (2012). *Cambridge IGCSE Travel and Tourism*. Cambridge, UK: Cambridge University Press.

Souza Bispo, M. (2016). Tourism as practice. *Annals of Tourism Research*, 61, pp. 170–179.

Spaargaren, G., Lamers, M. and Weenink, D. (2016). Introduction: Using practice theory to research social life. In Spaargaren, G., Weenink, D. and Lamers, M. (eds), *Practice Theory and Research. Exploring the Dynamics of Social Life*. London: Routledge, pp. 3–27.

Sparks, B. and Callan, V.J. (1992). Communication convergence and the service encounter: The value of convergence. *International Journal of Hospitality Management*, 11(3), pp. 213–224.

Spitzberg, B. and Changnon, G. (2009). Conceptualizing intercultural competence. In Deardorff, D. (ed), *The SAGE Handbook of Intercultural Competence*. London: Sage Publications, p. 542.

Stadler, F. (1998)., Vienna Circle. In *Routledge Encyclopedia of Philosophy*, Taylor and Francis. [online]. Available from: www.rep.routledge.com/articles/thematic/vienna-circle/v-1 [Accessed June 2, 2019]. doi:10.4324/9780415249126-DD076-1

Statistics, O. for N. (2012). *Labour Market Statistics February 2012*. [online]. Available from: www.ons.gov.uk/ons/rel/lms/labour-market-statistics/february-2012/index.html.

Stirling, D. (2002). Mathematicians need careers. *MSOR Connections*, 2(2), pp. 16.

Suh, E., West, J.J. and Shin, J. (2012). Important competency requirements for managers in the hospitality industry. *Journal of Hospitality, Leisure, Sport & Tourism Education*, 11(2), pp. 101–112. 10.1016/j.jhlste.2012.02.005.

Surprenant, C.F. and Solomon, M.R (1987). Predictability and personalization in the service encounter. *Journal of Marketing*, 51(2), pp. 86–96.

The Dearing Report. (1997). *Higher Education in the Learning Society*. [online]. Available from: www.educationengland.org.uk/documents/dearing1997/dearing1997.html.

Tobin, S.J. (2012). Attribution. In *Encyclopedia of Human Behavior: Second Edition*. London: Elsevier, pp. 236–242.

Torkildsen, G. (2005). *Leisure and Recreation Management*. 1st ed. London, UK: Routledge.

Torkildsen, G. (2011). *Sport and Leisure Management*. 5th ed. London, UK: Routledge.

Tribe, J. (2005). New tourism research. *Tourism Recreation Research*, 30(2), pp. 5–8.

Trilling, B. and Fadel, C. (2009). *21st Century Skills*. John Wiley & Sons.

Tuckman, B.W. (1965). Developmental sequence in small groups. *Psychological Bulletin*, 63(6), pp. 384–399. [online]. Available from: www.ncbi.nlm.nih.gov/pubmed/14314073.

Tuckman, B.W. and Jensen, M.A.C. (1977). Stages of small-group development revisited. *Group and Organization Studies*, 2(4), p. 419.

TUI (2019) Strategy. Available from: https://www.tuigroup.com/en-en/about-us/about-tui-group/strategy [Accessed on June 5, 2019].

Van der Duim, R. (2007). Tourismscapes: An actor-network perspective. *Annals of Tourism Research*, 34(4), pp. 961–976.

Van der Duim, V., Ren, C. and Jóhannesson, G. (eds). (2012). *Actor-Network. Theory and Tourism: Ordering, Materiality and Multiplicity*. London: Routledge.

Van der Duim, V., Ren, C. and Jóhannesson, G. (2013). Ordering, materiality and multiplicity: Enacting actor-network theory in tourism. *Tourist Studies*, 13(1), pp. 3–20.

Van Der Heijde, C. and Van Der Heijde, B. (2006). A competence-based and multidimensional operationalization and measurement of employability. *Human Resource Management*, 45(3), pp. 449–476.

Van Lier, H. and Taylor, P. (1993). *New Challenges in Recreation and Tourism Planning*. 1st ed. London: Elsevier.

Voss, U. et al. (2014). Induction of self awareness in dreams through frontal low current stimulation of gamma activity. *Nature Neuroscience*, 17(6), pp. 810–812.

Vroom, V.H. (1964). *Work and Motivation*. New York: Wiley.

Wall, G. (1983). The economic value of cultural facilities: Tourism in Toronto. In Lieber, S. and Fesenmaier, D. (eds), *Recreation Planning and Management*. State College, Pennsylvania, PA Venture Publications, pp. 15–25.

Wallace, M. and Wray, A. (2011). *Critical Reading and Writing for Postgraduates*. 2nd ed. London: Sage Publications.

Warhurst, C. and Nickson, D. (2007). Employee experience of aesthetic labour in retail and hospitality. *Work, Employment & Society*, 21(1), pp. 103–120. [online]. Available from: http://wes.sagepub.com/cgi/doi/10.1177/0950017007073622 [Accessed November 6, 2012].

Warhurst, C. and Nickson, D. (2009). 'Who's got the look?' Emotional, aesthetic and sexualized labour in interactive services. *Gender, Work & Organization*, 16(3), pp. 385–404. [online]. Available from: http://doi.wiley.com/10.1111/j.1468-0432.2009.00450.x.

Weiner, I.B. and Craighead, W.E. (2010). *Attribution Theory. The Corsini Encyclopedia of Psychology*, Vol. 1, (4th ed), (pp. 184–186). New Jersey: John Wiley & Sons.

Whatley, J. (2012). Evaluation of a Team Project Based Learning Module for Developing Employability Skills. *Informing Science and Information Technology, 9*, pp. 75–92.

Williams, C. (1998). Is the SERVQUAL model an appropriate management tool for measuring service delivery quality in the UK leisure industry? *Managing Leisure*, 3(2), pp. 98–110. [online]. Available from: www.tandfonline.com/doi/abs/10.1080/136067198376102 [Accessed November 27, 2013].

Williams, C. (2008). Beyond ideal-type depictions of entrepreneurship: Some lessons from the service sector in England. *The Service Industries Journal*, 28(7), pp. 1041–1053. [online]. Available from: http://swww.tandfonline.com/doi/abs/10.1080/02642060701846770.

Wilson, E. and Hollinshead, K. (2015). Qualitative tourism research: Opportunities in the emergent soft sciences. *Annals of Tourism Research*, 54, pp. 30–47. 10.1016/j.annals.2015.06.001.

Witz, A., Warhurst, C. and Nickson, D. (2003). The labour of aesthetics and the aesthetics of organization. *Organization*, 10(1), pp. 33–54. [online]. Available from: http://org.sagepub.com/cgi/doi/10.1177/1350508403010001375 [Accessed August 8, 2011].

WTO. (2011). *Travel & Tourism 2011*. Available from: https://cf.cdn.unwto.org/sites/all/files/111020-rapport_vellas_en.pdf [Accessed on March 1, 2012].

WTO. (2019). Travel and tourism: Generating jobs for youth. *Research report*, p. 1. [online]. Available from: www.wttc.org/economic-impact/social-impact/generating-jobs-for-youth/.

Yorke, M. (2006). Employability in higher education: What it is – What it is not. *Higher Education Academy*. Available from: https://www.advance-he.ac.uk/knowledge-hub/employability-higher-education-what-it-what-it-not [Accessed on June 5, 2007].

Yorke, M. (2012). Employability challenges for the future. In *2nd Employability and Citizenship Skills Conference*. Manchester, p. 20.

Zinser, R. (2003). Developing career and employability skills: A US case study. *Education + Training*, 45(7), pp. 402–410.

Zuckerman, M. (1979). Attribution of success and failure revisited, or: The motivational bias is alive and well in attribution theory. *Journal of Personality*, 47(2), pp. 245–287.

Index

Locators in *italics* refer to figures and those in **bold** to tables, though where concurrent with related text these are not distinguished from primary locators.

For Product Safety Concerns and Information please contact our EU representative GPSR@taylorandfrancis.com Taylor & Francis Verlag GmbH, Kaufingerstraße 24, 80331 München, Germany

Printed and bound by CPI Group (UK) Ltd, Croydon, CR0 4YY

02/05/2025

01859335-0002